THE GROUNDWATER DIARIES

Also by Tim Bradford

Is Shane MacGowan Still Alive?

THE GROUNDWATER DIARIES

Trials, Tributaries and Tall Stories
from beneath the Streets of London

TIM BRADFORD

Flamingo
An Imprint of HarperCollins*Publishers*
77–85 Fulham Palace Road,
Hammersmith, London W6 8JB

Flamingo is a registered trademark of HarperCollins*Publishers* Limited

www.**fire**and**water**.com

Published by Flamingo 2003
1 3 5 7 9 8 6 4 2

Tim Bradford asserts the moral right to
be identified as the author of this work

A catalogue record for this book
is available from the British Library

ISBN 0 00 713084 8

Set in Birka with Caxton display

Printed and bound in Great Britain by
Clay Ltd, St Ives plc

To Cindy, Cathleen and Seán

Contents

SPRING

SUMMER

List of Illustrations

Acknowledgements

It all seems so long ago now that I embarked on this series of journeys, the last one on September 11th 2001. Several of the walks in this book were first done with friends or fellow map obsessives — thanks to Tracey Bush, Doug Cheeseman, Karen Johnson, Dave Ludkin, Andy Lyons, Ian Spry, Kelly Thomas and Dominick Weir. Also my parents, Rhona and Tony.

Thanks as well to Ian Plenderleith, my flatlander writer mate, for his unswerving inspiration and morale boosting; Tony Davis for his photographic genius; Lee Marple for local history tips; Neil Ruane for Bank of Friendship discussions; Jill Sterry for getting me inside the sewage works; Rob and his gang for my trip under the streets; Jonathan Wright for help with early research; Rebecca Skeels for her supply of creative ideas; Edna Crome for local history knowledge; and Andy Major for help with bar surveys in the West End. Thanks to Dominick for dragging me round Portobello Road searching for cheap records all those years ago and helping me find the old volumes which started this quest. And to Seth Weir for walks, pub-crawls, ideas and writing workshops.

I have met lots of librarians over the last three years. I'd like to say there are too many to mention but the truth is I can't remember their names. All except for Isobel of Hornsey Library in Crouch End. Librarians are the guardians of our culture. And they've got cheap photocopiers. Cheers, library people.

On the publishing side: thanks to Rosemary Scoular for her positive input; Kate Morris for her keen eye; Terence Caven for designing my pile of doodles and sketches into a book; Philip Gwyn Jones for getting the whole project off the ground; and Georgina Laycock for her sympathetic understanding of the East Midlands magical-realist bollocks school of travel writing.

The most special thanks are due to Cindy for her love, encouragement and belief and to Cathleen for help with local research and for the loan of her Pingu videos. And hello to Seán, watching patiently (and dribbling slightly) as I write this. You're probably wondering what sort of shite your dad is on about this time.

AUTUMN

1. A Bloody Big River Runs Through It

- **London's forgotten rivers**

Dream of a big river – river obsession – Danish punk explosion – Samuel Johnson – London – electric windows – pissed-up Jamaican grandads – Hemingway – burning Edward Woodward – global warming – the underground rivers – old maps – lots of rain – roads flooded – blokes digging up the road

I have a recurring dream. I'm standing in the shallows of a silver-grey mile-wide river. My wife, in a blue forties-style polka-dot swimsuit, is next to me, with our daughter. We are picking bits of granary bread out of the river and putting them into black bin liners. On the shore stands a big wooden colonial-style house. I first had the dream before my daughter was conceived, in fact long before my wife and I even got together. Dream analysts might say I was crazy. But they are the crazy ones, thinking that punters will be fooled by fancy titles like 'Dream Analyst'. I contacted a dream analyst, anyway, because I can't help myself. It was one of those Internet ones with swirly New Ageish graphics which denote a certain amateur-cosmic badge of quality. You had to type in your dream, then your credit card details. I'm no mug, so I chose one that only cost sixty dollars. A few days later my dream analyst (whose name was Keith – I had expected something a little more along the lines of Lord Sun Ra Om Le Duke de Dream Chaos Universale) sent me an email.

> It is a pleasant dream showing you the very positive
> feelings of the family. You are together, safe, gathering
> and storing food. We survive best in a family and 'tribe',
> and this very primitive dream stimulus prompts you to
> make the most of that. You are lucky, most of the dreams
> like this work the other way by having the unit
> threatened. You might see your daughter drowning, thus
> frightening you (the objective of the dream) into
> increased protection in life.
>   I like it! A good dream. You even had it before the
> event, stirring you on to make the union and reproduce
> the species.

But I wasn't totally satisfied. Why did my wife's swimsuit have polka dots? Did the bread have something to do with religion? From my description, would he say the wooden house was designed in an Arts-and-Crafts style? And why were we in a river? Dream Analyst had gone quiet. Except for a ghostly hand that reached out from my computer terminal with a note that said '60 dollars please'.

OK, I am obsessed with rivers. Especially dark ones, like the River Trent in the East Midlands, 20 miles from where I grew up. It's deep and unfathomable. Like time, but with fish and old bikes at the bottom. My mum used to tell me a story about a local man whose daughter fell from a boat into the river. He jumped in and saved her, but was carried off by the tide. Is his body still there, in the river? Maybe. So how deep is it, then? Very deep, my parents would say, shaking their heads and sucking in their breath. Fantastic. I'd lie in bed thinking abut the river and what it must be like to drown. I couldn't imagine the bottom. It was like visualizing a million people or the edge of the universe.

I remember everything in the town where I grew up being smaller than elsewhere in the world (the cars, the voices, the people) and this was especially true of our 'river', the Rase. At its highest near the mill pond, the Rase could be up to 2 feet deep, but it usually flowed at a more ankle-soaking 8 to 12 inches. In early 1981, the placid river burst its banks and many people, my aunt included, were flooded out of their homes (ironically, my new copy of *Lubricate Your Living Room* by the Fire Engines floated off past her sofa). A couple of months later my friend Plendy and I decided to try and placate the Rase by making a pagan sacrifice. It was important to give something that we both treasured, but in the end were too stingy and instead nailed down a copy of *Bullshit Detector* (an anarcho-punk compilation album I'd bought some months earlier) to a wooden board, placed it in the water and watched it head off downstream. We liked to think it eventually found its way to the North Sea then travelled the world, spreading its gospel of three-chord mayhem and anarchist politics.

> *The men with the power*
> *Have pretty flowers*
> *The men with the guns*
> *Have robotic sons.*
>
> 'The Men with the Guns'

At the very least, most Scandinavian punk music must be down to us.

Scene 1: A farm in Denmark. A big-boned farmer finds a record nailed to a board on the shore near his house. He

6 removes it then puts it on a record player. It's good. He starts pogoing.

Scene 2: A few days later, in the farmer's barn, a punk band is practising. The farmer is on lead vocals.

Scene 3: A tractor lies half-buried beneath long grass. There are cobwebs on the steering wheel.

Scene 4: A painting of the farmer and his wife in the style of Gainsborough's *Mr and Mrs Andrews*. The farmer has a mohican. The wife looks very, very angry.

Before   After

The birth of the Danish Punk Movement

Long before we were offering third-class punk records to the water spirits, rivers were worshipped as gods. Those red-haired party animals, the Celts, threw things they most valued – shields, swords, jewellery, and other anarcho-Celtpunk memorabilia – into them (a residue of this is our need to chuck loose change and crap jewellery into fountains). To different cultures across the globe, rivers have represented time, eternity, life and death. It is believed that our names for rivers are the oldest words in the language, some predating even the Celts. Many major settlements were located at healing springs sacred to the pre-Roman goddesses, and many rivers, such as the Danube, Boyne and Ganges, were named after goddesses. The Thames is one of these, its name apparently

deriving from a pre-Indo-European tongue and referring to the
Goddess Isis. Some posh Oxbridge rowing types still call it that.
Well, we've got names for posh Oxbridge rowing types. Like 'big-
toothed aristo wanker', etc.

⓪   ⓪   ⓪

London is beautiful. Samuel Johnson, in the only quote of his
anyone can really remember, said, 'When a man is tired of London,
he is tired of life.' He may have been a fat mad-as-a-hatter manic
depressive in a wig, but there is something in his thesis. London's
got its fair share of nice parks and museums, but I love its under-
belly, in fact its belly in general – the girls in their first strappy
dresses of the summer, the smell of chips, the liquid orange skies of
early evening, high-rise glass office palaces, the lost-looking old
men still eating at their regular caffs even after they've been turned
into Le Café Trendy or Cyber Bacon, the old shop fronts, the rotting
pubs, the cacophony of peeling and damp Victorian residential
streets, neoclassical shopping centres, buses that never arrive on
time, incessant white noise fizz of gossip, little shops, big shops,
late-night kebab shops with slowly turning cylinders of khaki fat
and gristle in the window, the bitter caramel of car exhaust fumes,
drivers spitting abuse at each other through the safety of tinted
electric windows, hot and tightly packed tubes in summer, the roar
of the crowd from Highbury or White Hart Lane, dog shit on the
pavements, psychopathic drunken hard men who sit outside at
North London pub tables. London has got inside me. I've tried to
leave. But I always come back. It's love, y'see.

As you can probably tell, I'm a sentimental country boy. No real
self-respecting Londoner would love their city the way I do (and
before you ask, Dr J. was from the Black Country).

My love affair started early. The first trip was in the late sixties.
We went to the Tower of London and some museums while the
streets were 'aflame' with the lame English version of the '68 riots

8   ('What do we want? Cheap cigarettes and decent central heating! When do we want it? How about Wednesday? I'm visiting my Auntie for a long weekend!'). Years later I visited an old college mate in a little flat in Finsbury Park. I slept on the floor and spent three days sitting in pubs where we were the only people without overgrown moustaches and some obscure connection to the Brinks Matt robbery. A drunken fat bloke with a moustache the size of Rutland showed me how to drink Guinness properly. Throughout these years it seemed that London was a place full of record shops, shouty Irish blokes, pissed-up Jamaican grandads and stoners. I've found it hard to shake off these early impressions.

In January 1988 I hit cold evening air at Highgate Tube, north London, a heavy-duty iron forties typewriter (a prerequisite for the aspiring writer) strapped to my body with a mustard and maroon dressing-gown cord, guitar on my back, clutching a bag with a spare pair of jeans, a couple of T-shirts and a change of underwear.

I had arrived, like Hemingway in Paris, in a grand European capital where I would soon become a famous novelist and songwriter. OK, not like Hemingway at all. Unless his music has been kept quiet all these years.[1] I had a simple plan. Within six months I'd have clinched a record deal and would be starting my second novel. I was here to scrape the gold off the London pavements and cart it back to Lincolnshire, to be held aloft in procession through the streets of my old home town, before sharing my booty with all and sundry in the market place.

And so twelve years on I'm still here. Pushing a pram around for an hour or so every day and watching too much kids' TV.

---

[1]   (Peter Skellern style number)
      Is it me
      Is it you
      We two
      Let's do
      It.

I love London in late summer/early autumn. Hot weather. Then 9
cold. Then it's cold-but-hot cold. Cold days have warm miasmic
breezes. Hot days have brittle, icy winds that hide behind hedges and
garden walls. Then it'll piss down. The weather going crazy. You
always start your books with stuff about weather, said one (pedantic)
mate. What do you mean always? I've only written one. Yeah but you
started that with weather and now you're starting this the same way.

But weather is important. People on
these islands have always been
obsessed with it. The Celtic people
worshipped the weather gods. The seasons. Agriculture. Sacrifice. Dancing
naked around standing stones. Burning
Edward Woodward in *The Wicker
Man*. Listening to ambient techno
while off their faces on magic mushrooms. The British Isles can have wind,
sun, rain and snow all in one day. My
mate agreed and pointed out that he
lived here too so also knew these
things. But now it's changing more and
more, What With Global Warming

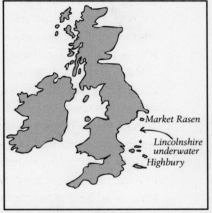

*Projected Map of the British Isles in 2050
showing results of tectonic plate
movement and rising seawater levels*

And That. The east of England could be underwater in a few
decades. I want to write a book about Lincolnshire some day. But
Lincolnshire may not be around for much longer.[2] London too. The
climate will get wetter rather than hot and dry. It could also get
colder in winter if the Gulf Stream gets clobbered by cold water from
the melting ice caps flowing into the North Atlantic, pushing the
warmer water further south. More importantly, my book about
Lincolnshire will then be about an area that no longer exists. Or one
of those Undersea-Lost-World-type things.

---

2 Reader: Does Lincolnshire only exist so that you can write a book about it?

'How do you know all this stuff?' asked my mate.

'I saw it on TV.'

Anyway after all the hotcoldrainsnowsuncoldhot stuff, it went cold again. Maybe we had gone straight from early summer to late winter. It became so consistently grey that my sensitivity to the London seasons became even more numbed than usual. As a kid, in rural Lincolnshire, every day held new smells and sensations. Cow parsley. Corn. Peas. Sugar beet. Rotting leaves. The perfume of a girl who'd just chucked me. Singed hairs on the back of a fat farmer's neck as he gets his 'winter cut' at the local barber shop. Rotting roadkill. Cow shit. Blood.

And after a few days of cold, the sun suddenly came out and I guessed, from stuff in the newspaper, it must be some time in August. On the way back I walked along the little avenue of trees in Clissold Park. This is a sacred space where we sometimes sit in the evenings, surrounded by people doing tai chi, yoga, reading, skinning up or snogging, and we watch some of the crap football lower down in the park. Fat women jog tortuously around the little running track. Above, breadcrumb clouds scud across a perfect sky, and a leather football hits a nearby tree.

🌀   🌀   🌀

For someone who finds rivers fascinating ('Yes, would you like to see my gold-embossed collection of nineteenth-century etchings of the tributaries of the Tyne?') underground rivers give me an extra thrill. As well as all that energy and ... water ... there's the fact that you can't see them. They're erotic, mysterious and magical because they're hidden and therefore may or may not really exist. In the early nineties when I lived near Ladbroke Grove I frequented a little second-hand bookstore at the northern stretch of Portobello Road run by a serious young Muslim with a goatee. His big gimmick was a job lot of poetry books by Reggie Kray, but my real find was a three-volume set called *Wonderful London* which he sold me for

twenty quid. The volumes were published in 1926 – lots of pictures 11
of London in the 1880s contrasted with the twenties with captions
saying 'Gosh chaps, look what a mess we've made of our city, eh
what.' If only they could have seen what was to come.

The books were brilliant – lots of highbrow columns, anecdotal
journalism and chummy recollections, but by far the best was a
chapter in Volume Two, 'Some Lost Rivers of London' by Alan
Ivimey. He described in exquisitely bright purple prose the undulations to be experienced in Greater London – the geography and
geology of the Thames Valley. London, said Alan, was an uneven
plain, bordered north and south respectively by clay and chalk hills
with a large river flowing through the middle of it, and in between
the hills and the river were undulations of sand and gravel and clay.
The once proud tributaries that flowed through this flood plain

were now little more than
'dirty drains beneath the
bowels of the earth, trickling
weakly along their old beds'.

There was a small map
showing the main rivers
that had disappeared –
around fourteen (though
possibly more) including the
Westbourne, the Tyebourne,
Bridge Creek, Hammersmith
Creek, the Wandle, the Effra,
the Neckinger, Falcon Brook,
the Holebourne (also known
as the Fleet), the Walbrook
and the New River. For
hundreds of years people had
been shitting and pissing and
throwing their dead relatives

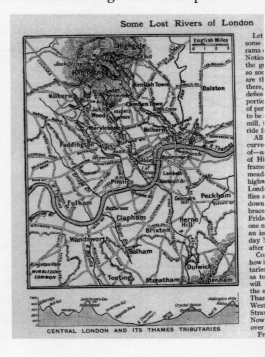

12   into these rivers so that, by the start of the nineteenth century, most had become open sewers.

Travel back in time. Imagine I've a Public-Information-Broadcast-type voice:

> (Swirly ethereal New Age synth music). Once upon a time London was full of vales with water meadows, woods and streams. Man first inhabited the area in Neolithic times, the Celts had a trading and fishing settlement near the Thames. Since then Romans, Saxons, Vikings and Normans invaded ... blah blah Tudors and Stuarts ... Georgians ... lovely squares ... Victorians - nice train stations ... then Edwardians then wartime then the sixties, seventies ... design nightmares ... eighties ... nineties ... modern London, a teeming fumed-filled post-modern high-tech metropolis where once was once rolling countryside.

I like to look at urban landscapes or, to be more specific, how urban landscapes would have looked before the industrial revolution. I can see the past, although it takes a lot of concentration. I walk down a street, look up at the old buildings then look down again at the winding lanes that once would have been filled with shit, rats and corpses. I've invented a special virtual reality gizmo that allows the user to input map co-ordinates then choose a year and the display will show the scene as it was then. So, for example, if I'm walking up Blackstock Road in Finsbury Park and I input 1760, it'd be a sandy lane leading from Stroud Green Farm to the heights of Highbury. A button would allow you to turn off all modern interference, such as cars or other people, but, of course, this would only be advisable in very safe conditions. Actually, by

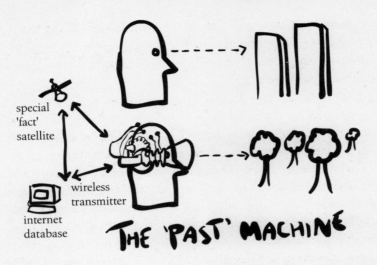

THE 'PAST' MACHINE

special 'fact' satellite

wireless transmitter

internet database

'invented', I mean had an idea and talked to my wife about it. She smiled and asked, 'Are the dreams still bad?'

After doing some research (half an hour on the Internet looking for 'underground rivers'), I discovered that living above an underground river, or groundwater, is bad for your health and should be avoided. This is to do with radiation and 'bad' spirits – that's why feng shui experts, hippies and mad country folk practise water divining. I'm always on the lookout for unified (and easy) theories of everything and it occurred to me that my insomnia, strange dreams and fragmented state of mind could be due to the fact that, since coming to London I had always lived above subterranean streams.

I got a surveyor to come round to investigate a little damp problem we had noticed and, as he was walking around with his damp detector, I tossed a casual question in his general direction:

'Do you think the ... er, damp ... could be caused by ... er ... the lost underground rivers of London like the New River, Fleet, Westbourne, etc., ha ha, as it were?'

'What a load of bullshit,' said the surveyor. He moaned that people were always banging on about underground rivers. Were

14 they? I said. I'm the only person I know who does – everyone else seems to be very bored with the whole concept already.

I live on a road with a watery name so thought that should be enough evidence, but decided to check out my theory on various old maps I'd picked up. Two Victorian maps showed the New River, which seemed to run along where our road is now. Then, during a visit to Stoke Newington library, I found an old leaflet about Clissold Park which showed that the raised avenue of trees was where the heavily banked river ran and continued past the brick shed at the park gate (actually an old pump house), then it went under Green Lanes and along our road before heading north. 'My God,' I thought to myself, slapping my forehead, 'so the tai chi people, crap footballers, snoggers and dopeheads are perhaps inexorably drawn to the electro-magnetic currents of the river!' I was so excited I got goose pimples and had to go for a shit immediately.

ↄ   ↄ   ↄ

At the eastern end of my street, opposite Shampers Unisex Hair Salon (cut £3.50, blow dry £7.00), water is bubbling up through the cracks in the pavement in about six places. This little spring is clear and shiny in the morning sun and I want to reach down and drink from it, only it's flowing over fag butts, withered banana skins, discarded ice cream wrappers and dog shit. It babbles and swirls for a few moments at the side of the road among a narrow band of cobbles, then pours along the kerb to a shallow trough in the road, where a pool is slowly forming. An empty can of Strongbow is already floating in it. As the water level in the pool increases, a group of middle-aged black people start to arrive at this end of the street. They are all impeccably dressed, the men in dark suits and blazers with ties, the women in dazzling summer dresses and hats. A tall man in specs issues instructions then they fan out, rapping fastidiously on doorsteps in twos, clutching their books and spreading the word.

'Who is it?'

'We want to talk to you about Paradise.'

'Fuck off,' says a bloke from an upstairs window.

'The end of the world is coming.'

'Who gives a fuck?'

It has been raining on and off for forty-eight hours, melancholy vertical summer holiday rain with an afterscent that's like faint pipe tobacco mixed with petrol and oranges. Plump droplets hang from the trees. A quick sortie around the neighbourhood shows that many of the area's drains are rebelling. In the network of streets to the north east of the Arsenal Tavern pub small lakes are forming in the roads. It's as if the tarmac and concrete have been pushed down and the area is reverting to swampland.

By early evening, the pool of water stretches across to the other side of the road. It's still flowing heavily from the same cracks and along underneath the iron railings. Half an hour later, four men are standing in the pool, one with a clipboard. They're all looking down at the water.

'Have you got a burst underground river, then?' I ask, smiling. The man with the board looks at me nervously and smiles, but doesn't say anything. As I walk down the road a mechanical drill starts opening up the pavement Er er er er er ererererererererererererereeererere. Down below, the New River flows on, biding its time.

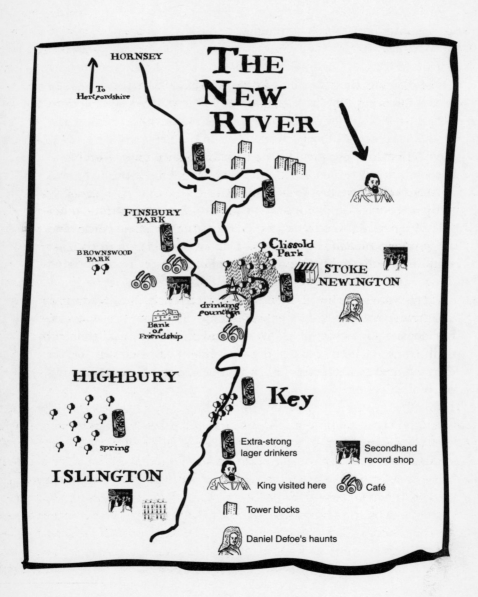

THE
NEW
RIVER

HORNSEY

To Hertfordshire

FINSBURY PARK

BROWNSWOOD PARK

Clissold Park

STOKE NEWINGTON

drinking fountain

Bank of Friendship

HIGHBURY

spring

Key

ISLINGTON

Extra-strong lager drinkers

King visited here

Tower blocks

Daniel Defoe's haunts

Secondhand record shop

Café

2. Special-Brew River Visions
(No Boating, No Swimming, No Fishing, No Cycling)

• The New River – Turnpike Lane to Clerkenwell

*Invisible rivers – Sex File – magic glasses – more dream analysis –
in the library – Turnpike Lane – Clifford Brown – Patrick Swayze in
Albanian Ladyboys – Finsbury Park – Woodberry Down – Swedish
prisons – Highbury Vale – Clissold Park – Canonbury – Islington –
Clerkenwell – Special Brew visions – the floods*

Another dream. I'm walking along the bank of the New River in the
park with my wife and daughter. The path is very narrow and the
water is full of crocodiles. We start to throw golf clubs at them
(irons, not woods) to stop them climbing onto the bank. I throw
the whole bag in and tell the others to run for it.

London is a city of invisible boundaries. Areas alter in atmosphere
or architecture in the space of a few yards, and a reason for this
might be that the rivers which once flowed were often the border-
lines between ancient parishes and settlements. You might walk
down a street now and suddenly notice a change in the air.
Chances are you have walked across the course of an underground river. The New River would have been no different.
Although a recent addition to the waterways of London (about
400 years old), when it was built it would have run through

18   mostly open countryside and settlements would have grown around it.

Some portions of the New River are visible to the naked eye. Yet these sections (for instance, Turnpike Lane to Finsbury Park), which flow silently behind housing estates and terraced streets, seem somehow not as alive as those which have disappeared. It's the ghost parts of the river, now covered by houses, gardens, shops, parks and roads, that get me going more than the algae scum[1] cuts I can see filled with bikes, shopping trolleys and empty plastic Coke bottles.

Searching for lost rivers is, in a way, a spiritual journey, searching for things that I once valued but have lost, like my Yofi acoustic guitar, God, my grandfather's retirement watch, a sense of childlike wonder at the universe, old girlfriends' phone numbers, a large cardboard box containing copies of the *New Musical Express* 1979–82, and my Sex File. Actually, my Sex File, one of the Really Big Things in my life that was truly lost (or, rather, forgotten about – it's often the same thing) – a pink four-sided A4 folder plastered with pictures of models from a stolen late-seventies edition of *Playboy*, with notes and drawings (and even coloured in areas) by me – was recently rediscovered by my father. He found it folded up in an old cobwebby red-brick chicken shed in the field behind the family house, where it had lain untouched (except by spiders) for over twenty years. The Sex File was a snapshot of my early teenage

While Rupert dowses for the stream, Algae Scum's boot makes him scream

---

1   Wasn't Algae Scum a character in Rupert Bear? A Borstal Boy piglet.

desires and fears, in many ways a mystical (almost religious) document – sort of like an East Midlands Dead Sea Scrolls but with leggy blondes, huge breasts, erect nipples and adverts for penis enlargers.

Before I could track the exact course of the New River I needed to do some research at my local library. However, I was immediately faced with a problem. I wouldn't be able to take any books out because I was currently a library Non-Person as I had a couple of books that were seven months overdue. One was an earnest tome about water spirits (the author had apparently lived with the spirits for several months and had been accepted as one of them), the other a teach-yourself aikido manual written in the fifties.

> Aikido is a jolly nice way to get fit and beat up chaps who are giving you a hard time or staring at your wife. Rather than going into the ring with them you simply give them a couple of hefty aikido chops and, hey presto, their nose cartilage has been pushed up into their brain and they're stone-cold dead! Crikey! You'll be the talk of the Lounge Bar. I say, old chap, here come the rozzers. Remember, this is the fifties. The forces of Law and Order don't take kindly to fellows who are dressed up as Chinamen. You'd better leg it, old man. Aiiee banzaaai!
> **The Gentleman's Guide to Aikido**

To go with my new habitat I also had a new look, a pair of mid-seventies National Health glasses. I'd originally got them when I was thirteen but never used them, having been anxious in my early teenage years to appear both tough (to stave off the hard cases who roamed the playground like carnivorous dinosaurs with feather cuts) and cool (to try and impress just one of the many girls I fell hopelessly in love with every week). Janus-like, I looked in two directions, at the birds and the bullies. Pity they weren't in focus.

20   Like the Sex File, the glasses had been forgotten about for a couple of decades until I recently found them at the back of a drawer in my parents' house and brought them back to London. Now I wanted to reclaim my swottishness. If I hadn't been so hung up on not being beaten up and getting a snog I would probably have been a pupil who enjoyed learning ('Ha ha, not really, Togger. Only joshin', mate!') Now I was going to recreate the Anal Years and spend weeks in libraries. The National Health specs would give me the vision of an inquisitive and swotty thirteen year old. Without the spots, the Thin Lizzy albums and the contraband porn mags.

Leaves were already blowing across Clissold Park. The skies were now grey and heavy. Then, just as an autumn melancholy was descending over north London, summer started up again, with muggy days and tropical drizzle and dragonflies dancing around the park. Then came a full-blown three-day heat wave while all over the country irate lorry divers were picketing garages due to a petrol shortage. A sense of unreality was in the air, culminating in England winning a cricket series against the West Indies. Then the rains came again.

An email arrived from Keith the online dream analyst:

> **Water in dreams is a consistent symbol for emotions. (Some people speculate that our first emotional memories are created when we're still floating in our mother's wombs. This may explain the correlation between water and emotions.) Accordingly, floods and tidal waves and other dream visions of rising water usually are associated with periods of 'heightened' emotion in our lives.**
>
> **Keith**

This was getting annoying. Keith the online dream analyst hadn't analysed my dream – he'd completely ignored the stuff about crocodiles and golf clubs. This highlighted a major problem with the online world. Things don't get done properly and you, the consumer, have no come-back because even the biggest corporations are actually run from some student bedroom in the LA suburbs. With razor-sharp clarity I realized there was only one way to sort this out – go to a better and more expensive online dream analyst.

ॐ   ॐ   ॐ

More rain. The old tree-covered New River embankment in the park was dotted with pools of murky water. Beneath some of the trees were clusters of magic mushrooms. A few years ago I would have been tempted to pick them to find out what strange dreams the river might offer me. Now, my drug of choice was a strong cup of tea. Maybe with a biscuit. While splodging around at the edge of the park I noticed that the gate to the little Victorian pump house was open and I just had to peek inside. Expecting to find lost and magical artefacts relating to the New River's past, I found only empty cans of strong lager and cigarette packets. I stood in the building trying to imagine what it would have been like 150 years ago, but all I could picture was a couple of blokes in tatty leather jackets with beetroot faces swearing at each other. I then walked to Stoke Newington Library and sat there surrounded by books on London, place names, rivers, architecture. For the first hour I flicked through free leaflets on yoga and local arts courses, then read the papers. The other people, mostly old or worn-out looking folk and the odd goateed library employee, seemed to be there because they didn't have anything else to do. But not me. No, ha ha, not me.

ॐ   ॐ   ॐ

(*Adjusts National Health glasses*) When James VI of Scotland arrived in London in the hot summer of 1603 to be crowned King

22   of England, he soon discovered to his horror that his new capital
had a foul and unhealthy water supply. Most of the city's medieval
wells and streams had been used up and the water in the larger
rivers was undrinkable. The largest of the tributaries, the Fleet, was
little more than an open sewer, while the Thames was also, literally,
full of shit. Small-scale conduits were piped in from outlying villages such as Paddington, but these had little impact on the now
rapidly rising population. James knew that something had to be
done quickly because he was thirsty.

۞ ۞ ۞

After my first book *Is Shane MacGowan Still Alive?* was published in
the spring of 2000 I began to consider the idea of myself as Travel
Writer. Travelling, jotting things down on the back of beer mats and
being paid for it seemed too good to be true. Emboldened, I decided
to embark on my second book. One idea was provisionally titled
Heartbreak On The Horizon, a sort-of-travel-book about (me) trying
to make it as a country music songwriter, incorporating my experi-
ences in a group which once nearly supported Eric Random and the
Bedlamites at Nottingham Ad Lib Club.

However, I'd also been plugging away on a book about my experi-
ences of London. It had developed from a novel I'd written in 1988
about tai chi film-buff bikers, set in and around a squat in
Leytonstone (with free jazz, Leeds United and the history of the
pullover thrown in) and had entered in the P. G. Wodehouse Comic
Novel competition. After getting the rejection slip back I buried it in a
field somewhere – I still get backache just thinking about it. Now I
dusted down the idea. Travelling in London seemed more intriguing
than roaming the planet in search of the exotic. The stuff happening
at the end of any street in London is far more interesting than, say, the
antics of someone stuck on a didgeridoo farm for a year. The idea of
finding mystery and adventure on the other side of the world has been
hijacked by the tourist industry and TV travel shows. There's nothing

new to find out there so people are turning in on themselves and looking for enchantment closer to home, looking at the things they'd forgotten about or possibly never even looked at. Like the Hare Krishna food delivery van parked across the road, the bloke at the end of the street who shouts 'Grandad Grandad' at the top of his voice every evening, the 125-year-old Greek woman who sits at the top of her front steps and waves to passers by. It was now obvious to me that my only course of action was to attempt a book about real life, a diary about my various journeys along the courses of the underground rivers of London.

The underwater country music project

Maybe I could do the rivers book and incorporate the country music stuff – get C&W stars to don wetsuits and swim in some of the subterranean water courses. For charity. Then record a concept album about the whole experience.

ঔ   ঔ   ঔ

Using the old maps, I traced the course of the New River – as close as I could get – onto my *A to Z*. I had decided to start the walk just up the road in Hornsey, near Turnpike Lane tube, where the river reappeared after an underground stretch. There are also various sections further north – an original loop, an ornamental waterway, now flows around Enfield Town (it was replaced by a straight section of underground pipes in the thirties) and there's also a section to the north of Wood Green. I took the Piccadilly line to Turnpike Lane, then ambled east along Turnpike Lane with its flaking Edwardian buildings, mostly small red-brick shops with awnings, selling fruit and vegetables, kebabs, the odd estate agent. It's a tight squeeze. You almost have to move sideways to get past the people staring at the traffic, at each other, at that nowhere-in-particular place in the middle distance that many bored people look at. There also seemed to be some kind of work-for-all scheme going on – it took five people to

24   transport a crate of satsumas or packet of toilet paper from van to
      shop and the pavement was full of blokes nattering to each other
      about the news of the day ('Oi, Memhet, the bloke next door has got
      seven blokes outside his shop and there's only six of us. We need
      another bloke – can we hire someone?')

⊚ ⊚ ⊚

What is a turnpike? The name derives simply from a 'lane beside a toll
barrier'. Many of the major thoroughfares into London had these barriers, presumably to pay for the upkeep of the roads. However, whenever I hear the word turnpike I think of Clifford Brown, the jazz
trumpeter who died driving off the Pennsylvania Turnpike. It sounds
so much more glamorous than, say, smacking into the back of a bus
near Turnpike Lane tube (it'd be the 341 or 141). That's American
roads for you. If there was a road in the US called the North Circular it
would seem romantic and mysterious. We've all been brainwashed,
somehow. Maybe through hamburgers or subliminal messages in rock
'n' roll records and Hollywood films.
They're much better at that sort of
thing than us Brits. Our idea of subliminal messaging is backtaping on
LPs so when spotty fourteen-year-old
introverts at boarding schools in the
seventies played their Led Zeppelin
records backwards they would hear
stuff like 'You must worship the deviiii-
iiiiiilllll. If you are a girl you want to
shag Jimmy Paaaaaaaage.'

⊚ ⊚ ⊚

I scrutinized the squiggly blue biro line
I'd drawn in my *A to Z*. The section of
the New River I was looking for was

*The New River, alongside
Wightman Road, with old crane-
winch-sluice type thing.*

at the junction of Turnpike Lane and Wightman Road. The New
River appeared not very majestically behind a high, half-rotten
wooden fence crusted with barbed wire. It snaked from around a
small housing estate into a bit of a straight.

⸙ ⸙ ⸙

Four years after James's succession to the throne, his patience was
at an end. The cleanest drinking water on offer in the capital, for
which you had to pay good money, was now suspiciously brown.
James invited some of his most celebrated engineers to consider
solutions and think 'out of the box'. In those days the phrase meant
that if they didn't sort it out they would soon find themselves in a
box, six feet under.

There was an idea knocking about to build a man-made water
channel that would bring in fresh supplies from the boring but
clear-watered countryside of Hertfordshire to the north of the City.
It was a madcap plan, but it needed someone with a posh-sounding
name to bring it to fruition. Step forward wealthy Welsh goldsmith
Hugh Myddelton, a man whose life so far had been a classic rags to
riches story – young boy leaves the Valleys to find fortune in
London, flukes a job at a jewellers in the City, works hard and gets
own business, chosen by King to become Royal Jeweller.
Myddleton not only offered himself up as the engineering genius to
oversee the project but also put up the money as well (the projected
cost was £500,000). Work began on the water channel – already
called the 'New River' – in 1609, starting out at two springs at
Amwell and Chadwell in Hertfordshire.

⸙ ⸙ ⸙

The New River, as if bored with hugging the main drag of
Wightman Road, meanders off to the south-east between the
houses of the Harringay Ladder, a row of long parallel streets than
run down the hill to Green Lanes. I spotted an opening next to an

old school and saw the river stealthily heading south. The path was inaccessible, with heavily bolted steel fences and Water Board signs telling people to keep out. I zig-zagged up and down a few of the streets just to peer over walls and railings to spot sections of the river, then walked down to where the river eventually crosses Tollington Road. Further down is the Albanian video shop and its window full of movies by Albanian Patrick Swayze lookalikes with film titles like I Love A Patrick Swayze Lookalike Ladyboy (possibly my translations are not 100 per cent correct).

ॐ　ॐ　ॐ

At one point Myddleton ran out of money and asked the Corporation of London for help. He was refused so turned to King James who agreed to take on half the costs (and profits). Work was finished in 1613, the river ending at an artificial pond called New River Head just off Rosebery Avenue in Clerkenwell, from where water was distributed to houses in wooden pipes. Over its 38-mile course the New River had many long twists and turns as it followed the contours of the land to maintain the steady drop from Hertfordshire to London. The New River was hailed as a great success and Myddleton became a hero. Statues of him can be seen at various stages along the river's route.

ॐ　ॐ　ॐ

The river travels under the road and reappears in Finsbury Park where it snakes across the 'American Gardens'. Finsbury Park is one of the few areas in this part of north London which doesn't seem to have had the clean-up treatment in recent years, possibly due to the fact that three borough councils – Haringey, Hackney and Islington – are responsible for different parts of it. It still has, according to official figures, a higher proportion than most parts of London of crazy nodding people, walking around talking to themselves, staring in glassy-eyed gangs outside the tube station, bumping into you and asking for money, then looking forgetful and wandering off.

Two of my favourite buildings in Finsbury Park were music venues. The George Robey, a Victorian pub which in its time had been the birth place of many third-division punk bands (though no Danish ones) is now some kind of dance club with blackened windows, a fence surround and the ubiquitous 'security' hanging around.

As the wooden-sided river passes the cricket pitch and under a little bridge, it's a bizarrely rural scene, a snapshot of how the whole landscape might have looked when the river was first built. Trees hang down over the banks, the water is clear. The river winds quickly across the north side of the park then disappears under Green Lanes, in the direction of the Woodberry Down Estate, where it disappears behind a fence and railings. Woodberry Down sounds like something from Rupert Bear. By all accounts it was actually like that (not the talking animals bit) until relatively recently – photos from 100 years ago show the New River meandering gently through water meadows past trees, stationary men with big moustaches and a little country cottage. The view is still good, though, and it's easy to imagine standing on a gentle hill looking down into a green valley of farms and rolling fields, and across Tottenham and Walthamstow marshes.

ᘓ   ᘓ   ᘓ

Naturally there was a danger that, people being people, the New River would soon get clogged up with all the usual debris – shit, blood, pigs' intestines, sheep's brains, the rotting heads of traitors, bloated corpses of drunkards who'd fallen in, everything that at that time clogged up most of the waterways of the city. The New River Company decided to combat this by building paths on each side of the river and employing walkers, big burly moustachioed men who would patrol the river and have their pictures taken when photography was invented. These walkers had the power to fine or even

28 imprison anyone they caught throwing rubbish or simply pissing into the river.

By the mid-nineteenth century most of the water supplies in London were once again polluted. The cholera epidemic of 1849 would eventually be traced to the contaminated water supply at Broad Street in Soho. Thanks to the New River Company's vigilance, their water remained pure and drinkable but as a result it was too expensive for the poor of London. The philanthropist Samuel Gurney spotted a gap in the charity market and under the auspices of his new and snappily named the Metropolitan Free Drinking Fountain Association, opened London's first drinking fountain in Snow Hill, from water pumped (and bought) from the New River.

ↄ ↄ ↄ

I cut across past Manor House, named after the old manor of Stoke Newington which stood nearby. Manor House is a big strippers' and showbands' pub, or at least it would have been in its glory days. I walk along the rumbling and dusty Seven Sisters Road for a quarter of a mile until the New River appears on my left looking very sad, chained up, covered in green American algae, another of those crap Stateside imports up there with grey squirrels and confessional TV, with a shopping trolley and plastic football set fast in the gunge. At Sluice House Nine (Kurt Vonnegut's London novel), on Newnton Close, in the shadow of three big tower blocks, I am finally able to get back down to the river and walk alongside it as it

Sluice House Nine near Newnton Close, Woodberry Down

winds past the East Reservoir, still covered in algae scum. There's a
sense of boundary here between the self-conscious bourgeois charm
of Stoke Newington to the south – with the reservoir and trees, a
church spire, Victorian rooftops, it could be
the countryside – and the more uncontrolled
and more recently built-up area around
Seven Sisters Road to the right, a canvas of
white council slab flats, shopping trolleys
left upturned, kids playing football (two kids
are trying to juggle a ball then the smaller of
the two nicks it off the big one. The big kid knocks
him over), an old people's haven with three plastic benches like a
prison. These tower blocks, another part of the huge Woodberry
Down Estate, are quite spectacular.

The scheme had originally been planned in the early twenties
when it was decided to get rid of much of the Victorian architecture
in the area (Victorians hated Georgians, Modernists hated
Victorians, we hate the Modernists – those fucking bastards),
although not finished until 1952. Its four eight-storey slab blocks
with projecting flat roofs in parallel rows were designed in a 'progressive Scandinavian style coloured in the pale cream like Swiss
municipal architecture' according to the bloke in the little Turkish
grocer's shop across the way on Lordship Road.

The reservoir is a haven for birds and their fat human sidekicks,
birdwatchers. Looking back, where the river meets the road, is my
favourite view of the New River – a blanket of green covers a small
sluiced section dotted with cans, blue girders, a red plastic football,
aerosols and bottles coming up for air like gasping fish, the three
identical tower blocks of Stamford Hill rising in the distance like
silver standing stones. There's ducks too, one old lad with four
duck chicks – well, not chicks, they're ducks, and one younger male
with a dodgy leg who's just been beaten up, probably in a fight over
the duck harem, which waits in the background ready to change

30 allegiance at a moment's notice should the old fella peg it suddenly.

Across the road on Spring Park Drive is a fifties estate. A fat woman shouts out of a sixth-storey window to her daughter below, 'Oi, get me some leeks.'

'I don't want to get leeks,' says the girl.

'Get me some fucking leeks, you little bitch,' shouts her mum.

'I don't want to,' says the girl and the mother is looking very, very angry. Get the leeks, go on, for a quiet life.

'I don't know what leeks look like anyway,' the girl shouts up, then runs away. A right turn and there's an old wooden bench on a patch of grass that once would have had old lads sitting down looking over the view, now it just looks onto the health centre. Look, there's the window where they had the wart clinic. Ah, those were the days. Across Green Lanes again into the back streets and onto Wilberforce Road, with its rows of massive Victorian houses where there are always big puddles on the tarmac. Only 150 years ago all this area north of here up to Seven Sisters Road was open countryside with two big pubs, the Eel Pie House and the Highbury Sluice alongside the river, where anglers and holidaymakers would hang out. Then, in the 1860s, the pubs were pulled down and everything built over in a mad frenzy. If you compare an 1850s map of the district and the 1871 census map you can see the rapid growth of residential streets in Highbury and south Finsbury Park.

On Blackstock Road there are a couple of charity shops and a huge Christian place, all with great second-hand (or more likely third- or fourth-hand) record sections. Their main trade, however, is in the suits of fat-arsed and tiny-bodied dead people and eighties computer games (i.e. Binatone football and tennis – which is just that white dot moving

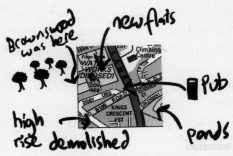

Handwritten annotations: "Brownswood was here", "new flats", "Pub", "high rise demolished", "ponds"

Collating useful information

from a line one side of your screen to another). They also have a fine selection of crappy prints in plastic gilt frames – mostly rural scenes, Italian village harbours and matadors. I buy a lot of crappy pictures in gilt frames and paint my own crappy pictures of London scenes over them, most recently Finsbury Park crossroads on top of a Haywainy pastiche. It's cheaper than buying canvases and you get the frame thrown in too.

Now on Mountgrove Road, the old accordion shop is empty, the estate agents have moved, the graphics company has closed up, the electrical shop has been turned into flats. This was originally a continuation of what is now Blackstock Road, called Gypsy Lane, but it's been cut off, like an oxbow lake. Cross over my road and you're suddenly into very different territory – there's an invisible border I call The Scut Line with cafés and corner shops on one side, nice restaurants and flower shops on the other. It marks a boundary of the old parishes of Hornsey, St Mary's and Stoke Newington. The mad drunken people of Finsbury Park and Highbury Vale don't stray south of the line, marked by the Bank of Friendship pub ('bank' possibly alluding to a riverbank). People would stand on one side of the river here and shout at the poncey Stoke Newington wankers – 'Oi, Daniel Defoe, your book is rubbish!'

The course of the New River has been altered several times in the last 400 years. Originally it flowed around Holloway towards Camden, but in the 1620s it was diverted east to Finsbury Park and

32 Highbury. Since these early days most of the winding stretches were replaced by straighter sections and its capacity was increased to cope with the capital's increased demand for water. This meant taking water from other streams, to the fury of people whose livelihood relied on the rivers, such as millers, fishermen and fat rich red-faced landowners who just liked complaining. Later on, pumping stations were put up along the route which pumped underground water to add to the river's flow. Until recently the New River still supplied the capital with drinking water, 400 years after completion. It's obsolete now that Thames Water's new Ring Main system is operational.

The river now runs only as far as the reservoirs to the north of Stoke Newington. South of here it's mostly been covered over – this happened in 1952 when the Metropolitan Board of Works, eager four-eyed bureaucrats with E. L. Whisty voices, made it their policy for health reasons.

ه   ه   ه

Across Green Lanes yet another time, past the little sluice house and the White House pub where skinheads drink all afternoon, and into Clissold Park. Originally called Newington Park and owned by the Crawshay family it was renamed, along with the eighteenth-century house, after Augustus Clissold, a sexy Victorian vicar who married the heiress (all property in those days going to the person in the family with the fuzzy whiskers). The now ornamental New River appears and bends round in front of the house. It ends at a boundary stone between the parishes of Hornsey and Stoke Newington, marked '1700', although it would originally have turned a right-angle here and flowed back west along the edge of the park. Where there used to be a little iron-railed bridge over the stream is the site of a café where the chips are fantastic and the industrial-strength bright-red ketchup makes your lips sting. This is the very edge of Stoke Newington (origin: 'New Farm by the Tree

New River, Clissold Park, eighteenth century – posh people search for fish

New River, Clissold Park, early twenty-first – illustrator knocked down by car shortly afterwards

Stumps'). The area, once a smart retreat for rich city types and intellectual nonconformists such as Daniel Defoe and Mary Shelley, went downhill badly after the war and by the seventies was regarded as an inner-city shit hole. Over the last ten years or so the urban pioneers (people with snazzy glasses, sharp haircuts and a liking for trendy food) have moved in and the place is on the up once more. I walk down the wide Petherton Road, which has a grassed island in the middle where the river used to run, towards Canonbury.

At Canonbury I enter a little narrow park where an ornamental death mask of the river runs for half a mile. This is a great idea in principle but in reality it's faux-Zen Japaneseland precious, some sensitive designer's idea of tranquillity, rather than reflecting the history of the area and its people. Completely covered in bright green algae, the river looks more like a thin strip of lawn. Here, too, the river marks a boundary, between the infamous Marquess estate on one side and Tony Blair Victorian villa land on the other.

Canonbury Park, further south, is a more typical London scene: silver-haired senior citizens in their tight-knit Special Brew Appreciation Societies sit and watch the world go by (and shout at it now and again in foghorn voices). More and more people walk around these days clutching a can of extra strong lager, as a handy filter for the pain of modern urban life. Out of the park and into Essex Road – a statue of Sir Hugh Myddelton stands at the junction of Essex Road and Upper Street on Islington Green.

34   The walk ends at Clerkenwell at the New
River Head, once a large pond and now a
garden next to the Metropolitan Water
Board's twenties offices. Above the main
door is the seal of the New River Company
showing a hand emerging from the clouds,
causing it to rain upon early seventeenth-
century London. I go into the building and
take a photo, then ask the receptionist if
there are any pamphlets or information
about the New River. He shrugs, although
apparently the seventeenth-century wood-
panelled boardroom of the New River Company still exists somewhere in the building.

Georgian house, Colebrook Row, Islington,
New River flowed through their
living room.

ꙮ ꙮ ꙮ

A few days later I mentioned the walk I'd done to my next-door
neighbour. She was already beginning to sense that I was obsessive,
as it's all I ever talk about to her these days, and told me about a
book that mentions the New River. A family friend had lent it to her
years before. Would I like to have a look at it? Ha ha. Give me the
book, old woman, I screamed, twitching, and nobody will get hurt.
It's a crumbling old volume on the history of Islington, printed in
1812. Inside is a pull-out map from the 1735 which shows not only
the New River but also a 'Boarded River' not on any of my other
maps. What is this? I re-read the chapter in *Wonderful London* on
the lost rivers and searched the net. Up comes *The Lost Rivers of
London*, by Nicholas Barton. A couple of days later I'm eagerly
poring over its contents – a survey and histories of many of the lost
rivers – including the map he's included with the routes of various
underground rivers. According to him, it's not the New River flowing under my road, but something called Hackney Brook. This is
confusing.

But then I remembered the can of strong lager in the old pump house. Could it have been a clue to the New River's mystery, a key to a parallel world? Naturally, I decided that it was – mad pissed people can see the barriers that are hidden from the rest of us, that's why they stick to the areas they know. Perhaps, if I got pissed on extra strong lager and wandered out into the street I too might see the invisible lines and obstacles opening up before me. I promptly went out and bought a selection of the strong lagers on sale in my local off-licence. Kestrel Super, Carlsberg Special Brew, Tennent's Super and Skol Super Strength (they'd run out of Red Stripe SuperSlash).

'Having a party, mate?' asked the shopkeeper.

When John Lennon first took LSD he apparently did so while listening to a recording of passages from the *Tibetan Book of the Dead* translated by Timothy Leary, some of which ended up as lyrics in 'Tomorrow Never Knows', the last track on *Revolver*. Looking for a more modern psychic map I decided to watch one of my daughter's videos, *The Adventures of Pingu*.

Skol Super (*'A smooth tasting very strong lager'* – alc. 9.2% vol.) 7.30p.m.: Tastes salty, tar, roads, burnt treacle. The side of my head starts to pulsate almost straight away. After five or six sips I feel like I've had a few puffs of a high-quality spliff; I should stop now. But no, my need for scientific knowledge is too strong. Sounds are much louder. The radiator behind the settee suddenly comes on and I nearly jump out of my skin. I'm becoming superhumanly sensitive already. I feel that my powers are increasing. Like someone out of the X-Men – actually, that's not a bad idea for a comic book series, a group of superheroes who are all pissheads.

Carlsberg Special Brew *('Brewed since 1950, Carlsberg Special Brew is the original strong lager. By appointment to the*

Royal Danish Court'- Blimey, must be hard work being a royal in Denmark – alc. 9.0% vol.) 9.30p.m.: Took ages to finish the first one. This has a dry-sweet taste and lighter colour with a damp forty-year-old carpet smell. Could possibly do with another couple of years to age properly. It sobers me up after the Skol. Pingu, on its fourth re-run, is getting a little bit boring. Fucking throbbing in my head. This feels like poison in my system.

Tennent's Super *('Very strong lager. Consumer Helpline 0345 112244. Calls charged at local rate'* – alc. 9.0% vol.) 10.20p.m.: Sweet, more like normal beer with a nice deep amber colour and a thick frothy head. A few swigs of this and I'm really starting to feel pissed. I can feel large areas of my brain closing down for the night. But which parts, that's the question?

'On a scale of 1–100, how much shite am I talking now?' I ask my wife.

'Well, it's difficult to say. You regularly talk a lot of shite.' (I look hurt.)

'But, yeah, any more than normal?'

She doesn't answer. A police car, siren blaring and lights flashing, zooms down our road. I quickly rush upstairs and search for a copy of *The Golden Bough*. I don't have one – never have. I'm drunk. I phone the Tennent's Super Consumer Helpline and leave a message about the dangers of living over groundwater.

Kestrel Super *('Super strength lager – an award-winning lager of outstanding quality'* – alc. 9.02% vol.) 11.20p.m.: Smells of Belgian beer. Very complex taste, with strong malt notes, flowery like a real ale. I stroke my chin. I want to unbutton my

itching head which feels like it's covered in chicken wire yet
strangely I feel very focused. I have also started talking to
myself in hyperbabble while thinking I'm actually very nice
looking. Actually.

I suddenly realize that we are in deep shit – the evil water
spirits are everywhere. Maybe they're nice, not evil. I think the
house might be haunted. I'm doing lots of pissing
and have bad gut rot. But I also feel clear headed.
Then start to feel a bit sick. I go to the wardrobe,
take out a coat hanger, break off the 'curvy
bit' and snap it in half, bending
each piece at right angles. I then get
two old pen cases to use as handles
and da daaa I have dowsing rods!
First off, the sitting room. I wander
around and the rods are going crazy
– there's water everywhere. Or is it
because I'm a bit pissed or walking over
the house's water pipes? I spend the next hour wandering
around our road and the nearby streets, charting the areas above
water, and noting down my findings on bits of crumpled-up
paper. According to my calculations the river (whichever one)
misses our house by about 10 feet and comes up the adjacent
road then crosses over and runs under the pavement for a while
before going underneath the houses and coming out again at the
used car lot next to the White House pub. Back at the other
end of the road I check out the Scut Line. It's the start of a very
steep hill heading towards Highbury Village. People who are
pissed cant wolk up it gravity take sover superbrew legs. I am
startinf to git a hedache or is it my riverline-seeuin 3rd eye?
Uuuuuuuuuuuuuuuuuuuuuuuuhh.

🌀 🌀 🌀

38   At the end of the month the heavens opened yet again, but this time they didn't stop. Waterfalls of rain, thunder and lightning, dark grey skies. The local streets once more began to turn into small lakes and streams. Down on Blackstock Road where, according to the old book the Boarded (New) River and Hackney Brook crossed, ponds formed in the road. Around the country people were flooded out of their homes. And the London rivers seemed to be rising too.

The problem with burying rivers is that we can't see, and know, what they're doing. In times of heavy rain it's not that the rivers themselves will burst – they are encased in concrete – but that the small springs and streams that would originally have flowed into them can't get into the concrete culvert that the river has become and simply follow the old course, spreading out over the river's flood plain. Four million people in London live on the flood plains of the lost rivers. One night in early November, Church Street was completely flooded at exactly the point where the New River used to cross over and head south towards Canonbury. The next morning, after more rain, there were huge floods in Clissold Park just where the Hackney Brook would have skirted around the ponds. At the end of Grazebrook Road, pockets of people wandered around in wellies, staring with disbelief at the expanding pool. We've got so cocooned in our soft, warm modern urban world that we've forgotten that nature is just outside the door. Some day these nineteenth-century shelters of bricks and mortar won't be able to protect us any more.

༚ ༚ ༚

One morning the tall smart-blazered Jehovah's Witness appeared again at my front door and begged me to take a copy of the *Watchtower*.

'See all this weather. It's the end times. Just like the Bible says. Read this leaflet. Promise me you'll read it.'

༚ ༚ ༚

Film idea: The Hugh Myddleton Story

Adventure. Big budget/People dying. There's a race on to see who can come up with the best idea. Myddleton wins but others try to sabotage his project. Love interest: she gets pinched by opposition but he wins her back at end. He also foils Gunpowder Plot and saves King. Not entirely accurate historically. Maybe played by Matt Damon. Shakespeare in there too. And the Spanish Armada. Maybe the fleet can only set sail when they've all had enough to drink. Triumphant music at end and high fives as Myddleton blows up Spanish ships. English all played by Americans, Spanish all played by posh English.

London Stories 1: The Dogpeople

The Dogpeople, mostly fat people in their fifties, congregate on the eastern side of Clissold Park, a good distance from the lesbian footballers and just slightly away from the pigeons (who they view as a rival gang. The pigeons ignore the Dogpeople and are more concerned with annoying the ducks.) The Dogpeople shout loudly at each other in high-pitched voices about flea powders and Pedigree Chum, as well as more risqué cries of 'Johnny, Johnny! Come! Come!!' A vague smell of urine wafts from their general direction. Various little rat-like dogs scamper around wearing the same kind of stupid sleeveless quilted jackets as their owners. I try to kick them as they run past, but they are always too quick for me. The dogs, that is. The Dogpeople are easy targets. Their bottoms – invariably covered in green corduroy – are so large and soft they wouldn't feel a thing.

On our street lives one of the Dogpeople ringleaders. Her dog is a pedigree, called something like Chormingly St John Carezza Jane Birkin O'Reilly. They've nicknamed him Petrocelli. Every night she puts a bowl out for Petrocelli in her back yard, and he laps heavily at it. Jokingly I once decided that it sounded like a village idiot wanking. Now I can't get this thought out of my head. I sometimes wake up in the early hours and can hear Petrocelli drinking away and want to scream, 'Run, run to the hills – the crazy man has cast his seed onto our front lawns!' One great idea I had for Mrs Dogperson was that they could fill their dogs with helium and fly them like kites. They could then do loads of great aerobatic tricks – catch the stick, flying bottom sniffing. It then occurred to me that I'd have to find a solution to the problem of dog shit dropping out of the sky at regular intervals. Perhaps some sort of municipal London version of the American Star Wars defence system. My brother has worked with lasers. He might be able to sort that. Or attach buckets to the dogs. Or put helium into their food so that the shit flies upwards as well. And before you ask, I have a grade C physics O Level.

When the Dogperson was ill I offered to walk Petrocelli through the park in the mornings on my way to the childminder's, thinking I might be able to ingratiate myself with the Dogpeople. It worked. Suddenly lots of

A dog with a Dogperson

earthy types in wellies started saying hello to me and pointing at the dog. So I had loads of new mates. The downside was the dog shit. I began to smell of it. Mrs Dogperson gave me polythene bags to scoop his poop, but the stupid dog kept shitting far too much and I'd get it all over my hands. Then when I tried to put it into the special dog-shit bins they had a spring-loaded door so I'd get my hand caught and the pooh would ooze out though the plastic onto my skin. I was also pushing a pram, so it was like driving a car using two different-sized rudders. Petrocelli would always try and force the pram in front of oncoming traffic so he could have me all to himself. Eventually I had to withdraw my offer of help and let Mrs Dogperson fend for herself. I wanted to be able to bite my nails without fear of disease.

The authorities are getting wise to the Dogpeople Problem. Already, police helicopters hover for ages at night over Stoke Newington and Finsbury Park. There are various theories about this (drugs, crime, drug crime), but my guess is that they must contain highly trained police marksmen, who are paid a hefty bounty to take out Dogpeople using airguns. Next time you see a lone mutt running down the street and you smile at the absence of a big-arsed minder waddling behind, remember that it's the taxpayers – you and me – who pay for the bullets.

WINTER

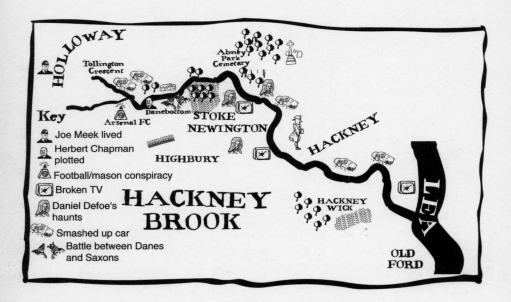

3. Football, the Masons and the Military-Industrial Complex

• Hackney Brook – Holloway to the River Lea

Arsenal – the football conspiracy – Beowulf – the weather – the Masons – Record Breakers – Holloway Road – Joe Meek – Freemasons – Arsenal – PeterJohnnyMick – Clissold Park – Abney Park cemetery – Salvation Army – Hackney – Hackney Downs – tower blocks – Hackney Wick – Occam's shaving brush

Want to hear something amazing? If you look at a map of the rivers of London then place the major football stadiums over the top of it you'll see that most of them are on, or next to, the routes of waterways. Does that make you come out all goosepimply like it did me? Well, here's the hard facts that'll send you rushing for the bog: Wembley – the Brent; Spurs – the Moselle; Chelsea – Counters Creek; Millwall – the Earl's Sluice; Leyton Orient (sound of big barrel being scraped hard) – Dagenham Brook; Brentford – the Brent (too easy); Fulham – the Thames; Wimbledon – used to play near the banks of the Wandle; QPR – the exception that proves the rule; West Ham – OK, so that's the end of my theory. But what of Arsenal?

I have a tatty old nineteenth-century Great Exhibition map[1] on my wall at home on which the London of 150 years ago looks like a

---

1   *Tallis's Illustrated Plan of London & its Environs* (1851)

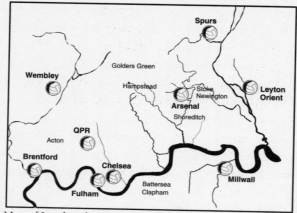

Map of London showing proximity of football stadia to rivers

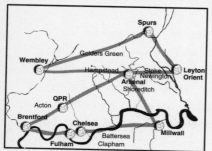

A double triangle. It must mean ... something.

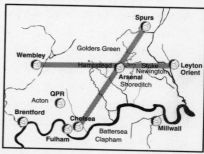

*When Arsenal's new stadium is built –
a Templar cross?*

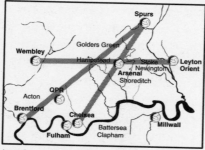

*Are the football clubs secretly run by
anarchist groups?*

virulent bacteria on a petri dish. I have always liked saying to friends, look, see where you live now? Well, look, it was once a ... field. Then I'll stand back with a self-satisfied expression while they shrug as if to say 'Who gives a fuck, have you got any more wine?' The Hackney Brook is marked on this map as a small stream near Wells Street in central Hackney. It also appears in various other sections, as a sewer along Gillespie Road, a small watercourse continuing off it towards Holloway and a river running from Stoke Newington to the start of Hackney, then stopping and continuing again around Hackney Wick towards the River Lea, before disappearing in a watery maze of cuts and artificial channels.[2] But when I transferred the route of this little stream onto my *A to Z* it struck me that Highbury Stadium, Arsenal football ground, lay right on the course of the stream.

Arsenal are planning to move to another site at Ashburton Grove, half a mile away. This too lies above the Hackney Brook, at a point where two branches of it converge. What's going on? Is there something about rivers that is good for football grounds? Water for the grass, perhaps? At one time they also wanted to move to an area behind St Pancras Station, the site of the Brill, a big pool near the River Fleet and, according to William Stukely, a pagan holy site.

And, while we're at it, how did former manager Herbert Chapman manage to get the name of Gillespie Road tube changed to Arsenal in the thirties? Did he inform local council members that Dizzy Gillespie (who the street was named after) was, in fact, black and so all hell broke loose? How did Arsenal manage to get back into the top division after being relegated in 1913? Some sort of stitch up, no doubt. And how did they get

---

[2]   In *The Lost Rivers of London*, Nicholas Barton tells us Hackney Brook is now 'wholly lost' but at one stage was a large stream which at flood could reach widths of 100 foot.

48   hold of this prime land in North London? Did they channel the magical powers of the Hackney Brook using thirties superstar Cliff Bastin's false teeth as dowsing rods?

A clue is in the club's original name, from its origins in south London. The fact that it was called Woolwich Arsenal and was a works team is all the proof we need that the club is part, or at least was once a part, of the Military-Industrial Complex. They are the New World Order. Their colours – red shirts with white sleeves – are also simply a modern version of the tunics of the Knights Templar, forerunners of the Masons. Maybe their ground is situated near a stream because they need the presence of sacred spring water for their holy rituals. You know, pulling up their trousers and sticking the eye of a dead fish onto a slice of Dairylea cheese spread.

A search on the Internet for 'Hackney Brook' reveals only eleven matches, some of which are duplicates. One of the most interesting is a listings page of Masonic lodges in London. Lodge 7397 is the Hackney Brook Lodge, which meets in Clerkenwell on the fourth Monday of every fourth month. Why were they called Hackney Brook? Maybe they knew why the river had been buried. The Masons know all about all sorts of 'hidden stuff'. Hidden stuff is why people join the Masons.

I love the idea of the lost rivers being somehow bound up in a mystical conspiracy. Maybe the rivers were pagan holy waters and the highly Christian Victorians wanted to bury the old beliefs for good and replace them with a new religion. Or what if developers – the Masons, the bloke with the big chin from the Barratt homes adverts (the one with the helicopter) – wanted new cheap land on which to build?

ə   ə   ə

I have a dream about Highbury and Blackstock Road in the past, a semi-rural landscape of overlapping conduits and raised waterways,

a Venice meets Spaghetti Junction.
I am walking over deep crevasses
covered by glass peppered with
little red dots. Water flies through
large glass tunnels, crisscrossing
one way then another. Purple
water froths over in a triumphal
arch. It's like some vaguely
remembered scene from a sci-fi
short story.

Water is flying, as if unsupported, crisscrossing one way then another.

Arches are always triumphal,
never defeatist. Why is that?
Because, when you think about it, an arch is like a sad face. A triumphal face would be like an upturned arch. I email the dream to my new online dream analyst ('Poppy') to find out the truth.

An email arrives:
(*In dippy American accent*)

> **Hi Tim!**
> **Dreaming of clear water is a sign of great good luck and**
> **prosperity, a dream of muddy water foretells sadness or**
> **sorry for the dreamer through hearing of an illness or**
> **death of someone he/she knows well. Dirty water warns**
> **of unscrupulous people who would bring you to ruin. All**
> **water dreams, other than clear, have a bad omen**
> **connected to them and should be studied carefully and**
> **taken as a true warning.**

I had already noticed a pattern emerging in the California textured world of online dream doctors. Take money off punter then cut and paste a bit of text from a dream dictionary. After a couple of weeks I wrote back to Poppy but the email was returned. On her website

50   was a 404 file not found. Perhaps the web police had raided Poppy's dream surgery and found her in bed with a horse covered in fish scales.

After a bit of searching around I found a sensible new online dream doctor called Mike. He didn't seem very New Age and replied promptly.

(Sensible Yorkshire accent)

> **I thank you so much for using our online Dream Diagnosis!**
> **I will interpret your dream as fast as possible.**
> **Thank you, and**
> **God Bless,**
> **Michael, Dream Analyst**

          ə   ə   ə

A river called the Hackney Brook? You have to admit it's a rubbish name. Some river names, like the Humber, Colne and Ouse, are thought to be pre-Celtic. The Thames is British in origin. Likewise Tee and Dee, and Avon. But the Hackney Brook? – the lazy fuckers just called it after Hackney. Didn't they? Of course, mere streams and tributaries would not have been given the importance of big rivers. All the same, the Anglo-Saxons yet again manage to show how dour and unimaginative they can be. So what about Hackney? Where does that come from?

There are three possible origins for the name Hackney. Firstly, the word *haccan* is Anglo-Saxon for 'to kill with a sword or axe, slash slash slash!' and 'ey' means a river. Or it is a Viking word meaning 'raised bit in marshland' – perhaps because Hackney was always a well-watered area, with streams running into the River Lea. But the most likely explanation is that the area belonged to the Saxon chief, Hacka.

Proof for all this? For once I can offer some evidence. Here is an excerpt from the great Anglo-Saxon epic poem *Beowulf*. In this short section Hacka, the founder of Hackney, makes a brief appearance.

> *Came then from the moor*
> *under the misty hills*
> *Hacka stalking under*
> *the weight of his river knowledge.*
> *That Saxon pedant*
> *planned to ensnare*
> *the minds of men*
> *in the high hall.*
>
> *He strode under the clouds,*
> *seeking Beowulf, to tell him*
> *about the river he had found*
> *near his new house.*
> *Nor was it the first time he*
> *had tried to name that stream.*
> *And never in his life before*
> *– or since –*
> *did he find better luck!*
>
> *For came then to the building*
> *that Beowulf, full of wisdom.*
> *(In E. L. Whisty voice)*
> *'Beo, there's this river that runs*
> *through my new gaff.*
> *What should I call it?'*
> *Quickly Beowulf's brain moved*
> *and he answered direct,*
> *(in John Major voice)*
> *'Call your new home Hacka's village.*
> *And the stream shall be named*

The Brook of Hacka's village.'
'That's original and catchy, O great chief,'
said Hacka, much pleased. 'Thanks a lot.'
As he went out, smiling.
He saw an evil demon in an angry mood
Pass in the other direction.
'Evening, mate!' said Hacka.
The demon had fire in his eyes.
That monster expected
to rip life from the body of each
one before morning came.
But Hacka didn't notice –
He was too excited about his new river.

I never thought I'd turn into the sort of person who talked about the weather incessantly, but the rain round our way was definitely getting worse. Big plump drops, vertical sheeting, soft drizzle, aggressively cold splashes, wind-blown white scouring sleet, peppery eye-stinging bursts and, of course, dull, wet London showers.

Holes have been dug in the nearby streets and small Thames Water and Subterra signs have been erected. They are obviously doing 'something' to the underground rivers. Cutting a deal with them, perhaps, urging them to be quiet. Or diverting them further underground in case they snitch. Or converting the waters of the river into beer. I got through to Thames Water and tried to find someone responsible for underground rivers, but with no success. Then I'm back in a queue: 'We are sorry to keep you. Your call is important to us. However, we are currently experiencing high call volumes. You are moving up the queue and your call will be answered as soon as possible. Thank you for your patience at this busy time.'

ॐ   ॐ   ॐ

Floods. Snow. Christmas comes and goes. Under a young tree lies a charred pile of stuff – pieces of clothing, books, aerosol cans and a small stool. A pair of men's shoes are still slightly smouldering. The aftermath of some apocalyptic festive break-up? Or perhaps a young graffiti-addicted accountant simply spontaneously combusted on his star-gazing stool while contemplating the sheer joy of life.

More lazy days in the library, looking at old maps of the area and the Hackney Brook valley. A book by a local historian, Jack Whitehead, shows the contours of the valley in 3D. The brook rose in two places, the main one at the foot of Crouch Hill, east of Holloway Road, with a smaller branch near the start of Liverpool Road.

Then my mind drifts and I stare at the faded chequerboard floor and listen to the beep of the book-checking computer thing, the cherchercher of the till, the murmur of African accents, the rumble of traffic going past the window. In Stokey library people eye each other up, but not in a good way – more 'Errr, you're walking along the lesbian crafts and hobbies section? You must be a poof.'

At last I find what I've been looking for. An old map, from some obscure US university, showing the course of the Hackney Brook in relation to the nearby New River and which corresponds with the old map from the Islington book that my neighbour lent me. It shows the rivers crossing over at a point parallel to the Stoke Newington ponds, about a quarter of a mile west. Thus 'the

17th/18thC
New River
carried over
Hackney Brook
by wooden conduit
(Boarded River)

Course of Hackney Brook

Course of New River

CLISSOLD
PARK

54 Boarded River' was the New River, kept at the correct gradient as it passed through the Hackney Brook valley and over the Hackney Brook. This is the point in the film where I turn to my glamorous assistant, as the Nazi hordes are waiting to pounce, and she kisses me in congratulation. I take off her glasses and realize she is actually quite beautiful. I then hand her a gun and say, 'Do you know how to use this?' Suddenly the door bursts open, she shoots five evil Nazis and we smash though a window and escape ...

I also had a look at John Rocque's famous map of London in the British Library (rolled up it looks like a bazooka). Rocque's depiction of Hackney Brook is a little sketchy – he has it starting further east and north than its true course and doesn't have it crossing Blackstock Road at all. This might have thrown me off course, but allied to various mistakes in the same area suggests that Rocque never actually visited Hackney and Stoke Newington. He was too scared. Probably got one of his mates to do it.

Rocquey

Mate: So there's this little river. I've drawn it on the back of a beer-stained parchment for you.

Rocque: Tis very squiggly.

Mate: OK, if that's your attitude why don't you go and have a look at it?

Rocque: Ooh no, I'm, er, far too busy. And I've got a cold.

⊚ ⊚ ⊚

I had a vague notion of walking the route of the Hackney Brook and then all the other rivers and streams in London, then writing to the *Guinness Book of Records* and appearing on *Record Breakers*.

Me: Yes, well, you have to bear in mind the substrata of London and its alluvial plane. Back in the mists of time there blah blah blah...

Then the studio floor opens up and there's an underground river. A little boat appears in the distance with a single oarsman and it's Norris McWhirter and he's holding a clipboard and tells the audience some factoids about the rivers. Then we listen to a tape of Roy Castle doing the unplugged version of 'Dedication' and the audience cheers.

ෙ   ෙ   ෙ

It's time to do some dowsing again. I buy a can of Tennent's Super and walk across the zebra crossing at the bottom of Blackstock Road, over and over again. I don't drink Special Brew so much as use it as a tool. I see myself as part of the same tradition as Carlos Castaneda. Whereas he got in touch with the spirit world through his use of Mexican psychoactive funguses, I buy cheap beer from Pricecutters in Highbury Vale and walk around muttering to myself, getting a clicking sound in my right knee (an old hurdling injury). I am also keen to reclaim these drinks from being the beverage of mad drunkards and to create a new form of Special Brew literature. Funnily enough, I found a book by Benjamin Clarke, a Victorian Hackney man who wrote a book called *Glimpses of Ancient Hackney and Stoke Newington*, in which he says that Hackney Brook used to be regarded as a river of beer. The Woolpack brewery, near Hackney Wick, churned out barrels of the sort of stuff that Londoners loved (and love) to drink – soapy mouthwash with no head. Discovering the alchemical secret of turning water into beer – it's every man's dream.

As my head buzzes pleasurably, I look up the road and see the river valley ahead of me. I'm ready to do the walk. But first I need a piss (beer into water reverse alchemy technique).

ෙ   ෙ   ෙ

The northern branch of Hackney Brook apparently starts at Tollington Park, around Wray Crescent and Pine Grove. It's just off Holloway Road, which is packed with people – dark-eyed lads with eighties jackets hawking tobacco; pale-faced chain-smoking girls with bandy legs and leggings tottering along with prams; huge-bellied tracksuit trouser blokes waddling from café to pub with a tabloid under their arm; Grand Victorian department stores turned into emporiums of second-hand electrical tat; eighties-style graffiti; students queuing at cash points; geezers flogging old office equipment piled high on the pavement. At no. 304 lived Joe Meek, the record producer of songs like 'Telstar', strange futuristic pop classics. Dang dang dong dong ding deng dang dung dooong. He must have been influenced by the strange atmosphere of this neighbourhood with its crazy adrenalin-fuelled rush of bodies, bumping against each other like electrons in matter, Oxford Street's ugly sister.

I had been hoping to see some kind of plaque or ramblers' guide at the start of the walk, possibly even a fountain bubbling with pure spring water. Instead I am faced with a large fenced-off mass of earth, a secret building site, with a lonely blue prefab building. Men with yellow hard hats stand around holding stuff – clipboards, balls of string, spanners, a spade. It's a tried and tested workman's trick. Hold something functional just in case the 'boss' happens to be driving past in his silver Jag and looks over. 'Hmm, good to see Smithy is working hard with his ball of string.'

There are two ways of looking for a river's source. You can do it the proper way with geologists, maps, digging equipment and people from Thames Water saying 'please hold the line'. Or you can look for puddles. And right in the middle of this mass of dirt is a large pool of standing water. This must be it. At the far edge of the site is a JCB digger-type thing with tank tracks next to a big hole. It looks as though the blokes with yellow hats are planning to cover the water with the big pile of dirt. Then it dawns on me that this is the Area 51 of London rivers. They were finally trying to eradicate all trace of the famous Hackney Brook. Why? And who are *they*?

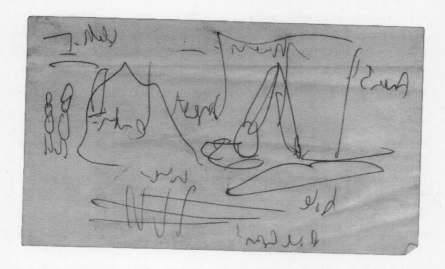

I quickly make a sketch of the scene on a Post-it Note, then retreat. One of the yellow hats spots me and mutters into a walkie talkie to one of his mates about five yards away, who is fidgeting with his ball of string. I quickly cross the road, staring into my *A to Z*, and pass a severe old grey brick Victorian house, the sort I imagine Charles Dickens had in mind when he described Arthur Clennam's mother's house in *Little Dorrit*: 'An old brick house, so dingy as to be all but black, standing by itself within a gateway. Before it a square court-yard where a shrub or two and a patch of grass were as rank (which is saying much) as the iron railings enclosing them were rusty ... weather-stained, smoke-blackened, and overgrown with weeds.'

And into a big estate. I keep looking behind me to check the men with yellow hats aren't following. Who are the yellow hats, anyway? Historically, the yellow hat has denoted royalty – crowns and stuff (or religious folk with yellow auras/halos). Geoffrey Plantagenet, father of Henry II and precursor of the Plantagenet dynasty, was so-called because he wore a sprig of yellow broom

58   (a Druid's sacred plant) in his hat so his soldiers would recognize him. His daughter-in-law, Eleanor of Aquitaine, is credited with the creation of the Knights Templar, forerunners of the Freemasons. Whereas I watch a lot of *Bob the Builder* with my daughter – the show is about a bloke with a yellow hat who talks to machines and a scarecrow that comes alive.

A quick detour around the modern Iseldon (original name for Islington) village with its strange dips in the road as it goes down the river valley, and where the two heads of Hackney Brook would have converged, and then I head onto Hornsey Road, alongside the Saxon-sounding Swaneson House estate with its dank sixties/seventies shopping arcade with laundrette, grocers and chemists. When I was a kid I used to have books which showed what the new exciting world would look like, and most of the pictures were like the shopping arcade of the Swaneson Estate. What a crazily drab world must it have been in the sixties, with its Beatles harmonies, cups of tea and cakes, that we were suckered into thinking these shopping centres were the height of futuristic sophisticated living? To the left are some tired swings, then further up some beaten-up cars. Some local creative has recently taken a crowbar to one, leaving it like a smashed flower, powdery glass on the road, bits of ripped metal folding outwards. There's a large pool of unhealthy-looking standing water, then another car, this time with no wheels. I have walked onto a set from *The Sweeney*, perfect for handbrake turns, jumping on and off bonnets, pointing a lot and calling people 'slags'. It's not so easy to find these bits of bombsitesque London now, even compared with five or six years ago. English Heritage should get areas like this listed.

Further up is a seventies-style Vauxhall estate car written over with some classic full colour graffiti. It should be in a gallery. But as a *Time Out* journo might say,

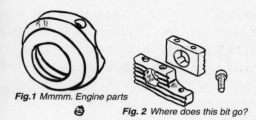

Fig.1 *Mmmm. Engine parts*

Fig. 2 *Where does this bit go?*

(Mockney voiceover) 'London is, in a very real sense, its own gallery.'

At the edge of the dirt track, near the road, is a sign for

the estate managers who own the site – 'state' has been cut out of the sign, probably by some bright spark anarchist. Smash the state, please fuck the system NOW. That's what Crass wanted, back on *Bullshit Detector*.

> The living that is owed to me I'm never going to get,
> They've buggered this old world up, up to their necks in
>   debt.
> They'd give you a lobotomy for something you ain't done,
> They'll make you an epitome of everything that's wrong.
> Do they owe us a living?
> Of course they do,
> Of course they do.
> Do they owe us a living?
> Of course they do,
> Of course they do.
> Do they owe us a living?
> OF COURSE THEY FUCKING DO.[3]
> **'Do they owe us a living?', Crass**

---

3   I expect that those lyrics have made their way into the Danish National
    Anthem by now. **King of Denmark**: Lave de skylde os en nulevende?
    Selvfølgelig de lave Selvfølgelig de lave. Lave de skylde os en nulevende?
    Selvfølgelig de [fucking] lave.

60 Back on Hornsey Road I walk through the tunnel under the main-line railway to the north. The walls have the peeling skin of a decade and a half of pop posters. At the edges I can make out flaking scraps from years ago – Hardcore Uproar and Seal plus multiple layers of old graffiti.[4]

I've wandered away from the course of the river. Access is impossible due to the railway lines and the Ashburton Grove light industrial estate, the planned site of Arsenal's new stadium. There's a seventies factory development, a taxi car park and another broken car, this one burnt out as well. A big-boned bloke in a shell suit is inspecting it. Was it his? Maybe he was on a stag night and his mates did up his motor for a laugh. The road is a dead end so I walk back and around Drayton Park station with the river valley off to my left under the Ashburton Grove forklift centre – for all your forklift needs. There's a beautiful big sky that'll be lost when Arsenal build their new dream stadium. To the right is Highbury Hill, with allotments on the other side of the road banking down to the railway like vineyards, a vision of a different London.

And so into the reclaimed urban landscape of Gillespie Park. It's an ecology centre developed on old ground near the railway, with different landscape areas and an organic café. I sit down for a while and stare out at the little stone circle and neat marshland pools, surrounded by grassland and meadow in a little urban forest created by local people, and listen to the sounds of thirteen year olds being taught about 'nature' by their teacher.

'Can we catch some tadpoles sir. Goo on.'

'No, now we're going to look at the water meadow.'

'Aww fuckin' boring.'

---

4 When we were kids we had a room that we used to cover in graffiti and drawings then, when the walls were full up, my parents would give us a tin of white paint and tell us to paint over it so we could start again. Like some weird communist job creation scheme.

The kid sticks his net into the pool anyway and swishes it around, while shouting, 'Come on, you little bastards.' The teacher, evidently of the 'smile benignly and hope the little fucker will go away' school of discipline, smiles benignly and begins telling the group about the importance of medicinal herbs.

I walk up the track past the 'wetlands' and can see Isledon village on the other side of the tracks. You get a sense of how the railway carved through the landscape in the mid-nineteenth century. Even then, when progress was a religion, people would have been aware of the landscape that would be lost:

> I am glad there is a sketch of it before the threatened railway comes, which is to cut through Wells' Row into the garden of Mr I. and go to Hackney. We are all very much amazed at the thought of it, but I fear there is little doubt it will come in that direction.[5]
> *local girl Elisabeth Hole to her friend Miss Nicols, December 1840*

In Gillespie Park it's hard to discern the real contours of the land because it's obviously been built up. There's a little tunnel into the trees, then down a dirt track to a wooden walkway and to the left is marshland. It's like a riverside. I stop and look across to the little meadow with another stone circle on the left. The rain lets up for a while and I sit down at a bench behind the stone circle with my note-book. Nearby, in the circle itself, sit four dishevelled figures. Two black guys, one old and rasta-ish with a high-pitched Jamaican accent, one young with a little woolly hat and nervy and loud, a tough-looking middle-aged cockney ex-soldier type and a rock-chick blonde in her late forties with leather jacket and strange heavy, jerky make-up. They look battered and hurt and are all talking very loudly, the men trying to get the attention of and impress the woman, as a spliff is passed around and they sip from cans of Tennent's Super.

---

5   Islington Past by John Richardson

62 They must be twenty-first century druids. The younger bloke, whose name is Michael, starts to shout out, 'Poetry is lovely! Poetry is beautiful! Chelsea will win the league.' I finish my quick notes and get up to go, as he smiles at me still singing the joys of football and poetry.

'You're right about the poetry anyway,' I say.

'Do you know any poems?' he asks. I recite the Spike Milligan one about the water cycle:

There are holes in the sky where the rain gets in
They are ever so small, that's why rain is thin.

'Spike is a genius. What a man!' he yells. 'We love Spike, Spike understands us!' and he starts to sing some strange song that I've never heard before. Maybe it was the theme tune to the Q series. Then the little Jamaican bloke with a high-pitched singsong accent jabs me in the chest, his sad but friendly eyes open wide, and he smiles.

'If ya fell off de earth which way would ya fall?'

'Er, sideways,' I say, trying to be clever, because it is obviously a trick question.

'NO ya silly fella. Ya'd fall up. And once ya in space dere is only one way to go anyway and dat's up. Dere's only up.'

'The only way is up!' sings Michael. 'Baby, you and meeeeee eeeee.'

'Whatever happened to her?' asks the woman.

'Whatever happened to who?'

'To Yazz ...'

At this strange turn in the conversation I wave goodbye and walk towards the trees. The little gathering is a bit too similar to the blatherings of my own circle of friends, confirming my suspicion that many of us are only a broken heart and a crate of strong cider away from this kind of life. I can see Arsenal stadium up to the right, looming over the houses. At a little arched entrance, a green door to the secret garden, I come out onto Gillespie Road.

This is the heart of Arsenal territory, where every fortnight in winter a red and white fat-bloke tsunami gathers momentum along Gillespie Road, replica-shirted waddlers dragged into its irrepressible wake from chip shop doorways and pub lounges, as it heads west towards Highbury Stadium. As an organism it is magnificent in its tracksuit-bottomed lard power, each individual walking slowly and thoughtfully in the footsteps of eight decades of Arsenal supporters. Back in the days of silent film, when the Gunners first parachuted into this no-man's-land vale between Highbury and Finsbury Park from their true home in Woolwich, south London, football fans lived a black-and-white existence and moved from place to place at an astonishing 20 m.p.h., while waving rattles and wearing thick cardboard suits in all weathers. No wonder they were thin. Going to a game was a high-quality cardiovascular workout.

(**Then:** Come on Arsenal. Play up. Give them what for (hits small child on head with rattle) spiffing lumme stone the crows lord a mercy and God save the King.
Now: Fack in' kant barrstudd get airt uv itt you wankahh you-uurr shiiiitttttt!!)

The source of this vast flow of heavily cholesteroled humanity is the pubs of Blackstock Road – the Arsenal Tavern, the Gunners, the Woodbine, the Bank of Friendship and the Kings Head. Further north are the Blackstock Arms and the Twelve Pins. To the south,

64 the Highbury Barn. The pubs swell with bullfrog stomachs and bladders as lager is swilled in industrial-sized portions.

Walk from the south and there's a different perspective. People in chinos with City accents jump out of sports cars parked in side streets, couples and larger groups sit in the Italian restaurants of Highbury Park chewing on squid and culture and tactical ideas gleaned from the broadsheets and Serie A. As I mentioned before, the scut line is around my street. Here, outside the Arsenal Fish Bar, which is actually a post-modern twenty-first-century Chinese takeaway, lard-bellied skin-heads stuff trays of chips down their throats to soak up the beer. Inside the café, on the walls nearest the counter, there's a picture of ex-Gunners superstar Nigel Winterburn looking like he's in a police photo and has been arrested for stealing an unco-ordinated outfit from C&A, which he is wearing (should have destroyed the evidence, Nige).

             ◈   ◈   ◈

In the Arsenal museum they have lots of great cut-out figures of many of the players who have long since departed. And a film, with Bob Wilson's head popping up at the most inopportune moments. He does the voiceover but materializes (bad) magically every time there's something profound to say, then dematerializes (good) in the style of the *Star Trek* transporter. Lots of nice old photos, and they make no bones about the fact that they never actually officially won promotion to the top division – in fact they're even quite proud of the shenanigans and arm twisting that went on. My main question, how Gillespie Road tube was changed to Arsenal, is never answered apart from the comment that the London Electric Railway Company did it after being 'persuaded' (tour guide laughs) by Chapman.

It's my belief that Arsenal were somehow involved in the shooting of Archduke Franz Ferdinand[6] and the onset of World War I so they wouldn't have to spend too long in Division Two. For lo and behold, the first season after the war they got promoted, despite only finishing fifth in the Second Division. How did that happen? It was decided by the powers that be (Royalty, Government, Masons, Arsenal) to expand the First Division following the end of World War I in an attempt to stave off proletarian revolution by giving them more football. By coincidence, Tottenham finished in the bottom three of Division One that year, yet were still relegated.

ӫ ӫ ӫ

I dive into the Arsenal Tavern on Blackstock Road for a quick pint of Guinness because it's only £1.60 during the day and I weigh up whether to ask the landlady about history but she is slumbering near the side door, arms like hams, chins on gargantuan bosoms, so I sit at the bar and chat to a gentleman called Dublin Peter, Cork Johnny, actually no I think it was Mullingar Mick, who anyway I've seen and talked to in here before and I notice that everyone is facing east. There are about twelve people in the pub – stare at pint sip stare at pint stare at wall stare at pint sip stare at pint stare at wall and repeat until need piss. The pub was called the New Sluice in the nineteenth century and I imagine they must have documents and photos of the pub back then.

The back room of the Arsenal Tavern is the exact point at which the boarded river crossed over Hackney Brook. I stand there for a few moments drinking and breathing hard, waiting for inspiration

---

6   Possibly an obscure relation of top centreforward, Les, who played for Spurs.

66   or some kind of sign. PeterJohnnyMick then appears again and starts explaining to me why Niall Quinn is still so effective as a front man for Sunderland: 'He's got mobility. Mobility, I tell you. He has the mobility of a smaller man. Have you seen how he can turn in the box?'

ಎ   ಎ   ಎ

I walk along an alleyway past a building site where the crushed remains of a tower block lie in mesh-covered cubes like Rice Krispie honey cakes. Nearby is a weeping willow, a nice riverside touch. I eventually come out at the not very aptly named Green Lanes then cross through the northern end of Clissold Park about 200 yards from the New River walk, by the ponds – the brook ran alongside them. It's an enchanted place, with birds and mad people sitting on the benches. For a brief moment, I imagine I am back a couple of hundred years. Through the gate and over Queen Elizabeth's Walk.[7] Then along Grazebrook Road,

Hackney Brook – Clissold Park ponds

where sheep, I suppose, used to, er, graze next to the brook. Then the land rises up to the right. And left. There's a school in the way so I go up to Church Street, which is full of young well-spoken mums, old leathery Irishmen dodging into the dark haven of the Auld Shillelagh, unshaven blokes in hooded tops sitting on the pavement asking for spare change, estate agents crammed with upwardly mobile families fecund with dosh or young couples looking longingly at places they can't afford, skinny blokes with

---

7   She walked down from Manor House, one imagines to buy drugs or procure a prostitute.

beards on bikes, kids, lots of kids, kids in prams, kids running, kids in backpacks, kids with ice creams, kids playing football, kids coming out of every doorway, Jewish guys with seventeenth-century Lithuanian suits, young lads with thick specs and thin ringlets, the odd big African in traditional dress, tired-eyed socialists and anarchists drinking in big, dirty old pubs and still dreaming of the revolution.

Turning into Abney Park Cemetery, I walk in a loop around its perimeter, past the grave of Salvation Army founder William Booth. It's quiet and boggy, with lots of standing water and a strange atmosphere like a temperature shift or pressure change. Or something else ... ghostly legions of Salvation Army brass bands emitting the spittle from their instruments. Branches curling down over old weathered stone, graves half buried in turf and moss, some with fresh flowers, which is strange as these graves are all well over 100 years old. I wade through big puddles as the track pretty much follows the course of the brook along the cemetery's northern boundary. My beautiful new trainers keep slipping into the water and I fear I'll be pulled down to an underworld by the grasping corpse-hands of the shaven-headed vegan N16 dead. The track ends at the main entrance on Stoke Newington High Street.

Just down the road is the Pub Formerly Known As Three Crowns, so called because James I (and VI) apparently stopped for a pint there when he first entered London and united the thrones of England, Scotland and Wales for the first time. Maybe he had the small town boy's mentality and thought that Stoke Newington *was* London (*'Och, ut's on'y gorrt threee pubs!'*) In those days Stokey was pretty much the edge of London. Up until that time the Three Crowns had been called the Cock and Harp, a grand fifteenth-century pub which was knocked down in the mid-nineteenth century just to be replaced by a bland Victorian version. When I first used to come to N16 the three nations had become Ireland, the West Indies and Hardcore Cockney, and the age limit was sixty-five and over.

68   Then it was the Samuel Beckett (Beckett wasn't from bloody Stoke Newington). Now it's called Bar Lorca (and neither did bloody Lorca. Bloody). How unutterably sad is that? (Puts on cardigan and lights pipe then walks off in a huff). There should be. A law against. That kind. Of. Thing.

I continue towards Hackney, with the common on the right. This used to be called Cockhanger Green, suggesting that Stoke Newington was a sort of Middle Ages brothel Centre Parcs, until someone, most likely a Victorian do-gooder, decided to change the name to the rather less exciting Stoke Newington Common. There used to be an exhibit timeline at the Museum of London showing a Neolithic dinner party. A nineteenth-century archaeological dig had unearthed evidence of London's earliest Stone Age settlers right here next to the Hackney Brook. The exhibit showed what looked like some naked hippies in a clearing holding twigs, and barbecuing some meat. These days they'd be chased off by a council employee or more likely a drug dealer. I buy a sandwich and wander onto the common then sit down to finish my snack, wondering if any evidence of my meal will appear in some museum 3,000 years hence ('And here we have artefacts from the time of the Chicken People ...').

At the junction with Rectory Road 'Christ is risen' graffiti is on a wall. A gang hangs about on the street corner, just down from Good Time Ice Cream, typical of gangs around here in that they are all around eleven years old.

A tall black geezer strolls up to me and cocks his head to one side.

'Aabadadddop?'

'What?'

'Aabbadabbadop?'

'What did you say?'

'Are you an undercover cop?'

'Argh?'

'An undercover cop, man? Talkin' into that tape recorder. What   69
you doin'?'

I spend about five minutes explaining to him about the buried rivers, in my special 'interesting' researcher voice, showing him the Hackney Brook drawn into my *A to Z* and how the settlements grew up around the stream. His eyes start to glaze over and he makes his excuses and speeds off towards Stoke Newington.

At Hackney Downs I can see the slope of the shallow river valley with an impressive line of trees, like an old elm avenue, except they can't be elms because they're all dead. At this point I should say what kind of trees they are, being a country boy, but fuck me if I can remember. I used to be able to tell in autumn by looking at the seeds.

At the Hackney Archive there are some old illustrations of Hackney in which the river looks very pretty and rustic as it winds

its way past various coun-
tryish scenes and one of the
Hackney Downs in the late
eighteenth century, with a
little Lord Fauntleroy type
looking down into a bab-
bling (or in Hackney these
days it would be 'chattering') crystal stream. Behind
him, where now there

would be muggers, dead TVs, piss-stained tower blocks and junk-yards, are bushes, shrubs, trees and general countryside.

Benjamin Clarke, writing 120 years ago, lamented how much it had changed in the previous 150 years and had it on good authority that in the 1740s 'the stream ["purling and crystal"] was quite open to view, trickled sweetly and full clearly across the road in dry weather but rapidly changed to a deep and furious torrent when storms along the western heights of Highgate and Hampstead poured down their flood waters'.

A few people are hanging out in the Downs but it's not a real beauty spot, more an old common. A battered train clatters past along the embankment to the right. Along cobbled Andre Street and its railway arches with garages, taxis, banging, welding, industrial city smell of petrol and chemicals, and those urban standing-blokes who never seem to have anything to do. And, of course, smashed cars and engine parts. People doing business, chatting, negotiating, and almost medieval noise among the cobbles. Are you into cars? If not what are you doing down here? We all love cars. Water drips along the cobbles. One day all this will be really shite coffee bars. I make it to the end of the street without buying a

car then turn left past the Pembury Tavern – alas, not open any more.

Here, the Victorian stuff blends with spoiled tower blocks/failed high-density housing projects, burned-out cars piled high behind wire fences; swirling purple, shaved-head speccy blokes jogging with three-wheeler prams; shaven-headed bomber-jacketed blokes pulled along by two or three heavily muscled dogs, nineteenth-century schools refurbished for urban pioneers with lots of capital. Hackney used to be shitty, now it's not so shitty (Tourist sign: 'Welcome to "Not As Shitty As It Used To Be" Country!') The brook in central Hackney was culverted in 1859–60. In his book, Benjamin Clarke visits the old church and finds a ducking stool in the tower which used to be near here and where they'd give scolds (women with opinions) the dip treatment. A bloke is following me laughing madly and loudly, then runs across the road into Doreen's pet shop, no doubt to buy a budgerigar for his lunch.

I head up towards Tesco, built on the site of old watercress beds – I reckon the stream goes right underneath their booze section. I hang around near the liqueurs for a while, checking the emergency exit, when the alarm goes off so I nip around the vegetable section and out by another door. Onto Morning Lane now, which follows the line of the river. There used to be a mill for silk works here and the Woolpack Brewery using Hackney Brook water. I love Benjamin Clarke's idea that this is a River of Beer. I wonder how easy it would be to turn a stream into beer. Just add massive amounts of hops, malt, barley and yeast, I suppose. Further down there used to be a Prussian blue factory. Lots of big blond lads with moustaches singin' 'bout how their woman gone left them *ja* and 'cos the trains are so damn efficient she'll be miles away by now. Woke up this morning etc., etc.' Oh, blue factory, that's ink, right? Now it's heavy traffic, cars, white vans, trucks, housing estates.

Large swathes of this part of Hackney must have been flattened by bombs in the Second World War. Or by the progressive council madmen who hated the elitism of nice houses and squares. Past Wells Street and little funky shops where the tributary marked 'Hackney Brook' on my map used to flow. Reggae blasts out from a shop – Rivers of Dub. People shouting, radios blaring, big arguments. At the end of Wick Road two guys in tracksuit trousers (or sports slacks) are giving hell to each other and pointing at each other's chests. Up above is the sleek black hornet shape of a helicopter, watching. On the other side of these flats, to the north, are the Hackney marshes.

Two pubs here, one a cute compact place, dark green and yellow Prince Edward, not the not-gay TV production guy but the Prince of Wales who became Edward VII, the fat bloke with a goatee who liked shagging actresses. I have an idea for stickers with a river logo and pint glass plus a thumbs up sign, like an Egon Ronay guide thing, that landlords of pubs along the routes of rivers could put on their front doors.

Benjamin Clarke wrote that when he was young that 'the popular name for the area around Wick Lane and beyond was "Bay" or "Botany", so nicknamed because of the many questionable characters that sought asylum in the wick, and were ofttimes not only candidates for, but eventually contrived to secure transportation to Botany Bay itself'.

More flats here, cubist and Cubitt mixed together. Then at the junction to Brook Road the roads rise up each side from the river valley. I keep straight on. There's a new Peabody Trust building site, announced by their little logo, which is two blue squiggly lines, like waves – maybe they only build on top of buried rivers. From Victoria Park, on a slight hill where the river once skirted round the north-east corner, I can see tower blocks in the distance of different shapes and sizes.

Back out and down into the river valley into the heart of the Wick under some rough-looking dual carriageways, past a lime green lap dancers' pub on the left. I turn right underneath both

roads of the A12 Eastcross route, onto the Eastway. A little old building says 'Independent Order of Mechanics lodge no. 21, 1976'. Their sign is a sort of Masonic eye with lines coming out from the centre. I pass the Victoria, an old Whitbread pub seemingly left high and dry by the road building, and St Augustine's Catholic Church, which hosts Eastway Karate

The Cut, Hackney Wick

Club. Then a beautiful thirties swimming pool in the urban Brit Aztec style. I look along Hackney Cut, a waterway made for the mills of the district so the Lea could still be navigable, as it stretched down further into the East End.

Now I am in Wick Village with its CCTV and sheltered housing. It's pretty dead, like the end of the line, a real backwater – dead cars resting on piles of tyres then a graveyard with hundreds of cars piled up. I climb up a footbridge to take a look around. It's still ugly from there, except I can see more of it. Lots of dirt in the air, windswept, everything is coated in it, blasted and bleached, grit in my eyes. Someone has dropped a big TV from a height and it lies in pieces by the stairs – perhaps in protest at the death of the *Nine O'clock News*. Great piles of skips here like children's toys, and lots of traffic. I cross over the Stratford Union Canal lock and to the Courage Brewery, where an army of John Smiths bitter kegs wait to do their duty.

A couple of old people dawdle up to me and I ask them about what they know about Hackney Brook.

Responses of local old people when you ask them about an underground river
  1. Outright lying
  2. Wants to unburden soul
  3. Does rubbing thing with ear suggesting they're contacting some secret organization
  4. Doesn't understand me
  5. Idea of underground river makes them want to urinate – 'You are my best friend!' etc.

There's a plaque for the Bow Heritage Trail and the London Outfall Sewer walk. Part of London's main drainage system constructed in the mid-nineteenth century by Sir Joseph Bazalgette. I can smell the shit. It's a shitty sky as well. But at last I can hear birdsong. There are scrub trees, wildflowers, grasshoppers, daisies and cans of strong cider.

Finally I am at the point where the newer Lea Navigation cut meets the old River Lea/Lee. The name is of Celtic origin, from *lug*, meaning 'bright or light'. Or dedicated to the god Lugh (Lugus). There are two locks here. This is the end of my walk, although the

74 path continues to Stratford marsh. Two big pipes appear, on their way down to a shit filter centre (technical term) somewhere out east. Maybe there is poo in one and wee in the other. I go down some steps to have a closer look at the river. The sewer is in a big metal culvert under the path. There's a small sluice gate on the other side, also an old wooden dock. Water rushes out a bit further up, and I'm happy. Maybe that is the Hackney Brook, maybe it isn't. It's good enough for me.

To the left is Ford Lock near Daltons peanut factory, on the right the placid winding waters of the old Lea. I cross over the locks and am blasted by the smell of roast potato and cabbage. It's deserted, like an old film set.

ə ə ə

My online dream doctor Mike's online dream interpretation arrives:

Hello Tim!

A very interesting dream indeed! It looks to me more like it is set in a future setting than in the past, and it sounds like a very beautiful place! (!) Water is symbolic of change, and it seems that your dream makes quite an artwork out of change. Walking over the deep crevices in the ground is symbolic of passing over problems in life successfully. If you were not passing over them successfully you'll be falling into or stumbling on the crevices. The glass over it covered in little red dots sounds to be very symbolic of health issues.

**The flying water sounds to be very symbolic of the
turbulent future, but the way you handle yourself
and your feelings about this dream make it sound like
everything will be fine. It sounds like this dream is
predicting some hard times ahead, but you are able
to overcome them and continue along a path.**

**I certainly hope this helped you, there really wasn't
a whole lot to go on. If I may be of further assistance
please feel free to write.**

**Sincerely,
Mike**

**ps: This is not to be considered medical or psychological
advice because I am not a doctor or psychologist.
I offer this as my opinion and should be evaluated
with this in mind.**

෧   ෧   ෧

I phoned up Arsenal F.C. and got through to the club historian,
who denied any knowledge of the underground river (he would)
but he did tell me that the site was purchased from the St John
Ecclesiastical college. The Knights of St John, the Knights
Hospitallers, acquired the Templars' land when they were outlawed
in the early fourteenth-century. Canonbury Tower, whose lands
stretched down to St John's Priory, Clerkenwell, has Templarism for
its foundations, and a cell in Hertfordshire, on or near, the old
estate of Robert de Gorham, was connected with the Order of St
John established in Islington. All of Hackney was owned by the
Templars, and large parts of Islington. Does this mean anything? Is
Highbury Stadium a Masonic stronghold?

The historian skilfully rebuffed my information-gathering technique which, I'll be honest, consisted of me saying, 'Blah blah underground rivers blah – so, are you a Mason?' in a Jeremy Paxman voice. He laughed and made a joke of it. Then I heard a very audible click, which could have been the gun he was about to shoot himself with. Or the sound of secret service bugging equipment. MI5 could be listening in. Or is it my hurdling knee playing up again?

Various people have attempted to explain Occam's Razor to me. Basically, if there are two explanations, you should choose the simplest.

> **Choice 1:** The land near reclaimed rivers was cheap and was bought up by football clubs.
> **Choice 2:** Something to do with mysticism and Masonry, paganism, choosing a river site and picking up on power vibe of ancient druids for occult football purposes.

Hmm. A lesser-known theory is Occam's Shaving Brush, in which you coat everything with a thin veneer of absurdity and then you can't see the chin for the stubble. As it were. By burying the streams they – the Victorian sewer maker, brick manufacturers, builders, football club chairmen, the Masons, Edward VII – were burying the last vestiges of the scared goddess worshipping holy springs. It was violent and anti-female, defiling London. No, I meant sacred goddess.

'What have you got to say to that then?' I asked the Arsenal historian.

He'd hung up.

ð   ð   ð

More religious people are starting to turn up at my door. It's the end times, they say. They are joined by an ever-growing band of needy folk who just want something. Yugoslavian immigrants who can only say 'Yugoslavia' and 'hungry', Childline charity workers, Woodland Trust, gas board people wanting to sell us electricity, electricity board people wanting to sell us gas, people from Virgin wanting to sell us electricity, gas, financial services and some of the thousands of copies of *Tubular Bells* by Mike Oldfield that they've still got piled up in an underground warehouse in the sticks, homeless people trying to sell us kitchen cleaning gear, cancer charity people, environmental groups. One day I opened the door and there was a chicken on the floor outside. It must be an omen. Actually it was a half-eaten piece of KFC with a few chips left behind as well. An urban trash culture post-modern voodoo juju hex. Without a doubt.

ॐ ॐ ॐ

Film idea – The Herbert Chapman Story

It's a mixture of *Foucault's Pendulum*, *Escape to Victory* and *The Third Man*. Takes over struggling Arsenal and gets in with the Masons to utilize the power of Hackney Brook. Have a spring. Players drink magical waters.

London Stories 2: A Young Person's Guide to House Prices

A while back I miraculously had a bit of money to burn and decided to buy a flat in Hackney before I spent it all in the local pub. I didn't really need the flat – I was already happily settled somewhere else – it was just greed. The theory was simple: buy something in a cheapish part of town, make some money on it, then sell and get a bigger place. Instant capitalism. Fast cars. Cigars. Shiny jewellery. Gadgets. Swimming pools full of beer. Beatles box sets. Er, big lorry loads of boiled lobsters. Hand-crafted living room furniture made of pasta ....

There were two flaws in my plan. First of all, I am Britain's most useless fuckwit capitalist. Secondly, the man I'd chosen to be my expert from the world of property was a Dickensian character in a shiny suit called Phil from a disreputable Hackney estate agents (let's call them Greed & Shite) who had, seemingly, come through a Narniaesque wardrobe from the Victorian era while searching for cast-iron Empire paper clips, and liked it so much he never went back. Through some outrageous personality quirk, Phil would manage to skirt me around the obvious and plentiful bargains of the area for enough time until prices went up so quickly that I was priced out of the market.

When I told Phil's boss my upper limit, he did an Elvis-type sneer with a little quiet laugh, then got our an old dusty file called Mugpunter Ramshackle One-Bedroomed Hovels That Haven't Been Modernised Since The Thirties. There was this little place on Mare Street, Hackney's central thoroughfare, that I really liked the look of. One bedroom, arched windows. I tried to look at it several times but Phil kept producing blocking manoeuvres. I'd phone up and say 'Can I speak to Phil?' and he'd say 'Phil speaking,' and I'd go 'Hi, it's Mr Bradford. I'd like to view the property in Mare Street,' and he'd say '"Ello Chinese laundry no understandee wrong number,' and put the phone down. Or he'd just play dumb. Eventually I got to see it with a crowd of about six other people. Phil informed me that the price had now gone up by six grand. How is that possible in six weeks, I argued.

'That's the market, innit.'

That's the market, innit. In some way that encapsulated everything I hated about capitalism. Unthinking

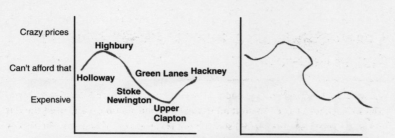

Graphs showing differences in price of one bedroom flats in the Holloway/Hackney area and the course of Hackney Brook - as near-as-dammit identical.

drones in shiny suits mouthing the ideology of their dad or boss thinking they're being somehow radical and exciting. This is Hackney, for fuck's sake. Take it or leave it, Mr Bradford. He then also informed me that I'd have to enter a contract race and I decided, at that moment, to renounce capitalism, forget about buying a flat and becoming a property magnate and concentrate on walking my daughter though the park, racing the old blokes in electric wheelchairs and laughing at it all.

Of course the flat is now worth twice as much. But I never liked the Beatles that much anyway. Shame about the lobsters though.

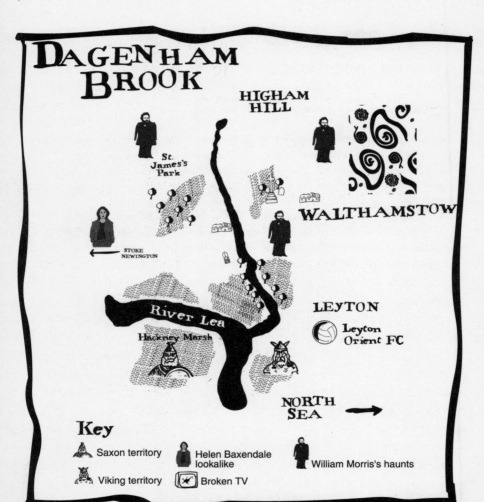

DAGENHAM BROOK

HIGHAM HILL

St. James's Park

WALTHAMSTOW

← STOKE NEWINGTON

River Lea

Hackney Marsh

LEYTON

Leyton Orient FC

NORTH SEA →

Key

Saxon territory

Helen Baxendale lookalike

William Morris's haunts

Viking territory

Broken TV

4. From Eel to Eternity: William Morris and the Saxon–Viking duopoly

- **Dagenham Brook – the Lea to somewhere in Walthamstow**

Seasonal Affective Disorder – the Danes and Saxons (what they represent), Saxons' ego, Danes' id, sensible and crazy – the river near Stevey's flat – flood plains – oh no, it's not the Ching – depression vs. positive thinking – William Morris – Dagenham Brook – walk it – go for lunch – look for source of brook – the Beard Brothers – Leyton Orient v. Blackpool – space eels

From the upstairs window looking down over Finsbury Park (the old Hornsey Wood) the sky is a sickly yellow-grey, prickling with TV aerials like broken winter trees. As a kid I used to love winter, the tranquillity and the hard feeling of cold brittle air in my sensitive asthmatic lungs. It gave me energy, as if I was sucking on a can of pure oxygen. Summer seemed frivolous and shallow. Plus it had cricket (sadistic PE teacher whacking a hard ball at you from about 5 yards away) and athletics (running while being shouted at by sadistic PE teacher). Now it's the other way round. Winter is neverending, annoying and wet. Maybe we are entering not an ice age but a new crap weather age ... (three dots ... leave it open ... 'Blimey', says reader ... 'profound thinker!' ...)

In February, people scowl at each other. It's bad and it's called

82 SAD. Sad Arsed Downer. Slobbedout And Drunk. Stoned And Depressed. Shit At Daytodayliving. Seasonal Affective Disorder. Sunlight disappears and people skulk in doorways. Mice shit on kitchen work surfaces when they're supposed to be in the expensive trap that's baited with peanut butter – 'It's what mice crave,' said the expert on rodent trapping from the local hardware store. Maybe mice prefer smooth. Pricecutters on Blackstock Road only had crunchy. (Wasn't the different consistencies of peanut butter the basis of Aesop's fable about the town mouse and the country mouse?)

Now I'd 'done' two rivers, in the sense that I'd walked them and drawn some pictures of local fat people, but I was already feeling a bit shagged out and worried that hanging around underground streams might be unhealthy. Research has shown that they can cause allergies, disease, poltergeist activity, madness and premature death. Or even spots. The next stream I was due to research was the River Ching in Walthamstow. The thing was, the Ching hadn't really gone. However, I spent three and a half years living in Walthamstow and I'd never heard of it. And seeing as I never knew it existed, it counted as lost in my book.

ð ð ð

For a laugh I take my daughter to a local music workshop, where a large-boned crazily grinning lady sings 'Kumbayah' and the

THE WOMAN WHO LOOKS LIKE THE ACTRESS HELEN BAXENDALE

'Grand Old Duke of York' while bashing away on an acoustic guitar like she's trying to smash ice with a chisel, while the kids stare with terrified eyes. 'Dance!' she cries, 'DANCE, YOU LITTLE FUCKERS!!!' Back in the park we take it in turns to look for amazing things. Cathleen likes nature ('Leaf!' 'Tree!' 'Pussycat!' 'Baby!'), while I'm into celebrity spotting. So far, we'd only managed to see a woman who looked a bit like Helen Blaxendale the actress, but I couldn't be sure. Similar nose, but she looked much smaller in real life. Famous people generally tend to hide away from me. In thirteen years of living in London the only other famous person I'd seen was Derek from Coronation Street in a toy shop in Covent Garden. He was buying a cardboard build-it-yourself puppet theatre.

Of course, Cathleen doesn't recognize as many famous people as me just yet. Except, whenever we pass a construction site she thinks she's seen Bob the Builder and forces me to sing the programme's theme tune with her while she jumps up and down in her pram.

ꙮ ꙮ ꙮ

Walthamstow is on the north-eastern edge of London. Actually, it's Essex really, even though it's got a London postcode. The name suggests that it was a Celtic area – *Wal* meaning 'foreigners' (Wales is the Saxon word for 'foreigners live here – let's buy second homes next door to them'). Another, perhaps more likely, interpretation is that it is a derivation of Wilcumstow (Welcomesville). In this area, at the River Lea, lay the boundary between the Danelaw and Saxon Wessex, a psycho-geographic buffer zone with crazy blond blokes in the east with mad expressions and sandy-haired sen- sible blokes in the west with bored complacent expressions. Positive thinkers in the west, melancholy downbeats to the east. The Saxon ego and the Danish id. Happy sad happy sad happy sad. People still dye their hair to look like Vikings – it's part of an ancient folk memory which basically says, 'Don't kill me! I've got relatives in Copenhagen!'

Saxons - sensible   *Vikings - crazy, man*

In 894 Alfred the Great successfully fought the Vikings on the River Lea. 'Alf' ordered the river to be blocked up and did this –

or rather told his men to do it – by cutting many channels in order to reduce water levels so that when the Vikings came back they were surprised that the river had virtually gone and they couldn't get any further. To celebrate, Alfred burned the cakes. Were they hash cakes? Walthamstow is now an enigmatic dead zone where London ends and Essex begins. It's cheap housing, big skies, teenagers with expensive clothes hanging around the shopping centre, burglaries, pie and mash shops, video stores, a thirties town hall that looks like a cockney Ceauşescu palace. Walthamstow Market is the longest in Europe, with stalls selling three-year-old fashions, batteries, Irish music tapes, training shoes, football wristbands, pots and pans, kitchen knives, fleeces.

I like it a lot. I lived in the Stow for three and a half years. During that time many amazing things happened.

The Amazing Things That Happened in Walthamstow between 1988 and 1991

1. We had dead pigeons in the water tank.
2. Tiny freshwater prawns once appeared in the cold water.
3. Dukey pinched a glamorous local barmaid from a geezer boyfriend with a fierce dog.
4. I did a Jackson Pollock rip-off painting on an old door in the garden which Dukey then gave away to his glamorous girlfriend while I was away.
5. Ruey blowtorched the grass in the garden.
6. The next-door neighbours shagged really loudly.
7. Our landlord asked how he could meet 'young ladies'.
8. We got burgled three times.
9. The pubs were full of fat blokes.

They were great days.

ð ð ð

I wrote to *The Guinness Book of Records* explaining my project to travel along London's streams and rivers and how it would work well on global TV – me racing along with Norris McWhirter by my side being pulled along in a boat on wheels by a car and reciting historical facts about the rivers and their uses. (Cue punk thrash version of the *Record Breakers* theme tune).

๑ ๑ ๑

In a bit of a downer mood I went out one night to meet my friend Stevey P. at a North London Short Story Workshop meeting. This group had been going on and off (mostly off) for about six years and now had only two members, me and Stevey. How we lost all the others I can't quite remember. I think Stevey slept with one of them and the other was his brother. His story was the first chapter in a mad London-based Dickensian sci-fi novel. My stories, on the other hand, were going nowhere. I couldn't concentrate on finishing any of them. My latest effort, *Run, Carla Djarango, Run Like the Wind*, consisted of three paragraphs of East Midlands magical realist bollocks. Stevey smiled patiently. He would have put his arm round me if he'd been the tactile sort, but instead he lit up a fag, narrowed his eyes and asked 'Pint?'

Five minutes later he read my half page short story then said, after taking a sip of his Guinness, 'Hmmm, it's got potential.' We both laughed. I then moaned on about rivers. He told me he had an idea. Great, I thought. What is it? A boat. Why don't you build a boat? Then dress up in nineteenth-century gear and get pulled around London. What a crazy idea. Thanks for nothing.

Stevey agreed to come out on a river walk in Walthamstow, where he lives. There was a river that runs very close to his house which I presumed must be the Ching.

'That's not a river,' said Stevey, a bit startled.

'It is.'

'It can't be.'

'What is it if it isn't a river?'

'It's a, a drainage ditch or something. A drain with some water in it.'

'No, I think it's a river.'

He started to gabble. 'No one told me about rivers when I bought my flat. Rivers flood and cause damage. That's a ditch, not a river. What happens if there's a really big flood? It'll ruin my hall.'

To add to his paranoia, soon afterwards Stevey got a leaflet though the door from the Environment Agency informing him he lived in a flood plain and offering some useful survival tactics. This was actually the River Lea flood plain but he seemed convinced that it must be referring to the small river ('drainage ditch!') next to his house. He began to fantasize about his street becoming like Venice. Fortunately he lived on the first floor. 'But what about the post?'

Now here's a factoid bit for all the research fiends and librarians out there (sounds of skinny blokes with thick specs sitting up suddenly and concentrating). I'd first seen a map containing the Ching in my old second-hand book and, looking at its location in relation to the Hackney Brook, had presumed it was in Walthamstow. But when I looked on my *A to Z* to check the course of Stevey's mystery river, I noticed that the Ching actually flowed south-west from Epping Forest and entered the Lea in south Chingford. It didn't really spend much time in Walthamstow, apart from flowing under the dog track. So Stevey's river wasn't the Ching after all.

(Scene: A gang of resentful-looking researchers, looking dead hard, hang around outside a library waiting to beat me up.)

ॐ   ॐ   ॐ

The trouble with SAD is that I get tired of people smiling and being positive at this time of year. Fortunately some new research has recently come to my aid. Apparently you've got more chance of being happy if you're pessimistic. This is because you have lowered expectations, so everything is a bonus. This corresponds with my own world view, what I'd term optimistic pessimism. In this, you go out there with a healthy can-do attitude while accepting that it'll probably all end in tears.

I also don't like fun. Or, should I say 'FUN!' Fun! is overrated. What I mean is, I don't like looking for fun! If fun! suddenly appears on my doorstep, that's great, I'll invite it in for a cup of tea. If a large candyfloss helterskelter funfair circus run by speedfreak laughing Zippo circus clowns sets up on our street, I'm happy. But the idea of going out and actively searching for fun! leaves me cold. I'd like to say I blame Thatcher – after all, I blame her for most things that are wrong in this country, or with me – but we have got the idea that 'fun! is our right' from the Americans. It's that thing about the 'pursuit of happiness' which manifests itself as a need for fun! It's a waste of time. It's only in fleeting moments that you'll ever actually experience happiness. Fun! is happiness with forced laughter, usually while dressed up.

I spent a bit of time in the States a few years ago and I used to feel really tense around happy people. Or at least people who seemed concerned at making the rest of the world think they were happy. Those 'I'm so pleased to meet you that I'm smiling, look, you make me feel good so you must be a special person' people. You can always spot them because they pepper their conversation with words they've nicked from New Age therapy-style literature. Tim, you look sad, Let Art Heal You. Tim, come into our Love Sanctuary. That kind of thing.

And yet, I realized that I was only going to be able to continue this rivers project if I got myself into a more positive state of mind. So I jotted down a few ideas to get me started.

The Groundwater Diaries self-help guide
This short course aims to turn you from a normal person (possibly even a well-adjusted one, but who cares about that?) into someone who is an incredibly annoying positive person

who never gets down about anything. People will run from you in the street when they see you.

For example, being positive isn't just about thinking, 'Yeah I can do that, I reckon,' it's also about showing the world who's boss, that you can do anything and that you've also got a very loud voice (possibly with a sort of American accent creeping in at the edges). Most self-help books work on the inner person (god how pathetic is that!?), putting over the idea that positive vibes will spill out from you into your universe in a kind of George Harrison sitar big beard huggy sort of way.

The techniques and exercises outlined here work in an opposite direction, making you look absurdly positive on the outside until finally, when you're head of IBM or you've won the Eurovision song contest three years in a row, you start to believe it yourself.

But as most psychology experts will tell you, 'We take Access or Visa.' OK, that's the first thing they tell you. The second thing is that everything is bullshit and pretending. People like to be fooled by others who seem more assured than they are.

Positive Exercises

Get yourself a new name
Ditch your old name that your parents gave you and grab a bright shiny positive new one. Here's some examples: Dong Powerlamp, Jemma Zii, Zak Backkaboo, Pandora Lightshower, Dalrymp Supercharger. These are positive and say something about you. If you don't want to go the whole way, why not get into the craze of Power Initials. John Smith becomes John Z. Smith, Ethel Jones become S. Ethel M. Jones. See? Hmm.

Affirmative thumbs
Put your arms straight out in front of you and stick your

thumbs up. Hold this position for thirty minutes while holding you mouth in a large wide grin. You can use Affirmative Thumbs™ at work if you are getting hassle from your boss. Half an hour of Affirmative Thumbs™ and he'll be happy to give you a pay rise. Possibly.

Power Smile

Sit with your arms by your sides. Take a deep breath. Now pull your arms up and insert your index fingers into the corners of your mouth. Pull your mouth as wide apart as possible and hold it. This is called a smile. Remember this facial expression when you are meeting new people or at a job interview. It tells people 'I am a positive no-holds-barred-get-up-and-go-live-for-today-smiley-doing sort of person.' It's more than a smile – it's a Power Smile™.

Within minutes of digesting that lot I was feeling like a buff-cheeked gibbon that's inhaled a year's supply of laughing gas.

Walthamstow is famous for two things. The jellied eel and William Morris. I'm not always keen on the Great Man theory of history, but in the case of Walthamstow I feel it's appropriate. I've always liked the idea of Morris rather than his art, which seemed to me to be a load of girly Laura-Ashley-style designs copied and repeated on a wall. Morris married Jane Bowden, a local girl with red curly hair who was discovered working in a shop ('I say, a SHOP don't you know!') by his friend Dante Gabriel Rossetti. She eventually become Rossetti's lover again after Morris became obsessed with discovering the perfect wallpaper glue. In portraits she looks a bit like Nicole Kidman.

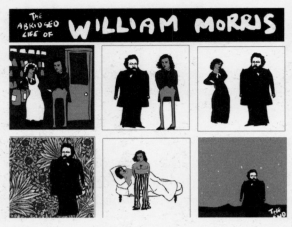

And jellied eels taste like slimy, dryish sick. My gran told me the whole point of jellied eels was that you weren't supposed to taste them, just greedily swallow great gloopy lumps like cheap oysters. Morris was obsessed with these small slippery creatures that lived in a pulsating glob of sticky goo. He felt that they were God's first creatures, living in the primordial jelly. Many of his most famous designs tried to capture the swirly essence of the jellied eel. People don't realise that the jelly is natural – it is their house and their food source. It's as if we all lived in places made out of pasta. Morris knew this. He saw the way jellied eels interacted with their environment and each other and it inspired him to try to create a better, more community-based and creative society. The Walthamstow jellied eel also represents, as Morris well knew, the serpent, life and pagan religion. The Vikings were pagan and their longboats had serpents/dragons/jellied eels carried on the front.

Other artists who loved jellied eels:
Pablo Picasso
James Joyce
Jean-Paul Sartre
Joan Miró

92   'It does not make a bad holiday' to go to Walthamstow, said
      Morris, evidently not bribed by the Walthamstow Tourist Board.
      The area was mostly countryside until the end of the nineteenth
      century. I used to love going running or walking around
      Walthamstow marshes on summer evenings, then lying down in the
      grass and watching the clouds scoot by, listening to crickets, cock-
      ney geezers with pit bulls threatening each other, car alarms going
      off and ambulances screaming. It's an area of interesting wildlife.
          History bit – The marshes were first drained for grazing pur-
      poses in Alfred the Great's time as a way of showing off to the
      Danes. They were so impressed they gave him their jellied eels.

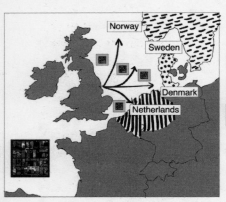

What did they get in
return? Over 1000
years later the Danes
would get punk music.
Yet something is not
quite right about my
punk theory. I've
been staring at a
map of the North Sea/
German Ocean/cold
slab of muddy water
off Mablethorpe and
wondering whether the

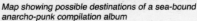

Map showing possible destinations of a sea-bound
anarcho-punk compilation album

      Bullshit Detector on the makeshift raft really made it to Denmark?
      How realistic is that? I could be fantasizing. When you look at the
      facts, it's much more likely that it ended up in Sweden or Norway.

                              ◈ ◈ ◈

      It was time to walk Stevey P.'s river. First of all I had to get in touch
      with the spirit of William Morris. I've never done channelling
      before. I remember reading about the great medium Doris Stokes
      whose ears used to go red when she contacted the dead. My whole

face goes red when I drink extra strong lager, so something must be happening. And it was to Tennent's Super that I turned when looking for a name for Stevey P.'s river. A couple of cans in and I was buzzing. Were those ghosts I could hear or my own voices: happy Tim and Morrissey Tim? I sat back and relaxed, taking deep breaths. And then it came to me. I had an urge to look on the *A to Z* again and I saw it almost straight away. South of the Lea Bridge Road came my answer. Stevey's river, the mystery river, was called Dagenham Brook. (Cue *Time-Team*-style ancient drums and flute music). But why Dagenham? This stream flowed nowhere near Dagenham, which lies 12 miles to the south-east – unless .... Walthamstow used to be near Dagenham and, like the Lost City of Atlantis, was engulfed by the waters of the Lea (but unlike Atlantis, then deposited 6 miles upriver to a spot east of Tottenham). I could see where Dagenham Brook entered the Lea and its course to there from Stevey's place. But north of that there was nothing. So I decided to take a different tack and walk towards, rather than away from, the source.

Of course, searching for the source is also in a sense a journey to rediscover one's own spiritual nature through personal exploration and self-cultivation. At least that's what Poppy, my ex-dream analyst, used to say before I dumped her for Yorkshire Mike. I kind of miss Poppy now, her madcap Californian optimism. I hoped to unlock the spiritual treasures of the universe and light the way to a life of internal and external harmony and fulfilment. And having already had some experience of Walthamstow, I surmised that this journey would have to take place in a pub full of fat blokes. During my Walthamstow years, our old local boozer was the Lorne Arms in Queens Road and it boasted three of the biggest lads in the whole of north London – the Beard brothers, weighing in at around 60 stone between them. Beard, the eldest, was around 23 stone, his younger brother Little Beard was about 20 stone and the baby of the family, Tiny Beard, was 17 stone. They all had the same beards. I thought they might be the living embodiment of the legendary giants of the City of London, known to most people as Gog and Magog (and Tiny GogMagogGog), who are carried around in the Lord Mayor's procession. They spend most of the rest of their year propping up the bar of the Lorne. Also there was Val the barmaid. We liked her to leave a decent head on our pints of Guinness rather than knife it off into the tray. 'You boys like a bit of head,' that was her catchphrase. 'I said, you boys like' ... And Landlord Len, denizen of the Grand Order of Water Rats, a sort of Freemasons Lite for cockneys, I suppose.

ᘒ ᘒ ᘒ

Walthamstow – the sludgeree years

When we lived in Walthamstow we all fancied ourselves as top chefs. Possibly the cheap local produce available at Walthamstow market inspired us. But it was also a good way to impress any woman who dared to come round. I had four specialities:

1. Marmalade paella – only wheeled out when we were absolutely desperate and about to starve, and which consisted of brown rice and marmalade.
2. Oxo porridge – a highly nutritious oat-based meal in beef, chicken or vegetable flavours. Ingredients: porridge oats, water, Oxo cube.
3. Angel-hair pasta with ketchup – what it says.
4. Sludgeree – buy lots of vegetables. Put in pan with water and leave for several hours and go down the Lorne to lose at pool to Dukey, until ingredients have merged into a thick, industrial sludge.

You're probably thinking, after seeing those recipes, that I was King of the Cooks, the alpha-male of the oven. But I certainly didn't have it all my own way. Plendy had this amazing dish called pasta and tomatoes. It consisted of pasta, about a hundredweight of garlic and a tin of tomatoes all mixed up together. If he was feeling really fancy he'd make a salad to accompany it. Dukey had tuna explosion, which involved him hiring a small plane and dropping a couple of tins of tuna fish from several thousand feet. He'd then scoop up the resulting mess and stick it in a pan with – a tin of tomatoes. Ruey had some kind of fishy bits thing. He used to get fishy off cuts from a local fishmonger. Tobe had pineapple curry. All I remember is tins of pineapple and curry sauce. Rich never used to cook, so we'd nick his dope and put it in our own meals, just to take the edge off the anger of those who had to eat it.

And we used to make serious money on these meals. If the food cost, say, £1.50 the chef would invariably ask for 70p each, thus making a handy mark-up. This would go straight into a savings account. Occasionally when a woman came round we'd stick on an album of French accordion music that I'd found at a jumble sale and try and schmooze them with top grub. Strangely, late eighties women just didn't appreciate fine food.

The house was split down the middle between English and Scottish tenants, but it was more complex than that. The split-personality fault lines of Walthamstow also meant that we were divided along organised (Saxon) and chaotic (Viking) lines.

ॐ ॐ ॐ

I go round to Stevey's flat to collect him for our walk of his river. He is still flapping a bit. He's cleared out his valuable seventies football card collection, in case the place gets flooded, and gives it to me in a Tesco bag, asking that I donate it to the artefacts library of my erstwhile employers *When Saturday Comes* (independent football magazine). It is a bit of a John Paul Getty III gesture.

We walk up to the end of Blyth Road to Bridge Road and look at Stevey's river, sorry, the Dagenham Brook, as it slowly snakes its way behind the little terraced houses. There are a few bits and bobs in the water – cans, bottles, old bikes. Soon, we turn into the Leyton relief road, which hasn't yet opened because they haven't finished building it. Concrete bollards bar access. A sign says that it's due to open in Spring 2002. A Somalian guy is in the little Portakabin office, all fenced off. We tell him we are on a research project, hunting for the Dagenham Brook. Right, OK. He seems a bit too laidback and cool for a security guard.

'Look,' says Stevey, 'Bywater on the skips. Are you noticing all these signs?' Stevey is a bloody teacher knowall. In a minute he's going to suggest we split up into smaller groups. We find the end of the river before it goes under the new Leyton relief road and under a light industrial estate to the River Lea. As we clamber into the undergrowth we suddenly come upon a group of very smiley people all pushing wheelbarrows. We've stumbled across some sort of gardening sect activity, which is alarming. I picture us being kidnapped and in a couple of days we'll be pushing wheelbarrows too. What are they carrying in their wheelbarrows? We have no option but to press on. But the barrow people are following us.

I confront one of the leaders, who explains to me that he's from the Environment Agency and these are volunteers helping to clear the lower reaches of the brook. He said they were planting stuff in and around the river, encouraging wildlife back. Kingfishers and that. I ask him about the route of the river. He says it disappears pretty soon after it crosses Lea Bridge Road. Stevey is jumpy, but manages not to ask about emergency flood procedures. As Stevey and I saunter past with our serious explorers' expressions, the not-barrow-people-but-voluntary-workers who are sweating hard obviously guess that we are pros or environmental activists and start to say hello. The brook then disappears under Leyton Wingate football club. There is a game on, but it's three quid to get in and we're not that desperate to find the stream. And that's the last we see of it, until it sluggishly flows behind houses then disappears

somewhere to the north in the vicinity of Markhouse Road. We celebrate our victory by repairing to the Hare and Hounds where we
have some god awful half-frozen-food and thin Guinness, surrounded by fat blokes.

ə   ə   ə

In John Rocque's 1746 map of Walthamstow there are several
country houses with ornamental gardens and ponds. Dagenham
Brook is called the Mill River and appears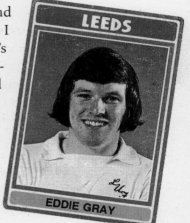
to be an artificial ditch, as Stevey had
hoped. I'll go round to tell Stevey but I
don't think he wants to talk about it. He's
recently given me some more old bubblegum cards, this time of my beloved
Leeds United, believing he can buy me
off so I won't keep going on about rivers
and we can get back to How It Was
Before – stories, politics, women and
football. He's underestimated me,
because ... bloody hell, between 1970
and 1974 Eddie Gray only played sixty
games for Leeds. I think he might have
been injured. I rub the back with a coin. Magic! A picture
appears. Then it disappears again! Ooooh.

ə   ə   ə

It's now late March. I walk from my house to Brisbane Road
stadium, which lies about 100 yards to the east of the Dagenham
Brook's southern section, to watch Leyton Orient play Blackpool in
a Third Division game. On the way I get caught up in a torchlit procession by hundreds of Kurdish demonstrators, some playing
medieval-sounding pipes, some banging drums. The rest are singing
a Kurdish version of 'All We Are Saying Is Give Peace A Chance'. At

least that's what it sounds like. A quarter of a mile further on someone lies dying at the side of the road, surrounded by a crowd of people, a victim of a hit-and-run driver. Blackpool win 2–1.

A few days later the USA pulls out of the Kyoto Protocol for climate control. Then Stevey P. phones me to say he is very worried about the river again. His bit is filled up with rubbish – old bikes, oil cans, car seats. Barely half a mile away, the Environment Agency are planting rare flowers and kissing kingfisher eggs. This is, he points out, the London of extremes. Dagenham Brook, once a river of mystery, is now one of contrasts – heaven and hell, London and Essex, Saxon and Viking, good and evil, kingfishers and used bicycles, something nice and jellied eels.

I needed sleep. I padded through to my study to get my well-thumbed copy of Albert Camus's *The Rebel*. I'd been reading it for about five years. (My other insomnia beater is *The Scarlet and the Black*.) In seconds I was drifting off.

ð   ð   ð

I went back to Walthamstow, bought some jellied eels and took then up to the William Morris Gallery. Didn't feel anything. I then went back to the Lorne after eating the jellied eels to show some William Morris prints to the Beards and Len the Landlord, plus my eel illustration. It was closed up. Then I walked back up Lea Bridge Road towards the roundabout at Clapton and decided to find out if there really was a psychic border at the River Lea. At the pub there I ran from one end of the bridge to the other to see how I felt. Saxon or Viking? Saxon … run run run run run run run run run run run run run run run run run … Viking … run run run run run run run run run run run run run run run run … Saxon…run run run run run run run run run run run run run run run run run … Viking … run run run run run run run run run run run run run run run run run … stop … gulp for air … dirty fumes … have coughing fit …

There was a rumour doing the rounds a while back that a bear had gone missing from a travelling circus in East London (maybe Zippo, maybe not). Eventually the authorities dragged the Lea in Hackney Marshes just south of here, near the Walthamstow pitch-and-putt course, and found the bodies of three bears, skinned. But not the one they were looking for, which turned up somewhere else.

ò ò ò

To: The William Morris Society

Hi there

I'm researching a book about underground rivers and William Morris crops up a couple of times. I was wondering if you had any information on whether rivers influenced Morris's work. I'm also interested in his time at Walthamstow – I've heard a story that he loved jellied eels! Have you ever heard this?

Hope you can help.

All the best,
Tim Bradford

ò ò ò

Dear Tim

Thank you for your enquiry. Morris was influenced by rivers and nature in general. His designs incorporate natural forms, especially foliage and flowers. In 1881, Morris & Co moved to larger premises at Merton Abbey, where the River Wandle was a ready supply of water and could be used for dyeing the textiles. There is a fabric named after the river, called Wandle, and Morris also produced a number of designs based on tributaries of the Thames.

Morris also had numerous opinions on food and drink. One of

the caricatures by Edward Burne-Jones is of him eating a raw fish while in Iceland. Morris spent his childhood at Walthamstow and his family home, Water House, is now the William Morris Gallery and is open to the public. For more information: www.lbwf.gov.uk/wmg

Please do not hesitate to contact me again if you require any further information.

Yours sincerely,

Helen Elletson
William Morris Society

ⓐ ⓐ ⓐ

Film Idea: 'Attack of the Jellied Eels from Outer Space'
Earth is being invaded by the evil eels who want to cover the world in jelly. Only William Morris can stop them. Helped by his friend H. G. Wells, he goes into the future and sees that they are growing their deadly eel spawn in the little Dagenham Brook. Morris creates some wallpaper which shows the plans of the eel spaceships. They throw Manze's pies up into the air to knock out the alien craft.
Starring:
Tom Cruise as William Morris
Nicole Kidman as Jane Bowden
Russell Crowe as Rossetti
Nicholas Cage as H. G. Wells

London Stories 3: Going to the Dogs

Scars on faces, all shapes and sizes, cockney aristos and Swedish tourists, coked-up crowds and serious punters, the smell of beer, shouting, loudspeaker, trendy crowd with nice specs, ladieeez in tight dresses, old blokes with sheepskin jackets, cheap cigars, scampi and chips, lose a fiver win a tenner, overhear some fellas talkin' near the bookies, take their advice then find your hound is a mangy bag of bones that wouldn't make a decent pot of soup even if you boiled it up for a couple of days. Ah, going to the Dogs is beautiful.

Last time I went, I lost loads of money, even though I won on a couple of races. I'd searched on the Internet for some betting systems. One, based in the Midwest USA, had all kinds of equations and maths you had to do before each race. It's all very well winning, but I think you've got to do it with the minimum possible effort. So I decided to develop my own system. It's the *Pogles Wood* connection system.

I'd pick any dog related to a character or event from this late-sixties kids TV programme. I talked very loudly about this and also wore a pair of pinstripe trousers to make me feel like a Serious Punter.

In the end I ignored my system and went with a dead-cert tip I'd got off the Internet. Rectobond Ace. Couldn't lose, they said. Race six.

They're off. Eager thin-snouted flesh

Greyhounds are bred to desire the flesh of electronic rabbits on wheels

torpedoes chasing a toy rabbit that's been welded to a turbo-powered Scalextric car watched by sinewy punters in Fred Perry shirts and shiny loafers, Yes. Yes. Yes Yes. Yes. YES. Y E E E E E E E S S S S S S S S S . YEEEEEAAAAAAAHHHHHHH-HHSSSSSSSSSSSS. Oh, shit. My bag of bones went off like the clappers then folded after about 100 yards.

However, my very sensible wife had bet on places for long-odds dogs and won enough to get some beers and a bag of chips. I went to the bar, ordered the beer and asked if there were any chips. A tall skinny bloke with a scar turned to me and said:

'I've got a chip on my shoulder mate ha ha ha ha ha ha ha.'

'I need more than one.'

His mate, an even taller black guy, said:

'Want chips do you eh eh? How about a kebab as well ha ha ha ha ha haha?'

'Or how about, how about some lobster ha ha ha ha ha?'

'First time out without yer mum is it ha ha ha ha ha ha ha?'

'I …'

'Ha ha ha ha ha ha ha.'

'I think that it's …'

'Ha ha ha hahahahahahahahaha-hahahahahahahahaha'

'I …'

'Ha ha haaaaaaaaAAAAAAA!!!!!'

Dickens, if he were alive today, would probably have included Walthamstow Dogs in a couple of his books (probably *Pickwick Papers* and *Oliver Twist*).

'Mr Snarzelwechumfuzz, do you have a canine selection for us this fine evening?'

'Indeed I do, Mr Pickwick, sir. It's Lady Hamilton Academical in race seven, the Puppy Breeders of the British Empire, Essex Division, Summer Trophy.'

Mr Pickwick laughed. 'I'll have some of that, Mr Snarzelwechumwack. Pray, what do you suggest?'

'A ten-guinea each way tipple, Mr P. And a couple of florins on Cholera Kid in race nine, the Tottenham Hale Open Cup.'

Mr Winkle piped up from the back. 'I say, Snarzelwechumpog, do they have fried slices of potato here?'

There was a snort from Sam Weller. 'Froyd slices uv potayto?!? Do you vink this is vee Savoy, Mr Winkle?' The others began to laugh merrily.

Etc.

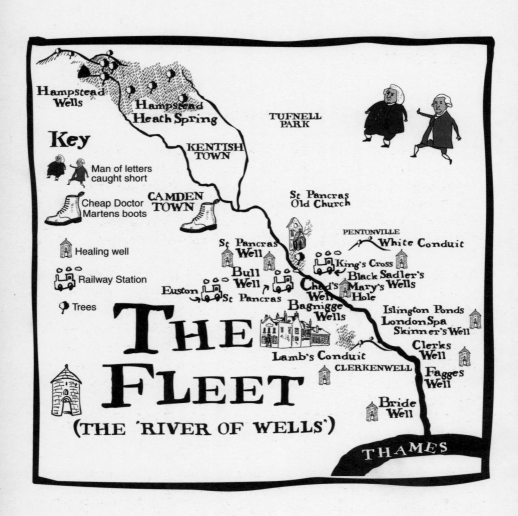

Key

Man of letters caught short

Cheap Doctor Martens boots

Healing well

Railway Station

Trees

Hampstead Wells

Hampstead Heath Spring

TUFNELL PARK

KENTISH TOWN

CAMDEN TOWN

St Pancras Old Church

PENTONVILLE

White Conduit

St Pancras Well

King's Cross

Black Sadler's Wells

Bull Well

Euston

St Pancras

Chad's Well

Mary's Hole

Bagnigge Wells

Islington Ponds

London Spa

Skinner's Well

Lamb's Conduit

CLERKENWELL

Clerks Well

Fagges Well

Bride Well

THE FLEET

(THE 'RIVER OF WELLS')

THAMES

5. Spa Wars

- ## The Fleet – Hampstead Heath to Blackfriars

Literary Fleet – Raquel Welch in bloodstream – the River of Wells – the London Spa Miracle – lucky pubs – Hampstead Wells – Pancras Wells – Old St Pancras Church – King's Cross – St Chad's Well – jazz – Bagnigge Wells – Black Mary's Hole – Islington Pond – Sadlers Wells – New Tunbridge Wells – London Spa – Clerkenwell – Faggeswell – Smithfield – Eric Newby is lost forever – Bridewell

The River Fleet, or Holebourne (as it was called in that Norman inventory pamphlet), is the largest of London's forgotten rivers. It rises in Hampstead and winds through Kentish Town, King's Cross and Clerkenwell before entering the Thames at Blackfriars. It creates a huge valley culminating in Ludgate Hill on one side and Holborn on the other. The valley can still be seen in the deep banks at each side of Farringdon Street, which follows the Fleet's course down to the Thames at Blackfriars, and Holborn Viaduct was built mainly because of the difficulties vehicles had in negotiating the steep fall then climb when travelling west to east across the Fleet's flood plain.

The Fleet has been written about a lot. According to my main source material, the book *Wonderful London*, it fell 'from a higher grace than any of its sister streams'. It appears in literature – Pope's *Dunciad* (thick blokes swim in the runny shit with the dead dogs), Ben Jonson's 'On the Famous Voyage' (a couple of madsers in a boat sail down the Fleet in a precursor to the Raquel Welch film *Fantastic Voyage* in which a submarine is miniaturized and injected into the bloodstream of a dying man, played by Donald Pleasance, to try and revive him and Raquel gets her kit off but you don't see anything), James Boswell (big-mouth Samuel Johnson's laugh heard from Temple Bar to Fleet Ditch, Johnson doing lots of craps in the river), Dickens's Mr Pickwick searches for the source of the Hampstead ponds (putting forward cutting-edge 'Tittlebatian theories'), and, more recently, Aidan Dun's poem *Vale Royal* (Fleet Valley ancient druidic site, St Pancras church omphalos, consumptive young poets top themselves at the beauty of it all) and U. A. Fanthorpe's 'Rising Damp', about the 'little fervent underground/ Rivers of London', whose buried names are still followed through the city, and in the papers every few years, usually in the context of pressure groups trying to restore it to its former glory.

Before its inevitable descent into a health hazard, the Fleet had flowed through orchards (Pear Tree Court, Rosebery Avenue), meadows (Smithfield – 'the Smoothfield') and Italian women (Little Italy in Clerkenwell). It has, at different stages of its course, been called Turnmill Brook and Battle Bridge Brook. It was also known as the 'River of Wells', due to the numerous healing springs which lined its banks. Strange to think that this river that now lurks beneath the roar of Farringdon Road was once venerated for its healing properties.

ॐ ॐ ॐ

One balmy night, during the never-ending Britpop summer of 1996, I sat with three friends at the bar of the London Spa in Exmouth Market and watched England beat Holland 4–1 on the big screen. When the fourth goal went in we held each other and exclaimed that Truly It Was A Miracle. And, being superstitious in a sad medieval country boy sort of way, I decided that the result was down to the pub's lucky vibe, rather than the skill of the players.

The Spa then became our 'lucky' pub for a couple of years, until   107
England lost to Romania at the 1998 World Cup and, like a gang of
fickle eighteenth-century hypochondriacs, we went in search of a
new lucky pub.

The Spa appears in census records dating back to 1851, but there
has been pub there for over 250 years. The name refers to a nearby
spa garden and the area surrounding it, also known as Bagnigge
Marshes, from which flowed chalybeate springs. These were at one
time used as holy wells and by the eighteenth century had been
rediscovered and turned into pleasure gardens. These days a pleasure garden is a can of strong lager and a place to piss, but then it
meant threepence for a glass of murky liquid and some songs and
rhymes. I decided I would trace the Fleet's course via its spas
and wells, seeing if I could pick up on the ancient healing vibe and
celebrate its traditions with a modern-day version of taking the
waters. Drinking Beer.

Hampstead Wells 1 (The Flask, Flask Walk)

I hold in my hand a glass of Young's bitter. It's got a hoppy, salty
taste with a soapy head. The Flask refers to the jars people would
take to fill with well water. A few blokes are sitting around half
watching football on the telly. A ginger bloke is eating chips.

Outside people are promenading. A
player gets sent off and everyone
cheers. The start of a pub crawl is
always dead exciting.

Hampstead Wells 2 (Wells Tavern, Well Walk)

A drinking fountain in the street
nearby has an inscription:

Drink Traveller and with Strength revived
Let a kind Thought be Given to Her who has thy thirst subdued.
Then render thanks in Heaven.

Chalybeate water springs were discovered here in 1701 and, as the pub sign says, gardens soon opened offering 'Good music and song

all day long and accommodation for water drinkers of both sexes. Court ladies all air and no dress.'

The Wells Tavern stood near the springs. It's a big late-Victorian family boozer, 'Dedicated to live music' (says the flyer), with a flowery carpet, hard blokes with dogs, tired mums with kids and, the centrepiece, a glamorous nineteenth-century-style barmaid in a black satin dress. I bet she's called Flossie. R&B plays on the jukebox. The Green King IPA tastes of chocolate bubblegum. I leave the pub and walk across the Vale of Health along the Fleet valley. You can see the fledgling stream in places around here. At the junction of two little tributaries I find what looks like a Neolithic flint tool and stick it in my bag.

Hampstead Heath Spring (The Garden Gate, South End Road)

After walking around past Keats's house, I'm back on the Fleet's route. Now I'm on London Pride, a slightly darker beer. It's watery to start with but has an aftertaste like milky coffee. Very refreshing. The sides of my head start to hurt. Could be the booze and heat. People used to drink this stuff to quench their thirst. I feel good, so it must be working.

The pub has a thirties Tudorbethan exterior with a nineties shiny wood interior. Lots of people with sunglasses on the top of their head. Barmaids with crop tops, tans, six packs, hipsters and pierced belly buttons. Outside is a public bog with classic Victorian big white enamel urinals. Winos sit nearby, no doubt enjoying the luxurious toilet facilities. Opposite, on a green, is a big drinking fountain with some little offerings tucked into it – some long-dead daffodils, a CD and a bike repair kit case. And a black donkey jacket. Three people sit nearby on a bench,

guarding the well – a big witch-like gypsy-looking lass, a young Peter Tosh type and a Donald Pleasance character. I'm happy to see they're all drinking Special Brew.

Pancras Wells (The Prince Alfred, Pancras Way)

Quite a way from the well, which was opposite St Pancras old church, this is the nearest pub I could find. A local boozer underneath a small sixties tower block, it's got a big screen, keg beer and a load of hard-looking blokes standing around smoking and talking loudly. Little plates of mashed-up half-eaten shellfish are dotted around the place. Arsenal are on. I buy a half of John Bull and sneak into a corner. The beer has a cold, metallic seventies taste. Bergkamp is clean through but misses. 'Yaaaaayyyyyy ooooohhhh!!!' shout the hard blokes.

Two guys are playing pool and arguing; a skinny man in his seventies in a suit with jet black hair and thick specs keeps repeating to a bigger younger man 'Look, I say it how I see it.' They're arguing over a foul shot.

Outside, I walk down to St Pancras Churchyard. What with the old Hospital for Tropical Diseases, the embanked railway line, the

110   giant Victorian gas holders and the roaring traffic, this spot feels
about as urban as London could possibly get – the beating heart of

the city experience. I sigh apprecia-
tively, as if sipping a vintage wine, er,
I mean John Bull keg bitter. And
then, suddenly, a beautiful green
space appears in front of me. St
Pancras Gardens – a little park filled
with gravestones, gnarled old trees
and a small, strange-looking church
– St Pancras church, supposedly one
of the oldest in Europe. The Fleet
would have flowed alongside it.

A smartly dressed old man with a
walking stick appears in the middle
of the graveyard. He watches me as I
stare at the various parts of the cemetery. I go into the church,
where I expect to see something ancient and Gnostic, but St
Pancras church feels like village England personified. Smiling, well-
groomed middle-aged women, all vicars' wives – are in the
entrance to the church, selling cakes, rolls, buns and other whole-
some goodies. I feel a tightness in my chest. The blood isn't reaching my brain properly, I panic as they all smile at me and swivel
round to look at the pamphlets. I pick up one that seems to be
about the church – 'History of St Pancras' – and hand over two
quid. It turns out to be all about the church's patron saint. Little
Pancras. 'You like saints do you sir? We like people who like saints.'
I escape, gasping for air. Apparently the church was attacked by
Satanists in 1985 and was closed to the general public until
recently. Maybe they'd met the vicars' wives. Might it have been
dyslexic satirists?

The old man suddenly reappears next to me and starts to talk in
a posh Irish accent about the gardens, which were derelict and have

been done up recently. He's the sort of fellow who might accompany you on a Bloomsday breakfast ('More gizzard there? Splendid!') and be an expert in the life and works of St John Gogarty. Then he disappears. Seconds later he appears again in another bit of the churchyard, under the unattractive clock tower that looks as though it was stuck on by some crazed Victorian enthusiast. Behind the church is the Hardy tree, a twisted tree surrounded by piled-up gravestones. When part of the churchyard was dug up to build the railway line in 1866 Hardy, who trained as a surveyor, helped in the construction of the line and the piling up of the many stones against this tree. The Midland railway destroyed much of this area when St Pancras Station was built in the mid-nineteenth century. Now that initial digging 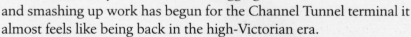 and smashing up work has begun for the Channel Tunnel terminal it almost feels like being back in the high-Victorian era.

Ah fookin 'ell. I need a slash. And this seems to be happening more and more frequently. Socio-Urinary Historians would say that my obsession with the flow of water underneath London has triggered a physical reaction in me – I want to somehow free the rivers but am becoming plagued by the threat of bodily incontinence. And the lack of physical evidence of the rivers perhaps has led me at times to need to create my own – the rivers of piss flowing downhill. I search for a bog, but in the end walk on to King's Cross and home.

St Chad's Well (Cooper's, King's Cross Station)

Next day I set out again but I'm not feeling so good. I haven't been ill for ages, but my first explorations of the healing wells have left me with a foul cold. Sore throat. Thick head. I come out at King's Cross feeling a bit pissed off with the Fleet.

Prostitute-soaked drugsbust wasteland it may be, but I've always liked King's Cross. Perhaps because, for me, it's the gateway to another world – Lincolnshire and the North. In the highly artificial station pub, Cooper's, squat blond blokes in stonewashed denim waiting for a Great North Eastern Railway train that'll take them home, clutch pints to their chests and look out at the world through suspicious squinty eyes and tight-pursed mouths while droning on about Leeds United. Oh, just a minute, ha ha, that's me. It's my reflection in the barman's red shiny nose!

It's a normal day in King's Cross as I leave the bar and make my way to the site of the well. A drunk collapses near the phones and rolls over on his back like a dead beetle. Police pull a young black girl to the ground and handcuff her, while her mate shouts at them. At a King's Cross bus-stop, traffic, hollow-faced girls in leggings stand around in groups craning their necks to look for buses, dead-eyed guys with stubble try to catch your attention, old blokes are smiling and staggering into doorways, people are constantly moving, not staying to contemplate the boarded-up shops, and severe dark grey Georgian streets just off the main drag that offer no comfort.

The well is down a side street called St Chad's Place. Where it stood is now the site of the Thameslink Station platform. But above, on the road, I see water spurting out of from a little crack in

Boswell tries unsuccessfully to stop Dr Johnson doing a crap in St Chad's Well

the pavement. That's good enough for me. Back on Gray's Inn 113
Road, I go into Mole Jazz to look for something with a wells reference. But the nearest I can find
is the Gordon Wellard Septet.

Bagnigge Wells (The Water Rats, Gray's Inn Road)

I have a Boddington's, which is
cold and keggy, like it's come
straight from your fridge. On a
day like this, with all the fumes,
that's not such a bad thing. Two
Irish girls are behind the bar,
two middle-aged men sit at a
new brown sofa doing a deal, another one is on his mobile. Bands
playing here soon include Flickknife Rickshaw and Triphop
Disciples.

The pub was known as the Pindar of
Wakefield[1] until about fifteen years ago.
Marx drank here. Several decades later, so
did Lenin (who lived in nearby Percy Circus).
I wonder if he sat at the same table. But much
more importantly, The Pogues played their
first gig here in the early eighties.

There were two Bagnigge wells, discovered (or rediscovered) in 1767. There
seems to be some confusion about them
because they were so close together, but
the official spot for Bagnigge Wells
House is 31 King's Cross Road, a
Victorian terrace.

---

[1]   The Pindar of Wakefield fought Robin Hood and Little John.

114 At nearby Calthorpe Community Gardens, I go into the office there and chat to an Australian woman who seems to be in

charge. Their lease is up soon and she fears the council may sell the land. I ask her what she knows of Bagnigge Wells. She's never heard of it. We quickly concoct a plan to relaunch the gardens as New Bagnigge Wells. 'The council would have to agree to that,' she laughs. I celebrate by getting a can of Red Stripe from nearby Gray's Inn Wines and sitting on a wall next to an old bloke. It soon gets the sides of my head throbbing.

Dr Johnson gets caught short at Bagnigge Wells

Black Mary's Hole (The Union Tavern, King's Cross Road/Lloyd Baker Street)

The strange name comes from the fact that:

1. The well was once owned by the Benedictine nuns of St Mary's, Clerkenwell, who wore black habits.
2. There was once a well keeper called Mary who kept a black cow.
3. One keeper of the well, a Mary Wollaston, was black.
4. It had been a holy well dedicated to Black Mary, the dark

Madonna, who represented the dark side of the moon, and originated from the ancient moon goddess.

5. There was a basement club owned by a goth called Mary.

Black Mary's Hole was enclosed in 1687. Smart gardens and a hamlet grew up around it, taking its name, and it became a popular chalybeate healing well, particularly good for curing sore eyes. An estate called Spring Place was built over the gardens in 1815 and the well was turned into a cesspool. It reappeared briefly in 1826 when the footpath above it collapsed and a pump was erected, but it's all long gone now.

In honour of Black Mary I have a Guinness in the Union Tavern, a few yards from where the well was. Although it's been done up recently it's still late high Victorian in style with loads of fantastic mirror work and strange swirly patterns on the ceiling. U2 is on the jukebox. Two people at the bar arguing are about the direction of their company's sales force. Significantly, one of them is a woman dressed in black. She's holding a cigarette and blowing smoke everywhere.

Islington Lands (Filthy McNasty's, Amwell Street)

There's a real villagey atmosphere round here, though it's rapidly changing with all the new building work. I settle down into a smashed-up old leather sofa in Filthy's and enjoy a pint of Guinness. The walls are covered in paintings by one of the bar staff.

Islington Lands was a pond in a field called 'a famous ducking land' (Strutt's *Sports and Pastimes*). The sport consisted of hunting a duck with dogs, the duck diving when the dogs came close to elude capture. Another mode was to tie an owl upon the duck's back; the duck dives to escape the burden when, on rising for air, the

wretched half-drowned owl shakes itself, and, hooting, frightens the duck ; she, of course, dives again, and replunges the owl into the water. The frequent repetition of this action soon deprived the owl of its sensation, and generally ended in its death, if not that of the duck also.

This was also where witches and scolding wives were ducked. These days people would pay good money for that sort of thrill.

Sadlers Wells (The Stage Door Café, Rosebery Avenue)

There was a holy well here in medieval times famed for its sacred healing powers. The priests belonging to the Priory of Clerkenwell used to attend there, and made the people believe that 'the virtues of the water proceeded from the effi- cacy of their prayers.'[2] It was stopped up during the Reformation. When a Mr Sadler, who worked on the roads, discovered the well while digging for stones, he decided to profit from it and built a music house around it.

In the theatre I have a chat with Well-Groomed Tessa the Events Manager about the well. It's still there but covered by a hologram of water. 'There's a water gremlin who

2 *The Legendary Lore of the Holy Wells of England* by Robert Charles Hope

appears when you put money in,' she says. I put in 40p but nothing
happens apart from a lot of over-acted gurgling. She tells me the well
is still active and that they've bored down 600 feet lower than the
original well. The water is on sale in the café. I pop next door and buy
four bottles. It's kind of salty.

Islington Spa/New Tunbridge Wells (The Shakespeare's Head, Arlington Way)

I wander up to the Shakespeare's Head, a local pub with pictures of luvvies from the theatre on the walls. I only rec-ognize Stefan Dennis who used to be in *Neighbours*. I sit down with a glass of Courage Best and observe a crowd of old geezers at the other end of the pub watching racing on the telly.

I sit for a while on a bench in Spa Gardens and try to imagine how this little patch of green was once part of an impressive area of walks and gardens.

London Spa (O'Hanlons, Tysoe Street)

The horror! The horror! The London Spa is no more. It's all boarded up with a 'For Sale' sign outside. What about the beautiful mirror work? What about the lovely cubicles? What about the (nearly) lucky big screen? What about the lucky barmaid? Nooooooooo. It's going to be turned into crappy flats, you can tell.

Fuck it. O'Hanlons is across the road on a side street and has been done up recently moving

The London Spa, formerly the luckiest pub in the world.

away from rustic country boozer territory and into the 'trendy shiny bright colours for people who've only just started drinking' zone. Only a few months before I'd seen Chelsea beat Man United at home on the big screen. A sort of miracle, I suppose. A pint of honey ale goes down well but doesn't make up for my crushing disappointment.

Clerk's Well (The Betsey Trotwood, Farringdon Road)

One of the earliest writers on London, William Fitzstephen, wrote in his *Description of the ancient City of London in 1173*

> There are, on the North part of London, principal fountains of water, sweet, wholesome, and clear, streaming from among the glistering pebble stones. In this number, Holy Well, Clerken Well, and St Clement's Well, are of most note, and frequented above the rest, when scholars and the youth of the city take the air abroad in the summer evenings.

The stone Clerk's Well is still visible in a glass-fronted office on Farringdon Lane, along with a display about the history of the wells. A few yards away is the Betsey, run by a bloke called Steve, whose business success was founded on my thirtieth birthday being held in his pub. The amount of beer my family and friends put away that night set him up for life. I have a pint of Spitfire and a quick chat with Steve, then head off into the evening, feeling healed as a newt.

Faggeswell (The Hope, Cowcross Street)

I don't know much about Faggeswell, except that it was situated around no. 18 Cowcross Street, close to Smithfield Market. Centuries after the last stand of the Britons, the river once again ran red with blood but rather than spurting from the veins of tattooed shouty longhairs it was the blood of cattle, sheep, pigs, otters, chickens, skylarks and all other beasts that medieval Londoners liked to eat. This area was originally called Smoothfield – large tracts of low-lying meadowlands just outside the city walls. Huge fairs were held here where animals were bought and sold and eventually it became the site of a huge permanent meat market, Smithfield. In the Middle Ages the butchers did their own killing, slicing up animals in the streets facing the river and allowing the blood and offal to slide down into the Fleet. Dead animals, industrial and human waste turned it into a foul sewer. In Ben Jonson's 'On the Famous Voyage', the two lunatics who travelled down it described it as eclipsing the four rivers of Hades in foulness. At one stage the river must have seemed split fifty-fifty between water and blood/offal. The Fleet had at one time more meat products floating in it than any other European waterway: 'It makith a horrible stench and foul sight' (*Ludgate Priory Record*, fourteenth century).

Smithfield still has a powerful mystique. Farmers I know in Lincolnshire usually slumber politely (but boredly) while I bang on about London and its charms. But the mention of Smithfield has them sitting bolt upright with eyes shining maniacally. 'MMMMmmmmmmmm, Smithhhhhh fieeeeelllldddddddd.' Not really sure if that proves anything, but it impresses me.

Various laws and statutes were passed by the City burghers to address the problem but the Fleet had been clogged up for years when, in 1589, the Common Council granted money for it to be cleaned up so that the water could be used for drinking. After the Great Fire Sir Christopher Wren had the bright idea of turning the cesspit stream into a canal to rival the best of Venice. It looked great but it didn't make any money for its owners. One of the reasons it failed was that the architects hadn't factored in the rogue Smithfield butchers, who continued to do what they'd always done – throw their carcasses and entrails into the Fleet – and so it once again became a disgusting river of liquid meat and shit by the

120   middle of the eighteenth century, so much so that if a pedestrian fell in he was unlikely to drown but highly likely to be asphyxiated by the fumes. Eventually, in 1765, the Fleet around Smithfield was filled in for good and now it flows underneath the big traffic thoroughfare that is Farringdon Road.

By 1841 the remaining section of the Fleet, to the north of Ludgate Circus, was proving to be such a hazard to public health that the entire central stretch was arched over. Now it is a dark subterranean channel, although the mouth of the canal can be seen at low tide.

St Bride's Well (The Punch Tavern)

A quick detour to West Smithfield and the beautiful St Bartholomew's church, one of the few areas to escape the Great Fire and the only sacred building I visit that isn't a pub. Then I cross the ravine of Farringdon Street.

In the Punch Tavern, all done up like a ritzy Victorian sitting room, I buy a pint of murky brown liquid and stand at the bar. I catch the eye of a barman and explain to him that the last time I was in here, my mother left a new copy of an Eric Newby travel compendium on a seat.

'How long ago was that, sir?'

'Hmm. Dunno. About five years possibly.'

He says he can't help. Bah. The food was crap anyway, I mutter.

It's now the last part of my journey, down onto New Bridge Street

 at the bottom of Farringdon Street. At one time there were five bridges over the Fleet round here. This is where Fleetway Comics used to be based, the producers of all those classic football annuals and army comics (War Picture Library) in the sixties and seventies.[3]

---

3   Arrrgggh. Achtung! Aieeeeeeeeeee!

Bridewell is an ancient holy well and also the site of the old
Bridewell women's prison, which in turn took the place of a mansion called Baynard's Castle. It's just office buildings now. I stagger down to the edge of the Thames, craning to see the tunnel of the old storm drain beneath, but there's only the lapping high-tide waters.

London Stories 4: The Secret Policeman's Bar

Back in 1994 I was out with my mate Dom in Clerkenwell and, after we'd been kicked out at half past twelve from a bar for (I think) dancing on tables, and we both really needed more beer. We stood around near Smithfield market saying 'beeeeeeeeeeeeer' loudly to each other and looking very melancholy. Then, as if by magic, a friendly policeman appeared.

'All right then lads?'

'Beeeeeeeeeeeeeeer!'

'What seems to be the problem?'

'We were just out for a beer and all we wanted to do was drink until we couldn't stand up and it was coming out of our ears but this landlord in the pub we were in, right, chucked us out, right, at half eleven so we went to another bar and they kicked us out at half twelve and we couldn't have had more than a gallon it's not like we're training for the London Marathon or anything it's not fair don't they want our money or what?'

This sad tale must have tugged his heart strings. He smiled. 'I know a place you can go.'

'Where the cops don't know?' I said.

'Well, actually there'll probably be quite be a lot of police in there.' He laughed.

He gave us directions – through the market, left, right down an alleyway, left, on a bit, right, left, left. Turn round three times in the shadow of St Bartholomew's church, see some steps go down and mention him, PC 9392 (not his real name), to the old man on the door.

Why had he decided to help us? Perhaps it was a set-up. Were we heading into a trap? We didn't care. At this stage of the night, as long as we could get a pint of Guinness we'd be the fall guys for anything. We staggered off. It appeared that, after Cloth Fair, there was some secret street that only very drunk people could find. You then had to piss in a doorway and walk down a bit further. No sign of anything. Then, just before the end of the street, we saw a glass door. It seemed to be locked up but we gave it a gentle shove and it opened. Sitting in the twilight was a leathery old man, just as PC 9392 had said, perched on a high stool guarding the main entrance. Beyond him was a flight of steps and the faint sound of conversation.

'Can I help you lads?'

'PC 9392 sent us.' I said, expecting him to tell us to fuck off.

'Right you are.'

We walked down some more steps, then it opened out into a bright room full of cheeseplants. Dotted around the room were small groups of thick-set villainous-looking characters in light grey shiny suits with heavily made-up women in skimpy dresses by their side. It was as if all the extras from all the police dramas ever had been invited to a party.

'It's fifty–fifty cops and robbers, I reckon,' whispered Dom, as we grinned at each other and made our way through the crowd to the bar on the far side of the room, in a confident way as if we'd been there before. People looked at us – blimey, it's Starsky and Hutch! Dom got to the bar first.

'Where you from then, lads?' said the landlord.

'Who wants to know?' joshed Dom, in a winning parody of north London TV villain-speak. 'Two Guinness' please,' he said, smiling.

But it was nothing doing.

'Sorry, lads. I can't serve you.'

Eh? We stood our ground for a couple of minutes trying to persuade him to change his mind and that we weren't really north London TV villains, but our lack of Mr Byrite style formal wear had exposed us. We trailed out sadly, refusing to look back in case the bar disappeared for ever, and made our sad way home.

The next day, during my lunch break, I walked up to the area but couldn't find it. Nothing. No sign of a bar. Just the door to an office or lock-up. But, a few months later, completely pissed up, I returned with two other mates and somehow found the bar again. This time it was packed with a fifty–fifty split of coppers and nurses and we posed as off-duty doctors. It's that most modern of places, a public-sector theme night bar that only exists when you've consumed twenty units of alcohol.

INVISIBLE STREAMS

Some of the smaller forgotten water-courses mentioned by early historians may simply be myth and never actually existed. Here is an in-depth history of three such streams - The Cranbourne, the Oldbourne and the Shoreditch...

The Cranbourne allegedly flowed near the Convent Garden (now Covent Garden).

By the Elizabethan era it had already been covered over and virtually forgotten

But some experts maintain that a stream called the Cranbourne never existed.

IT NEVER EXISTED!

RIVERS EXPERT

And so, Cranbourne Street, in Covent Garden, is named after an Elizabethan nob, Lord Cranbourne.

EXCELLENT!

It is said that *the Oldbourne* flowed down what is now Fleet Street into the River Fleet.

For years, most experts either ignored the stream or doubted its existence.

RIVERS EXPERTS

IT NEVER EXISTED

THAT'S RIGHT!

But in 2000 archaeologists found evidence of a Roman channel on the course of the Oldbourne.

Who is right? River experts or archaeologists. Whatever, neither group is very good at fighting.

Experts can't agree on *Shoreditch*. Was it part of the Roman battlements that kept out the Britons?

FASCISTS!

But some claim the name is a derivation of *Shitditch* - and that the river was simply a cesspit.

However, the area is famous for shoes. Perhaps the *Shoeditch* was a footwear graveyard.

GOODBYE FOR EVER!

Most likely, the existence of these streams depends on whether you're a realist or a romantic.

NO! *YES!*

London Stories 5: Triumph of the Wilf

I was standing on the steps that lead up from the Peabody Estate to Bowling Green Lane in Clerkenwell, trying to work out whether the sharp stomach pains I was getting were due to the lukewarm seafood salad I'd just eaten or prolonged exposure to football memorabilia, when a bald old man in a long grey raincoat who looked like William Burroughs walked down the steps towards me.

'What's that?' he said, pointing at my green and orange striped Punk Doctors T-shirt. 'Is it a rugby shirt?' he said.

I told him I got it from a German friend of someone I worked with during the Euro 96 football tournament. I'd got it in exchange for one of my highly valuable hand-painted T-shirts that said 'Go!'

'Ah, that was a good 'un, that Euro 96. Nobby Stiles. Bobby Moore.'

'No' I insisted, 'it was 1996.'

'That's right, 1996. We won the World Cup. Bobby Charlton. He was in that plane crash. They was a good team. Duncan Edwards. Frank Swift, he had the biggest hands in football. It was a shame about Bobby Moore.'

He told me his name was Wilf, then made some enquiries as to my reasons for being in the vicinity. As if he was a bouncer for the Bowling Green Road steps.

'Are you George? Bob's son.'

'No,' I told him, 'I work on Pear Tree Court.'

'What, the *Guardian*?'

'No, that's Farringdon Road. Pear Tree Court. It's just there, about 15 yards away. The Betsey Trotwood pub is at the end of it.'

'Oh, you're Steve from the Betsey, are you? Nice beer in there.'

'No, I'm Tim. I work round the corner, at a football magazine.'

'So, Vic, it's your sister that goes out with that black gentleman, isn't it? Up in Peabody. Got a big car. Better be nice about him, seeing as he's family.'

I did that 'looking at watch' gesture.

'Course, we have this van here to take us around. But since the coons come in there's hardly enough room. There's Asian families that gets houses straight away.'

I guessed that Wilf was regurgitating this stuff from the National Front pamphlets that he'd just finished delivering in the local area, and as he rattled on I started to move away. Just then another old boy came down the steps from Bowling Green Lane, effectively cutting off my getaway.

'Hey,' said Wilf to the newcomer, 'do you know Tom? George's son?'

The new old bloke looked me hard in the eye and scowled. I could tell he thought that I was pulling Wilf's leg.

'Never seen him before,' he growled.

A few days later I was walking a bit further north, down Rosoman Street, past the little Spa Fields park near what used to be the Thomas Wethered pub but is now called the CrapChrome Bar (or something), with its neatly clipped hedges, rich and damp aroma of flowers. I stopped for a couple of minutes taking in the sound of the birds and sniffing the heavily scented air. Some kids were messing about on a big tyre in the play area on the other side of the road.

'Yeah, I can smell it too. It's urine, innit?' I turned round. It was Wilf. I smiled weakly. I sensed he had been waiting behind a bush for several days, until someone walked past whom he vaguely recognized. ('Great it's George's son! Time to turn on the charm.')

He shook his head. 'They come out the pubs and they just piss against the wall and into the road. Disgusting.'

SPRING

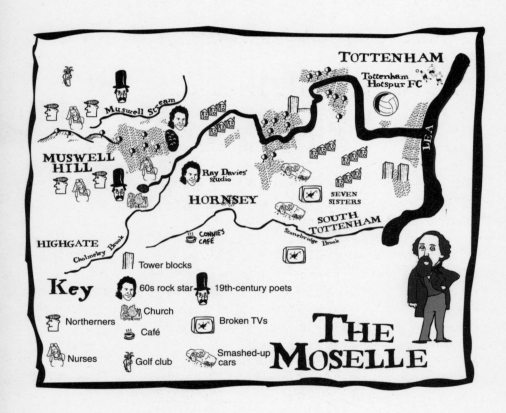

TOTTENHAM

Tottenham
Hotspur FC

Muswell Stream

LEA

MUSWELL
HILL

Ray Davies'
Studio

HORNSEY

SEVEN
SISTERS

SOUTH
TOTTENHAM

Stonebridge Brook

CONNIES
CAFÉ

HIGHGATE

Cholmeley Brook

Key

Tower blocks

60s rock star

19th-century poets

Northerners

Church

Broken TVs

Café

Nurses

Golf club

Smashed-up
cars

THE MOSELLE

7. The Pot and the Pendulum

• The Moselle – Hornsey High Street to Tottenham

Northerners – two lost streams – loads of nurses – Ray Davies of the Kinks – Littlehampton Boys – Alain de Botton no no no – Dickens's Sex Thriller – a short history of Muswell Hill – 'Little Fluffy Clouds' – pot and pendulum – Hornsey Church – Wood Green Shopping City – Spurs are rubbish

When northerners come to London they need to acclimatize first by staying in a halfway house, somewhere that isn't the sticks but isn't quite London either. A place where they can kip down for a couple of weeks, get used to the accents, then continue their journey to London proper. Muswell Hill is such a place. Real Londoners don't bother going there. It's so far north that it seems as though it might be in Yorkshire. Yet if you stand on top of Muswell Hill, in front of Alexandra Palace, and look down on London you're somehow fooled into thinking the city is much closer.

Up here it's London suburbia-by-numbers, everything knocked together by the same architect in the first half of the last century; a Broadway here with a roundabout there, thirties shops with flats

132   above, piece of piss, lah de lah, time for lunch, do a bit of the Charleston. The Victorians didn't get a chance to cover it with their gloomy urban vision. Muswell Hill has two underground streams: the Muswell goes to the north on the far side of the hill; the Moselle is much bigger and runs west–east to the south.[1] That's one for locals and one for newcomers.

As well as lots of northerners, quite excitingly Muswell Hill has the highest proportion of women to men in London. Most of the area was built up in the twenties because of the influx of nurses, who invaded London between the wars and decided to stay. The nurses come out on Mayday and dance around a big pole in Alexandra Park, until they are whisked away one by one by rich city traders.

Maybe this is why a lot of celebrities choose to live in Muswell Hill. Such as Maureen Lipman and Tom Watt (Lofty out of *EastEnders*). OK, scrub that theory. Ray Davies of the Kinks was brought up here and is still probably Muswell Hill's most famous son. Some of his lyrics seem to try to make sense of the rural/suburb/city aspect of Muswell Hill, making him feel like an outsider on the edge of town.

                        ॐ   ॐ   ॐ

Got no time for Muswell town
Gonna look around now
My old town was good to me
But oh…

Guess I'll say so long now
Don't even say a word

---

[1]   At least according to the Ordnance Survey map from 1865, along with an older map from 1771 and one from 1829. Also mentioned in *The History of Muswell Hill* by Ken Gray and *People and Places – Lost Estates in Highgate, Hornsey and Wood Green* by Joan Schwitzer.

I'll turn my back and walk away, but oh ...
The day that I've seen everything I promise to return

So long, so long
Now I'm on my way
So long, so long
See you all some day
So long, so long
Now I'm on my way
So long, so long.

'So Long', Ray Davies of the Kinks

Music/Rivers critic says: Ray Davies of the Kinks recognizes that Muswell Hill is an epicentre of nurses but says that although he has had a few nurses in his time – and let's face it, who hasn't? – he is not ready to settle down with one yet. But it is also a reference to the buried Muswell Stream, which has had enough of being used as a sewer and has retreated far underground. 'See you all some day' suggests that the river knows it will one day come back to the surface. The nurses might represent the public health fears that forced the river to be buried, which is why Ray Davies of the Kinks is angry with them.

Muswell Hill was my halfway house. In 1988 I moved to London and into a house with three other blokes who were also recent arrivals. The Scotsman was an old mate from university who let me camp down on his floor. He'd legendarily walked around the City for weeks in a pinstripe suit two sizes too small, looking for a job. Everyone wished him the best but didn't hold out too much hope. So when he got a job as a Eurobond dealer at a Japanese bank it was a major triumph for all of us wasters. The bankers had been impressed by the fact that he was a regular in the London Scottish first team. Which was true in the sense that he was Scottish and lived in London.

Living with the Scotsman was an intensely cultural experience:

> **film review** – *Midnight Express*. The Scotsman has got a big lump of dope from a local loudmouth but I tell him it's not dope, it's part of a stock cube. We can't agree so, to resolve our argument, we eat half each. I'm taunting the Scotsman for his naivety and watching the bit where Brad Davis bites someone's tongue off when the next thing I know I'm lying on the floor laughing my head off and the Scotsman is laughing too and every time one of us opens our mouths the other pisses himself. The film is the funniest one of all time, though I can't remember what happens.

My other new flatmates were the Swede and the Canadian. I'll call them The Chessmen. The Swede was an Edward Fox clone with ultra-blond hair. The Canadian was a thick-set fellow with a big toothy smile and a big selection of heavy knitwear. Together they played chess morning, noon and night. Speed chess, with a clock. Nice blokes. Things started to fall apart in Muswell Hill when The Chessmen got new employment. One evening they took me and the Scotsman out for a drink and told us they were moving to Costa Rica, I presumed for a big chess tournament, but no, it was some kind of property scam, er, I mean business development scheme. The Swede was the sort of person who in a previous era would have been an eccentric Victorian explorer. It was his sort of scheme. Great, we said. Good luck. They asked if we'd like to go with them, but I was too busy writing on my old forties typewriter to bother with trifling concerns like having a job and the Scotsman was too busy earning proper money and shooting up champagne in City bars. A few months later they returned, lucky to have escaped with their lives. Money owed, guns to the head, crazy women who turned into snakes in the bedroom, magic galleons in the street, butterflies everywhere etc. etc.

The departure of the Chessmen had meant that I moved into a room of my own. It also meant a new flatmate, one of the most fascinating characters I'd ever meet. I'm not sure how we got to know the Businessman – he was a friend of a friend of a friend of a friend of a friend. Of a friend. He looked like a Brat Pack actor and had his own folk song, which he'd sing at moments of high emotion:

> *Littlehampton boys, we are here*
> *Shag your women and drink your beer.*
> *La la la la la la la la la.*

The high point of Littlehampton Boy Fascination was when Anneka Rice appeared in Arundel, just up the road from Littlehampton, in that programme she used to do with Kenneth Kendall, him standing in a room with a load of middle-aged saddos and her bouncing around breathlessly in a tight tracksuit. That was avante garde TV in the late eighties. The Businessman was ecstatic.

'Littlehampton boys! Littlehampton boys!' he screamed at the TV.

Anneka went running down a street he knew. 'Littlehampton boys, Littlehampton! beeeeeooooooooyyyyyeeeees!' squealed the Businessman. I think he might have ejaculated in his trousers after that, but I had to leave the room. For a while, after that episode, the Businessman became my mentor. We went to the pub and he told me about his theories of personal development.

'Tim, when you shake someone's hand you should squeeze it really hard to show them who's boss. It's called "body language".' He even did the 'rabbit ears' thing with his fingers. I sipped my beer and nodded silently, happy to be in the presence of a guru. An interesting thing about the Businessman was that he had a powerful animal magnetism. What some might call a strong 'personal

136   scent'. It may have been a ruse to attract females, but I wanted to
       talk to him about that. Could he, possibly, do something about it?
       A friend of mine had stayed in his room, while the Businessman
       was away drinking beer, singing folk songs and squashing people's
       hands in Littlehampton, and nearly asphyxiated from the fumes
       emitted by one of the Businessman's shirts.

       The Businessman was quite proud of his system. He'd wear a
       shirt for a week then hang it up and start wearing another one.
       When it was time for the first shirt to come back into rotation
       he'd spray it with aftershave. He'd have three, maybe four, shirts
       on the go at any one time and slowly the pheromonal odours
       would build up until it was like a stink glacier, smashing every-
       thing in its path. Of course, there'd always be crowds of women
       hanging around outside, strangely attracted to our flat, though
       they didn't know why ...

       In the Muswell Hill days, unable to leave behind my northern-
       ness, I used to sit and stare at people on tubes trying to make eye
       contact. People don't like you looking at them. One evening I was
       reading *Portnoy's Complaint* on the way home, I laughed so much I
       banged my head against the wall. An old woman sat down next to
       me and started having a go. 'My daughter's dying of cancer. How
       can you laugh?'

'Cos I'm a Muswell Hillbilly boy,
But my heart lies in Old West Virginia,
Though my hills are not green,
I have seen them in my dreams,
Take me back to those Black Hills,
That I have never seen.

'Muswell Hillbilly', Ray Davies of the Kinks

Music/Rivers critic says: Ray Davies of the Kinks is refer- ring to his unrequited love for Olivia Newton John – West Virginia (she sang 'Take me Home, Country Road ...) but he is a yokel 'hillbilly boy' unversed in the sophisticated ways of the world. 'I have seen them in my dreams,' he sings, perhaps suggesting he is using an online dream analyst.

🌀 🌀 🌀

It was good to be high up on a hill and every morning I'd go for a walk in Alexandra Park and look down on the city. It seemed easy then to fix the idea of London in my head, to encapsulate the city in one thought. Not so easy now, of course. 'There was London. I lived here. Whatever was going on in London was whatever I was doing.' So whether the 'happening' was drinking ten pints of bitter in the historic Green Man pub at the top of the hill, trying to avoid the eye of the local nutter who had loads of dogs, talked to himself and allegedly owned several machine guns, or whether it meant a shambolic evening of improvisation at Finsbury Park Community Centre or just sitting in watching TV with a pizza, that was the only thing that was happening in London at the time. At the risk of paraphrasing Lou Reed really clumsily, if you're brought up in a small town you get used to the idea that not much happens. And if it does happen and you witness it there won't be anything else going on so don't worry. Fuck. Sorry, Lou Reed.

🌀 🌀 🌀

And there's a tap by a reservoir, leading to a stream, that turns into a river estuary that eventually opens to the sea.

'London Song', Ray Davies of the Kinks

138   Music/Rivers critic says: Ray Davies of the Kinks believes that the world needs to be healed, and this can be achieved by everyone visiting the old Mossy Well in Muswell Hill. This was a healing spring and became the subject of pilgrimages from far and wide. The stream could be the Muswell Stream or the Moselle.

ə ə ə

A research day. I walked from Highbury to Muswell Hill library, through Stroud Green and Crouch End. From the top of Crouch Hill the City looked like Manhattan. Well, a bit. At one stage all the traffic was held up because someone had burst a water main – a plume of water rose 20 feet in the air like a geyser.

Naturally, I hadn't rung up to check library opening times and naturally the library was closed, so I went down the hill a bit and stood outside our old flat. Everything seemed much neater than I remembered. I decided to go for a quick pint. The old local, the Green Man, had been a pub since 1552 and would have been my normal preference, but I was concerned I might run into Dog Gun Bloke, so I went for a pint in the Swiss Village across the road. I sat with a pint of Guinness, crap R&B playing on the jukebox. The Swiss Village has a deep red carpet with a black pattern (could be William Morris, hard to tell – did he do pub floors?), worn away around the bar area. In 1988 it seemed brash and new.

I sipped my beer and read a few pages of Alain de Botton's *Consolations of Philosophy* that I'd picked up in WH Smith's half an hour earlier when I'd needed to get some change for the phone so I could find out if Highgate library was open, which seems like a bloody expensive phone call when you analyse it, but at the time I thought hey it's on special offer so I'm making a saving here. A loud Cockney bloke at the bar was telling his mates about the operation he'd just had on his stomach.

And then something dreadful happened. Something that often happens when you read books that try to make you think. I thought to myself, 'What is my philosophy of life?' Arrrgh, fuck. Before I had time to put my hands to my ears and shout 'LA LA LA LA LA!' or hurl the book over the bar and leg it out of the pub, I was thinking 'Hmmm. Bingeing on love, sausages, beer, art and country music while transcending capitalism in some way.' After some deep breathing and heavy concentration, I managed to get back to my former state of mind, a sort of shallow reminiscence mixed with an inability to concentrate on one thing for very long. And casual eavesdropping. And I relaxed. Aaaahhhhhhhhhhh.

My mind started to wander again and I looked at a photo screwed onto the wall, a portrait of a Victorian bloke, 1860s or 1870s at a guess, with short hair, a big moustache, clipped beard and fuzzy whiskers. Posing at an angle of 45 degrees he looks slightly startled as if observing something that's happening out of the shot, say his collection of rare butterflies were being stolen, or the Corn Laws had been unrepealed. He then started to look at me and I went into a stream-of-consciousness thought process, thinking about how lots of travel books these days follow in the footsteps of some intrepid explorer from the past. Particularly if it's a posh Victorian. And you're far more likely to get a book reviewed in the big papers if it's a biography of a dead posh person (preferably from the eighteenth or nineteenth century). Maybe this is because the descendants of said posh Victorian are now working in the literary pages of the press. Now, *that's* a good idea. I decided his name was Charles Foster ('C. F.') Talgutt and, in the space of about seventeen years in the mid-nineteenth century, he was almost solely responsible for the covering over of London's rivers. Talgutt had hated running water ever since a rabies scare he experienced in India. Talgutt was a vicar's son from the Midlands who had moved to London in the 1880s after a failed love affair with a wealthy landowner's daughter. He became a Victorian renaissance man – a

140   muscular Christian who liked the ladies, martial arts and visionary writings, who wrote bad poetry and did mediocre watercolours. A writer, poet, fighter and musician. He sailed a boat through Clissold Park, boxed Jem Mace, the Swaffham Gypsy, was a friend of Dickens, had affairs with actresses. One of his most strongly held views was that a man should not ejaculate during intercourse. Connected to his phobia about running water, perhaps. He did have a theory – that the semen went to a large storage container in the afterlife, which would come in handy when you eventually pegged it as all the other old duffers would be pretty much sperm-less by then. Dickens was going to write a novel about it but instead wrote *Little Dorrit*. Shame. Talgutt was a mystery man. He hadn't produced much work but he had somehow achieved mythic status. He was seen as a philosopher- poet, and various Talgutt societies had sprung up in Ireland, Britain and America. Even in France there had been an article in *Paris Match* entitled 'La Philosophé de Talgutt. Qu'est ce que c'est et qui est il?' His poetry was beginning to be taught in universities and schools. Maybe, though, Talgutt existed before, not before the nineteenth century, but before in my head. I did invent what literary critics call a madey-uppy character a while back when I started writing a novel about Lincolnshire, set in the nineteenth century, with the working title of *Dickens Sex Thriller*. Dickens visited Lincolnshire a few times and slagged it off. He had an un-named travelling companion who got into scrapes with local ne'er-do-wells. *Dickens Sex Thriller* got shelved when I gave my old Amstrad to my brother and bought an Apple Mac. The Amstrad disks were incompatible with any other computer and I couldn't afford to transfer all the data – thirty quid a pop from some little bedroom com-puter shop in Hanwell. I still have them, somewhere. Maybe I could do this rivers project as a novel from

the point of view of a Victorian who was obsessed with covering up
the rivers (for whatever psychological reasons). As well as the main
story, the book would contain pictures of Talgutt, his drawings, old
maps, old photos, his inventions and old posters.

I had another sip of my beer. No, it's a rubbish idea. I had to kill
off Talgutt before this went any further.

London is a metropolis of open pustules, running sores that blight
the fair city's visage. A foul stench permeates the surrounding areas,
a disgusting wetness. How grand it would be to walk down the
course of the evil Fleet river and not be waylaid by the rotten fluid.

Letter to the Royal Geographical Society, 1842, from *Perambulations
Along the Watercourses of Our Great Metropolis* by C. F. Talgutt

No, no, stop it. He does not exist.

I finished the Guinness quickly and headed for Wood Green
library.

*I love sitting down by the riverside,
Watching the water go flowing by.
Oh, golly gee, it is heaven to be
Like a willow tree.*

'Sitting by the Riverside', Ray Davies of the Kinks

Music/Rivers critic says: In 'Sitting by the Riverside', Ray Davies of
the Kinks is imagining what the Moselle would have looked like
before it was buried. The willow tree in question is on
Brook Road, at the bottom of the hill. The willow grows
where there is water, sometimes when it cannot be seen.
Ray Davies of the Kinks would like to be a diviner. The

142   river is also a stream of ideas – Ray Davies of the Kinks can pick out the ideas as they float by.

ॐ   ॐ   ॐ

In the library I found copies of various maps: 1822 OS, 1894 OS, 1819 Greenwood, 1741 John Rocque, 1815 Edwardes. The Muswell Stream ran down the hill along the line of the present-day Albert Road.

I ask for more information and am advised to go to the history archive at Hornsey Library, Crouch End. At the archive Isobel, a librarian, excitedly tells me of a local historian, David Harris, who knew all about the underground rivers of the area.

'He would have been able to walk them with you and tell you all about them.'

'Er, "would have been?"'

Her face drops. 'I'm afraid he died three weeks ago."

But she gives me some maps of the routes of the Muswell and Moselle.

Pretty nurse: (takes drag of cigarette and blows the smoke in my face): So, big boy, tell me about the history of Muswell Hill.

Me: In what is commonly known as the dark ages but I prefer to call the 'Fuck Me, It's the Saxons and the Vikings!' years, the terrain of Muswell Hill seems to have deterred clearance and settlement so the woods and wildlife thrived and it eventually became a hunting park owned by the Bishop of London, spanning a huge area including what is now Highgate and Finchley.

Much of the land became owned by nuns from Clerkenwell. They'd been given it by a scrofulus king who was

At one time the area was called Muscle Hill

cured by the waters of the Mus Well – the mossy well in the heart of the village. The nuns built a chapel near it, 'bearing the name of our Ladie of Muswell'. The chapel disappeared in the Reformation, but the land remained with Clerkenwell parish until 1900, being known as 'Clerkenwell Detached'. Until the early twentieth century Muswell Hill was still a remote hamlet, due to its location. It was dragged into the modern age by a gruesome murder which took place in the village in 1901. The papers ran pieces on this crime of passion and people would embark on murder sightseeing trips and stand outside the house to get a bit of that badman juju. Muswell Hill became a sensation and new houses started springing up all over the hill.[2]

Pretty nurse: (looking sleepy): How interesting. Now, why don't you go off on a walk and leave me in peace.

ॐ ॐ ॐ

I tried dowsing again, this time without the aid of druidic hallucinogens (i.e. Special Brew). I wanted to test whether the ability to 'sense' the presence of water was innate or came as part of a free gift from the big brewers. I got hold of a pamphlet called 'Letter to Robin' by an American called Walt Woods.[3] You had to use a pendulum. Fortunately I had one and had used it mainly for Matters of High Level Importance such as football results and the lottery (without success). Unlike most of my stuff, it was still in pristine condition.

Research on dowsers suggests that they use extra frequencies of brainwave such as theta and delta. They are more 'aware' but are also searching for 'something'. I went out with my pendulum to find the Source.

I'm in Hornsey High Street opposite Bikerama, a wonderland of toys for boys – Yamahas, Kawasakis and Hondas. Across the road is the Magic Flute Banqueting Hall and further down there's the

2 http://dowsers.new-hampshire.net/lettertorobin
3 A Brief History of Muswell Hill
   http://www.muswell-hill.com/muswell/history/muswellhill

144   Great North Railway Tavern. That's pretty much it in terms of excitement. C. F. Talgutt is already waiting for me in his walking clothes and standing beside a large wooden structure, like an ark.

'What is this, Talgutt?' I ask.

'It's a boat. We're going to sail down the Moselle to the River Lea, collecting two of every species as we go, then have a fight with some locals and retire for dinner at a good inn.'

I shake my head vigorously to get rid of this creation, and continue alone.

There in front of me is old Hornsey Church, which is now just a tower, though in pretty good nick. I've got an old print that shows 'Hornsey Church in the County of Middlesex' surrounded by hills. There's birdsong in the tree-covered graveyard and for a few moments I'm imagining Hornsey past, trying to read the gravestones. Most are from the eighteenth century, some possibly even older but illegible. The sound of planes up above mixes with the birdsong. It reminds me of the opening bars of the Orb's 'Little Fluffy Clouds'. The comforting urban sound of police sirens breaks the mood. I light up the skinny spliff I've knocked up from old chippings found at the bottom of drawers and fag packets and take a few drags. Then I get out my pendulum and start the ritual.

Dr J looking to relieve himself near Hornsey Old Church

'Is this Hornsey?' I ask the pendulum.

Yes, it replies.

'Is there water here?' I ask the pendulum.

Yes, it replies.

'What's best, Kawasaki or Honda?' I ask the pendulum

Yes, it replies.

'Am I wasting my time?" I ask the pendulum.

Yes, it replies.

'Which progrock band did Rick Wakeman play keyboards for?' I ask the pendulum.

Yes, it replies.

There's lots of standing water around. Some stones are half buried. I look for a dip in the land and scribble some sketches. People are wary of someone with a notebook and a couple stop and stare. The traffic noise calls me out to the road, where there are cafés, estate agents and an interesting little cluster of shops, all pretty down at heel. There are shops that sell bathroom fittings, always a sure sign that the source of a river is close by. People in the Bathroom Fittings Industry know about these things on an unconscious level. You can actually use them instead of dowsing rods. I once got offered a job on a well known Bathroom Fittings Industry publication (as well as bathrooms they also reviewed bedrooms and kitchens). I said I wanted to think about it for twenty-four hours and the publisher was so enraged that he gave the job to someone else. When I suggested to him on the phone that this was not the way to do things, he snarled, 'The lad I have given the job to was made up. Made up, he was.' So he cared about his appearance. Big deal. Anyway, I had the last laugh. I dossed about for three more months then went to the World Cup in Italy with my mates, blew lots of money and puked in the shower a lot.

Laundrettes are always another good bet that there is an old river nearby, and in Hornsey there's the Crest. This must be the place. I look for a big puddle and find it at the start of Nightingale Lane,

146   near the Magic Flute, a big red idiosyncratic Victorian building.
Then I find two puddles at the edge of a road called the
Campsbourne. Is that another stream? A group of loud kids walks
alongside me then follow me, shouting rather than talking. Past a
Territorial Army Centre surrounded by barbed wire, with graffiti
'FIFÖ' and 'Brez'.

To the left are some more puddles on a little muddy lane. There's
some meat-and-potato drumming coming out of a council house
window – could be Ray Davies of the Kinks' Konk studios, laying
down tracks for Ray Davies of the Kinks' new album, except I think
they're a couple of hundred yards further east on Tottenham Lane.
These thudding dreams of stardom make me feel jaded and melancholy. The Nightingale is a bright red-painted Victorian local.
Turning a corner there are lots of modern flats and a weeping
willow next to the road. I can imagine the river flowing beneath it. I
follow the lie of the land along Pembroke Road, crossing over
Campsbourne and then Myddelton, onto Moselle Close, where
there's water all over the road, flowing out from a big car wash
place. It looks like a dead end, just a couple of people chatting, and
I'm just about to turn back when one of them walks off down an
alleyway with her two kids so I follow because this is the exact line
of the river according to David Harris's map.

Over the other side of the fence are great mounds of mud and
large pools of water. Some kind of works at the reservoirs connected to the New River – there's still an old waterworks building
on the main road. A bloke in a luminous yellow jacket and yellow
hard hat is on a walkie talkie, watching me. I look over the river
and there is a small stretch of water. It can't be the New River
because that lies abut 50 yards further west – is this a section of the
Moselle, being kept prisoner? I look at him then take a photo over
the fence. He talks into his walkie talkie again and I walk quickly
away, thinking is there some kind of organization which is keeping
these rivers a secret from the general population?

The 1741 Rocque map shows a pond at the Moselle's source –
this is now a used car depot, with bashed-up Ford Fiestas, East
German models and others. Then I cross over a dead straight
stretch of the New River, only a short distance to the north-west
from where I started my New River walk last year. There are real
country views here (although through a wire fence), with
Alexandra Palace in the background, and water birds' piercing
cries. The wind feels different, more biting. Then down into an old
dank tunnel under the railway – dripping water, old pipes, flaking
Victorian bricks, old-style eighties graffiti that should have a
Grandmaster Flash backing track – except for 'To Emma and
Bradley I love you, love Granddad 15/11/99', which I feel defies cat-
egorization.

Out the other side to a light industrial area, where a big old rust-
red gas holder dominates the skyline. When the path ends, the first
named street I get to is Brook Road, which still has a rural feel to it,
small and forgotten in the shadow of Wood Green's famous
Shopping City, itself directly above the course of the Moselle.

Inside Shopping City I first have to squelch through a smelly
food market hall full of music, squashy food underfoot like a covered street market. The main area is like a space station – wide
avenues and purple lights. The Shopping City logo shows the name
on a pool-like daub of blue, a reference perhaps to the river running
underneath.

'Is this the ultimate shopping experience?' I ask the pendulum.
No, it replies.
'Do the phones here work?' I ask the pendulum.
No, it replies.
'Did this complex win design awards?' I ask the pendulum.
No, it replies.
Outside is pandemonium. Wood Green is on the move, going
upwards, lots of money around, bustling, people packed down
with shopping bags. A walkway crosses the high street. I imagine it

148 as a conduit carrying the Moselle, like my dream. I am drawn towards a big pool of water near bus stops. The centre is a mad mix of styles, pick'n'mix, glistening Hollywood cinemas, thirties blocks, sixties modernist flats, Victorian houses and eighties and nineties shopping arcades. Likewise the people, a total heady London mix.

I cross the road then traverse Gladstone Avenue into the dead straight Moselle Avenue, with trees and Arts-and-Crafts-style small terraced cottages, which pretty much follows the course of the stream for half a mile. The light is different here, brighter, silver even, the land lower lying. It feels like a flood plain and would once have been wide open farmland. There's a great old sign – 'Jumping strictly prohibited'. A Spurs celebration poster hangs limply in a window, blue from age like a barbershop photo – possibly the 1991 FA Cup-winning team or even older. It must be tough being a Spurs fan. I see a wooden drumstick lying on the pavement, the second 'rhythm section' reference on this walk, then turn onto Lordship Lane, which at this point follows the curve of the Moselle's course. Offies, video shops, mini markets, laundrettes, the staple no-frills survival fare of any urban settlement in England.

Next, I am in Lordship Park. In the distance, at the other side of the park, is the Broadwater Farm estate, looking like a modernist

The Moselle flowing through Lordship Park, with the Broadwater Farm estate in the distance

cathedral, scene of the 1985 riots. On old maps there is a Broadwater Farm in the middle of open land, and they suggest that the river was quite wide here. At last the Moselle makes an appearance, but it's a thin channel running hurriedly across the park as though trying to hide. Huge pollarded trees run alongside the bank, majestic like stone megaliths – some trunks lie on the ground nearby, victims of storms. They must be 150 to 200 years old, remnants of what would have once been a wild rural setting. The

Recreation Ground is a kite-flying park, windswept and open like an   149
old common. A few people jog around the perimeter path. Graffiti on
the bridge reads – 'E-Dogg sucks Cyc-0'.

   Although it's great to see a 'live' river round here, I'm a bit disap-
pointed by the Moselle. Just a skinny channel coming out of a
concrete pipe. There seems to be more water in the standing pools
that chain around nearby, possibly from other channels and rivulets
flowing into the valley. There's a small greedy pond with what must
be the Moselle's water and more smashed-up trunks of giant elms.
The futuristic brightly coloured Broadwater Farm estate seems a
different world – tranquil, kids playing outside as the sun goes
down, people coming in from work – it all seems vaguely South
American. Yet the riots in 1985 are still lodged in my cultural
memory banks. I walk around the estate then turn left off Adams
Road and head due north through a thir-
ties estate of small cottages. Groups of
women and men are walking around with   1
blue, white and yellow Spurs scarves.

   Another estate in an olde Englishe style
has smart cars parked, people talking football. 'Should have played long ball in the
semi.' 'We were better off under Graham.'
On Flexmere Road now and I can feel the 2
gentle contours on my ankles and Achilles
tendons, and imagine the Moselle flowing
around bends.

   In the distance I can now see the White
Hart Lane stands gleaming orange in the   3
evening sun, tempting me. It's getting late. I
walk alongside the closed-up cemetery

then down a path and up to old White Hart Lane, still a rural lane
at the start of the twentieth century, where the river would have
come out between there and Moselle Place. A mate has given me

150   his ticket. Spurs are playing Bradford so he thought I'd like to go. Bradford are already relegated at this late stage of the season so they've nothing to lose. In the bogs I ask the pendulum if it'll go for a home win. Yes, it replies. But Spurs are rubbish and only kept in the game by good goalkeeping and the enthusiastic shouts of the fat kid in front of me: 'Come on yids!' he squeals. And all the time the medieval-sounding boom of a single drum boom boom boom 'YIDS!!!' shouts the crowd, boom boom boom 'YIDS!!!' drum drum drum 'Yids!' drum drum drum 'Yids!' like some kind of ancient battle cry. Studies have shown that the White Hart Lane crowd has the highest proportion of International Marxist Leninists in the UK.

Afterwards I leave the crowds and walk down Southend Green looking for Carbuncle Alley. It's black air. There are people out in there in the dark somewhere, I can hear voices, but I can't see anyone. Someone says 'injecting it like this'. I head towards the sound of the Lea rushing by in the distance and before it the redirected Pymme's Brook coming down from Edmonton. But it's the sound of traffic. After crossing the railway line, at a fastish jog pace now, I find myself in Tottenham Marshes. The Moselle has gone – I can feel it, I'm cold and tired and hungry. I tell myself I'll come back another day but I know I never will. I quickly head back to Tottenham High Road and get a bus back. From the top deck, North London seems like one big housing estate, street after street the same as developers sucked up the rural land and covered it in brick before anyone had a chance to complain. But who would have complained?

◎ ◎ ◎

Well I'm leaving town and I won't be 'round
'Til I reach my destination, tell the world I'm underground.

'Let Me Be', Dave Davies of the Kinks

Music/Rivers critic says: Ray Davies of the Kinks' brother, Dave
Davies (also of the Kinks) decides that he is giving up music and
will from now on devote himself to the study of underground
rivers. But his search is not just for water, it is for meaning and the understanding of the interdependent one-
ness of the universe. The song's hint at the Beatles' 'Let
it Be'. And an anagram of 'Let Me Be' is 'Beetle M' –
could this be referring to the so-called death of Paul
McCartney in the late sixties? Maybe Dave is about to fake his own
death. Conversely, it could also be Belt Meet (Beltane Meeting?) –
maybe Dave is a druid and is going to live in a cave.

London Stories 6: Catching Muggers, Starsky-and-Hutch Style

I had just finished a six-mile run around north London – up to Turnpike Lane then through Crouch End and got lost, then along Hornsey Lane to Archway – and was feeling pretty washed out. I was in training for running for the bus because I'd missed a couple recently. The 141 bus usually came down Green Lanes just as I was coming out onto it from my street, 150 yards from the nearest stop, and I'd have to sprint. Sometimes I have to run on to the next bus stop to catch it. The drivers do it on purpose grinning maniacally all the while. I've seen them do it to pensioners in heavy rain.

'Nuffink to do wiv me, mate,' they say with a sneer if you rant and rave.

Anyway, I had just slowed to a walk when, at the bottom of the Archway Road, as I hit the roundabout, I heard a woman shouting at someone. Naturally, I presumed it was either a high-spirited female piss-artist just staggering out of the Archway Tavern or a lovers' tiff. However, she was pointing at something as she was shouting, so I tracked her gaze and noticed, amidst the uninterested people going about their business, a man running away to the north in the direction of the Archway Road subways. I crossed the road to check she was all right but she just screamed at me – in a heavily pissed-off-Japanese accent reminiscent of Yoko Ono telling John the Beatles were shit and he should start doing thrashy dirges with her on backing vocals. She shouted something along the lines of

'Never mind me, you fuckwit, catch the evil villain.'

So I set off at top speed, with thoughts in my head of the headlines in the morning papers ('Writer Foils Criminal Mastermind'). My wife and I have a bit of a laugh sometimes and pretend to be Starsky and Hutch. I'm Hutch and she's Starsky. And, er, well, I don't think I should really tell you any more.

Anyway, owing to the tiredness in my legs due to having already run about six miles, my top speed was sadly not enough to stop the 'robber' escaping into the complicated tunnel system. I sniffed around down some stairs and in a couple of tunnels but all I picked up was strong piss odours. He'd vanished.

When I get back to the crime scene, the woman was being comforted by a big Irish guy who'd appeared from a nearby bar.

'Did you catch him?'

Oh yes. Here he is in this specially built Thief Net I'm carrying. Of course I had to render it invisible, which is why you can't see him.

'Er, no. You see, I've just been on a long jog and my legs feel like lead. And, er, no.'

'Fucking hell!' she shouted. It turned out all she'd lost was a chain and I asked myself, pragmatically, had I just risked life and limb for a trinket her boyfriend probably won at a fairground?

'You got a good look at him though, didn't you?' she said.

'Well, I saw the back of his head. And the way he ran.'

'So, could you be a witness?'

If a line of people stood up and showed me the backs of their heads, then ran off, maybe. She asked if I could write down my name and telephone number – I thought of putting down a comedy name, so the cops wouldn't be calling up. Roy Race 01 261 7193. We'd phone his hotline when we were kids to find out what was happening in the football world. We'd also nick my gran's ciggies. And pour boiling water over ants' nests. Urgh. Anyway, it wouldn't have been very gallant to be unhelpful so I gave her the information.

She was still pretty cross with me for not catching the mugger-who-might-have-been-armed-for-all-I-know. Whereas she was positively purring to the big Irish guy who was still hanging around. It seemed that they were about to have sex, so I headed off for the bus. Slowly. 'Bye, then,' I said in my best have-a-go-hero voice. But they weren't listening.

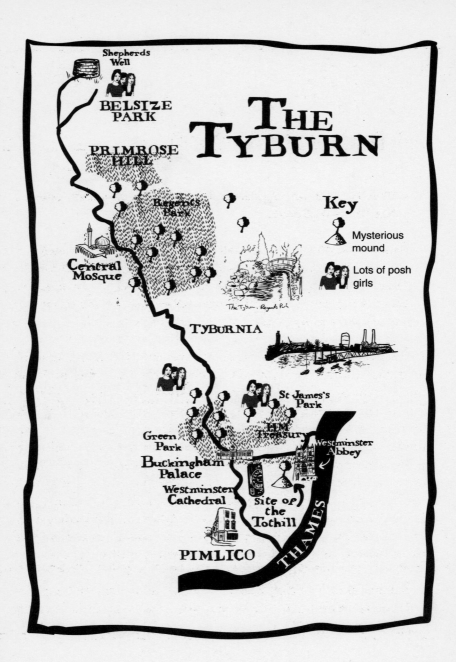

8. Can You Feel the Force?

- **The Tyburn (or Tyebourne) – Belsize Park to the Tachbrook Estate**

Westminster Abbey – brass-rubbing fat kid – Belsize Park – Swiss Cottage – Central Mosque – Regents Park – Marylebone – Oxford Street – Buckingham Palace – Mayfair – Green Park – Tachbrook Estate – Pimlico – Thomas à Becket – Special Brew time travel – 'Put you Watson, Kung Fu!'

FLASHBACK: It's 1988. I sit back in my seat. The cool medieval air of Westminster Abbey cloaks my face like a damp shroud. Faint muffled voices echo across the ancient walls, footsteps reverberate into the high space above me. I sink into myself. It's been a tough morning – I had to write a couple of letters and listen to the cricket on the radio. I close my eyes and tingle with the peace of meditation until all I can hear is my breath. In ... out ... in ... out ... in ... out ... in ... out ... in ... screeeech oout in screeeech out. I slowly open one eye. Sitting next to me is a five-piece American family. A boss-eyed, plump-arsed screechy adolescent is pleading with his dad, who is busy videoing a party of Italian girls as they wiggle past the pews while the mother watches, purse lipped and nervy.

Screechykid: Hey dad, can we do some more brass rubbings?
Dad (George Bush Senior whiny voice): You did the brass rubbings already.

Screechykid: Jeany's still doing them.
Dad: You can sit here.
Screechykid: Aww Dad, just one more brass rubbing.
Dad: I already told you, you did the brass rubbing.
Screechykid: But Jeany's done it twice. I wanna do another brass rubbing. I wanna do another brass rubbing. I wanna do another brass rubbing.

I open both eyes and jump out of my seat, then get up and walk quickly away, out of the Abbey, over the road getting faster, down Abbey Orchard Street then onto Victoria Street where I speed up so much I look like I'm in a twenties silent film. I only relax when I'm back at my desk.

ॐ ॐ ॐ

At a point directly under Buckingham Palace the Tyburn splits into two (possibly three) branches that run down to the Thames. This would all have been marshland and Westminster Abbey was built on what used to be known as Thorney Island, in the Tyburn's delta. The island was at one time flanked by two channels which flowed where Downing Street and Great College Street now lie. It has been suggested that on Tothill there was possibly a religious site, an artificial mound, thousands of years ago.

But it was only plotting the route of the Tyburn, which begins in Belsize Park, onto my *A to Z* that I noticed something striking about the stream. On its course, as well as the abbey and Buckingham Palace, were some of London's most famous landmarks: Lord's Cricket Ground, the Central Mosque, 221b Baker Street, Westminster Cathedral, New Labour headquarters at Millbank, the Treasury and the Paul Smith Sale Shop. Had I discovered something that no one else had spotted? Or, rather, had I blown the whistle on something that lots of people in power obviously already knew about? The Tyburn is the river of power and secrecy. Why else would it be the only river to have no streets or parks named after it? I charted the positions of these landmarks onto a map of London. The result, when a line was drawn though all the co-ordinates, was a picture of the Big Dipper. A famous constellation. I drew again – this time the CND logo.

Perhaps the stream had some kind of powerful energies which, as the Druids understood, could be tapped for religious or political purposes in the same way that the football clubs had fed off the smaller tributaries. After all, isn't it this hard-to-explain energy that is picked up by dowsers and water diviners when they're looking for wells or underground streams? With this in mind I set off on a Tyburn walk with a can of trusty dowsing juice – Tennent's Super – tucked away in my bags.

Belsize Park Town Hall
One branch of the Tyburn began at Belsize Park. Coming out of the tube I notice that everyone has sunglasses on top of their heads. The women are bra-less with long coiffured hair swept back and tied with bands, the blokes tanned and clean shaven, no socks, expensive leather loafers. White jeans, jumpers slung causally over shoulders, they look like the lead characters from French sixties show *The Aeronauts*. They sit around in cafés, discussing clothes or talking on mobile phones about which café they'll go to next.

The Tyburn's main source is what used to be a well round the back of the Town Hall, a majestic redbrick ornate building erected in 1877. Aldermen, burghers, councillors and mayors know the power of old holy wells and the pomposity and self-adulation of setting up shop above a former holy shrine – although whereas 700 years ago people would throw offerings to the well they now take their chequebooks along to pay council tax or parking permits.

The Swiss Cottage

The land slopes to the left towards the nineteenth-century Tyrolean-restaurant-style Swiss Cottage. Across the road is a big detached house, with a green iron front gate and metal grilles over the windows to deter squatters, green shutters and green doors. As the beer takes effect, I stare at the green door. Shaking Stevens, the Welsh Elvis, had a hit with 'Green Door'. Something to do with the Green Man and druidic altered states, perhaps? In the side streets there's a dip in the land as the gentle river valley heads into the heart of St John's Wood and the houses get smaller. In front of me is a fifties estate with balconies, called Turner house. Turner the painter or Tina Turner? 'River deep mountain high', that's the Tyburn connection spotted by a clever architect.

The Central Mosque

I turn into Regent's Park. Formerly forest, then hunting grounds, it was laid out in the early nineteenth century by Nash. Over to the right is Lord's Cricket Ground. It's a rural scene, green and beautiful with great views. Near the boating lake across the little bridge there's a loop of river where the Tyburn hits the pond.

To the right is the golden dome and the tall concrete white minaret of the central mosque. I wonder if rivers are of any importance when choosing a site to build a mosque? If you've ever made a spatula in woodwork class, the same technique is used for mosques. Layers of thin veneer bent into shape. I could have made a mosque. They never told us that at school. We were shown how to make those things you use to stab the turf of your garden with. And a box with a lid and finger hole. And, of course, a spatula using veneer. The woodwork teacher had a long term sports injury. We, generously, used to call him 'Gammy Leg'. Our impersonation of him owed a lot to Kenneth More's portrayal of Douglas Bader in *Reach for the Sky*. For years I thought the Baader Meinhof gang was something to do with the legless flying ace, still fighting the

German state decades later. Around the same time someone also told me that '66 World Cup hero Geoff Hurst's mum had held up a bank in the USA on behalf of the Symbionese Liberation Army. Respectable news sources were few and far between in Lincolnshire in the seventies.

A bloke dressed in white, possibly a cricketer, sprays fertilizer on the grass and it blows into my face.

221B Baker Street
After the park I cross a couple of roads then bend around into Baker Street. Baker Street is pure essence of Crap Tourist London – roaming herds of hollow-eyed Japanese heritage junkies looking for Sherlock Holmes and hanging outside the London Beatles Store still waiting for Paul to walk barefoot across the road in a deer-stalker hat. Concentrate hard and you can taste the grubby tail end of the sixties, acid trip comedown blues. 221B, Sherlock's Holme, is now an Abbey National office.

It gets worse. Straight over Marylebone Road. Mary le Bone. The Globe pub ahead is full of thick-necked Aussies here for a holiday – fish and chips to eat in and take away. The sound of a tape loop playing backwards in an echo chamber. Madame Tussaud's on the left, queues streaming down Euston Road. Look, Roger Moore! Look, Patti Boulaye! Look, Don Estelle! Look, Minder! Look, Prince Edward! To the right A40/M40 Marylebone flyover and West London traffic hell.

The American Intercontinental University – London
After Paddington Gardens, where plague victims are buried, I turn down an alley off Moxon Street. Here is one of Europe's top univer-sities and a famous CIA training centre. Outside various operatives are disguised as drippy teenagers and talking in a strangulated valley speak – 'Yeah like wow, you know?' Some are in dayglo waterproofs, eating sarnies.

160   Across the road is the William Wallace pub – Scottish ales, large Scottish measures. A car alarm goes off.

St Mary le Bone Church, Brook Street
Is it to do with St Mary by the Bourne or some kind of pagan/fertility/erection thing? Marylebone Lane follows the winding course of the Tyburn through a bustling area with little Edwardian-style shops. Like a village high street, except with poncey designer gear.

Paul Smith Sale Store, Avery Row
Across Oxford Street's rivers of people I struggle against the tide. It's almost impossible. Blokes in suits and sunglasses, women in tight T-shirts. Shaved heads. Bright red buses, flower sellers, Selfridges for shoes or records, HMV, Debenhams, boots, suits sweaty, fashions ... then suddenly it's quiet again. Down winding, dipping Davies Mews, then a claustrophobic old alleyway called South Molton Lane and Avery Row, another alley. I really need a purple dogtooth-check skin-tight three-piece suit. Oh look, there's the Paul Smith Sale Shop. It has all the stylish candy-striped bargains that no one wants. I look down a drain. I can see water. It's not flowing.

Berkeley Square
I stop for a moment and try to imagine this ancient scene – this would have been a lush water meadow on the bend of the Tyburn. But I'm slightly confused. It looks like the river should flow down the middle of the square, but apparently it flowed along the east and then bottom. There's an old map on a sign that shows the stream in its last (open) days, around the 1740s, as a smelly sewer or ditch.

At the end of the square I take a right onto an alleyway, Lansdowne Row, bustling with shops. 'The elegant, the prosperous, the polite Tyburnia, the most respectable district of the habitable globe,' wrote Thackeray about this part of town.[1] A sign says 'Medico-surgical procedures fifteen years experience'. A Japanese student stands before it in a bright green rubber dress and I wonder whether they are connected in some way.

Buckingham Palace

On Curzon Street the river cuts diagonally towards Shepherd Market and Mayfair, with its bistros and ex-Sandhurst types in v-necked jumpers talking loudly in the pub. Then, crossing over Piccadilly, you can see where the river would have flowed down into Green Park – the Tyburn valley. The Tyburn winds round beneath here, by Constitution Hill. The lake in Buckingham Palace is fed by the stream.

At Buckingham Palace the tourists are up against the railings like kids at a zoo. It's grey and depressing, with a dreary asphalt/gravel forecourt where the lads are doing their mini-goose step thing. The royals need something more vivacious, rococo and extravagant – a smart set of rooms in Mayfair would probably do for them, or a rambling old pub down in Sussex. I'd phoned Buckingham  Palace earlier and talked to someone in their press office. They'd never heard about the Tyburn (oh yer) and had no records of why the house was built over the stream but did say that originally it was a private residence, Buckingham House, and was bought for the royal family and extended by John Nash. But, sorry, no information about the stream. And they didn't mention the rumour that the palace was built on the site of an old witch's house.

There's a big pile of horseshit in the road. It's aligned exactly with the palace and some golden angel monument. Spooky.

I stop a policeman and ask him about the Tyburn. He scratches his nose ('sign language which means he's fibbing' – Body Language

---

[1]   Only joking.

162 Expert) and says, in thick Glaswegian that he doesn't know. It's around here somewhere, I say, looking serious and pointing at the blue line drawn onto my battered *A to Z*. He looks nervous. He's obviously picturing Prince Edward in the sewer, in his scuba diving gear, indulging in some strange pagan rituals surrounded by body-guards and wondering if the young royal is going to be found out. He tells me there's something near Tower Hill, obviously trying to get rid of me. I walk around to the other side of the palace and to Buckingham Gate, past the stalls selling postcards of Princess Diana's head. The road swings round and as I take a left onto Palace Street I can see dips in the road where the river winds round here, and what seems like thousands of Japanese tourists buying up Union Jack tea towels from a stall at the side of the road. Maybe they are a Tokyo branch of the Ulster Unionists.

Westminster Cathedral
After Palace Street comes Stafford Place. This is the south branch of the Tyburn delta. At the side of the road some high-class winos sit on a little bench watching the world go by. They're drinking bottles of Stella. Stella, for God's sake. They must have money to burn. Now out onto the crazy concrete of Victoria Street. Fifty yards up the road is the Albert pub, which is worth going into as it's the only old building in the vicinity and is an oasis, surrounded by the glass and steel modernist cliffs of the tower blocks. Nearby are newish pillars and walkways designed by some bright spark in the sixties who'd been on holiday to Bologna and simply copied the style but made a complete botch of it. The architects of Victoria Street probably said to each other, 'Pure form!' 'Bold geometry!' But it's a shit hole, plain and simple.

I eventually arrive at Westminster Cathedral. It's a Catholic church but wouldn't look out of place in a more eastern setting. It's got a big Italianate cross in front, with people sitting on the steps. Next to it are lots of redbrick Edwardian mansion blocks populated by old Nancy Mitford clones living in cologne-scented apartments with round-cornered thirties walnut furniture. All these women have poodles and thousands of pounds worth of crockery with the royal family on it, pre 1953, and they never go out to drink except to posh wine bars in Soho with their hairless man friend of forty years. And I'm not generalizing here.

Tachbrook Estate

Now I turn down into Tachbrook Street – same river, different name. Coming out of the Uniwash laundrette are two women with kids, one a little Asian in orthodox Muslim gear, the other permed and in stonewashed eighties denim. Both have loud cockney accents and are talking about porn. 'It's better watching it than having to do it' says Perm Girl and her mate roars a dirty laugh. They drag their washing in the other direction, pissing themselves.

And then the Tachbrook Estate. According to *The Lost Rivers of London*, the Tachbrook flowed alongside the flats until the seventies.

Tyburn House

I cross to the other side of the busy Grosvenor Road which runs alongside the Thames. There are two oldish buildings that have obviously been renovated recently. Tyburn House is 40C. First time I've seen the river mentioned. The house has a little patio and stairs down to their boat at an old dock, and the river apparently flows underneath it into the Thames. Next to it is all building sites – London Town Plc. A load of yellow hats are looking down a drain.

View from the mouth of the Tyburn

I walk round into Pimlico Gardens. It's much warmer now. Half-naked lasses lie spread-eagled on the grass. There's a statue to William Huskisson, MP for Morpeth and President of the Board of Trade, whose fifteen minutes of fame came in 1830 when he became the first man ever to be killed in a rail accident – he was run over by Stephenson's *Rocket* during the opening of the Liverpool to Manchester Railway.

It really is the back of beyond here. Why did they build these shit roads right on the river, when any urban planner worth his salt would have made it into a continuous market of indie record stalls, good pubs and cheap second-hand Paul Smith clothes.

Westminster Abbey
Dear Sir/Madam

I'm currently writing a book about London's underground rivers, one of which, the Tyebourne (or Tyburn), used to flow very close to Westminster Abbey. Is it known if there was any significance in the fact that the Abbey was located near such a stream?

Yours faithfully,
Tim Bradford

Subject: the river Tyebourne

I am not sure about any particular significance of having a river
around the Abbey boundary other than the fact that obviously
the monks would have needed running water to power their
mill, to flow into their fishponds, to flush the sewers and drains
etc. around the monastery. As the river and its tributaries ran
on three sides of what was known as 'Thorney Island' this was
very convenient. The other side was bounded by the Thames.
Drinking water was piped by conduit from Hyde Park and St
James's Park.

But maybe the water was for more than fishponds. So if, as some
dowsers have claimed, religious sites' spiral energy lines (they call
them dragons) appear over underground water, over wells and
streams because of energy, plus all that ace chanting from the
monks, it might add to the divine feeling of a site. What do you
reckon?

There is a theory that the masons who built the great cathedrals
believed that the energy of moving water could be accumulated in
other material and that people could act as capacitors for this
charge. 'Their position near water streams support their standing
energy contact. The water pipes below churches were able to regu-
late energy of the matter and the building by numerous megalithic
constructions.'(*Cosmic Energy*, Miroslav Provod.)

It was now time to do some dowsing so I make my way back to
the abbey. I find a spot under a tree in front of the church and crack
open my can of Tennent's Super. I'd been playing around with the
optimum dosage for a while and had come to the conclusion that
one can was about right for dowsing purposes. I take some deep

breaths then have three or four swigs and almost straight away start to enter the altered Superbrew state known as urrrrrgggghhh. I begin to observe characters at the north side of the abbey. A group of Japanese tourists talking very loudly become medieval monks chanting in strange harmonies. A team of red-shirted scouts are a band of knights. A statuesque blond woman walking past in slow motion in a long black dress is a twelfth-century princess with alabaster skin, tall and proud with long flowing hair, on her way to give Henry II a good seeing to. The bloke with the 8th Army shorts and Hawaiian shirt, sitting under a tree with a can of beer and eyes rolling around in his head, is a crazy fool.

On the face of the abbey are a few figures, some knights, a couple of bishops, some kings – a giant's chess set. They're all having a right laugh, vogueing, holding poses and bitching about the tourists.

Thomas à Becket: Look at the fat-arsed Yanks. (Sigh.) Don't you think fashions get worse?

King Richard: I don't know why they cleaned us up. I preferred being black.

Henry V: That's like that Steve Martin film.

Thomas à Becket: *The Man With Two Brains* – I like that, especially since I had mine kicked in.

Henry V: No, *The Jerk*.

Thomas à Becket: So I got it wrong – there's no need to get personal.

Henry V: It's a film. Called *The Jerk*.

Richard: So it's about someone who didn't want to be sand-blasted?

Henry V: No, he was white but thought he was black.

Richard: But I am black. Or at least I was.

Everyone else on the lawns is drinking foaming frappucinos or Coca Cola. I'm the only patriotic drinker here, with my Tennent's of Glasgow beverage. Brewed since 1556, served to Bonnie Prince Charlie's army just before they, er ... lost.

And then it's time travel time. I walk across the lawn and lean against the cold wall of the abbey and try to go back to the era of Edward the Confessor, to get some tips as to how they built the original abbey on such marshy ground.

Here's how it works. The Superbrew has kicked in. Listen to the traffic noise, then imagine your ears getting wider and wider apart until they're about half a mile away from each other. Then you concentrate the centre of the mind that's left, and try to imagine what the scene would be like at a particular time. Then imagine that you have two little toggles, one on each side of your brain, that you can push forward to go into the future and back to travel into the past. Slam them back into overdrive then slow down as you reach 1200 so you can finetune it to arrive at in the 1050's.

But I've reversed too quickly and gone back too far, to a time when Thorney Island is little more than a dark, desolate swamp. All I can see

168   is a broken tree, dead, with two branches and some men with beards underneath it discussing the weather. Maybe they have antlers on their head. Are they worshipping the horned god, who is manifested in the branches of the river? Or is it a pagan stag night? Can they see me? I take another sip and am blasted back to the present.

I open my eyes. The red scouts have become blue scouts, now there are twice as many of them and they're all fat ZZ Top lookalikes.

'Religion is the Special Brew of the masses,' says Karl Marx.

'Get the beers, in beardy!' replies Engels. I throw some bits of food to the pigeons and suddenly I am surrounded by birds, a sandwich bar St Francis of Assisi. A huge semicircle surrounds me. Outside that is a semicircle of people.

Time to have a bit of peace and quiet in the abbey. But – God –  it's now £6 to get in. I say God. God? He's not listening. Too busy counting the readies. So I sit for a while and stare at the can of Tennent's. The beer is still playing tricks on me and the circles on the front look like the lines of energy emanating from the river. The little 'put-your-litter-in-the-bin' logo seems to represent a man dowsing over a well with some kind of rectangular force-field in between them. And the big red T in the middle is like a dowsing rod. Or a Druid's oak tree. Or a blood-stained cross.

ல   ல   ல

When I was a kid a mate of mine wrote a letter to the Queen asking something about the swans in Lincoln. She wrote back, of course, saying, 'Yus. Ay doo own the swans. It is a craym for inywun to kill a swun.' etc. At the time I thought his letter was stupid and arselicky (as well as a way of getting free publicity in our local paper for the pub the kid's father owned), but I now, with the benefit of hindsight, realize it was a piece of inspired communication. Now it was time for me to do the same. I felt there was only one person who could sort this out for me. I needed to correspond with someone high up who might be an expert on the Tyburn. Someone – a sort of celebrity, perhaps – who grew up near its course, and would be in the know about the various histories involved. I decided to write to Ed, Prince Wessex of Windsor, head honcho at Ardent Productions (TV company) and former inhabitant of Buckingham Palace.

FAO: Ed Wessex

Dear Ed

I'm currently writing a book about underground rivers in London, called *The Groundwater Diaries*. The idea started out as research into a local stream which runs pretty much underneath my house in Highbury.

Recently I walked the course of the Tyburn from Hampstead/ Belsize Park area to the Thames and, as I'm sure you're aware, it splits almost directly underneath Buck Palace before going onto the river in three branches near Westminster Abbey, Whitehall and the Tachbrook Estate.

I'm writing to you to find out if you know of any information regarding the Royal Family and the river and also whether you personally have any memories of the Tyburn while you were growing up (floods, strange noises, dampness, mad dreams, etc.).

Yours sincerely,
Tim Bradford

He didn't reply.

ə   ə   ə

170   Later in the summer I picked up a felt-tip and traced the course of
the Tyburn, with all its heads and branches, onto the back of a
bank statement, then asked my daughter what it looked like. A
bird, she said. Hmm. It looked more like a short-legged big-lipped
rabbit to me.

Once again, I decided to embark on an expedition that involved
walking a tributary of the Tyburn which used to flow from London
Zoo and joined the main stream near the Regent's Park ponds. I took
along a crack team of research assistants. Cathleen (two), her cousins
Amy (seven) and Hannah (five), my brother Toby (thirty-five) and my
sister-in-law Michelle (thirtyish). Well, when I say 'walked the other
tributary', I mean 'went to the zoo and had chips for lunch'. At the
end of the walk I asked them all what was their favourite animal:

Cathleen: The lion. And the monkey. And the gorilla. And the
   monkey.
Amy: The lion.
Hannah: Nothing.
Toby: The gorilla.
Michelle: The giraffe.
Me: The buff-cheeked gibbon.

☙ ☙ ☙

**Film Idea: The Underground Prince (maybe a Disney kids'
cartoon)**
Westminster Abbey. Aliens say Tyburn is a power river. Royals go to
live underground after revolution. Become reptiles again as pre-
dicted by people like David Icke. Meanwhile, in Baker Street Super
Sherlock Holmes is a Japanese-anime-style cartoon.
   'Put you Watson. Kung fu.'
   Dr Watson has a magic Beatles plate. Meanwhile, Moriarty is in
the tunnel of the Tyburn singing Gerry Rafferty's 'Baker Street'.
Holmes has a bath and snorts charlie from the cover of a violin case.

Moriarty appears from the plughole and tries to strangle Holmes.
Big martial arts fight scene, lots of jumping in the air.

It's not all bad. Prince Edward is a goody who is on the side of the people. At the end they go back to their planet. Like the end of *ET*. Edward has been befriended by a little boy, modern version of Tiny Tim. Called Timmy. He is injured but makes it back to the last escape pod. Tearjerker ending. Edward played by Brad Pitt. Sophie by Kate Winslet. Holmes by Alan Rickman. Watson by John Sessions.

London Stories 7: Our Man in a Panama Hat

I was very skint when a woman at an employment agency said, 'Do you have experience of working in a property office?' so although I heard myself say 'no' what actually came out of my mouth was 'yes'. I was given the job of Sort-of-Surveyor.

'You'll have to wear a suit,' she said.

'No problem,' I replied. On the first day I turned up in an Oxfam suit, Panama hat and pineapple kipper tie to the offices of London Transport Estates where I was given my own desk and a little tape recorder. I talked into the tape recorder, ideas for novels and songs, and then gave the tape to some nice girls in the basement who typed up my thoughts as letters and gave them back to me so I could sign them and send them out. And I travelled around London, in my Panama hat and be-pineappled kipper tie with my special LTE tube pass, visiting property owners, sorting out boundary disputes, pinpointing the exact location of watercress beds, and talking some more into my little tape recorder. Then one day, a couple of months into my work, after we'd been to the pub (I think to celebrate the settling of yet another boundary dispute between two MOT garages under the arches near Latimer Road), the boss said 'Ha ha have you really had experience in a property office?' and I said

'Ha ha – no,' and the next day I was told that ha ha ha the job had ended.

But because I'd helped the LTE cricket team when they were short of players by drafting in various Lincolnshire refugee friends and members of my family – in fact given them Rob, my half-Trinidadian fast bowler gerbil-breeding cousin who was destined to play for the West Indies at cricket until he was cruelly relocated to the wilds of small market town Lincolnshire – they took pity on me and offered me alternative employment. Superintendent of Shepherds Bush and South Harrow markets. This was a big job with a lot of responsibility. I had to wear a suit without a Panama hat and pineapple kipper tie and carry around a big leather briefcase, collect the rents and sort out problems. I am no good at sorting out my own problems so I won't be much good at sorting out other people's, especially hard-bitten market traders'. But I didn't say this out loud because my big mouth had already lost me one job.

They took away my little tape

recorder and in its place gave me an assistant, Afdab, a middle-aged Moroccan with a pencil moustache. Afdab was eager to please and would constantly be bringing me mugs of tea – a pint mug with the teabag, water, milk and sugar all in together and generally flapping about in a late-seventies-sitcom manner. And he'd turn up at the little bullet-proof window of my office saying, 'Tim boss. Problem.' Actually when they'd first told me it was bullet-proof glass I'd laughed and said, 'You're joking,' and the boss had laughed back and said, 'Ha ha no I'm not.'

On my first morning there was a huge bag of frozen chicken drumsticks outside the office with a note from one of the stallholders saying he hoped I enjoyed my 'stay' at the market. What was I supposed to do with those? I'd been told not to accept presents so had to decline.

Later on, the psychic palm reader came to pay his rent and offered me a tenner to 'have a drink on me'. What had I done to deserve this? Or perhaps I hadn't done it yet. I thanked him for his kind offer, but told him that I was paid a good enough wage by London Transport (a lie). But then he should have known that already.

But I wasn't much good at the market stall business, particularly the wearing a suit-being bossy-getting up early on a Saturday morning bit. So after about six weeks I handed in my notice. On the last day I left in a hurry and left eight grand in a black zip-up holdall on the train. Nooooooooooo!!! I screamed in slow motion and ran back to the train, just catching it as it was about to pull out of Hammersmith Station.

But when I told them at the office, they just laughed.

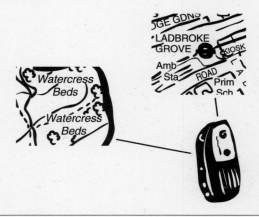

9. Danish Punk Explosion Dream

Some Danish punk bands – mad lyrics – letter to Morten – Morten replies – more Danish punk

'The Danish monsterquartet the Burnouts is putting the rock'n'roll into the punkrock and they bring loud'n'noizy two-chord action filled rock down to the basics, showing you rocksters what it's all about. Energetic, raw and dirty entertainment you can trust. Out from the dark Copenhagen underground scene they come flying on a shimmering, flaming turborocket.'[1]

Pooper scooper
Fast, melodic and Danish punkrock/skatecore. [2]

De Knòtne Hòttentòtter[3]
'Actually it all started in seventh grade when Kasper wanted to make a band because ... well because it would be cool. Kasper told his friend Laust about the idea, and there you go a new band was formed. Neither Kasper nor Laust could really play on anything (ANYTHING???), but they both wanted to play the guitar. After working hard and saving money they could afford to buy their first electric guitars (Kasper actually didn't work at all, he got some money as a present and bought a guitar with them). Kasper and Laust figured that they needed a drummer, so they picked up some bum called Martin in a club

---

[1] http://www.geocities.com/SunsetStrip/Stadium/1141/
[2] www.worldwidepunk.com
[3] http://knotne.freeyellow.com/

176   (actually they knew the guy, and he wasn't really a bum, anyway). The three guys now needed a bass player, so they had about five people coming to Martin's place at the same time to find one. But hell no, it didn't work at all so they decided that they didn't REALLY need a bass player.'

'Boyfriend'
She's got a boyfriend, i thought i were the only one.
Of course i knew that i wasn't, she just made me believe i were.

Find the guy, crush his head
Find The Guy, Make Him Dead.

The Hangdorks

'Balls'
I don't know why i feel the way i do
even though i try i can't talk to you
i hate myself 'cause i'm way too shy
i feel even worse now as the days go by

I wish i had the balls to talk to you
but like any normal guy i only got two
I wish i had the balls to talk to you –
but like any normal guy i only got two.

I wrote to the editor of a Danish music fanzine:

To: morten@_____
Subject: The Origins of Danish Punk

Hi Morten

I love Danish punk music. Unfortunately I haven't actually heard any of the music yet, it's more the idea I'm into.

A long time ago (1982) I nailed my copy of <u>Bullshit Detector</u> Volume 1 (Crass compilation album) to a plank of wood and sailed it off down our local river in the English East Midlands. Eventually, I surmised, the record would make its way to the River Humber and then the North Sea.

I now realise that the record must have floated all the way to Denmark, was picked up by a fisherman or farmer who, on hearing the music was inspired enough to sell all his possessions, buy a guitar and some amps and start off a high-energy Scandinavian punk movement.

How close is this version to the actual historical truth? Has anybody in Denmark heard <u>Bullshit</u> <u>Detector</u> (Volume 1)?

Yours sincerely,
Tim Bradford

ps: And if you need any articles for your magazine by people who haven't heard the music, I'm your man.

No jobs

Nothing seems like it's going
anywhere these days
nothing stays forever
and everything must go.

Young man trying to be true
to what's inside
wanna know what's keeping you down
take a look around.

No jobs
grey city
it gets me down.

Class war in the schools
the lesson they're teaching us
is give nothing away
unless you're sure to make it pay.

You have made it for the few
the shit is left behind
control my temper while I wait
democracy is gone.

The generation's doing hard time
they took away our pride
we're signed up and thrown away
will there be better days.

No jobs
grey city
it gets me down.

ॐ   ॐ   ॐ

Hi Tim,

That might be close to the truth, but then again - however cool the idea may sound, we don't have that many great Danish punk bands. Only a few. That's why we don´t review ´em, and that´s why quite a few of them are pissed at us.

If you want good and innovative punk rock, look out for Sweden, or even better Finland ... So maybe the record floated even further away?

But anyway, what are you interested in writing about? And thanks for your interest!! cheers Morten Gerdsen

chief-editor

The Tremolo Beer Gut: The Sleaz-e-nator[4]

'Copenhagen's Tremolo Beer Gut draw inspiration from the ultra-cool rough twangy guitar sound of fifties and sixties surf as well as the great film music of Mancini, Barry and Moricone.'

The Ultra Bimbos[5]

PMS 666 (No Man's No Good!?)
from: Jukka Perkele! 7"
available at: Bad Afro Records
label: Bad Afro Records

---

[4] http://stage.vitaminic.dk/the_tremolo_beer_gut/
[5] http://www.earpollution.com/vol3/jan01/album/album2.htm#theeultrabimbos

180 'If The Ultra Bimbos were not from Finland they would be a huge hit; the record mega-moguls would be scratching and clawing to sign them.'

Toybomb[6]
Peter Rasmussen, drums, vocals
Ulrich Basler, guitar, vocals
Johannes Pedersen, bass
Jonas Jakobsen, guitar

'We have played since 1995 with different drummers and bass players. In 1996 we met Peter and he started to play with us. We played for some time, but in 1998 our bass player Vinnie, left the band and we continued with me on bass, Jones on guitar and Peter on drums. Then in 1999 we met Johannes and he joined the band ... and that's the short version of our story.'

Did I mention that I have formed a Danish punk band? They're called the Stigmen. The members of the Stigmen are me and Danish ex-Liverpool midfielder Jan Molby. Jan plays synths and looks cool and translates our lyrics into Danish, although it's intentionally written as if badly translated from Danish into English. Of course, Jan's not really in the Stigmen. He coaches at a lower division English football team. But having an ex-footballer in the band might generate a bit of music press interest. Does that make sense?

At the moment the Stigmen only have one song, about the Tyburn, called 'Mr No Socks'.

> The women in Belsize Park don't seem to wear bras.
> Everyone seems to drive very smart cars.
> There aren't many old blokes' pubs
> Just trendy bars.
> It's a popular place for actors and rock stars.

---

6 http://www.toybomb.dk/

Yeah it really rocks
yeah it really rocks
yeah it really rocks
Look, here he comes, Mr No Socks.

Dear Morten,

After your comments about Danish punk music being shite
I've decided to form my own Danish punk band which
corresponds to the high quality Danish music myths I've
created. Would you be interested in running a feature
about my band, the Stigmen? We are a cross between the
Swell Maps and Karl-Heinz Stockhausen.

Cheers,
Tim

London Stories 8: Suspicious Mind

A couple of summers back I was sauntering through Leicester Square, enjoying the aroma of warm mayonnaise from the nearby sandwich bars, when I was collared by a beefy woman who looked just like the boxer Jake La Motta, except she was wearing a floral-print dress and had long grey hair tied up in a bun on top of her head.

'Lucky heather, love?'

'I, er, well, er, I, er, haa ha …'

'It'll bring you good luck.'

What she meant was, it'll bring you bad luck if you don't buy it. We did the deal and I walked quickly away, ashamed at my weakness. I'd like to throw the heather away, but each time I try it I see the gypsy woman standing next to me saying, 'Just you try it, sonny.' I'm not superstitious or anything. Far from it. But every time a gypsy woman stops me in the street and offers me some lucky heather, I am paralysed with fear at the thought of saying no.

Around that time Leeds United were embarking on their first foray into the UEFA Champions League. I arranged to meet up at a sports bar in Covent Garden called Evergreens to watch their first qualifier against the German side Munich 1860 ('Ha ha – sounds like a beer, dunnit?' said the landlord) with my old friend Andy. Our evening went something like this. Andy got there first and got the beers in, I turned up a couple of minutes after kick-off. We stood and stared at the screen for an hour and three quarters clutching beer to our mouths, occasionally going to the bar or the bog. At half time we'd have a quick conversation about work and family then it was back to business. Leeds won the game, then we retired to the nearby Freemasons Arms to discuss the game. For the return leg we did exactly the same thing and Leeds won again.

Now through to the Champions League proper, Leeds' first game was against Barcelona. I couldn't make it so watched the game on TV. Leeds got tonked 4–0. Next game I met up with Andy again and we went through the same ritual. Leeds won. We retired to the nearby Freemasons Arms to discuss the game.

Although both reasonably rational people (well, Andy is) we now realized that we were in a Magical Luck Ritual. In fact, we were pretty much locked into it. Any deviation from our tried and trusted formula meant that Leeds would lose. As if to prove our thesis, every time we didn't meet up, the team always lost.

I'm a firm believer in the lucky pub theory of football success. I've travelled all over London searching for the perfect venue. Certain boozers have stood out over the last few years the Winchester Hall Tavern, the London Spa, the Green Man In Riding House Street, the Boston Arms and the Birdcage in Stamford Hill. Of course, they always let you down in the end, but on the way it's good fun trying.

LUCKY PINT

LUCKY TELLY

LUCKY MATE

LUCKY HEATHER

Others began to cotton on to Evergreens' mystical powers. Namely, the London Leeds United Supporters Club. The London Leeds United Supporters Club seemed to be made up of about twenty thick-necked lads with skinhead haircuts, twenty tall blokes with specs and suits, a couple of well-built blonde lasses, a curly-haired former magazine editor plus Andy and me.

Leeds got through the first group into the second stage of the

Champions League, with an even harder group. But we were confident that if our system held, so would the team's luck. Leeds doggedly progressed. Then at the end of this stage, disaster struck. Evergreens closed down. Panic-stricken, we all moved 50 yards up the road to a bar called Rampage. The atmosphere changed. People started bickering because they couldn't see the TVs. And the Guinness was expensive. But the luck seemed to hold. Leeds won the first leg of the quarter final against Deportivo La Coruna 3–0.

Then – mini disaster. I arranged a holiday in Ireland with my family that coincided with the second leg, and didn't have the heart to pull out. I had to listen to a bad Talk Radio reception in the west of County Clare as Leeds went down 2–0. In the semi they were held to a 0–0 draw at home, but I was quietly confident of them progressing. An even bigger set-back was to follow. Andy and his wife had arranged to go on holiday for the second leg. He'd forgotten all about the football when he'd booked it. And neglected to tell me, the bastard – if I'd had time I could have arranged to go on holiday at the same place (Jersey) to meet up with him.

However, I arranged to get a photo of Andy and carry it about in my pocket, buy it beer, chat to it about tactics afterwards. But the only pic I'd got was of Andy at the Notting Hill Carnival with a couple of Jamaican grannies on his arm. It didn't have the necessary gravitas. I roped in a couple of other friends in the hope that providence wouldn't notice Andy's absence. But when I got to the bar I saw that it was completely full of Johnny and Jemima-come-latelys. My mates were standing outside, with a crowd of others, unable to get in. Crestfallen, we wandered around for a while to a couple of Australian bars, then sat in an Irish pub that was showing a Liverpool game.

Leeds got stuffed. Andy and his wife moved to Guildford. Heartbroken, I stopped watching Leeds on TV.

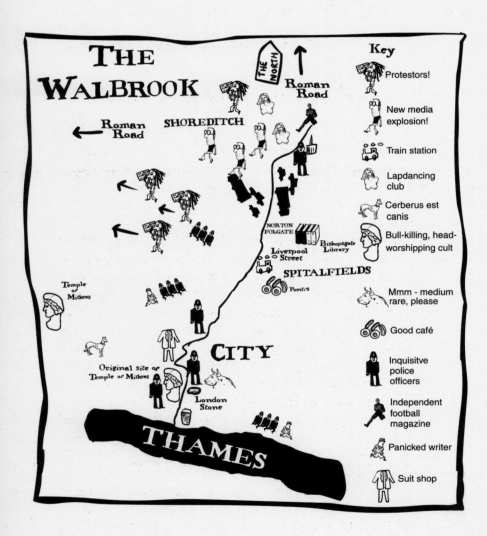

THE WALBROOK

← Roman Road

← Roman Road

SHOREDITCH

THE NORTH

Roman Road →

NORTON FOLGATE

Liverpool Street

Bishopsgate Library

SPITALFIELDS

Pontis

Temple of Mithras

Original site of Temple of Mithras

CITY

London Stone

THAMES

Key

Protestors!

New media explosion!

Train station

Lapdancing club

Cerberus est canis

Bull-killing, head-worshipping cult

Mmm – medium rare, please

Good café

Inquisitve police officers

Independent football magazine

Panicked writer

Suit shop

10. Big Sky Over Norton Folgate

• The Walbrook, Hoxton to Southwark Bridge

*TV – Val Singleton – Saxon shit – Temple of Mithras – Caecilius –
Mayday protests – Shoreditch – Internet – global capitalism –
Broadgate – Bank – police search – Christian security guard*

Media Event No. 1

I met up with a high-powered Person from a TV company who'd
heard on the media grapevine that I was going to attempt to be the
first person to walk the courses of London's rivers while giving a
high five to Norris McWhirter and singing Danish punk songs.
After all, reality TV is all the rage at the moment. I told her my idea
was for a public-information-type film narrated by ex-*Blue Peter*
star Valerie Singleton, with lots of old illustrations. I'd meet Val in a
pub and say 'Val, want to be in my film?' Then Peter Purves comes
over and threatens me – says 'Oi, are you chatting up my bird?'
Then there'd be a scene of me necking lots of cans of Special Brew
followed by a dream/dowsing sequence done in a Terry Gilliam cartoon style. Then some clips of Scandinavian punk bands. After this
I'd recreate the past using an illustrator but pretending it's my 'Go
Back In Time' headgear machine. Then meet different river groups
and discover their manifestos for world domination. I'd finish
building my boat, then cut to *The New River Story* – snatches of
film overdubbed with the river history in *Flashing Blade* style.

188   Maybe with *Scaramouche* starring Stewart Granger. Some montages of maps and diagrams, then a trance record called *Free the Rivers* played outside the mayor's headquarters. At the end Peter Purves (who's been stalking me throughout the film) attacks me and we have a fight, falling to our deaths through an open man hole into an icy underground river.

The High-powered TV Person nodded politely and smiled. 'Sounds like fun!' she said then rushed out of the room saying she'd be in touch soon. I hope the filming schedule doesn't interfere with my summer holidays.

ら ら ら

The Walbrook was the first of London's rivers to disappear, originally in Roman times, when it became choked up with old pottery, bits of mosaic, floor tiles, Latin textbooks and the like. The Romans left in 410 when the legions went scurrying away to protect Rome from the invading central European gloom mongers the Visigoths, and as London slowly began to fall to pieces it wasn't long before the Walbrook (if it wasn't already filled with rubble) was getting clogged up with Saxon shit. The Germanic invaders objected to the idea that the previous inhabitants had high-tech lavatories and bathrooms. Saxon lives were so high octane – what with their farms and stuff – they didn't have time to waste on going to the bog, so just did it at the side of the road or in each others' houses or, most often, in the river. The Walbrook was finally filled in in the mid to late fifteenth century when the fast expansion of the population led to a building boom – plus, houses needed to be bigger because of the billowing pantaloons and huge ruffs that were all the rage at the time, so land within the city walls became extremely valuable.

To lose a river once ... careless, to lose it twice ... bloody useless. As a result no one is exactly sure where the Walbrook runs, although various people have done excavations and builders to this day have problems. In the twenties, as Alan Ivimey notes in *Some Lost Rivers of London*, City buildings almost had to float, built up on piles up to 40 feet deep, to clear the soft mud and water. We do know that the Romans used the Walbrook to get to the Temple of Mithras. This shrine was built on the banks of the river around what is now Walbrook, a street near Monument. It was moved by the Corporation of London after it was excavated in the fifties because some director of an insurance company mentioned at a Round Table meeting that he'd like it in front of his office.

The Mithraic cult was popular among legionaries – in a way it was similar to present day squaddies' worship of Page 3 models. At the temple they cut off bulls' heads and (of course) bathed in the blood, while chanting stuff to a supernatural deity who shagged cows.

> Caecilius is in the temple. Here comes the bull. Clemens hands the sword to Caecilius. Chop goes the sword. Thud goes the bull's head against the floor. Spurt goes the bull's blood. Now they all swim in blood. 'All hail to Mithras, weird bull-like deity of the crazy Romans!' shout Caecilius and his friends.

Caecilius and Grumio kill the ball for the glory of Mithras

Q1. How does Caecilius chop off the bull's head?

Q2. Who is holding down the bull?

Q3. Did you see *Caligula* starring Malcolm 'Mad Eyes' McDowell? Helen Mirren was pretty damn impressive.

ð ð ð

In a way, the Romans still roam the City of London. Their helmets have changed slightly – they're more penis shaped now – and their uniforms are black. They do have the same shields, though now they're made of Perspex. They patrol the streets and look down on anyone with long straggly hair. They've dispensed with the stumpy swords and instead use terrifying batons. Look at a London police-man and it makes you realize how the past, present and future exist all together – overlapping, like the pieces in an old fuzzy felt set. Ever since I can remember I have always tried (John Coltrane record playing in background) to imagine the past in the present, with me in between things, straddling time and space, between cultures.

'Now put on this poloneck and say that in French,' said my wife. We both thought about time for a while and divided our lives up into little segments. (Is that how much I've got left? As a kid you see the world from your own point of view, then at twenty-two you understand, with a thud, you're going to die.)

'What's the point of anything?' we said to each other, in despair.

'Shall we get a video?' I said.

'Mmm, yes, as long as it's a romantic comedy. Fancy a Chinese?' And then we forgot all about time.

ð ð ð

Media Event No. 2

It's Mayday. Which means revolution is in the air. Originally a Celtic festival known as Beltane, the Day of Fire (Bel was the sun god) celebrated the spring planting of crops. During the Middle Ages the event became a time for carnival, fertility rites and dancing round a maypole, with characters such as the Green Man poking fun at authority. These events were looked down on by the church and state. Eventually it became an international workers' day – it used to be our public holiday, until the dunderheaded Thatcherites decided it was too socialist and scrapped it.

But now, it seems, the old traditions have returned and on 1 May mass anti-global capitalism protests take place in cities across the industrialized world, much to the annoyance of heavy-handed and paranoid governments – like our own. On this particular Mayday, while all self-respecting anti-globalists are in the West End getting their nuts whacked (Beltane?) by Red-Bull-addicted thick-necked Home Counties coppers, I'm making my own silent protest about something or other by walking the route of the silent Walbrook through the City of London while singing, at regular intervals, the lyrics to 'Do They Owe Us a Living' by Crass from the *Bullshit Detector* LP. I'm recording it for posterity on my crappy old Dictaphone and will try and splice some of the excerpts into a hardcore dance anthem later in the summer. Or maybe I won't.

I start at the source of the main branch of the river, on Waterson Street in northern Shoreditch, which runs between the Hackney and Kingsland Roads. North Shoreditch/South Hoxton is now famous for the Internet Revolution, when the bars around the area throbbed with the excitement of big-specced skinheads 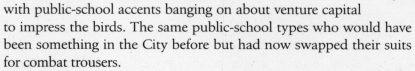 with public-school accents banging on about venture capital to impress the birds. The same public-school types who would have been something in the City before but had now swapped their suits for combat trousers.

Nearby is a collection of workshops and studios, one of which is home to *When Saturday Comes* magazine, a cult left-wing football magazine. It's been my (only regular) source of income over the last decade. One day every month I get an email from *WSC*, explaining that they need a cartoon of a footballer with very short legs, and I duly oblige. I've spent most of my time in London working for the magazine in one capacity or another (drawing players with very short legs, drawing players with big noses and very short legs) and it's still got pretty much the same crowd running (and reading) it. All around are trendy designers and photographers who are mostly fifteen years younger than us. We give them useful advice, like how to do a Harold Wilson impression and how to skin a rabbit.

After popping my head round the door and giving a little wave, I turn right onto Hackney Road and walk down to St Leonards Church, Shoreditch. Shoreditch High Street isn't a high street any more so much as a typical deathtrap French two-lane motorway transplanted, by some Euro trickery, to Central London. Actually, a typical deathtrap French two-lane motorway with two or three lap dancing clubs, to be precise. Maybe, somewhere down in central France, there is a strange little road in the middle of the country-side with butchers' shops, pubs and 'characters' hanging around on street corners trying to sell stuff. I cross over the road and see some anti-globalization protesters – skinny blokes with happy smiles, wispy beards and dreadlocks flapping in the wind, heading off in a small posse on rickety bikes, perhaps imagining their confrontation with armed and heavily padded-up police with their riot shields as similar to the fights of the Britons and the Roman legions.

There are people out on the streets, big policemen with uniforms and helmets. Are their penis hats an appropriation of the phallic maypole? Maybe they should go the whole hog and have ribbons put on. With little toy people flying around it. On Shoreditch High Street a crowd of policemen and women are piling into vans. There are police everywhere, standing around at the side of the road, laughing and joking. At the J18 protests of summer 2000, some Reclaim the Streets activists released water from a hydrant which erupted in a 40-foot fountain: 'people sang and danced in the water of the walled-up Walbrook River ... perhaps for the first time in 500 years, it bubbled up into the sun'.[1] The Reclaim the Streets supporters claimed that the rivers of London were 'commons': they were once freely accessible for swimming, drinking and fishing, but were then effectively stolen from commoners, first by pollution from factories, and later by the enclosure of the rivers by private developers. I like this idea, and it ties in with my Special-Brew-fuelled visions of freeing the rivers, creating small urban biodiverse parkways in the middle of the city with signposted foot and bike trails. It depends on technological pathways being open to all. If we all had wired up laptops at home, the City might cease to be the maelstrom of activity it is today. Instead you'd get people doing the markets while sat at home or in the pub with their mates, or even sitting in the park.

But this year there don't seem to be any river warriors. The focus is elsewhere. Some big branch of McDonalds in the West End that has brought out a new way of packaging extruded poultry pieces is crying out to be trashed, perhaps. After a bit more hanging around the police all drive off, heading west.

The tall buildings up ahead look like cliffs, and with Tower 42 (formerly the Nat West Tower) behind they form a deep river gorge or canyon. The City is money, and they need these big cock

---

1   'At the Mayday Protest' by Jay Griffiths (from *London Review of Books*, 22/6/00)

towers to convince others of their prowess – it's like those lads who get themselves penis enlargements just to impress other blokes in the 'locker room'. On the left is one of my (current) favourite areas of London. A huge building site which is a big new development at Norton Folgate – 201 Bishopsgate.

It'll eventually be yet another Massive Glass Structure but at the moment there's nothing there except for this beautiful big sky. You don't see big skies like that in the City any more. I treasure that sky. The City is a crazy place, its landscape always changing, as the old is pulled down and the new springs up. Circle of life. Death and rebirth. The jellied eel of existence. The skyscrapers might look great from a distance, say from a no. 43 bus high up on Archway Road, but not when you're right next to them. In *Wonderful London* there are plates showing the latest modern buildings in the exciting new world after the Great War. It never changes. Underneath that big sky they found the skeleton of an Iberian-Roman princess in a stone coffin. I saw it on *Meet the Ancestors*, I think. The bit where they recreate their faces with clay – it always gets me. Sends a shiver down my spine. This whole area of mud will be offices crammed with people in a couple of years. But that's not to say that we can't celebrate the big sky over Norton Folgate for just a little while longer.

I carry on to Scrutton Street, where there are some old shop fronts in a majestically Dickensian style. That's not really a style, is it – Dickensian? Lots of wood and little windows. The streets are still deserted. I pass an office with a glowing desk like the bridge of the *Starship Enterprise*. I follow the winding course of the stream, and looking back I can see the subtle dips in the landscape where the river would have been.

Past the London Transport Police building and loudspeakers are going off, it's like the end of a Bond flick, *Dr No* or *Moonraker* – the secret hideaway thing. Trucks are being moved around, vehicles are getting into position, blokes in uniforms are running around.

Alongside Liverpool Street Station I turn right at a little clump of young trees. Test signs are up – *veium exerci*. It's Latin, isn't it? Maybe it's some kind of Mithraic code.

Past some patrol barriers, then I walk through Broadgate, past the skating rink in the middle. Look at an old map and you see how Bishopsgate's and Broadgate's street layouts have changed completely. They could do with market stalls round here – it's all a bit too corporately slick. The river flows under what was Broadgate Station, which I remember was already dilapidated in the mid eighties. I liked the building. Liverpool Street Station used to be pretty depressing, dark and cavernous. They've done a pretty good job doing up that. A big group of police walks past, done up to the nines in all their padded gear, and I skirt into the darkness of the Broadgate catacombs to avoid them, then re-emerge behind the Espresso à la Carte Bar near the Liverpool Street modern-art sculpture that 'looks like someone left a few slabs of steel out in the rain' (angry anti-art critic). In WH Smith's I am confronted by forests of men's magazines with headless tits on the cover – a fat bloke with glasses is flicking through a love-making manual, maybe he's going on a hot date tonight. I buy a film, then out and cross onto Blomfield Street, with the Savoy Tailors' Guild on the right, then over another road and under an archway, left down Throgmorton Avenue. It's shit for traffic but exciting for the walker that London was never built on a grid system.

ð ð ð

I worked in the City for a while when I first arrived in London. It was at SG Warburg. I met a systems bloke recently who also used to work there and we talked about old times. Or at least we attempted to. What did you do, he said. Filing. What, database? No, putting paper files in a filing cabinet and flirting with middle-aged West Indian ladies and young strapping bawdy Cockney girls.

196 I remember Black Monday. Or was it Purple Tuesday? But I won't forget the sight of the City boys sitting around shell-shocked.

❧ ❧ ❧

Near the Bank of England (the river flows right underneath it and can been seen from the vaults), I'm approached by a policeman, who stops me and says, 'Can you tell me what's in that bag?'

'A notebook. *A to Z*. Water.'

He asks me to empty the bag. Then he frowns and asks:

'Why are you talking into a Dictaphone?'

I'm liaising with the head of the protest movement who's directing operations from his laptop in space.

'I'm walking the course of an underground river.'

'Really? That sounds interesting. Oh, I know all about them.'

'Do you?' I asked.

'Yes. You're doing the Walbrook now.'

'Do all police know about them then?'

He went quiet, then smiled in a 'Move along sonny, God-I-love-the-Masons' sort of way.

'Sorry about that, but it was the Dictaphone – for all I knew you could have been a terrorist.'

I wave him off.

I'm feeling pretty damn smug about my one-man protest against Capitalism and Stuff when I hit a snag. I'm walking past Austin Reed and I see a nice summer cotton suit in the window that I really like. I go in and take a closer look. A young bloke is in charge. 'Oh it's sir's colour isn't it would you like to try a pair of shoes on?' He takes the shoes from a dummy. God, capitalism is great. I almost go for it, then realize I never wear suits. Back out again, past

Mansion House, the stock market and Poultry. I used to be fascinated by the Gothic fripperies of the tall, wedge-shaped Victorian Mappin & Webb building at no. 1 Poultry. They – blokes in yellow hard hats – knocked it down and built the clever-clever new no. 1 Poultry. Lots of people I know reckon it's great and architects-like-it-so-it-must-be-good but although it is an expression of the times, I think it's a vacuous confection of shit. It smells of evil.

Still, that's the history of the City, and you can't get too attached to the old buildings. And something good came out of it. Archaeologists were allowed to dig extensively under the site in the nineties before the new No.1 was built.

Archaeologist's voiceover: Meandering silt-filled palaeo-channels associated with the Walbrook and its tributaries were located and sampled at various points across the site. The western side of the stream valley was cut by small streams fed by natural springs, with tributary streams to the north and south-west creating a raised gravel 'spur' which extended part way across the site towards the main channel of the Walbrook.[2]

Through Bucklersbury Passage, which would have had houses along it in Roman times (there's a mosaic in the Museum of London that was dug up here), now a shopping arcade, past St Stephens Walbrook church – the vicar here formed the Samaritans and there's a glass case outside with the first ever help-line telephone from the fifties – where the Walbrook flows under the vaults. The Temple of Mithras was right here. Now there's a Mithras wine bar and a Slug and Lettuce pub.

---

[2] English Heritage Archaeological Archives
(http://www.eng-h.gov.uk/ArchRev/ner95_6/poultry.htm)

Now I head straight down to the end of Walbrook. On Cannon Street is a pub with little round olde world windows, called Cannons. I take a picture and log it onto the tape. Then I'm stopped by two policeman, one a typical straight-backed Big Cop, the other a wry-looking burly Scots bloke. They ask what I said about the pub. I tell them about the rivers.

'So are you saying that it's a kind of guide for pissheads to go in and out of pubs while walking along rivers?'

'Er, yes, pretty much.'

'Hmm. sounds pretty good,' says the Scotsman.

But Big Cop isn't satisfied and wants to hear what I've said on the tape, so I play it back, but go too far and it's the bit about me going on about Samaritans and suicide and despair. They look at each other then search my bag. The Scotsman starts going on about ley lines.

'What have ley lines got to do with it?' I asked, intrigued.

'Well, the drunkards, they'd go down the leylines I suppose.'

Bloody hell. How did they know all this stuff? They knew about the rivers and, like the first cop, were very excited. I thought back to my earlier theory abut Masons controlling the powers of the underground wells and streams. Maybe there is an underground network of policemen in little rowing boats. It might sound a bit Flann O'Brien, but that doesn't mean it isn't true.

The PCs disappear and I walk about 20 yards, blathering into my tape recorder in an ironic way about police oppression when I'm stopped for a third time, by a big red-faced officer of the law with a 'tache. He asks what I'm doing. I say I'm looking for the Walbrook because I'm doing a project on the Temple of Mithras.

'Oh, its not here, it's further down the street.'

'Why did they move it?'

He shrugs his shoulders. I ask him for proper directions and he forgets that he'd stopped me in the first place which is just as well because he'd want to hear the tape as well and either I'm banged up or in a few months' time the police bring out a walks book of underground rivers and steal all the glory. The temple, or rather its foundations, are a couple of streets along in front of the Legal and General building, a little rectangle of Roman bricks with stones inside it and a little fence around. I'm about to take a picture when a little security guard appears and says I can't. What do you mean I can't? It's a national monument, for God's sake. There follows a heated discussion. Then two other guys come out and start discussing me and talking on two-way radios. This bloke wants to take a picture of the Temple of Mithras. What do you think? Eventually the little guy relents and says I can but I can't take a picture of the office. Why the hell would I want to do that? I ask. The other security guard asks why I want to take a picture. Not only is it just a load of old stones but it's a danger to Christianity.

'They worshipped bulls, you know.'

Then it's back down the street and onto Dowgate Hill, where the Walbrook rushed along before finally reaching the Thames, then I finally reach the big river. I go to the Banker pub and over a pint or two of London Pride I watch on the TV as men in black uniforms hit little blokes with beards on the head in the West End. And I wonder to myself, can the sensitive (tanked up on Special Brew) walker feel anything while following the Walbrook route? Maybe. If you can ignore the paraphernalia of the City you can tune in to the different atmosphere in, say, Spitalfields, Houndsditch, Leadenhall Street and Fenchurch Street compared with Cannon Street, Cheapside and St Pauls. In *The East End – Four Centuries of London Life*, Alan Palmer puts forward the theory that, as early as the fifth century, the Walbrook was already a border, with the victorious but dull Saxons settling to the west of the River Walbrook, and the defeated crazy Romano-Britons (Celts) confined to the east. An earlier template for what would happen between the Saxons and the Vikings at the River Lea 300 years later. Some have suggested that Walbrook or Wallbrook comes from the fact that it flowed through the City wall. But more convincing I think is that Wal Brook means 'stream of the British' (or 'foreigners') in Old English.

Barman: A likely story.

Then I go outside with my beer and look down at the pebbled shore, and after three pints I get an idea of what this area might have been like centuries ago – stone foundations, water lapping gently against the shore. Here, between Cannon Street Rail Bridge and Southwark Bridge, were the lock gates of Walbrook Dock, which until recently led to the depot where domestic refuse was processed before being conveyed down river in barges. The depot has now been converted for container traffic. A few yards up river is a metal drain cover, which is all that can be seen of the Walbrook. Apart from the puddles.

ə ə ə

Film: Mithras the Movie
The Romans. Temple of Mithras. Emperor trying to bring in Christianity. But maybe the Mithras worshippers are the goodies in this. They'd be played by Americans. Haughty Christian emperors would be played by Brits. Alan Rickman is Claudius (or whoever – cinema audiences won't care). Reprising his *Gladiator* role, Russell Crowe is the kindly priest of Mithras who just wants world peace. Got a plan to oust the Romans and bring in a new order of New-Age-type Celts who'll rule Britain fairly. He is double-crossed by jealous Celt who is double agent. Could be a cartoon – Mithras would be like the Genie. Maybe Robin Williams could be Crowe's comedy sidekick. Voice of Mithras done by Woody Allen. Leads to Battle of Boudicca. Not accurate but, again, who cares?

London Stories 9: Hidden Art Soundscapes in the Aura of Things

At the gallery behind Stoke Newington library, several earnest young people are attempting to show Stoke Newingtonites that sound art terrorism can be sexy. We are about to witness a happening. There are pictures by local artists on the four walls. In the middle of the room stands a man who looks like a young Tony Blair – slim, pale-faced, and with an earnest I-Want-To-Change-The-World-While-Listening-To-Genesis expression. On his right hand he has an electronic pad attached to biker gloves which is all wired up to a mixer and amplifier and various other little effects boxes. After he is finally happy that the device is connected properly, he walks over to the nearest picture and brushes the glove against it. Shards of ear-popping white noise come bursting through the speakers: Cchhhhoooooowwwwwooooeeeeeeeeeeeeeeeeeeeeeeeeeeeeeeeeeeeeee eeee wwwwwwwwwww. There are a few people with glasses sitting on chairs who grimace and nod politely. Then one of them gets up, opens an instrument case, pulls out a saxophone and jumps onto the stage. 'Baa de lee beee yeee parrrpppp ee oowww rarrch honk blaaaaa!' he wails, blowing his stuff like a real north London daddio. A middle-aged man with wild hair then walks up to a chair on the stage, sits down and shouts, 'Bleee blman bok pooo dow nying!'

I look around. People are trying to nod their heads in time to the music. But the music doesn't have any time, so they look as though they've all got nervous twitches, or some strange illness where the patient suffers from permanently agreeing with everything.

Glove Man walks further along the wall to a big abstract picture with a metal frame. His expression gets a bit more serious, then he brushes his glove along the frame. Schhhhhhffff ffffffffffffffffffffzzzzzzzzzzzzsssss sssssssss goes the white noise glove mix electronic box amp thing. Bla baaa paaaeaarrrp goes the sax. Nyang pow pop goes the man with the funny voice, sorry, sound art vocalist.

Three lads come in wearing fancy Bermuda shorts and swigging from cans of Red Stripe. They are talking loudly to themselves and stand at the back of the hall. One of them murmurs, 'This is shit,' and the others laugh. But it's a frightened laugh. They are left dumbstruck, unable to take the piss out of something that is beyond pisstake. A young guy with a

quiff comes into the hall with a small case, opens it up, takes a trumpet out and starts bashing out some staccato phrases while the sax player packs away his gear. Then a magnificent Goth in a shimmery skirt plugs an electric violin into an amp and lets fly with some discordant screeching and scratching (imagine the violin bit from 'The Devil Rides Down to Georgia' played backwards at 16rpm and blended through a fuzzbox and local garage radio). Meanwhile, Glove Man has found a nice piece of hot water piping and eyes it up lasciviously (though in a cerebral way). He caresses the painted metal with his magic glove and a shimmering 'sffffwwoooooaaaaaaoooorrrgghhhhh Sssshhhhhhhhh' fills the hall. 'Zong tangà neeeek eek!' replies the singer. 'Paprp pep pip' says the trumpeter, 'Eeerooo wwneeeeooooeeeeeaaaa' says Goth Violinist. The hall is beginning to empty. Now there are only four other people plus me, and they are all musicians. Then vocal man and trumpeter leave the stage, followed by Goth Violinist, so only Glove Man is left, earnestly wandering the walls of Stoke Newington's Library Gallery loõking for Hidden Art Soundscapes in the Aura of Things.

Whether you're a middle-aged ex-punk or a youngster eager to discover more about London's heritage, **English Punk Heritage's** *Westbourne Trail has* something for everyone.

For those walking with their guitars, we offer three chords – G, C and D7 – for free.

English Punk *Heritage*
Kicking over the **statues** then putting them back **neatly**

THE WESTBOURNE TRAIL

G
C
D7

HAMPSTEAD
WEST HAMPSTEAD
KILBURN
BAYSWATER
Hyde Park
The Serpentine
KNIGHTSBRIDGE
PIMLICO
THAMES

Key
1. The Sex Pistols
2. The Police
3. Joy Division
4. The Damned
5. The Adverts
6. The Clash
7. Shane MacGowan
8. Mark E Smith
9. The Jam
10. The Sex Pistols
11. The Clash
12. The UK Subs

11: River of Punk

• The Westbourne – Hampstead to Ranelagh Gardens

Hampstead – Sting sex – Damned in Hot Rod sleeve – Kilburn – modernist flats – Paddington – Westway – Ken Boothe UK Pop Reggae – Mark E. Smith (anti-fashion) – Bayswater – Hyde Park – Knightsbridge – Lady Di lookalikes – Westbourne Tunnel

'Let us, in imagination, open some old, quaint-looking panorama of the City as it used to be ... All the landscape is dinted and curved – and behind it the uplands of Highgate and of Hampstead frame the prospect. In the lush meadows of Westbourne, near the highway to Harrow, the citizen of London could once see dragonflies and loosestrife, or, lying face down in the buttercups, tickle a brace of trout against the coming Friday'.

'Lost Rivers of London', *Wonderful London*, Alan Ivimey

> *The ice age is coming, the sun's zooming in*
> *Meltdown expected, the wheat is growing thin*
> *Engines stop running but I have no fear*
> *'Cos London is drowning and I live by the river.*

'London Calling', The Clash

꩜   ꩜   ꩜

The Westbourne, a river of similar size to the Fleet, flowed from Hampstead down through Hyde Park to Sloane Square and into the Thames at Chelsea. Like the Tyburn it, too, had a couple of sources and a tributary. In an attempt to get to the heart of the stream I tried the visual approach again, sketching its course on a piece of paper then testing it out on my family. I felt it looked like a running stag and that the Westbourne might be related in some way to the ancient fertility custom of Swearing on the Horns, which still takes place in the odd real ale pub on the hills around Highgate.

'A reindeer,' said my wife.

'No, it's a camel, said my daughter. Scrap that idea then.

According to Victorian pedants, the river was originally called the Kilburn (Cye Bourne – royal stream) but has been known, at different times and in different places, as Kelebourne, Kilburn, Bayswater, Bayswater River, Bayswater Rivulet, Serpentine River, Westburn Brook, the Ranelagh River and the Ranelagh Sewer. But one name for the stream that the historians have mostly ignored, in their race to be right, is the one that is perhaps the most apt – the River of Punk. For, back in the mid to late seventies, a wealth of bands sprang up around the Westbourne's banks and in the pubs and clubs that mark its course. Had not the river been buried just like the hopes and dreams of thousands of kids across recession-hit Britain? Somehow, these kids had picked up on the energy of the buried stream and transformed it into three-chord guitar gold. I looked at the picture I'd drawn again. Could those branches I thought were antlers actually represent a badly maintained spiky punk haircut?

I head out on a hot early summer day to follow English Punk Heritage's Westbourne Trail, which starts on Hampstead Heath near Jack Straw's Castle and goes through the winding lanes of

Hampstead Village. Hampstead always seems to do something to my internal navigation systems, which are not that good at the best of times, and after two or three minutes' walking I am already off course, but just thrust on downhill anyway and hope for the best. I wander around some dark treed lanes, not understanding which way to go and staring at my *A to Z* waiting for it to spit out the answer. I arrive at a big black manhole cover over a drain which seems to me to indicate the presence of the stream. It reminds of a big vinyl LP.

There aren't really any punk bands from Hampstead. Sid Vicious and Johnny Rotten had a squat in the area in the mid seventies and 'Hampstead' was an early song by Adam and the Ants. But really it's known as Sting territory. The Police were punkreggae bollocks with helium vocals. They brought out 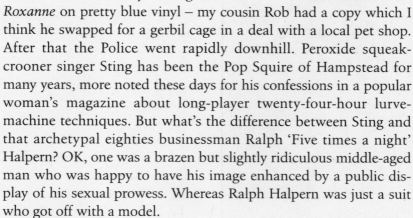 *Roxanne* on pretty blue vinyl – my cousin Rob had a copy which I think he swapped for a gerbil cage in a deal with a local pet shop. After that the Police went rapidly downhill. Peroxide squeak-crooner singer Sting has been the Pop Squire of Hampstead for many years, more noted these days for his confessions in a popular woman's magazine about long-player twenty-four-hour lurve-machine techniques. But what's the difference between Sting and that archetypal eighties businessman Ralph 'Five times a night' Halpern? OK, one was a brazen but slightly ridiculous middle-aged man who was happy to have his image enhanced by a public display of his sexual prowess. Whereas Ralph Halpern was just a suit who got off with a model.

I make the mistake of aiming to follow the river's course exactly through the mazy streets of West Hampstead. I try as much as possible to follow the contours of the land, but the preponderance of railway lines makes this difficult. It was here that the Moonlight Club on West End Lane was a big punk venue in the late seventies

208 and early eighties. The Damned recorded tracks there in 1979 that were eventually released on the *Eternal Damnation* collection. In the back of *NME* there was a mail order record place that was always advertising 'Damned Album in Hot Rods sleeve' for £25, which I could never quite get my head around. Bizarrely, my own copy of *Damned Damned Damned* went walkabout after a party and now all I have is the sleeve. Is it worth anything as a collector's item if I put another record inside it?

Joy Division played three gigs at the Moonlight Club in 1980, just before Ian Curtis died. They recorded a version of 'Sister Ray' which appears on their last album, *Still*. I foolishly turned down the chance to go and see them play at Retford around that time, preferring in my thick-headed yokel way to go to the local disco with a bottle of rum and black in my pocket in the hope that I'd get a snog from some teacher's daughter I fancied. The morning after Curtis died I wore a black armband to school. Actually it was a brown elastic band. The other option was an orange Day-Glo armband. Not long afterwards, the myth that 'Ian Curtis died for us' started to do the rounds and people who'd never even heard of the band a few months previously started wearing long coats and looking miserable, which left me with a choice of either upping the ante and being even more down, to show what a true fan I was, or to forget all about it. Which I did. Another less famous post-punk death was that of the Swell Maps' Epic Soundtracks, who died at his flat in West Hampstead in 1997. The clockwork-toy influenced 'Big Maz in the Desert From the Trolley' and the guitarythrash 'Let's Build a Car' remain two of my favourite punkpop songs of all time.

Eventually, tired of doing detours, I double back down the back streets towards Kilburn. Ian Dury's band Kilburn and the High Roads took their name from a local road sign. Around here is also the spiritual home of the Pogues – I imagine them hanging out in one of the big Irish boozers after doing some water divining using the metal bits in their teeth as dowsing rods. Shane MacGowan had previously been in a group called the Nipple Erectors, a reference to the holy springs that flowed from the nipple of the mother goddess. They probably created their own holy springs by pissing on the seats.

At the Priory Tavern there is lovely Truman's beer and hunting pictures on the walls. The Westbourne flowed by here and was crossed by Hermit Bridge. Around 1100 AD a hermit called Godwin built a little cell or hole in the ground next to the stream here, like the toilets in a punk club. There's a plaque nearby which doesn't mention the hermit. Instead it says, 'Thomas Creswick, preacher, died 1868. His last sermon was delivered at the bridge near this spot one week before he fell asleep in Jesus.' 'Fell asleep in Jesus' sounds like a Nick Cave album. The Bad Seeds? No, they weren't really punk as such – more OzGoth post punk voodoo thrash.

The river follows Kilburn Park Road for quite some way, and the land starts to open out into a wider valley. On the right is a school where people are moving boxes of Liebfraumilch and a chain-smoking cleaning lady guards them at the door. The headmaster and a senior teacher look serious. This is a big job – the staff room's whole consignment of sweet white wine for the summer term. Huge sky emptiness and the sweet smell of marijuana as a group of beautiful people walk past, chatting happily. On the right are blocks of mad modernist West Kilburn flats. Two girls in pretty summer frocks and long Rasta hair sashay past. Sashay is a good word. It's a bit more sensual than wiggle and more graceful than waddle.

I'm getting cramps in my right foot. More red brick creeping in now. Don't think the two are connected. Old shirtless blokes with leathery tans sit outside the done up Truscott Arms. Skin cancer? Who gives a shit – I am the brownest! There's a strong smell of piss from the nearby phone box.

210   Gaye Advert, of the Adverts, apparently lives in Paddington, still
with TV Smith I think. The one Adverts song that sticks in my
memory is 'Looking Through Gary Gilmore's Eyes'. When I first
heard it I naturally took to be a reference to the Australian fast
bowler Gary *Gilmour*, who was first change along with Max
Walker, supporting the front-line duo of Dennis
Lillee and Jeff Thomson. As a batsman he still
holds the Australian record for a seventh wicket
partnership of 217 with Doug Walters against
New Zealand in Christchurch 1976. But in
fact in June 1972 – in Furman v. Georgia –
the United States Supreme Court effectively voided forty death penalty statutes
and suspended the death penalty. Four
years later in Gregg vs. Georgia, guided discretion statutes were
approved and the death penalty was reinstated.[1] Gary Gilmore, a
convicted double murderer, was the first person to be executed in
the United States since the reintroduction of the death penalty.
Gaye Advert was the sexiest punk musician after Debbie Harry.

From Paddington, (Oh, and Elvis Costello was born in Paddington
in 1954) under Harrow road and the Westway, going in a line
straight down to Porchester Road. The Westway is Clash territory.
'Drove up and down the Westway, in and out the lights' ('what a
great traffic system, it's so bright!') London's Burning … *dial nine
nineninenine.* They came from here, under the Westway and
further west on Ladbroke Grove. I'll never forget the first time I
heard the Clash in the summer of 1978, two years after they'd hit
the big time (Lincolnshire, behind the times, no electricity, horses
and carts etc., etc.):

---

1 'Paying "Decent Respect" to World opinion on the Death Penalty' by Harold
   Hongju Koh (Edward L. Barrett, Jnr. Lecture on Constitutional Law, University
   of California Davis Law Review)

Meernah ta sizzmun
Forty thirsty why d'ya make her?
Dillingence is Leroy Sparks
Delroy Wilson, cool operator.

Ken Boothe UK pop reggae
A backy bah Sow's sister
And ivva annarin azai
Amaunblabiigoerizan.

Singer Joe Strummer was born in Ankara so was weaving Turkish or Arabic words into the lyrics. Hard thrash Joycean genius.

I pass Royal Oak, a pretty little station but sort of lost, named after an old coaching inn which is long gone. The noise levels have increased now. Shops, cafés and restaurants lead down towards Queensway, originally a country lane but named Queens Road in 1837 after newly crowned Victoria. I always thought Queensway never felt like London – more like Babylon Five with lots of different people milling about, all drinking espresso and buying foreign-language newspapers. When I was skint I used to go up there and pretend I was on holiday. If you go to Whiteleys, the big old shopping centre, you can go on a world gastronomic tour – you know, the usual stuff, 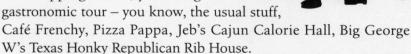 Café Frenchy, Pizza Pappa, Jeb's Cajun Calorie Hall, Big George W's Texas Honky Republican Rib House.

The only pub in view now is the Dean Gooch, inside a block of modern flats near Budgens. A beautiful fish and chip smell wafts in on the breeze and I stop and savour it for a while, then go left into Bishops Bridge Road, where William Blake used to fish when he

212 was a young man. Any visions in store for me? I have a look around but everything seems normal.

To the right is Westbourne Grove, where Shane MacGowan was hit by a taxi in 1986 while getting into a car. He was thrown into the air and left unconscious on the pavement. Seconds later, as I walk past the bus stop at the end of Westbourne Grove, two lads come flying out of the crowd of pedestrians, whacking seven kinds of shit out of each other. Actually, it's one guy, much bigger, hitting a skinny guy with no shirt on really really hard in the head. Some others, mates of the big lad, start getting involved, kicking at the skinny guy and the scene changes from a bit of sub Queensberry Rules argy bargy to something more dangerous. Now the big lad knocks the skinny bloke over and just starts kicking him in the face. His nose disintegrates and blood splats out onto the pavement. People at the nearby bus stop are just standing around. All this happens in the blink of an eye, but the action seems to be in slow motion.

I stop and shout 'Hey! Lads!' but they are too engrossed in trying to separate the skinny bloke's face from his head. 'Hey, come on lads!' The big guy hits him again, then stops and looks at me, then pulls out a big leather strap and snaps it menacingly.

'There's kids around. Look – there's mothers with their families and you're going to hurt someone else in a minute.' I say in a really soft unthreatening voice. I'm only a few inches away now – though make sure I don't touch him. The big lad looks at me and his eyes do something and he sort of calms down and wakes up, while his mates stare at him waiting for a sign. The skinny bloke, who's been looking at me and then the big lad, then just gets up, runs into the road and legs it at Olympic speed in the direction of Royal Oak station. I decide to get away quickly before the mood changes again so walk fast in the other direction past the commuters who are still watching the scene in a daze.

Rough Trade, now on Talbot Road, started up in 1976 in nearby Kensington Park Road, first selling reggae then early punk stuff. It then became a distributor and a record company, distributing early Factory releases and releasing records by Stiff Little Fingers, one of my favourite bands of the late seventies. The first gig I ever went to was SLF at the Cleethorpes Winter Gardens in early 1980, me and my mates trying to look hard in our donkey jackets and trying to talk in really deep voices.

Punk: Got a light, mate?
Fifteen year old in donkey jacket: (*high pitch*) No (*changes to Lee Marvin growl*) No.

My cousin Rob, who had in the meantime become a successful gerbil breeder, got back into music with SLF and used to write to SLF's singer Jake Burns on a regular basis.

Mark E. Smith of the Fall used to stay at Bayswater's Columbia Hotel when he visited London.[2] I still have it in my head that the Fall are a newish band but they've been going nearly twenty-five years. 'Are you doing what you were doing two years ago? Well don't make a habit of it.' he shouted on one of their early live albums. Which I

---

[2]   *The bed's too clean*
     The water's poison for the system
     Then you know in your brain
     LEAVE THE CAPITOL!
     EXIT THIS ROMAN SHELL!
     'Leave the Capital' The Fall, from the album *Slates*

214 always thought was dead profound. Mark E. Smith still looks like seventies Leeds striker Allan Clarke, who went on to be a manager. I like to think they could have swapped places without anyone notic- ing. Mark E. Smith of the Fall would certainly have been a good manager, shouting slogans at players through a megaphone. And he'd have been great as a pundit during World Cups. As for the Allan Clarke Project, it would have been dour Yorkshire poetry over a John-Cale-style screechy viola. Could still happen.

SNIFFER

Out onto Bayswater Road where the river flows right into the north part of the Serpentine. The Swan, a 300-year-old boozer packed with tourists used to be the last drinking place before criminals got hanged at nearby Tyburn gallows. Rather confusingly for people like me who get confused easily there's a tributary of the Westbourne called the Tyburn Stream that starts a bit further to the east and flows into the Serpentine in Hyde Park. I go into Hyde Park at Marlborough Gate and walk on the left-hand side of the ponds. There used to be eleven natural ponds here which eventually became just a huge cess pit, and you can see quite a bit of the shape of the river valley. The park to the left is long grassed like a water meadow, with a more natural feel than I remember. For some reason I always think of this as a neat, trussed-up park.

It brings to mind a neat, buttoned-up band. On the Jam's first album *In The City*, in the song 'I've Changed My Address', Paul Weller sings:

> You'll probably find me in Hyde Park
> Try the hotel first, then a bench.

Could it be the same hotel that Mark E. Smith stayed in?

Years later, Weller would write the ultimate song about the lost river Westbourne, 'Going Underground'. But the Jam are ultimately positive about the fate of this lost stream – 'Give it a chance to breathe again,' sings Bruce Foxton in 'London Traffic' (from *This is the Modern World*, 1977).

Anyway, back to Hyde Park ... In the film *The Filth and the Fury* Sid Vicious hangs around there, talking to the camera about himself and heroin. Sid was just the first of several pop stars to peg it from heroin overdoses in the next year – including Malcolm Owen from the Ruts and the two from the Pretenders. It's hard to imagine any of today's clean-cut musicians dying from anything other than being crushed by a large sack of cash. Could be a game show idea there.

The Serpentine opens out into a big expanse of pond. There's a church in the distance and Westminster Abbey off to the east, little paddle boats in the foreground. You get a sense of the unchanging lives of Londoners – in old illustrations of the Serpentine people are behaving exactly the same, promenading, sitting around chatting. A middle-aged guy with a big nose and glasses with big brows, tweed jacket, shirt and fedora is sauntering along behaving exactly the same; one young couple are talking about Europe; another couple on a bench are all over each other, his hand in her bra; some lads are chatting about football, whilst a kid wearing a gaudy Union Jack shirt with 'England' on it skips past, people are slumped into deckchairs or spreading all over the place as if on a beach. This is seaside London, all life is here.

I come to a little bridge with three arches, where the Westbourne goes, then disappears underground again, down into a little valley through the Rose Garden. I follow the valley and head towards a French flag at Albert Gate and Knightsbridge.

The Clash mention Knightsbridge in their song '1977'.

> *In 1977*
> *knives in West Eleven*
> *it ain't so lucky to be rich*
> *Sten guns in Knightsbridge.*
>
> *Danger stranger*
> *You better paint your face*
> *No Elvis, Beatles or the Rolling Stones.*

Was this a reaction against what they saw as a wealthy and privileged part of the city? Or did they, with their Situationist slogan T-shirts, feel a certain rivalry with the punk boutiques in the West End? But the Clash weren't all talk – they lived the revolutionary vibe. In early 1978 bassist Paul Simonon and drummer Topper Headon went on a Baader-Meinhof-style rampage against what they saw as the forces of oppression. From a rooftop in Camden Town they took potshots at racing pigeons, those evil birds that shit on your head and that in their competitiveness are the very embodiments of capitalism. They were arrested and fined £800. But their point had been made.

Sadly, I hero-worshipped the Clash and decided to make myself a pair of bondage trousers, using an old school uniform and a load of zips. I think I ended up accidentally sewing them to the jeans I was wearing, which wasn't very punk. I also decorated my guitar, Simonon style. Where he used Jackson Pollockesque splashes of paint, I rubbed on some Batman transfers.

Heading south, I pass Doric columns on big fuck-off houses, the streets full of BMWs, Mercedes and Jags.[3] A group of middle-aged workmen are repairing the stucco of one of the old houses, reeking of strong perfume. Maybe they're part of some ancient City company,

---

3   The Jags were a post-punk power pop combo who had a minor hit in 1979 with 'I Got Your Number (Written on the Back of my Hand)'.

guild or sect which insists on fine bodily odours. The Worshipful
Company of Nice-Smelling Gentlemen? Cross onto Lowndes Street
and there are seventies flats with balconies, Ray Ward gunsmiths
(does he sell Stens?), sleeveless green quilted 'Jobo' jackets and general
hunting products for folk who like to blast stuff out of the sky, shops
with leopardskin picture frames, art galleries with Constable copies in
gilt frames. Left down Cadogan Place and straight on, past bald cockney blokes with tattoos, skinny loud blokes pushing barrows around,
everyone jabbering to each other or themselves, daytime radio bland-
pop blaring out of car radios. I have a peek in an estate agent's
window and there's a three-bedroom flat in this square going for one
and a half million. It's got a marble bath, so that's all right then. I start
sneezing, that psychosomatic thing I get when I'm allergic to an area.

'Gardens. Private. No dogs. No cycling. No ballgames. No music.
No vandalism.' No working-class people. No Elvis, Beatles or the
Rolling Stones? William Wilberforce lived in one of these houses. I
look through a door, the interior is in traditional style but is cold
and austere, empty and drab. Beautiful pinched brown statuesque
sixty-something women totter about, hints of their glory days in
the way they hold themselves.

Through Cliveden Place and Sloane Square and into Bourne
Street, then back to the river again. Battersea Power Station towers
over the rooftops. This is a forgotten Georgian village crammed
with little cottages. It's got everything
the villagers need – a posh women's
hair stylists and an upmarket estate
agent. Looking at the chicks walking about here, they don't eat much
anyway – lots of fit, tanned, not
exactly pretty Lady Di-lookalikes
with shopping bags, wearing white.
There's a factory round here churning them out.

218   Down from Sloane Square, Malcolm McLaren and Vivienne Westwood had a shop, Sex, in the King's Road, where they put together the Pistols in 1975. It was like an early version of that *Popstars* programme – they'd check out the kids who came into the shop to see if they'd look good in the band. The Pistols was a marketing and branding phenomenon years ahead of its time. Unfortunately for Malc, they forgot to choose people who'd go along with the plan indefinitely. One of the myths of punk is that the Sex Pistols and the Clash all went to public schools and would all have gone on to lucrative jobs in the City if they hadn't been plucked from the ballroom circuit by their respective managers. At that time Britain was toff crazy and the escapades of the royal family and other aristocrats filled the newspapers. Although they came from the same smart set, there was intense rivalry between them, due to the fact that the Pistols went to Eton and the Clash were Old Harrovians.

Over into Pimlico Road/Ebury Street area with a little village green, Orange Square and a statue of Mozart. He lived round here for a few months and it's where he wrote his first symphony in 1764. He was born in 1756, which means he was eight when he wrote it. Eight! If it happened nowadays the news headlines would be 'Composer writes symphony in British house'. He stayed there for about seven weeks but couldn't practise because of the noise, so he spent his time composing. He did his first public concert in nearby Ranelagh Gardens in 1764. I look in the window and there's a tanned middle-aged bloke in an armchair, as if listening to classical music. Looks like an advert for something – Cup-a-Soup maybe or mail-order golden-oldie classics. Perhaps it's a rule of the property that the owner can only listen to Mozart and he's gone mad.

Chelsea were an early punk band who lost most of their members

(like Billy Idol and Tony James) to other, more famous, groups and 219
never really hit the big time. The singer was Gene October, who
sounded a bit like Rick Astley. I never had any of their singles but I
think my mate Kev did, possibly buying it off a bloke at school called
'Moorey' Moore, who once had a big purge of his record collection
and who possibly spent the cash on more school dinners.

There's a toilet in the square that is right above the Westbourne.
Nearby, Travis Perkins' Victorian wood yard is under threat of demo-
lition after 150 years of continued use. There's a save the wood yard
campaign that I expect will get thousands out on the streets. I pop
my head round the corner to look and it is indeed a beautiful thing,
and seems familiar from televised Dickens novels. If I could find that
spatula I made in first-year woodwork I would donate it to the cause.

UK Subs guitarist Nicky Garratt first moved to London at the
start of 1977 and had a flat in Pimlico.
In my mind the UK Subs were famous
for having the oldest punk singer in the
world. Vocalist Charlie Harper was
absolutely ancient (thirty-one in
their heyday, which obviously I now
think is incredibly young).

The Westbourne flows under the
army barracks at the end of Bloomfield
Terrace. Is this the terrace where the
Stranglers' Duchess lived? There's a big old early Victorian house
right next door to the barracks and a bit of wall with a gap where
it's broken down. The garden is full of junk and standing near the
back door are four blokes with white hats. Maybe it is the
Stranglers. They all look middle aged and one of them certainly has
a beard. One is digging in a big hole while the others look on. Are
they trying to get into the barracks, a sort of reverse *Escape From
Colditz*? Or maybe they've just escaped and they're filling in the
hole? And who are the white hats anyway? Templars? Knights of

220 St John? Yellow hats, red hats, white hats. It's getting confusing. I start to do a quick ten-second sketch of them. One of them looks up and sees me, then points out to his mates that they're being watched. I do the chameleon thing where I try to merge with the bricks, but it doesn't work so I smile awkwardly and quickly walk away.

I'm on Ebury Bridge Road now (presumably there was an Ebury Bridge over the Westbourne). At the back of the Ebury Bridge Estate, past a car park bloke in a green shirt slumped in a red chair reading a tabloid. There's some massive block being demolished, a big old forties aircraft-hanger of a building with its guts pulled out, wires everywhere sticking out, metal twisted and spewing. Out onto Chelsea Bridge Road. Past some posh Peabody Trust flats and Jerome K. Jerome's old gaff (no. 104). According to all sources the Westbourne flowed through what is now Ranelagh Gardens, then hit the Thames. There's a dip in the road just in front of gardens' main gate. I cross over Chelsea Embankment and the tide is pretty high up. There's a whiff of drainy sewer and when I lean over the Thames wall I can just see the top of the tunnel arch where the Westbourne/Ranelagh Sewer enters the Thames. Like punk, the Westbourne was once clean and pure then got filled up with shit and eventually forgotten about. But to some people it will never die. Its spirit lives on.

> *Down in the sewer*
> *Picking up on a lot of empty Coca Cola cans*
> *And there sure are a lot of them around here.*
> *How did I get down here*
> *Well it's a long story.*

'Down in the Sewer', the Stranglers
(by kind permission of Complete Music)

ॐ   ॐ   ॐ

Film Idea: the Story of Punk.

Malcolm McClaren lives in a house boat on the Serpentine with Vivienne Westwood. He hangs around in a local library and discovers that it used to be the Westbourne. He feels that rivers being covered up is like the working class being downtrodden. He starts the music movement which also has environmental goal of getting rivers brought back to surface. Glen Matlock is the river lover who wants to bring this about. But then McClaren becomes power crazy and decides river project is unimportant. Matlock wants the Pistols to be vanguards of movement for Jubilee. He is sacked, shot and dumped in river.

Helen Mirren – Vivienne Westwood

Gary Oldman – Malcolm McClaren

Tom Cruise – Glen Matlock

Ewan McGregor – Johnny Rotten

London Stories 10: The Secret Life of the Market Trader

In the early nineties I spent a year in South America and, while there, found that I had a gift, the sort of thing that can change people's lives. I discovered I could hand-paint T-shirts and sell them for cash. When I saw the look on people's faces when they went away with their painted clothing items, I realized that I had to share this gift with as many people as possible.

So when I returned to London in 1992 I decided I'd become an entrepreneur. I would get a stall in nearby Portobello Market and sell my hand - painted T-shirts and help create a happier world. I joined the National Market Traders' Association and arrived early on Saturday morning to get my pitch. At first I was in a little covered market just before the railway bridge, then moved to a spot down the side of the Westway. It all went rather well. Although advertising slogans like 'Get your expensive hand-painted T-shirts here!' and 'Wow! Fake iron-on transfers of Tommy Lawton!' didn't seem that clever, I sold five T-shirts the first week and eight the second. I also made some nice new mates, like the photographer, the hairdresser and the crazy old knife woman. Any kind of knife you wanted – pen knives, flick knives, hunting knives, butchers' knives – the crazy old knife woman had got it. She'd sell them to anyone, but her main market seemed to be

shifty hot-tempered adolescents. My only real competition was a bloke at the other end of Portobello Road who sold T-shirts with pictures of beefeaters, double-decker buses and Princess Diana for £2.99.

I saw myself becoming a permanent market trader, eking out the decades at my little stall. Then one evening I made the fatal mistake of taking my 'business' a bit too seriously, and wrote down some figures. What a shock. I calculated that I'd have to work 400,000 hours to make a million. OK, I thought, I can do it. I've

THERE'S NO MONEY IN HAND-PAINTED T-SHIRTS

got stamina. Trouble was, I would have to live to the soggy old age of 16, 660 if I was to achieve my goal. And that's with no time off for sleep, sex, food, TV or beer. Flat out. Twenty-four hours a day. For 16,660 years. So if I decided to do the normal entrepreneur sixteen-hour day, what then? I was looking at 25,000 years. A nice round number. I'd have to discover the elixir of life. But if I did that I'd have no need for producing hand painted T-shirts. Basically the whole thing was such a non-production-line idea Henry Ford would have spun so fast in his grave he'd have melted.

But he's decomposed anyway so who cares.

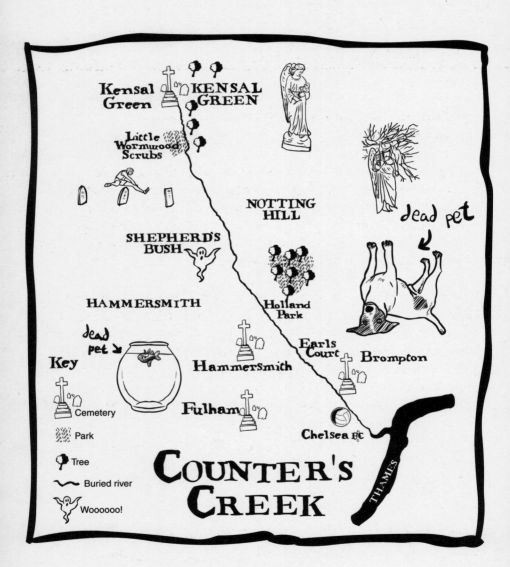

Kensal Green

KENSAL GREEN

Little Wormwood Scrubs

NOTTING HILL

dead pet

SHEPHERD'S BUSH

HAMMERSMITH

Holland Park

dead pet

Earls Court

Brompton

Key

Hammersmith

Cemetery

Fulham

Chelsea FC

Park

Tree

Buried river

Wooooooo!

COUNTER'S CREEK

THAMES

12. Fred the Cat and the River of the Dead

Dream: A trip over lakes and rivers with a coffin. My grandad.
Have to catch a train to get to the funeral. Trains keep getting can-
celled. Going to miss the funeral. And I'm out in some sort of
Everglades in England. Nice sunny day. There are fish in the water,
which is beautiful and clean, can see the bottom. Worried about a
shark I've seen so I don't swim in it too long.

I phone my mum to tell her what's happening – that dad and I,
along with the body, will be late for the funeral. She says that she's
not sure he's really dead now. Just gone missing. The police think
they'll be able to find him.

So whose body have we got, then? Nobody knows.

ॐ   ॐ   ॐ

If you chart all the tributaries of the Thames onto a big map of
London and stick it up on your wall (use Blu Tak, not those little

white foam buds, which will tear the paint or wallpaper off leaving bare plaster) then stand back, two things become evident.

1. London looks like a big jellyfish.
2. Many of the rivers, deriving from springs, start in cemeteries. The connection with cemeteries originates in the development of Christianity – pagan shrines and places of worship were appropriated and turned into Christian sites. The old shrines would once perhaps have been holy wells, revered by the local population and thus, possibly, used as burial grounds.

Counter's Creek, originally named after a Countess of Oxford who owned land in west London in the Middle Ages (Earl's Court was named after her husband, Earl), rises in Kensal Green Cemetery, one of the most famous Victorian burial grounds in the capital. As the numbers of London's middle classes expanded they grew tired of being comfortable, keeping servants and reading Jane Austen and were looking out for the next big thing. Death. And for a while, death became big business. Considering they were the kings of common sense, the Victorians were pretty barmy. The middle class saw aristos being sent off to the next life in mad quasi-Egyptian mausoleums and wanted a piece of the reincarnation action. They demanded high-class transport to the land of the dead with all the fantastic trappings offered by this life – rubbish gas lighting, top hats, side whiskers, corsets, sexual repression – plus immortality. And, so, they got it – and their gateway to paradise and immortality lay at the western end of the Harrow Road.

The nineteenth century made death exciting again. We are terrified of death in a way the Victorians – in fact most of our ancestors – wouldn't have understood. Death is different now. When self-obsessed free love guru Timothy Leary died, his ashes were rocketed into outer space. Imagine the day when some alien life forms find his casket, think it is a gift of cosmic druggy stardust from hedonist planet Earth and snort it. Infuriated, and with noses full of powdered prophet, the aliens will probably obliterate the earth in a massive vengeful strike.

So far the London rivers have seemed like a life force but they can also represent death – that underworld journey. Counter's Creek is London's River Styx, particularly now it's been buried itself. (Maybe that's where the phrase 'out in the styx' originates, referring to places in the suburbs with no life.) The last time I had visited the area, *Paradise by Way of Kensal Green* was a bar on the main street with a comedy club upstairs. There were various up-and-coming stand ups that night and my friends and I were merciless in our heckling, reducing one guy almost to tears. In fact he completely died on stage. At the bar afterwards he asked why we did it. I didn't have an answer. Perhaps, unbenownst to us, it was the influence of the nearby buried river, which flows in an almost dead straight line to the Thames, like an aquatic funerary path.

On a bright early summer day, I walk down through a gentle valley in the graveyard towards a burnt-out truck up ahead. Around it was a small rubbish dump and, behind that, the Grand Union Canal with an embankment on this side – there's an old iron gate but it's locked. I get the feeling they used to bring bodies here by barge. Reminded me of the death boat in *Don't Look Now*. Except that film was a bit unrealistic – in real life would Julie Christie have even gone near Donald Sutherland, let alone shag him?

Somehow the area near the gate has mutated into an impromptu landfill site. Shopping trolleys and the usual detritus of city life (why go to all that effort to dump stuff here of all places?), mixed with more plaintive paraphernalia of the dead – 'Daddy' spelled out in lights made of red plastic plants. Nearby is a small, melancholy, grave-grey stone.

It's like walking though a country meadow full of 150 years' worth of stone wheels, plinths and crosses, maybe a trick of a cosmic computer artist's palette, dusted with wildflowers. Some of the graves are recent and too shiny, others are worn with time and the weather and seem comfortable in their anonymity and sleepiness, the illegible names long forgotten: Charles Babbage, Charles Blondin, Isambard Kingdom Brunel, Wilkie Collins, Mary Gibson, Thomas Hancock, John Hobhouse, Thomas Hood, Joseph Hume, Leigh Hunt, Fanny Kemble, Freddie Mercury, Annabella Milbanke, William Molesworth, William Mulready, Robert Owen, Terrence Rattigan, Henry Russell, William Makepeace Thackeray, Anthony Trollope, John Waterhouse, Lady Jane Francesca Wilde.

Another 'Dad' sign lies discarded in a rubbish bin. I clamber over a large stone set into the ground and feel a familiar sharp jolting pain under my kneecap. Ex-hurdlers will recognize this as a case of hurdler's knee. Mine is something more. As well as inflamed tissue I also have my invisible great-grandad in my knee. He was very small, so when the knee swells up, it's accommodating his actual size. Just about.

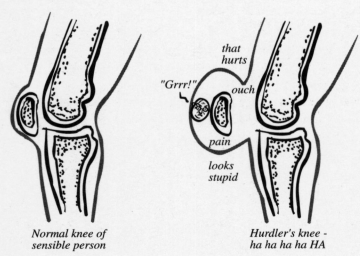

that hurts

"Grrr!" ouch

pain

looks stupid

Normal knee of sensible person

Hurdler's knee - ha ha ha ha HA

Even when alive, my great-grandad could make himself invisible – he'd disappear for what seemed like days on end to a 'shelter' near where he lived in Cleckheaton (West Yorkshire), to play dominoes and talk loudly about cricket. Children and women were not allowed to set eyes on the shelter – an old Yorkshire custom, apparently. I always imagined it as a small wooden building, packed with little old blokes with shiny bald heads, trousers pulled up to their nipples and lots of dominoes trophies on the walls. 'I'm off down t' shelter,' he'd say, then he'd be gone. But whenever there was anything good on their massive old black-and-white TV with the sliding door he'd miraculously reappear, scowling because he'd lost at dominoes, then he'd turn the TV over and there'd ALWAYS BE RUGBY LEAGUE on another channel – ALWAYS – which was a game with simple rules: a fat lad with long sideburns would crash into another fat lad with long sideburns and push the ball back with his foot to a player behind him. Most games ended 2–0, due to a penalty kick between the posts midway through the second half.

My great-grandad was an Ultra-Competitive Sportsman. He hated losing at anything (unless he was playing cards with my youngest brother, Snake, who hadn't yet worked out how to let someone else win). He had been a good athlete in his time (he said), an 880 yard runner, whose technique was to sprint out from the gun, wait for the other runners to catch up, then shout 'Weh heeeeyy!' and sprint out again with a big grin.

When he died, his funeral was on the same day as our school sports day. And I was faced with a dilemma. After years of being a perennial second/third place chugger in events like the 100 metres – that year, the last in which we could compete – I was favourite to win something. The 110 metres hurdles. At last it was the big time. I'd been looking forward to it, to the extent that I'd possibly over trained, banging my knee often on hurdles – occasionally it would swell up. But as long as I raced with good form, I reckoned I would be fine.

230   So, I could sit with my relatives in a cold northern crematorium listening to tributes to my great-grandad's dominoes ability while a wobbly electric organ played in the background, or I could test my body against the clock in De Aston School fourth-year 110 metre hurdles, representing Ancholme House. Should I choose death or glory? I decided that death would be more appropriate in the circumstances but was eventually persuaded that I should do the sports day rather than go to the funeral: 'It's what he would have wanted.' But on the day of the funeral it poured with rain and the race was called off. I moped in the damp, feeling sorry for myself, occasionally clutching my knee and thinking about my great-grandad scowling down from his Yorkshire heaven and shaking his fist. Somehow his death, my guilt at not going to the funeral and the fucked-up knee all merged into one. Even now, if I'm climbing the narrow stairs to my daughter's bedroom, and feel a painful click behind my kneecap and instinctively think 'I am a glory-hunting bastard who doesn't care about his family,' and am consumed with guilt for a brief moment.

But then I look at the gravestones in the brownish light reflected from the gothic rust-coloured gas holders that loom behind the trees and, as the music to *Chariots of Fire* starts to play on a small electric organ set to 'church' sound (the kind beloved of crematorium cemeteries), I imagine accelerating down the slope with speed and fluidity, hurdling over each stone with perfect form, in slow motion, as all my dead relatives cheered me on, and my great-grandad turns to his mates up in Yorkshire heaven, smiles and proudly says 'Ee, that's my great-grandson,' before frowning and adding '...but 'e's a bit bloody slow, i'n't 'e?'

I've even planned my own funeral. There was the time I thought I was going to die from alcohol poisoning, uncontrollably puking up in a pub toilet in Lincoln. I wanted to die there and then, but couldn't help wondering how I would be remembered. As a normal bloke? As a loving and giving son, friend and lover? As a brilliant,

charismatic and dynamic sexy success story? **231**
As a loser? As a misfit? As a loner? As all of
the above? Or none? I can't be the only sad
bastard fascinated by their own death.
And, of course, there's the important question of the musical
arrangements for my departing cere-
mony (at the time of the toilet episode it would
have consisted of Kid Creole and The Coconuts'
'I'm a Wonderful Thing'). But later in another near-death experience on a flight from Houston to London, as the plane shuddered
and gasped over the Atlantic, I wrote out a working list of possible
tunes on the paper sick-bag that the airline had generously stuck in
the pouch in front of my seat.

1. 'White Man in the Hammersmith Palais' – The Clash
2. 'Nice and Easy Does It' – Frank Sinatra
3. 'Harvest for the World' – Isley Bros
4. 'Atmosphere' – Joy Division
5. 'Ain't Love Good, Ain't Love Proud' – Dave Clarke

I looked at it for a couple of minutes, soon realizing it wasn't right.
Too 'pop musicy', not enough gravitas, which suggested I was a bit
shallow. More specifically, Joy Division was too depressing, the
Clash too tinny. 'Harvest for the World' too Saturday-night-disco-
had-too-many-rum-and-blacks-looking-for-a-snog for a funeral.
Sitting next to me a 230 lb Texan had stopped reading his, er, 'gentleman's' magazine (photo captioned: 'She will do it any way they
fancy') and was earnestly scrutinising my Death List. I folded the
bag up and tucked it back in with the newspapers in front of me.

ஓ ஓ ஓ

232   A report in the early sixties, *The Geography of London Ghosts* by G. K. Lambert, showed a correlation between underground streams and hauntings. European folklore has similar stories about underground rivers and goblins (You want evidence? That Czechoslovakian sixties kids' show *The Singing Ringing Tree*), and in the case of the UK's most famous haunted house, Borley Rectory, a nun's ghost is said to walk the route of an underground stream, only disappearing when the river comes into the open. The sceptics – people like Daphne in *Scooby Doo* – point out that the sound of running water is similar to ghostly moanings, and that the preponderance of mosquitoes and midges around water might look like ghostly apparitions. A different theory is that underground water creates an energy – the earth force that dowsers pick up on.

But another kind of ghost is that sense of the past that exists purely on an emotional level, as if energy is stored in the very fabric of a building or area.

> A place used for rites and ceremonies throughout the centuries will keep within itself the influence and the power poured into it through the work of those who have used it in the past – thus the 'atmosphere' felt so often by sensitive, and even not sensitive, people in certain places.
>
> *The Western Mystery Tradition*, Christine Hartley

I have always been interested in this. It evidences itself in my fascination for the past manifesting itself purely as a desire to eat and drink in places where people have been eating and drinking over many years. It's why I am addicted to London's pubs. I really believe that, somehow, the spirit of past times can be felt in old pub seats and beer-stained floors. Maybe even in the piss in Victorian urinals. When I arrived in London in the late eighties, I was reading *The Pickwick Papers*. The characters seemed to spend the whole

19th Century　　　　　　　　*21st Century*

time sitting in little rooms in inns drinking brandy and hot water. I decided to find these drinking dens as an introduction to the Capital. And with the office where I was a temp as a starting point, I spent the evenings tramping the streets hunting for boozers, holding my book in front of my face. I spent several fruitless days looking for the Magpie and Stump on Fetter Lane. I couldn't see it so would head off down side streets then double back in the hope that it had been hiding. Sadly, I had to give up. The only pubs seemed to be new ones. I have a love of the mystical mundane, and nothing seems to typify this more than a fruitless hunt for an old boozer.

After the cemetery I need to head west, but first I go over the canal down onto Ladbroke Grove where a pub called the Narrow Boat used to be. It disappeared when the bridge was widened to accommodate the new Sainsbury's traffic. I can hear the ghosts of my friends and myself ten years ago playing darts and talking shite, where now there is just bare concrete and scraps of grass, and a lot for used cars that says 'Warning these premises are protected by razorwire.' What's to protect? An old car or two? Or are they worried someone might come along in the night and rebuild the pub? Yeah, scaredy cats, that sounds more like it. Then a Canada goose takes off from the spot where the dartboard used to be. Just further down the road I have a vision of the Notting Hill Carnival in 1989,

234   I can taste the Cockspur rum I drank again; hear the heavy drums, hips and flashing bright red of the iron bridge over the railway. It all kicked off when someone lobbed a bottle and the lads on police horses waded in, threatening anyone who tried to reason with them. But now there's just traffic.

After a long walk past a thirties terrace I reach Little Wormwood Scrubs recreation ground, a very rough field of wild grassland where the river used to flow. Counter's Creek once ran from the graveyard, under the canal then through the Eurostar depot, where there are huge stationary trains looking futuristic and incongruous behind the park. There's a winding path which probably follows the course of the river, down a very gentle slope from Sainsbury's.

But I end up wandering down Latimer Road and on past confusing pedestrian signs through temporary corridors and walkways made of grey boards. It looks like they're trying to create a garden among the building works. Lots of workers in red hard hats milling about. This is Notting Dale – I bet that's just some Rupert-the-Bear-style estate agent's urban-ruralesque invention. Nearby is Wood Lane tube, one of two ghost stations in the area (the other being Brompton Road further south). Then I get to Shepherds Bush Green, the home of a famous haunting – Dylan Thomas's ghost has reportedly been seen at the back of the Bush Theatre at the bottom of the green.

At the edge of the green is a crushed snail. Possibly a much-loved family pet, now a squirt of slime and crackly bits of shell. This evening some kid will be saying 'Mummy, why hasn't Sammy Snail come home?'

My own pet/death ratio during adolescence was so high that it shaped my personality. I remember a day in 1980 when I was enjoying my usual cooked breakfast, tussling with an exceptionally rugged piece of bacon rind, when my dad appeared at the door.

'Tim, can you put your boots on and come outside for a moment? I need a bit of help.'

I followed my father to the old outside toilet, which we only used on occasions we wanted to sample a bit of life in the Victorian era. It hadn't been used on a regular shitting basis for well over half a century. The door to the little privy was half open and I pushed inside.

'Look in the corner, under the leaves.'

I parted the leaves with my hands and felt cold, dry fur. Fred the cat's lifeless body was stiff and heavy. I let out a cry when I saw our pet's mouth was stuffed with dry leaves.

'How ... did it happen?'

My dad didn't know. Maybe he'd eaten something nasty, poison from a crop sprayer, then tried to eat leaves to make himself sick. Together we carried Fred's corpse to the vegetable garden and I dug a deep hole.

'I'll plant some carrots here,' said my dad. 'I expect Fred will make them grow.' I tried not to cry. We lowered Fred into the grave and covered him with soil. Then the two of us stood motionless for a few moments and I thought about life's injustices. How come Fred had to die when rapists and murderers are allowed to live?

And yet Fred was by no means the first of my pets to meet an untimely end.

Bit (goldfish)
Named after one of the famous Playschool goldfish, Bit died a few days after being won at a fair when I was five. I think the bowl had been put too close to the window and the sun made him overheat.

Bot (goldfish)
Named after the less-celebrated Playschool fish with the slightly more risqué moniker, Bot lasted about a fortnight in the little round bowl, before he too departed to that large ant-egg factory in the sky.

236   Morecambe and Wise (goldfish)

My mum and dad bought me a larger tank to accommodate these two new members of the family. I hoped they would have lots of baby fish, who I had already decided to call the Two Ronnies. Naming beloved pets after conventional British comic double acts was all the rage at the time.

Morecambe[1] and Wise lived for a couple of years, until a mystery virus, perhaps passed on by infected ant eggs, claimed the life of Morecambe. In true show-business tradition Wise gamely soldiered on alone. But it was no use. I ended up flushing him down the toilet when he appeared one morning on his side, floating on the surface. After which I gave up goldfish for ever.

Atom (dog)

Atom was impossible to train. We tried for a while but gave up and instead my dad erected a big gate to keep him in the yard. He was a fantastic footballer, much better than me. Atom was a great pet but alas his favourite hobby was dodging traffic. This would have been OK if he'd been any good at it. But he should have stuck to football. Atom had his back broken by a car and had to be put down. I was devastated and didn't get over it until ...

Fluff (wombat – ha ha, no, cat of course)

This originally named animal never really caught my imagination. It was only when my dad informed me, one morning, that he'd found Fluff at the side of the road flat as a pancake that, in death, I got enthusiastic.

---

[1]   In the Find Your Porn Name game, in which you use the name of a favourite pet and your mother's maiden name to find what you would have been called in the sex industry, I always used Morecambe. Morecambe Sowden has a certain English end-of-the-pier raciness, I feel.

Joey (cat)

Joey was a homely cat who didn't stray too far from the house. The one time she did was obviously a night to remember; for, a while later, we found her with four newborn kittens. Joey was obviously not cut out for motherhood, for the next day my dad found her all squashed up at the side of the road. But my brothers and I were determined to be good friends to the kittens and bring them up as if they were our own kids (even though they had to sleep in the airing cupboard).

Horace

A handsome tabby who bossed the others about. The fact that he was brought up by humans not only gave him delusions of grandeur but also failed to give him the requisite survival skills. His desire to become a traffic policeman ended in the inevitable thin crust pizza/side of the road discovery for my, by now possibly traumatized, father.

Rosie

This pretty and intelligent little cat had hopes of travelling the world and meeting people. She didn't get much further than the top of the drive. Dad ... spade ... dustbin bag etc. etc.

George

Prosaically named, George was well within his rights to jump into a builder's van and escape to the other side of town, where he was renamed something along the lines of Simpkins or Fortescue. My mum didn't have the heart to ask for him back when she heard the builder's daughter had fallen in love with him. The builder's daughter had fallen in love with him ... it sounds like something from a folk song.

Fred

Fred seemed so thick and slow, yet outlived his brothers and sister by at least six years. He and George were the only ones not to die a rock'n'roll death on the infamous A631. After his demise, we went to a local farm to choose another cat, but my heart wasn't in it any more. I'd recently got into Joy Division, feeling that their brand of rock despair was a suitable soundtrack for the ever expanding pet cemetery in our vegetable garden. Of course, not long after, Ian Curtis died.

ॐ ॐ ॐ

And, anyway, what were we talking about? Oh yes, the river. Hereabouts, it flowed towards Earl's Court. A few hundred yards to the west is Hammersmith Cemetery. This has big angels and Celtic crosses all packed up to the main thoroughfare, but bare grass over the rest of it, like a work in progress. It's as if they ran out of dead Victorians at some point and simply gave up. The river then travels along what is now the railway to Fulham Broadway. Next to it is the famous Brompton Cemetery, whose high-profile burial customers have included Emmeline Pankhurst (Suffragette leader, wore big hats, chained herself to railing, got arrested, achieved the vote for women), John Stow (chemist and public health campaigner, identified cholera hotspots, got a pub named after him in Soho) and Lone Wolf (American Indian war hero, member of Buffalo Bill's Wild West Circus, remains eventually sent back to the USA at the end of the nineties). The creators of West London's cemeteries must have liked the River of Death, because just down Lillie Road to the east is Fulham Cemetery.

Past Stamford Bridge, Chelsea's ground, where the stream was traditionally the boundary between the parishes of Fulham and Kensington. From Stamford Bridge I walk the short route to the Thames where the lower part of the stream, the tidal inlet known as Chelsea Creek, is still there. Some of the creek has already been covered over, but on the bits that remain gangs of shirtless lads sit in the scrubland, fishing. Further down, two smaller kids chuck sticks in. There's lots of development on old industrial land, bland new luxury flats in keeping with the desire of planners to pack the riverside with people earning a minimum £100,000 a year, who in turn desperately want a part of the London experience for themselves. While the Victorians clamoured to get into classy mausoleums, our new middle classes prefer a living death – crammed into soulless luxury estates with no shops, no pubs, no gardens, just a view of one silver-grey river winding off into the distance.

Public information: The cat we got to replace Fred was called Willie. That was my great-grandad's name as well. One of the Countesses of Oxford was married to Edward de Vere who, allegedly, wrote all of Willie Shakespeare's plays. Spooky.

SUMMER

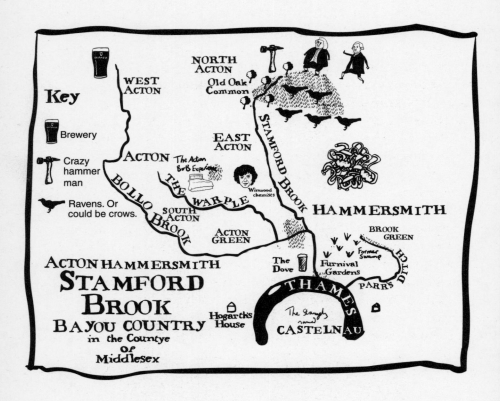

13: Acton Baby!

- **Stamford Brook – Wormwood Scrubs to Hammersmith**

Hogarth dream – confessions – Weedon and Arthur – three streams in one – Hammer Man – St Elmo's Fish Bar – Ravenscourt Park – Hammersmith Creek – 'Rule Britannia' – Hitchcock's The Birds

Dream: I was travelling around the dark cobbled streets of eighteenth-century London with the illustrator William Hogarth. 'Fancy a drink?' he said. 'I know a good bar.' I followed him through slums and winding lanes, then up some rickety stairs to an old wooden shack. Hogarth (whose face looked as though it had been drawn by himself) rapped on the door until a light came on and a tired-looking landlord came to the door. He led us through to the bar (behind which was his

244 bed and living quarters), and made us some cocktails. It was dark and sleazy inside. As we sipped our drinks, the bar started to fill up and a George-Melly-style jazz band began to play. Then Hogarth took the mike and started to sing.

ك   ك   ك

Confessional writing is big business these days. Reveal a big secret, something bad that happened to you, and people love it. I want a bit of that My Life Used To Be Shit action. Here goes.

I lived in Acton. Phew, that feels better already. It was only for three days but it's stayed with me. I'd just returned to London after a year in South America and after kipping on friends' floors for a while I just sort of ended up in Acton. It was a small B&B which seemed miles from anywhere and certainly miles from London. Now I'm going back, on a river walk. I'm very excited. I've got two books in front of me. One is *Ludgate Monthly* 1893–4, which my parents kindly bought me as a birthday present to help with my research. At the back is an advert for Mellins Food Biscuits, 'for infants and invalids'. Lots of poor portraits of men and women staring out at the camera and looking startled at the fast onrushing twentieth century.

MR. ARTHUR NELSTONE IN "JAUNTY JANE SHORE."

MR. WEEDON GROSSMITH, MR. J. D. BEVERIDGE AND MISS GLADYS HOMFREY.

And photos of two of the top comic actors of the day, Mr Weedon
Grossmith and Mr Arthur Nelstone. The other book is the *Oxford
Dictionary of London Place Names*, edited by A. S. Mills. It says:

> Stamford Brook: Hounslow. Marked thus on the Ordnance Survey
> map of 1876-77, district called after a small stream (now covered in)
> flowing into the river Thames just east of CHISWICK, recorded as
> Stamford Brooke in 1650 and named from Staunford 1274, that is
> 'stony ford' from Old English stan and ford. The original ford was
> probably where the old main road to the west crossed the stream.

Weedon: Chiswick? It gets on my wick more like.
Arthur: How's your father?
Weedon: Exactly.
Arthur: No, I really am enquiring after the health of your pater.

What we river enthusiasts now refer to as Stamford Brook is actually
three streams. The main branch, the Stamford Brook that would
have been forded over Goldhawk Road, started at Old Oak

246 Common in East Acton at what is now Wormwood Scrubs. The second Stamford Brook, which locals called the Warple, rose near present-day Acton Main Line Station. The third Stamford Brook, known sometimes as Bollo Brook, rose in what is now Park Royal. All three branches joined up around Ravenscourt Park then flowed to the Thames as the Hammersmith Creek. Life is far too short to do three walks in and around Acton so I choose the two main branches, Stamford Brook and Bollo Brook – and leave the third as just a permanent sad blue line in my *A to Z*.

I come out of the tube at East Acton, then turn left and left again up Erconwald Street, crossing over Wulfstan Street. A wiry, shaven-headed bloke with a really long neck is walking in the opposite direction on the other side of the road, brandishing a large hammer. Every time he goes past something hard he hits it. Whack. I glance briefly at Hammer Man and he stares back as if to say, 'YOU GOT A PROBLEM WITH ME SMACKING THINGS WITH THIS HAMMER, HAVE YOU, MATE?!?-EH? EH!?!' I do that looking-down thing with the eyes which says, 'Ha ha no, Hammer Man, I am thoroughly tolerant of others who like to hit metal objects with DIY tools and now I'd just like to go somewhere else quickly please', and I walk on. Taaaaaanggg!!!! I look back. Hammer Man has hit a post box. It's as if I've come face to face with a modern incarnation of Hammersmith (a Marvel Super Hero, a slightly less-than-fantastic Germanic deity and contemporary of the Viking god, Thor). He turns a corner, out of my life (and, unfortunately, probably back into someone else's), and I continue to the end of the road and come out at Wormwood Scrubs.

Wormwood Scrubs is a great name for a Dickens character. It's also a strange, wild, windswept open space. Not really a park so much as some land that the developers didn't get to build on due to some obscure sub-clause in a medieval land lease. I really like it, especially in a contrast to the manicured and designed areas that are the majority of London parks. Not that there's anything wrong with them, mind.

Weedon: Ooh the poor liberal *Guardian*-reading fence-sitting writer doesn't want to hurt the feelings of any of the park keepers.
Arthur: Mustn't upset the park keepers!

๑   ๑   ๑

The first thing I notice are what seems like hundreds of ravens, all standing in the grass facing west. Though they might be crows. A few flap off lazily as I walk through their midst, but most stand their ground. They're like the little cousins of pterodactyls. And I can't help thinking, quite unoriginally, of Hitchcock's *The Birds* – I'm glad I've got my shades on, so if they do try to peck out my eyes at least I'll have some protection. But if they really decided to try and have me they would, no bother. Why am I so on edge? Could it  be the preponderance of Germanic/Norse symbolism already – the Old English street names, the raven gods, the comic book hero Hammersmith I have just seen.

To the north is grassland, like the Serengeti, but full of sunburnt fatties slugging beer rather than herds of wildebeest, then a artificially raised high bank and the main depot for Eurostar trains, which looks down over the Scrubs like an elongated space-age castle.[1] These spaces are wider and more open than I'm used to, the sky much bigger. It helps that it's hot, the cyan sky is empty except for the billowing vapour trails of Heathrow jets. I quickly draw the geometric patterns they've created, looking for some interesting signs. i + v x w. And then there's the kites. Wormwood Scrubs is full of kites. Two of the red-torsoed lads, the indigenous creatures of the

---

[1]   Counter's Creek rises a few hundred yards to the east.

248 Scrubs, stand transfixed as their kites billow and swoop in the thermals. Further back a bandy grandad in slacks shows his grandson how to control a model aeroplane. Just behind them, nestled into the remaining clump of trees, are a couple of small dome tents. Their owners stand and sit in a line in front, two skinny boys with bare chests smoking spliffs watching the kites, the well-built girls stripped down to their power bras, sunbathing. In the distance, over to the left, past the Linford Christie Stadium and Wormword Scrubs prison, is the Post Office Tower.

Hard to believe now, but Wormwood Scrubs was once a fashionable hang-out. Except that two hundred and fifty years ago it was called Acton Wells, a trendy spa resort for the primped, cosseted, heavily made-up and bewigged denizens of west London. And their wives. Dr Johnson used to visit regularly.

The river was, like many of the others at the time, a crystal-clear brook. It's amazing that it got snarled up so quickly. Quite possibly Dr Johnston did one of his gargantuan turds, which would have dammed it pretty much straight away. The good doctor's travel book *Shitting My Way Around London's Rivers* (alas) never saw the light of day. It was a diary of his long-term project that involved him trying to clog up every river in the city, in the hope of winning a wager he'd made in a pub with Tobias Smollett:

> **Excerpt from Johnson's diary**: Today was estimable in the extreme. In the morning I breakfasted at Highbury on hog's head and chaffinch lard cakes, then a brisk three-hour walk to Acton Wells, one of the few rivulets not yet to feel the effects of my fervid stool. Flesh is good as the stool then sinks to the bottom of the stream, rather than the floater as created by too much bread in the diet.

The Stamford Brook rose just north of the park at the eastern end of
the Eurostar depot and that's where this walk begins. A track seems
to follow the course of the stream that I've jotted down in my *A to
Z*. It could be that this is a regular pilgrimage. I walk west in the
direction of some more trees in the distance – the remnants of Old
Oak Common. A church spire suggests a village and a sense that I've
only just missed some evidence of ancient London. I pass by the
school that stands where the Acton Wells pavilion used to be.

Acton. There's so many to choose from – East Acton, North Acton,
West Acton, Bloody Acton. I cross over the huge Western Avenue,
constant traffic, the sweet smell of car fumes and impeccable Tudor
styling on the houses. I start counting the amount of cars with only
one person (90 per cent) then write an imaginary letter to a newspaper but that's too melodramatic so instead I send it to my old penpal
Denis, over in France. '*Cher Denis, il y a beaucoup des autos.
Incidentement, merci pour le lettre à Nathalie.*' (When I was thirteen
I'd asked him to write me a letter to the local small-town French
beauty I'd fallen in love with on my first exchange visit. He was too
enthusiastic, turning it into a piece of porn literature.

A police van, with siren blaring out, roars past. A Muslim woman
with long black robes and just a tiny slit for her eyes goes by with a
couple of kids. I'm staring at my *A to Z* with the river drawn in and
suddenly a man appears asking if I need help. 'No thanks, I'm fine.'
'Are you sure?' he asks rather quizzically. 'No, I'm OK.'

Cross over and down Askew Road and I can see the river valley,
first on my left and then on the right. Past Adam's café, a high-class
couscous joint and St Elmo's Fish Bar. St Elmo's Fish Bar could
have been a low-budget British version of the famous American
movie of the eighties. Phil Daniels would have been in it, as well as
Patsy Kensit and William Roach, though it would more likely have
been a soap opera.

Ravenscourt Park is full of activity. Kids sitting on benches
blathering on their mobiles, guys chatting up schoolgirls, rugger

types huffing and puffing on the basketball court, posh kids running around the smart play area. A load of hippies are sitting around a pollarded tree, meditating, playing guitar and being beardy. I sit down near them and draw a 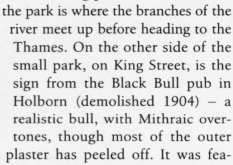 sketch. The big pond in the middle of the park is where the branches of the river meet up before heading to the Thames. On the other side of the small park, on King Street, is the sign from the Black Bull pub in Holborn (demolished 1904) – a realistic bull, with Mithraic overtones, though most of the outer plaster has peeled off. It was featured in *Martin Chuzzlewit* and bought by William Bull, the local MP, who also gave the park to the people of Hammersmith and wrote articles about local streams for the parish magazine of St Mary's Stamford Brook.

I'm hungry so walk down to Hammersmith Station to buy some sushi and noodles. The station is like a beating heart. Every couple of minutes or so, a huge tide of people come spurting out of the entrance. Then other travellers move in the opposite direction. People are being pumped out over towards King Street, and Shepherds Bush Road. I then go past the Hammersmith and City line tube to Paddenswick Road, where a branch of the brook called Parr's Ditch snaked around east Hammersmith towards the Thames.

Next to King Street. What used to be Hampshire Hog pub

(it appears on an 1830s map of Hammersmith) is now called the Hampshire and has had a lick of paint, and a trendy new bar installed (well, they – the dunderheaded modernist designers – think it's trendy) and some bland new tables and they've changed 150 years of history. For what? A couple more affluent punters and some wine bar girls? It's sad. There should be a Pubs Czar to deal with all this shit.

This bit of Hammersmith is great, a mix of restaurants and cafés, little second-hand places and crap pubs. And an art deco cinema that used to be called the Flea Pit but is now like a glistening thirties neon marshmallow. I headed down Nigel Playfair Avenue where Hammersmith Creek – the name of the lower reaches of Stamford Brook – was culverted in the thirties in order to create land to build the Town Hall. The building's sixties add-ons are desolate concrete post-modern stuff with walkways. The coat of arms is a castle or crown with two hammers. Hammer Smith? It's a bit literal. Of course they might not be hammers, but dowsing rods.

And then to the beautiful A4, which splits Hammersmith in two, and quickly under the subway, where there's loads of standing water, to Furnival Gardens, where the creek met the Thames. The traffic sound is like the sea bashing against high cliffs. Looking back I see an old building with Friends Meeting House written on top. It would be nice to think I could go in there and find all my lost mates. I stand out in the now sheeting rain with my sushi and noodles and stare out at the river. In the distance is Hammersmith Bridge and before that the big houseboat community. Some of my noodles get caught in the wind and fly off into the Thames. I look over the river wall and watch them hit the low-tide mud down below, bizarrely forming a unique noodle-based river map in the sludge. Then I look around and see the creek, or the remains of it – a big arch, the size of a canal tunnel, with shut iron sluice gates and a sludgy channel down to the Thames. There it is. I feel like I'd just found Tutankhamun's remains. No, not on the river but in a

252 pyramid. Yeah, OK, so they're in a museum. I mean finding them. I know I wasn't born then. Look, fuck off will you.

I'm very excited. This is a magic bit of London. I am floating, this has made it all worthwhile – the crap walk, in fact the whole project. Magic. A bloke jogs past space-style, on his toes, taking huge Juantorena-style strides. Magic. But anyway, here we are in the twenty-first century with our clean water and clear air and Hammersmith Creek looks like slimy sludge. What would it have looked like 100 years ago? My romantic view of Hammersmith's past takes a bit of a knock. I always imagine the past in colour, but

now it becomes black and white. I have a spring in my step. Sometime I wish I lived by the Thames again.

The Jellied-Eel-Art Beardy Socialist William Morris also lived by the river in Hammersmith. He pegged it in his front sitting room there, exhausted after a life making hand-printed wallpaper for his mates ('Oh, another home-made card, William, how, er, *lovely*!').

There's only one thing left to do. I repair to the Dove, the nearby seventeenth-century public house, with the smallest snug bar in Britain (4 ft 2 in by 7 ft 10 in), where Charles II shagged Nell Gwyn and where Hemingway used to get smashed. It is, however, most famous for being the place where 'Rule Britannia' was composed by the, er, composer James Thomson. Britannia rules the waves. But what kind of waves? Brain waves? I go in and sample a few pints of ESB, Fuller's fine and hallucinogenic strong ale, and my own brain waves start to scramble nicely.

I then tried to compose my own tune, a new national anthem, along the lines of the old Grace Jones track: 'Slave to the Rhythm'. Britons are Slaves to the Rhythm.

Slaves to the rhythm
Hurrah for the Brits!
Obsessed with the Germans
And page three girls' tits
Slaves to the rhythm
Britons always always always shall be
Slaves to the rhythm.

Film Idea: Alfred Hitchcock's *The Byrds*

At a magic well in London bathers are being terrorised by flying floppy-haired country rockers. Dr Johnson defeats them by cleverly laying little packets of pure heroin for them to find and soon they are all addicts. Everyone retires to St Elmo's fish shop to celebrate.

London Stories 11: How to Fuck Your Knees Before You're Fifty

As Dr Johnson would have said had he a decent pair of training shoes, was about four stone lighter and the streets of the eighteenth-century city hadn't been completely covered in horse shit, there is no better way to see London than while jogging. In fact, whenever I move to a new part of the city I always put on my smelly old trainers and go exploring the housing estates, terrace-lined streets and little scrubby parks. I've jogged in more bits of London in the thirteen years that I've been here than I've had hot dinners at expensive Italian restaurants. And although I've occasionally stepped in equine manure (on Wimbledon Common, while 'checking the form' of a runner in front of me), the experience has mostly been a positive one. I'm healthy and my knees and ankles are only a little bit fucked.

Granted, not all my runs have been jogs as such – running for a bus, or because you're late for an interview, or because the big bloke in the pub didn't like the way you said, 'Your lips were made for kissing, angel features,' (to his girlfriend), doesn't really count.

One of the great things about jogging is watching other people. First there's the normal jogger like you or me, with tense, red faces screwed up with effort, wobbly and knock kneed, their dough-like buttocks seeping over the top of maroon tracksuit bottoms. And then come the proper runners, who glide past you gracefully with barely a sound, slim-hipped and spare, the fucking bastards. And why is it that attractive people of the opposite sex only ever see you right at the end of a long run. You want to say to them, 'Hey, I've just done ten miles!' And then, of course, you start sprinting. It's a reflex action. Ridiculous, but you just can't help yourself. Knees up, shoulders back. But how many women, when asked about what attracts them in a man, would reply, 'Someone who runs on his toes with his knees up.'

The occasional straight-backed chap will shout 'MORNING!' very vigorously as if he's wearing a bowler hat and swinging a golfing umbrella under his arm. And then there's the thick-necked centre-threequarters from a local rugby club, blasting through fifty or so short interval training sprints with an expression of pure agony on his face as he atttempts to beat his

the attractive ones, laugh at you or, as was the case with me in south London, the problem of overtiredness due to the fact that you keep getting lost in the parks and commons. 'Darling,' you say in your best purringly seductive voice, 'wouldn't it be nice if we moved to a bigger house? And here's a map of potential jogging routes, er, I mean properties.' Another problem is that when I'm jogging, pubs often look heart-rendingly beautiful and I have often been tempted to stop my run there and then. OK I have stopped it there and then. But not very often. It was raining. What?

Jogging may completely shag your knees and back over the long term, make you feel like a twat as you heave and puff your way past attractive sensible people, pollute your lungs from all the traffic fumes as well as send excess saliva to the brain, where it builds up in a big wedge, blocking out any sensible thinking patterns (been proved, honest). But it's a glorious way to travel if you like looking at fat people's arses.

personal best (before heading off to the gym, to work a bit more on that neck). They're usually too tired to say anything other than 'Bleeuaargh!' But I never talk back, preferring instead to adopt a feeling of Zen-like calm while trying to make it look easy. The most imperceptible of nods usually is enough.

A downside is that there's only so long you can run in one particular area. Then, if you're an addict, you have to move on. It might be boredom, because the pollution is getting to you, or because all the locals, especially

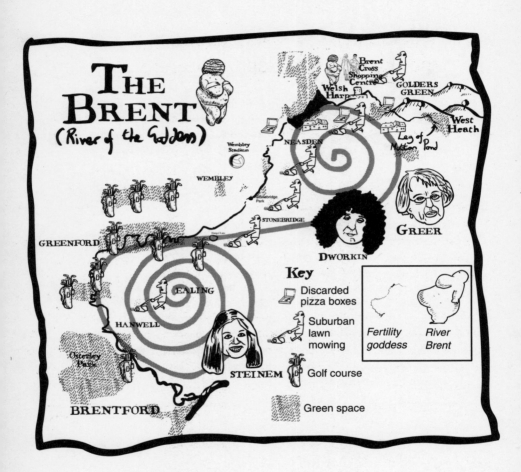

14. The Suburban River Goddess at the Brent Cross Shopping Centre

• The Brent – Hampstead to Brentford

*The Sweeney – Goddess – ha ha it's the riverman – the Hollybush
– Ada Maltz – Hendon – Brent Cross Shopping Centre – chocolate –
Welsh Harp – Hanger Lane – golf is evil*

The Brent. Brent. What is it about that name? Perhaps something clapped out from the seventies, like a character from *The Sweeney*. Bent coppers. Rent books. Say it slowly over and over again for maximum effect. Brent. Brent. Brent. B...r...e...n...t. And, believe it or not, 'Brent' is not a mockney villain in some shit new Britflick crime caper or a crappy British Leyland family car (i.e. the Austin Brent). It turns out the Brent is a holy river – the pre-Celtic name comes from *brigantia*, meaning holy, or high, water. Its ultimate source is the Goddess Bridgit. It's like the Ganges, except it runs through Neasden and has a load of golf courses on its route. Something in my head – a half-forgotten lyric by some post-punk feminist band, perhaps, or clever brainwashing by Miss Rylands, my attractive rad fem English teacher from the late seventies – tells me I must walk the goddess's river.

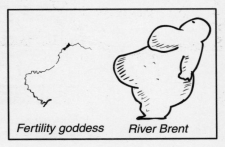

Fertility goddess   River Brent

258   Most of the Brent is still on the surface, which immediately makes it less interesting (though this sits a bit uneasily with my desire to see some of the rivers unearthed). I'd been avoiding the river because a) it seems really long and b) goes through parts of London I hate – miles and miles of semi-detached houses full of people on Prozac with *Haywain* prints on the wall and an Astra in the driveway. But I shouldn't let my prejudices get in the way of some nice exercise.

I mentioned my rivers project to a friend. 'Is there a deeper meaning?' she asked. 'What do you mean?'

'Your unconscious?'

'Er, dunno.'

'So I suppose you've heard about the hard-core feminist group who walk the lost rivers of London?' My eyes did that cartoon thing and leapt out on stalks. 'Eh? You're having a laugh.'

'No, really,' she said, 'a friend of mine, Mad Maureen, has been out with them. They see the rivers as being symbolic of female sexuality. They were buried by the Victorians, you see. And the Victorians repressed female sexuality.'

This was it. My grail. My path was to find the hard-core feminist river walking group. At last, my life had meaning. I could meet them, have a rant about how feminist teachers and writers were to

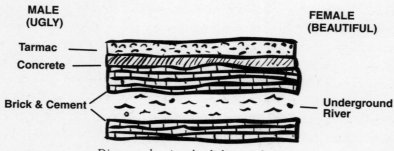

Diagram showing the dichotomy between
vibrant earth juices and man-made materials

THE ADVENTURES OF
THE HARDCORE
FEMINIST
RIVER *
WALKERS

INCLUDING SCENES OF NON-PHALLOCENTRIC DOWSING!

BETTY

ANDREA

GERMAINE

GLORIA

KATE

SUSAN

blame for me not getting shagged when I was a teenager, then I'd be sorted. I'd be able to walk away. So how can I get in touch with them? Er, you can't. They're quite secret. And I don't think they like blokes.

What a brilliant notion. Loads of feminists tramping around London knocking holes into the concrete and trying to free the rivers. Of course, finding them might prove difficult. But the search would be the thing. So ... (strokes beard, Blofeld style, and arches eyebrows) the Hardcore London Feminist River Walkers were out there somewhere, walking over silent forgotten streams just like me. Perhaps I'd walked past them once or twice and not noticed. Those girls in Hackney Wick. The school kids on the Tyburn. Their motivation may have been different (men are evil, free the rivers), but the their aim was the same as mine – to understand London, sex, history, politics and magic while getting out and about in the fresh air and having a beer or two. This was like the race for the South Pole, with the Hardcore London Feminist River Walkers as Roald Amundsen and me as Scott and Captain Oates.

Actually, I was a feminist once. This East Midlands feminism (we were too far north for me to claim it as '*fen*inism') was a result of

a) Being influenced by young, attractive feminist teachers. 'So this is how the world works,' I thought. It tied in with what many of the bands I was into at the time (late seventies/early eighties) were saying. Jon King, lead singer of Gang of Four, had explained in the *NME* that he wore big baggy shirts because they were androgynous and therefore non-sexist.

b) A strategy for getting shags. Sensitive to feelings. I hear what you're saying, baby. It was totally misguided. At sixteen I'd take a girl's bra off at a party then put it back on again because I respected her feelings and wanted to empower her. With girls I really fancied I'd concentrated on what they had to say but then rather than falling at my feet they'd run off with older blokes with flash cars. At university in the mid eighties studying English and film, feminist critiques like the seminal *Feminism and the Western: How Guns Are Evil Because They're Phallic, Not Because They Kill People* were all the rage. I also happened to be in a band called Simone de Beauvoir. Me (a student twat with a rubbish flat-top haircut) on guitar, a philosophy undergraduate with a quiff on bongoes and a big-lipped girl called Joolz singing. Simone de Beauvoir folded after one session when we realised we were not only shit but pretentious too.

I can laugh at it all. It hasn't served me too badly. Like all the men in my family, I'm a dreamer. All my big relationships have

been with women who are strong, clever and opinionated. And 261
I've learned not to put bras back on.

The Brent's source is on Hampstead Heath, further west from where
the Fleet and Westbourne rise. Once again I come out of Hampstead
tube dressed in 8th Army gear topped off with a T-shirt advertising
Venezuelan beer. 'Ha ha, it's the river man!' laugh the local shop-
keepers and point at me. 'Der – I'm lost already. Have you seen a river
ha ha ha ha?' Bouncing off the huge chest of a wealthy Hampsteadite
walking her dog, like a pinball, I cross over the main road and go up
Holly Hill, past the famous Hollybush pub on the right.

> *Come come come and shout loudly*
> *in a music hall cockney accent*
> *down at the old Hollybush*
> *tra la la la la.*
>
> *Chase around the room*
> *Holding your lapels*
> *And grinning like*
> *A synchronized swimmer*
> *down at the old Hollybush*
> *tra la la la la.*
>
> *Ooh look*
> *Here comes the First World War*
> *Let's wave our little flags*
> *And wade into storms of machine gun fire*
> *In the name of King and Country*
> *Tra la. Because we're told to!*
> *down at the old Hollybush*
> *tra la.*

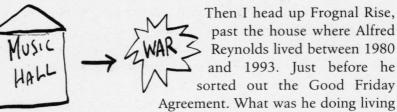

Then I head up Frognal Rise, past the house where Alfred Reynolds lived between 1980 and 1993. Just before he sorted out the Good Friday Agreement. What was he doing living in Hampstead when he was supposed to be Prime Minister of Ireland? Maybe running a little cafe somewhere to earn extra dosh. From teashop to Taoiseach.

No, please, don't put the book down. I agree, that was terrible. It won't happen again. Of course, that was Albert Reynolds. Alfred Reynolds was a Hungarian poet.

Things they said:

Alfred: Jesus remains a living figure reminding us of our humanity – the kingdom of Heaven which is within us.
Albert: If we were to have peace and stability on the island, the North of Ireland domestic market would go up by 100 per cent. The South of Ireland market – domestic market – would go up by 50 per cent. We could have a sharing of the overheads as to how to run the country and save us all money. How much money are we paying, as Irish taxpayers, to try and sustain the security position that we have? We're actually paying four times more than the British taxpayers.

There are some big houses here, five storeys – one each for parents, kids, nannies, agents and mistresses. Narrow gothic windows. Does Glenda Jackson live down here? I remember her in *The Music Lovers* and *Women in Love* and that thing with George Segal. I used to fancy her, mainly because I was on a one-man (boy) crusade to wangle staying up late to see some European film with a bit of nipple and Glenda never failed me. She was interesting looking rather than straightforwardly pretty. Whenever I've mentioned to people that I think early period Glenda was a sex goddess, they don't understand. In fact, they laugh. They just didn't watch the right films. I think Julie Christie lived round here as well. She was completely gorgeous but inaccessible. You imagined Glenda being a sixth former who you'd try and get a snog out of when you were thirteen.

Hampstead is the centre of the so-called Chattering Classes who annoy the *Daily Mail*. Maybe the *Daily Mail* would rather nobody talked about any ideas. At Heath Road – named after Ted Heath, in fact the whole of Hampstead Heath is named after him, in gratitude for his defeating Labour in the 1970 election – I take a left then wander down a bit until I find the path up east to Jack Straw's Castle, which is a high point on the Heath and nothing at all to do with a heavily guarded compound owned by the right-wing Labour politician. It's a medieval term given to a high point from which you could see a long way. There's one in Highbury as well where the peasants of the Revolt met up before being double-crossed and disembowelled by the establishment. Should'a done those negotiation skills evening classes.

I come to a clearing and a little dried-up brook. Forest sounds – birds, humming, different squeaks and whistles. This is the start of the Brent, and I think it's called Mutton Brook at this point, metamorphosing into the more goddess-friendly Silk Stream a mile or two down. Further on there's thick brown water. Jumping from one bank to the other, I try to find a decent path, ducking and weaving through undergrowth and lots of holly. Things are rustling in the undergrowth, something running. Wild boar? Wildcats? Faeries? I get caught in a holly bush then push through some more bushes until the scene opens out and becomes quite marshy. I notice a piece of multicoloured rag hanging from a branch of the holly bush.

ð ð ð

Blessing of the Brat Bríde: *During the day before Imbolc the woman of the house or women of the grove should take a small piece of cloth* *(larger if it is for the entire grove) and lay it on a bush outside. During the night, as the goddess roams to bless the houses of her followers, she will pass by, touching and blessing the cloth. Collect the cloth in the morning and tear it into small pieces. These pieces of cloth, individually called a Brat Bríde (BRAHT BREEJ), should be distributed among the children and females of the household. The Brat Bríde will give them protection throughout the year wherever they go. These pieces of cloth may be sewn into the clothes or jackets of the children to ensure that it won't be lost.*[1]

CLOTH

ə   ə   ə

Bushes. I don't know if it's significant but I went to an exhibition by an artist called Tracey Bush, who has created a limited-edition handmade book called *The Lost Rivers of London*, as well as doing lots of other idiosyncratic river-related projects, poring over old maps as inspiration for her illustrations. Her rivers are narrow bumps on home-made paper which look like pale veins and arteries. This exhibition – of limited-edition litmus paper books that had been dipped in Thames water then sealed in little polythene bags – was in Clerkenwell. I had a browse around the little gallery, looking at Tracey's litmus books, then at some other stuff that was being exhibited – a load of models with toy snakes and lizards all stuck together. The model artist, a middle-aged beardy bloke, was holding court, explaining his work to an admiring crowd. I nabbed a glass of wine and ducked into a corner, where I got stuck in conversation with a nice and loquacious old duffer who was writing a history book about London and said he carried a can of hairspray around with him to ward off muggers.

---

[1]   from 'Brigit – Behind the Veil'
(http://www.msen.com/~robh/slg/deities/bridol.html)

'You don't know who I am, do you?' he kept saying. It's true, I didn't. Possibly Sir Roy Strong, or Brian Sewell. He took out his can of hairspray to show me. It was the sort my mum used to use in the early eighties.[2]

ॐ   ॐ   ॐ

It's good to be out in the wild. Of course, the shops of Hampstead High Street are only half a mile away. It's more a state of mind. Nature reminds me of my grandmother. She wasn't religious in the traditional sense of kneeling down in a tall old building before a man in a dress then taking a piece of rice paper in her mouth then drinking wine and pretending it was the blood of an omniscient deity's son. Her religion was nature based. In fact, she believed in Mother Nature. The bounty of the goddess was everywhere in her small but beautiful garden. Don't get me wrong, she wasn't some kind of Edwardian hippy chick – she believed in hunting, hanging and flogging. She also believed that the people who put those hard plastic wrappings over the top of sauce bottles should 'have their heads cut off'. But to see her scrabbling about outside, connecting with her plants – this old country girl kneeling before her goddess – was to see her at one with her universe. For Mother Nature was in everything – the tiny shoots, the beautiful flowers, the birds in the branches, her grandchildren as they told each other to 'fuck off' then kicked a ball through her greenhouse. After she died we scattered her ashes on her garden so she could continue her good work.

---

2   Scene: Night. An old man is walking down a dark street. Two muggers are lying in wait. As he approaches, they jump out, taking exaggerated kung-fu poses. The old man calmly takes out a can of hairspray and lets it off in their faces.

Mugger 1: Owwwwwwww. Aieeeeeee.
Mugger 2: Hey, my hair suddenly feels full yet bouncy.
Mugger 1: But it's quite a natural look...

Old man runs off, leaving the muggers stroking each other's hair.

I look up and the sun does that dapply thing behind trees like on pop videos. Someone should be singing about a skinny girl they used to know. In front of me is Leg of Mutton Pond, with sweet wrappers and paper tissue scattered around on the sandy paths. I walk through to Golders Hill park and the next section of ponds. There are benches next to the track inscribed with names of dead people.

'In memory of Ettie Picard, who loved benches and parks.'

'Cyril Horrocks, who loved this park.'

(Maybe Cyril's relatives phoned up the bench makers and said 'he really loved the Sparks' and they misheard.)

'Ada Maltz 1921–1990 who spent many a happy summer's day in this park with her family.'

I sit down on Ada's bench and try to imagine her in the park with her family. Fifty years ago, maybe, hanging around here with her kids. She'd have been thirty-six, my age, in 1957. Not that long ago. That generation had lived though the war, had cool fashions, a changing optimistic world, consensus politics and free jazz. What was Harold Macmillan's famous phrase? 'I say – let's cook up some noise, Daddio!'

Will I have my name on a bench one day? Yes, maybe a bench in an old boozer. I wouldn't mind that: 'Tim Bradford 1965 –2095, who spent many a happy evening in this pub with his beer and his wrongheaded theories.'

I've got a present from Ada, or rather her bench – some chewing gum is stuck to my leg. Down below is the water garden. On one side of a bridge is a dammed still pond with a light dusting of algae, below it are waterfalls with lush foliage, lilies and other water plants. The river comes cascading down then, at the edge of the pond, trickles down between two iron grilles and flows under the road – then right underneath a big detached Tudorbethan house. I ring the doorbell. No answer. Ring again. Then I hear movement in the garage and pop my head round. A skinny bloke with a moustache is moving stuff around.

'Hi there, I was wandering if there's a way through your house to follow the underground river?'

'You what?' He's a gruff Geordie.

'Is there a way through here? A river flows right underneath.'

'What are you talking about?'

'An underground river.'

'A river?'

'It flows underground, yes.' I'm jabbing the *A to Z* now as if that will give my request some legitimacy.

'Listen, mate, I don't know the first thing you're on about – I had enough trouble finding this place myself. Sorry.' And he continues rummaging.

A river guardian? One of Bridgit's warriors? A garage box thief? Or a northern river enthusiast who doesn't want to share his research?

These roads have smart houses, semis, mock Tudor beams, shiny cars, nice lawns, a sense of the futility of existence. The melancholy of the suburbs. People doing gardens. Hedge trimming. Washing their cars. Swigging gin straight from the bottle through a funnel. Waiting to die.

Over Finchley Road it's suddenly very quiet. I can see the river valley to the left, but there's no way through. When they built these housing estates and streets why didn't they think that people would want to walk the river's route? If you didn't have an *A to Z* I'd say it would take years to get out of these parts of London, this semi-world. No shops. No pubs. Silence broken only by a lawnmower.

Where is the goddess taking me?

London is in conflict between the new urban chic of city living and the continued suburbanization along American lines[3] – out-of-town neoclassical shopping centres with fake restaurants from around the world, big car parks, big roads, nice detached houses

---

3   Plus the small minority who'd like to trash it all and turn it into a big urban park.

with big gardens, fat arses, lots of telly. Yet, are the suburbs all bad? A lot of English post-war culture has been created by suburbanites stranded in the cultural crossfire. David Bowie. Er, *The Good Life. Terry and June*. The feeling I get in the suburbs is the same feeling I get when walking around large department stores or shopping centres. My breathing gets shallow and I start to feel trapped. I used to be dragged around big shops in Bradford and Leeds by my mother and grandmother. The shops all smelt of groomed, perfumed women. Women's voices. Women shopping. My shoulders would slump and my feet would drag.

A postman is jumping over fences to save time. Posties have changed. Now they're all skinheads in surf shorts. Even dogs are scared of them. In the Penny Black pub in Farringdon I once saw a postie set fire to an ash tray then start shouting 'Har haaarrrrrr!' Maybe it's all part of the rebranding as Consignia. The letters might not arrive on time but those lads are hard as nails. And they know where everyone lives.

The gardens are looking more and more overgrown. A faded Homer Simpson comedy 'D'oh!' towel hangs in an upstairs window. Car after car streams past in a never-ending flow. I stand there and wonder how to view London as a whole. The only place you can do it is at the Thames in the centre of town. Most of the time, you can't get your head around London. Try too hard and you'll burn out your brain cells, which probably feels like heading a fifties leather laced-up football that's been left out in the rain.

Towards Hendon I turn down a footpath into Clitterhouse Recreation Ground, home of Hendon Football Club. Although, Clitterhouse sounds like an eighteenth-century bordello, I believe it must be connected in some way to the 1938 film *The Amazing Dr Clitterhouse*, starring Edward G. Robinson and Humphrey Bogart. I can smell the pungent fragrance of softly flowing shit. The river must be nearby. And there it is. Stagnant at first, with brick sides, then slow moving and overgrown.

The park is like a snippet of bright open moorland. A whitish butterfly flits near my head. I find some treasure, a slightly burnt offering – some pieces of paper with scrawled writing. Is it a secret parchment of the Feminist Rivers, maybe *The Essence of Rivers* by Andrea Dworkin? No, it's a child's history essay. A turquoise rope hangs over the river from a nearby branch and in the water underneath it is a motor scooter and two shopping trolleys, with another rusted moped further up. Then a bit of a car. Like me, these unconnected, unwanted transportation items seem somehow drawn to the flow of water. Two teenagers sit up on a bench at the edge of the park, no shirts, white baseball caps.

I *must* have a go on the rope. I do a concealed run and leap onto it, then sort of dangle, arms and shoulders hurting because I haven't done this for years, then swing back and try again. I do a proper run and throw myself out towards the rope. I still don't make the other side. My legs are pumping furiously like a cartoon character running in mid-air. It's a lot harder on the arms and shoulders than I remember. I'm twenty-six years out of practise. Someone has spray-painted on the opposite bank 'This Swing belongs to J King'. Jon King of the Gang of Four? Or Billie-Jean King?

One of the kids sees me and turns to his mate. They both stare. I stagger past, shorts flapping, holding my shoulder and trying to look dignified. It could be dislocated.

There's graffiti in red and white everywhere – on the fence and all over the path. Three shopping trolleys lie in a row, half submerged. Maybe the Hardcore London Feminist River Walkers did it, blocking up the river with objects that supposedly represent femininity in the capitalist world – shopping, domesticity – trolleys are feminine objects, spaces in which things are put. Or it could just have been twattish pissed-up blokes. What else? A kid's bike. A flat football. Empty Coke bottles. Fag packets. Cans. Smelly. The river bends then goes around the back of the houses through a pipe and disappears.

270   I'm at the North Circular, where the traffic flows like a huge river and is just as difficult to cross. On the other side of the road are the enormous shells of sixties buildings, like schoolrooms but much bigger, with blue panels, lots of glass and a chessboard effect at one end. It could be something in a war zone. Everything is boarded up at ground level and covered in graffiti. Once these were new and beautiful modernist constructions, and now they're rotting away. I try to picture the day they were opened. A few cars would be pootling along the North Circular, everything would be slightly shiny. People would be smiling. God, sometimes the sixties seem further away than the nineteenth century.

There doesn't seem to be anywhere to cross the road. An old faded sixties sign points pedestrians to a crossing area, but there is no longer a way across. Maybe it's from a time before the North Circular was built, when this was just a medieval sandy track. Two hundred yards away I can see a footbridge to the left. But busy watching the sea of traffic, I bang my shin on some jutting concrete – blood trickles down my leg. Across the bridge I pass a big and completely empty car park, with weeds growing though it. To the left is a very sad-looking funfair with merry-go-round and bouncy castle. There's a solitary shopping trolley, which means that the river can't be far away. Blue and yellow pennants[4] flap in the light breeze along the path, leading me onwards. And there, with the Brent flowing in front like a moat, is the Temple of the Goddess.

The Brent Cross Shopping Centre was built in 1980. Inside it sounds as if we are underwater, with a constant hum or murmur of women's voices and the shrieks of kids. There are all the usual big shops – clothes, electrical goods, music, Marks and Sparks, computers, a food hall at the top. People are pushing kids around in

---

[4]   Maybe one day, when we're all sick of nationalism, shopping centres will be bigger and more popular than countries.

little yellow trolleys shaped like cars, with a steering wheel so the child can pretend it's tearing around London on the North Circular, swearing just like Mummy and Daddy.

Bright, advertising voice: This summer will see a wealth of new and exciting retail changes at the centre. We are pleased to welcome Benetton, who have recently opened their new store in the West Mall (opposite Suits You), and look forward to the arrival of River Island and an H&M ladieswear, who will be opening shortly on the lower ground floor. Another new store to the centre is the Gadgetshop, who will be opening their doors later on this month. For those of you Next-lovers you'll be pleased to hear that they are soon to move to a bigger store which will be located on two floors. The new store should open its doors during September. In addition to the exciting retail changes at Brent Cross, we are also pleased to welcome Costa Coffee and BB's Muffins to the wide range of restaurants and coffee bars at the centre. So if you're in urgent need of retail therapy (*laughs falsely*) or just fancy a coffee and a chat – Brent Cross has it all.

That was a quote, by the way.

ॐ ॐ ॐ

Imbolc Feast: On the eve of Imbolc a family or community feast should be held. When all is prepared and the table is set the persons who were involved in the making of the Brídeog should go outside and retrieve her. The doll should be placed on the outside of the building next to the open door. The men should get on their knees before the doll (the traditional gesture of respect for the Brídeog) and shout into the house, 'Go on your knees, open your eyes, and admit Brigit!' The celebrants inside should answer, 'Welcome! Welcome! Welcome to the holy woman!' The

TABLE

272 *Brídeog should then be carried into the house and leaned against a leg of the feasting table. Begin the feast with a prayer of thanks.*

ঽ   ঽ   ঽ

I sit and watch the people go by. It feels like an undersea world of women. Happy, confident, heavily made-up women of all ages, shapes and sizes (including the largest concentration of leopardskin print leggings in Northern Europe) walk purposefully around, some pulling along tired-eyed men, but most on their own or in pairs. I guess it's women who hold capitalism together, keep economies ticking over with their 'If somebody's gone to the trouble of making a new thing I should go to the trouble of buying it' kind of attitude. If it was up to blokes, stuck in their sheds with their hobbies and saying things like 'Why do we *need* that, darling?' the wheels would soon come off the free market juggernaut.

I decide to count the first hundred passers-by. It's four women to every bloke – the same as Nottingham, Muswell Hill or the Ritzy Bar Niteclub in Soho (sorry, members only). The blokes here all look a bit knackered and furtive. As if they don't really belong. Then, looking at a plan of the centre, I notice it bears a striking similarity to the female symbol of a circle with a cross.

I try the lunch of kings. Burger King. It seems strangely, exotically male in the context of the Brent Cross Shopping Centre. When it's my turn to order I hesitate and someone jumps in front of me. Normally I'd turn round and tell them to sling it but I'm strangely nervous. I don't know what to do. What is all this stuff? I finally order a double cheeseburger. 'Is that a meal?' asks the girl in the orange uniform. 'How do you mean? What else is it going to be?'

'Well, in a meal you get a drink and fries as well.'

'No, just a burger.'

'So just a sandwich. The meal is better value'.

'No thanks.' I can see everyone in the restaurant pointing at me and silently laughing. 'He didn't order chi-ips. He didn't order chi-ips!!'

The girl rolls her eyes and takes the order. She then moves my tray   **273**
to the side so the next customer can get in. Phew. Done it.

I sit at a little dark grey table at a little red plastic seat and inspect
my burger. It's tiny. I'd always imagined cheeseburgers to be huge. I
bite into it and it's got a thin metallic taste. In fact, most of the taste
comes from the pickle. The meat is grey and looks like churned-up
windpipe. I suddenly imagine myself sucking on the entrails of rotting
farmyard animals. A burger is the crappy bits of cows (or bulls, whatever) put into a special black-hole machine that makes it incredibly
dense then spews it out in a burger shape. How to save the planet?
Ban meat eating, cars, cigarettes and guns, all fine American products.
Can't be doing with saving the planet. When it's completely fucked
we'll bugger off to space stations with reg-
ulated atmospheres.

On the floor is a little free Burger King
toy that some kid has discarded. Next
door in the toy shop I marvel at how far
apart Action Man and Barbie have come.
When I was a kid their physiques were
comparable. Neither had any nuts, Barbie
had little tits and AM had a crew cut. He
was the universal fighter who knows no
fear, you needn't worry 'cos Action Man is
here. Now AM is a steroid muscleball
who probably assassinates anti-globalism

*Action Man and Barbie in the
1960s (a gentler age)*

protestors and Barbie has the equivalent
of 44GG breasts. She is all-powerful. Is
she the river goddess? I walk around for a
while trying to find the Hardcore London
Feminist River Walkers. There is a group
of young girls hanging out in Benetton. I
try to observe them without coming
across as an obvious stalker. In Marks and

*Action Man and Barbie in the crazy
21st century*

274   Spencer a couple of well-built women are buying bras. Is that
Germaine Greer? And Naomi Wolff buying knickers! OK, maybe not.

But the atmosphere is catching. I buy some underwear in Marks
and Spencer, then wander around in a daze until I find Godiva's
chocolate shop, where I stare at the soft mounds of milk and sugar
confectionary. I buy a small box for my wife, then the pretty
Frenchwoman behind the counter asks if there's anything else. And
I never buy chocolate for myself. I might eat it if someone leaves it
lying around but it's not really my *thing*. However, I find myself
pointing at the largest, whitest, creamiest-looking lump of choco-
goo in the shop and grunt shyly, 'That one. Please.' Just one. She
wraps it up lovingly in a little bag and I walk out of the Brent Cross
Shopping Centre, slowly *un*wrapping it. As I pass the crowds I start
to nibble. It tastes like it comes from a country dairy where the
cows are raised on magic sugar grass. Past a sad playground, up
over a concrete barrier then through a path on a little island of
gorse and over another footbridge, and I'm still breaking off tiny
shards of chocolate and cocoa mulch.

As I swallow the last bits I look around and see that I'm trapped,
surrounded by cars. Where do pedestrians go? The infernal combus-
tion engine still lords it over us. All of this was open fields not that
long ago. I'm not saying it would have been better, in many ways it
might have been worse, boring land, possibly hard to farm. At least
now you can drive round and round this big roundabout – Staples
Corner (the Staples Bedding factory used to be nearby) – going
yaaaaay while listening to crap CDs or Talk Radio, with the air
conditioning on. Now that's what I call progress.

I forgot the river. But now I can see it again. Then it goes underneath the road near a sign for M1 and the North. There's a little
triangle of countryside with three trees and a bit of sloping bank:
goddess pubic hair. There are roads on three sides and a big fuckoff
road going through the middle on stilts. That's a neat scale model
of what England will be like in fifty years time.

Another sign says 'No Pedestrians no stopping'. That's a shame. I was thinking of walking up the M1 to see my mum. There are garages underneath the railway arches. Cars, bits of engine, tyres, a clutch place. Two hours ago I was in the Hampstead countryside. Now I'm in the centre of the urban dream. I seem to have sped forward in time. Concrete and cars, noise, fumes, and hardly any of that horrible nature stuff. I feel disorientated, so try to concentrate on where I should be going. I head towards a North Circular Wembley sign, up a footbridge onto a web of smaller footbridges, a footbridge spaghetti junction. An Indian woman in a sari leans against the side of one of the footbridges and stares out as if sightseeing.

On the other side of Staples Corner the North Circular still has a bit of that sixties optimism about it, with little businesses and light industrial units at the side of the road. The traffic is speeding up now. I feel kind of light headed. Then – as if by magic! – there's a little path off to the right and I'm in parkland. Very quickly the sound of traffic recedes as I walk along a track towards the Brent, or Welsh Harp, reservoir. Wooded slopes, a spire in the distance, butterflies in wild grasses, the sound of insects. And Wembley Stadium a few miles away, the twin towers gleaming white in the sun. Fields and traffic, good and evil, light and dark, beauty and the beast (although Beast was beautiful inside and Beauty only fell in love with him to help her father out financially). The Welsh Harp reservoir nearby is named after the Welsh Harp pub which I think got knocked down when the M1 was built. There's a derelict building up to the left, completely covered in graffiti – in front, there's a pile of ashes where someone has recently had a fire.

ॐ   ॐ   ॐ

Bride's Bed: *As the evening of the Imbolc feast winds down the women of the household or grove should gather up the last of the straw and fashion an oblong basket in the shape of a cradle called*

276   *'leaba Bríde' (LAWA BREEJ) or 'the bed of the Bride'. Place the bed near the hearth if you have one. Then place the Brídeog into the bed and place a small straight wand of birch with the bark peeled in the bed beside the figure. This wand is called 'slatag Bride' (SLAH-TAHG BREEJ) or 'the little wand of the Bride'. If you have burned a fire during the evening the ashes of the fire should be scraped smooth. In the morning check the ashes for Brigit's wand or better yet, her footprint to prove that she had visited during the night. If no marks are found, burn some incense in the hearth or near the spot where the bed was placed, as an offering.*

ASHES

❧   ❧   ❧

I come out on Neasden Lane, with the river valley down to the right. There are iron gates next to the river and an old path, but it looks like they've been locked for decades. Instead, I cross over the river and go through a little park into a sixties low-rise estate. There's lots of building work and crowds of workmen in white hats drilling, digging, grit flying around in the air. My river route is completely cut off by the railway. I'm due for a massive detour now.

As I climb a slight incline, following a curvaceous woman in leopardskin leggings, water spurts out as if from a spring and trickles down the hill. A little fat black kid with a basketball says 'Hey nice legs!' Thanks, I say. 'Er, I meant nice shoes,' he says, pointing at my black Nikes. 'Er, OK, thanks anyway.' He follows me for a while, getting an eyeful of my trainers. Asda is across the road, and I go in for camera film and come out with a Winnie the Pooh video and a free dinosaur backpack for my daughter.

I've had enough of this and decide to get the tube. I'll walk to Wembley[5] Park and it's only one stop to Stonebridge Park, from where I can continue the walk. It's cheating, but who cares? I go

---

5   'Wemba's forest clearing' – Local History Buff

past a working pub at last – the Torch – built for the 1948
Olympics. On the wall is an ad for Spearmint Rhino gentleman's
club, 'the hottest table dancers in town'.

ð   ð   ð

Fucking railways, roads, golf courses, building sites, cars and super-
markets. Parts of London are just completely unconnected thanks
to our pea-brained way of building. All those railways cutting communities in half. The Victorians didn't think they'd be shunting
their working population into ghettos: why should they?

> **Gravelly voiceover:** What reason would a yokel from Neasden have
> to visit Wembley where it is all yokels, except for to steal the pig of
> another yokel? I am doing society a favour by building these rail-
> ways. Yokels, your pigs are safe.
>
> · 'Report on the Railway-Caused Inaccessibility to the Local Yokel
> Populations of Neasden and Wembley', Isambard Kingdom Brunel

Although to the Victorians the covering up of the rivers was a sign
of progress (as well as a repression of female sexuality, naturally), a
badge of their modernity and ability to tame nature, now I think
our idea of 'progress' has shifted. It certainly doesn't just mean
using the latest technology to achieve a short-term solution, but
changing our thinking. So maybe we'll free the rivers some time
soon. The Victorians thought in narrow channels and I'd like to
believe that these days we are more open minded. But so much of
our morality and manners come from them that sometimes you
wonder whether we'll ever gain a wider perspective. Or at least stop
taking organized sport so seriously.

On the tube I realize that to get to Stonebridge Park I should've
got on at Wembley Central – about a mile away – not Wembley
Park. This train is a fast one to Baker Street via Finchley Road.

278   (Non-London readers look away now ...) Gahhhh. Fuck fuck fuckity fuck. Fuck the railways, fuck the Victorians. I look around and a woman is chuckling away at me cursing out loud to myself.

Opposite me is a skinny middle-aged man in denim with a can of Tennent's Super. Next to him is a bombed-out bloke staring off into the vortex. They are dowsing. I smile at them in recognition, like we're all in on some big secret. By the looks of Vortex Man, it's not a very nice secret. The carriage snakes along, following the one in front in some strange public transport belly dance. I get to Baker Street and change onto the Bakerloo Line. The next train only goes as far as Queen's Park. Then I wait for a train to Willesden Junction. And finally I get a train to Stonebridge Park an hour and a half after leaving Wembley. Holy river? Cursed river, more like! I could have crawled to Stonebridge Park, I want to cry.

I come out at Stonebridge Park and there's a sign for Neasden Hindu Temple, the biggest outside India. I feel I should check it out, but the blood is still running down my leg so instead I head west, the Winnie the Pooh video once more bashing against my cut leg. I bet Sir Ranulph Fiennes doesn't have to put up with this sort of hardship. A poster says 'Are you getting enough?' It's the 'Brent Benefits Takeup'.

The river is just up there to north, parallel to the road. I see World of Leather up ahead. 'We are all on herbs', says the sign painted on a door. 'No reasonable offer refused.' In the same way that you might invest in a drinks company when you're thirsty and drink seems like the most important thing in the world, so it's dangerous going in a place like this when you're knackered. Luckily for me, it's all expensive pastelly fuchsia shell-like stuff. I stagger on towards Hanger Lane, the video still banging against my leg, and sit down in the middle of the roundabout, as the traffic goes round and round. And round. And round.

ॐ   ॐ   ॐ

Brídeog Procession: *This is a special type of procession, similar to carol-ing, that members of your grove can do on the eve of Imbolc (or one of the preceding nights if necessary). Arrangements should be made ahead of time so that people can sign up for a visit and know what to expect. They should also be advised that it is best to do the spring cleaning before the Brídeog visits. Assemble a company of participants, called 'Biddys' or Brídeogs and prepare your songs for the event. Then take the Brídeogs from house to house to offer blessings and entertainment to the families who live there. Dressing in unusual clothes and wearing funny hats will add to the fun of the event and is quite traditional. A young lady, traditionally the prettiest of the crowd, should be selected to carry the Brigit doll with them. When you arrive, ask for admittance to the house (it is considered very bad luck to be uncivil to a Brídeog) and everyone should file in. Entertain the household with a couple of songs (traditionally song, rhymes and music on flute, violin, and later, accor-dion) and recite a prepared Brigit blessing for them. If the household does not already have one they should be presented with a Brigit's cross for protection and blessing through the year. Before going the family should present the Brídeogs with an item of food, especially one associated with dairy to be used at the community feast (or as an alternative you can collect non-perishable food items for a homeless shelter).*

FUNNY HAT

As the traffic goes around me, I flick though the *A to Z*. Brentford is famous for two battles (one in 1016 between Canute and Edward Ironside, the other in the Civil War which had a spin-off – the Battle of Turnham Green), then there's Brentford Nylons and the football team called Brentford FC. I'd like to go there one day, but not today. You see, between here and Brentford the Brent flows through four big golf courses and I just can't face that. Not after Staples Corner and World of

280 Leather. It's *Hang Her* Lane. Mother Nature destroyed by cars and sport. Is the goddess having a laugh? Or is she screaming?

And what the hell is this river walking all about? Is it about needing validation from women? Or a search for lost shags? Or just craving my mother's attention? Or breaking out of feminised domesticity? *Iron John*? Liquid Tim, more like.

London Stories 12: Swedish DIY Fascism

Earlier on, I modestly claimed that I invented Scandinavian punk music by nailing a Crass LP to a big wooden board and sailing it across the North Sea. But it's just occurred to me that those resourceful Vikings would have taken one look at the wooden board and tried to make something with it. In other words, IKEA is all my fault too.

But whereas Scando-punk is harmless fun, IKEA is evil. I was wandering around the Brent branch of IKEA with my wife one Saturday afternoon – in the kitchen fittings section, as it happens – when it suddenly dawned on me that I fucking hate DIY and I hate IKEA and all that modernist lemming-like interior fashion consciousness let's do up our houses bollocks. I didn't say that out loud, I just looked pained and let out a Big Existential Sigh.

'Are you all right?' said my wife.

'Uh' I grunted, and carried on pushing the trolley along the stupid little yellow line that eventually leads to the check-out, then to the car park, then to the North Circular. Clutch. Brake. Accelerator. Brake. Clutch. Brake. Usually I'm safe from these kind of temples of the house proud because you have to drive to them and we don't have a car. But a friend of ours had unthinkingly lent us her car while she went off to change her name and write the Great Feminist Novel, so I had no get-out excuse. The whole DIY/IKEA thing gave me an insight into why so many Scandinavians are depressed – remember, Norway and Sweden have the highest suicide rates in Europe. It's because of their boring fucking kitchens and living rooms – all those ash floors and clean lines. It's enough to make you want to batter yourself to death with a maple and chrome book-shelf.

During the second half of the nineties, style gurus teamed up with prat designers to push a new lifestyle choice – a sort of bastard modernism with lava lamps thrown in. A kind of 1984ish non-individuality cult took over, where everything looked the same – stripped floors, chrome, sparse minimalism, cold.

In the same way that my eyes start glazing over when my mates start talking about cars, DIY really turns me off. But before I lose all my disgusted male readers here, I do have an ongoing DIY project. (Come back, lads!) An electric guitar. An electric guitar? Pretty impressive, hey? Actually I just made the shape of an electric guitar body in a solid lump of wood. Then

NEW! The DIY
DIY BRAIN
Kit

Replace your rubbishy
old brain with a brand
new DIY-crazed brain!

made the neck with another bit of wood and joined them together with two big nails. Then carved out the bit for the pick-ups (humbuckers). It was Strat shape with a Gibson pick-up system. It's a long-term project, actually. I started it a while back – I remember doing it around the time that General Jaruzelski was putting down the Polish Solidarity strikes, so that would make it about 1980. I'm not quite finished. I need to take it to a guitar shop to get the machine heads fitted.

I ended up buying a work desk shelf unit thing from IKEA. It's deliberately designed to lean to one side, like the way a compassionate Scandinavian cocks their head to listen to you pour out all your troubles. This lopsidedness makes me angry. Which makes me depressed and sad. Still, after putting up the crap IKEA shelves my jaw became squarer and my brow slightly more furrowed. I then drilled a couple of holes in our living-room wall and put up some kind of huge, fake Regency anti-modernist mirror with fancy gilt frames (my family is running a book on when it will come crashing down).

Then I retired from DIY forever.

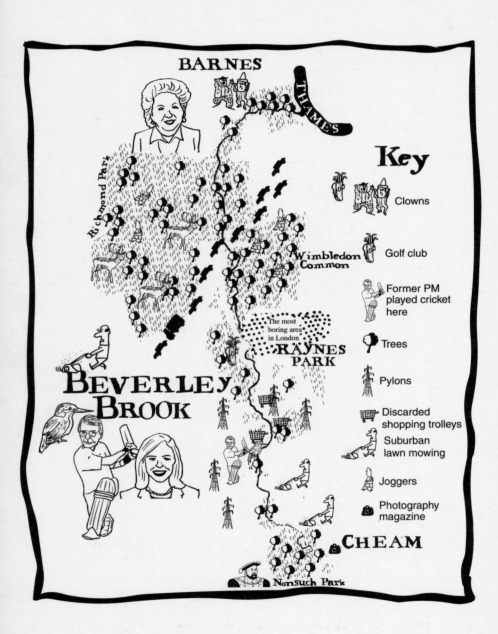

BARNES

THAMES

Key

Richmond Park

Clowns

Golf club

Former PM
played cricket
here

Wimbledon
Common

Trees

The most
boring area
in London

RAYNES
PARK

Pylons

Discarded
shopping trolleys

BEVERLEY
BROOK

Suburban
lawn mowing

Joggers

Photography
magazine

CHEAM

Nonsuch Park

15. The Unbearable Shiteness of Being (in South London)

• Beverley Brook – Nonesuch Park to Barnes

South London travel guide – Raynes Park – Cheam – Photography mags are not porn, no way – Henry VIII is a sports fathead – Canadian actress – John Major – Egyptian turkey god – World of Golf – Raynes Park model shop – Glaswegian deer – Zippo's Circus – hole in space-time

Just before I briefly moved south of the river around six years ago I went to a bookshop in Notting Hill and asked for a travel guide to south London. 'Ha ha ha,' said the shopkeeper, 'good joke. Why would anyone want to travel to south London?'

'So have you got one?' I asked, deadly serious. They didn't. And I thought, afterwards, that I should write one myself and send it to Lonely Planet or Rough Guides. Because, basically, people need to know about places like Raynes Park.

Where is Raynes Park? asks the smiling, happy, well-adjusted reader who's never lived there (or the walk-on character I've paid to appear in this paragraph). Stand in the centre of Wimbledon, on a wet and windy day when there is nothing to do (except perhaps watch kids spitting at pigeons), then walk vaguely south-west for about twenty minutes, until all the decent shops and amenities run out. You are now in Raynes Park. Possibly the most boring area of

286   London. Don't stand still too long or you'll get covered in really crap graffiti.

I lived here for two years and, I think, spent a lot of that time in a low-level depression brought on by my surroundings. If you look up Raynes Park in the *A to Z* it seems to be surrounded by a mixture of parks, sports grounds and big dual carriageways. This is certainly a heady suburban mixture. It also means that there is less space for other things, such as book or record shops. As an alternative to reading, ha ha, why not try walking around a football pitch fifty times followed by half an hour spent trying to cross the road. It soon makes you

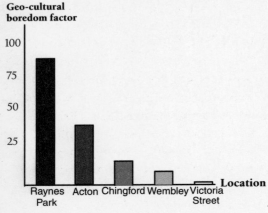

The most boring place in London? According to the latest figures from recent studies (i.e. stuff in the author's notebooks) it pips Acton by some distance.

appreciate the finer things in life. My favourite piece of highway was the stretch from Wimbledon Chase post office to the A3 roundabout, known as Bushey Road. This dual carriageway is the symbolic edge of London – on the other side of the road is Surrey, the south-east, a different, smarter suburbia. Nice lawns, Rotary Club meetings, Simply Red albums, big white modern kitchens. It's quite scary, don't you think. At night, when the sky is clear and full of stars, you can almost imagine yourself as a medieval traveller, fearful of falling off the edge of the known world.

As luck would have it, Raynes Park has its own river, called the Beverley Brook. This stream, which starts around Cheam and runs into the Thames at Barnes, hadn't been culverted, hadn't been forced into pipes, hadn't been manhandled, filled in, buried, hadn't been forgotten, you don't need to go into a library to find out about

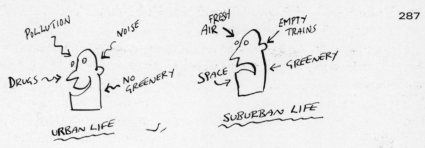

it. It's on the *A to Z*. You can throw sticks into it. You can smell it. One of the reasons that it hadn't been concealed was that it flowed through some of the most boring parts of London, like Raynes Park. The buriers, the culverters, the pipers, whatever those guys called themselves, just couldn't face having to spend time in shittily dreary south London suburbs. So they said to whoever it was made the decisions about burying rivers, 'Hey, that's a great river. We didn't need to do that one. And it's so beautiful, and healthy. Not got any shit in it. At all.' And because the People Who Made the Decisions About Burying Rivers probably never really thought things out that much, they just said, 'Er, yeah, OK.' and stamped a piece of paper with their River Killer rubber stamp. Hooray. Can we go home now? And so the Beverley Brook survived. I have decided to confront my fears and hang-ups about south London by revisiting Raynes Park in the guise of a walk along the Beverley Brook.

First, a long journey down to Cheam. In the early nineties I was one of London's few reverse commuters. I'd do the normal commuting thing from Walthamstow to Victoria, but then I'd keep going, heading back out again into the outer reaches – and further, to Cheam. They were exciting times. I was twenty-five and (at last) had a glamorous London media job. Testing cameras on a photography magazine. According to my mother, it was classed as top-shelf porn in Lincolnshire, but that I'm afraid says

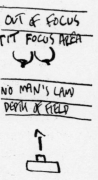

288   more about the East Midlands than it does about the magazine. I mean, you'd be pretty sad if you went to the trouble of buying a photography magazine just to have a wank over it.

Cheam is a nice but dull little village, with loads of Tudorbethan fripperies. I cross into Cheam Park across grassland, and an upward sweep towards Nonesuch Palace, one of Henry VIII's massive country retreats. I eventually see a murky, milky, stagnant stream with lots of black flies in a piece of marshy forest, leading into a tiny stagnant pool swarming with green flies.

I do feel that Henry VIII has been misunderstood. Some say he was principled and patriotic. I say he was a crazy thick-necked sex-addicted sports fat-head who liked gold. I try to conjure up an image of Henry VIII and all I can think of is a rugby player shagging his bird in the bushes then bullying pocket money out of little kids.

෧   ෧   ෧

Beverley Brook has got a girl's name. In fact, it's named after a Canadian actress. OK, she's called Beverly Brooks, but it's pretty damn close. Beverly appeared in the Kanata Theatre Company Production of *The Prime of Miss Jean Brodie* as Jean Brodie. And a couple of other things. I imagine she'd be pretty stunned if she

knew there was a river named after her. But I don't know how to contact her. I wrote to her theatre company in Canada.

Hi there

I'm currently writing a book about London's rivers, one of which is
called Beverley Brook, and am trying to get in touch with some of
the Beverly Brooks(s) throughout the world with the idea of orga-
nizing some sort of internet creative workshop on a virtual river
bank some time next year.

If you could forward this to Beverly I'd be very grateful.

Cheers,
Tim Bradford

ॐ   ॐ   ॐ

Twee pre-war semis, with leathery old blokes in shorts pushing
rotary mowers. These houses have the added attraction of
looking like they've only just been finished. It's deathly
quiet and pristine. Maybe the Beverley Brook valley is
in some kind of Bermuda-Triangle-like time warp, a
hole in pan-dimensional space-time that means it's
always lagging behind the rest of us. One can imagine
people, with their couple of kids, coming down here
from the city centre in the thirties, moving in wearing
their Sunday best. The only twenty-first-century
thing I can see is a post box which has been graffi-
tied pink. People slag off graffiti. I do. But it can be
a comforting sign of humanity, people marking their environment in the same way as the
old cave painters. Well, OK, that's what I'd
tell the police if I was caught doing it.

At Cuddington Recreation Ground I sigh with pleasure at the fantastic sloping football pitch with a view over London. What more could you want? A quick glance at the *A to Z* and a compass shows that it's actually a view over Morden, which is not quite so exciting. A long narrow strip of trees and bushes runs the through middle of the park. There's a pipe at the start of it with bricks all around. The same flies, the same murky liquid, though it's flowing just a tiny bit now. The little river is all grown over and covered with bushes and trees, including a lovely weeping willow. Suddenly it disappears underground and reappears in a weird rock pool dammed with pages of an *A to Z*, some old phone directories, plastic bags, receipts and magazines.

ے   ے   ے

There's also a Beverley Brooks in Dallas, Texas who is a Bankruptcy Analyst on ext. 233 – Beverly Brooks, Bankruptcy Analyst: Chapter 7 Regional Co-ordinator. There was an e-mail address for her. I wouldn't have been doing my job if I didn't get in touch with her. What am I doing? I mention a couple of American women and I start coming on like Philip Marlowe.

> **Beverly.Brooks@_____**
> **Dear Bev**
>
> **I'm currently doing a book of walks over all the rivers of London and have been doing some research on the Beverley Brook, which runs from Sutton to the Thames at Barnes. There isn't much information about the stream on the Internet, but I did get quite a bit of info about you. Have ever heard of this river?**
>
> **There are several other Beverly Brookses around the world and I'm thinking of having a Beverly Brooks get**

**together later in the year: would you be interested in
something like this?**

**Yours sincerely,
Tim Bradford**

ॐ   ॐ   ॐ

There's an old bloke on the other side of the road in a dark blue
suit. Old people still wear fashions of their day. Old Bloke Gear
used to be heavy suits, now it's light sports wear – slacks, bomber
jackets. When we're old what will we (as in, the postpunk thirty-
somethings) wear? 501s, leather jackets and DMs? The seventy year
olds were the same age as me in 1966. They probably bought
Revolver and 'dug' it. Now that is scary.

I'm in Worcester Park. There's a dumped bike in the stream in
pretty good nick – better than my own bike. I cross over the small
metal bridge to Worcester Park Athletics Club, which is famous
for being the ground where the dashing and handsome young
John Major (the nearest the UK has ever come to JFK) learned the
game. John grew up near the Beverley Brook at 260 Longfellow
Road and probably played Pooh sticks and other interesting
games in it. His dad's successful garden gnome business
was near Worcester Park station. His mother worked at
the local library. It's time the local council set up one of
those big tourist signs saying 'Welcome to John Major
Country!'

John somehow represents the suburbs, even more
than Thatcher who self-consciously allied herself with
Essex/Suburban man to curry favour. In fact, John
Major's vision of traditional England – old maids cycling
from evensong with a quart of homebrew strapped to
their back (or something like that) – seems quite like this
whole area.

292   I'm approached by a leathery old guy with smiley eyes, who comes right up to me and says, 'Are you looking for wildlife? I thought you might have heard about the kingfisher.'

'Is there a kingfisher? I hadn't heard.'

'Well, I saw one. Just a bit further up. Just the other day. And I thought to myself the river must be getting cleaner if the kingfisher is about.'

He beams brightly and tells me he's lived in the area since 1936. It was his parents who moved in wearing their Sunday best. I tell him I'm walking the river's route. 'Do you know there used to be an avenue of huge elms here when I was a kid, they used to go all the way up to Morden Priory. I think it was a kind of ceremonial path. I remember there used to be minnows and sticklebacks in the forties. I've fallen in it a few times. When I was six or seven it froze over and we played Scott of the Antarctic down there on the stream.'

I'm nodding enthusiastically. I ask him if it had always been so overgrown. 'No, it was more accessible in the old days.'

We both look off into the distance for a few moments.

'So ...' he says, 'are you going to look for this kingfisher then?'

'Yeah ... maybe.'

We say our goodbyes and I watch him speed walk off towards the centre of Worcester Park. Further up I sit down on the bank for about fifteen minutes and look for the kingfisher, but all I see are two Carling and Fosters cans side by side, squashed on the riverbed, and some ducks.

As Green Lane heads towards woodland there's an abundance of wildlife and birdsong. The road becomes shitty tarmac in terrible condition, then fades into an old track going through the forest. Unfortunately it heads off at right angles to the river, possibly towards Morden Priory. To the left are what look like ancient hay meadows. A sign says 'No right of way'. A small malt kiln sticks up above the woods in the distance, there are horses, hayricks and kids' laughter from the nearby school, floating on the wind. I walk down a farm track then across a field to the river. There are two huge electricity pylons in the field, ugly giant metal insect legs things.

I wade down through tall grass-land towards the river at the end of the field, and walk along its banks in jungle grass as tall as me, surrounded by birdsong. Under the pylons something like a wave goes through my eardrums and ends in a deep, dull 'crump' sound. The sound of my brain being cooked, perhaps.

South London Countryside

   ò   ò   ò

There's a Beverly Brooks who is a careers and life coach for high achievers and potential leaders in the UK business environment. And a Beverly Brooks who is in charge of a big army tank depot in Alabama. And a Beverly Brooks who works in a history of art museum in Illinois. I hoped to be able to get the Beverlys together and get them to do a fun run along the banks of the Beverley Brook. How to do it without them thinking that I'm taking the piss? It could be called the Beverley Brooks Classic.

   ò   ò   ò

There's a road of strange bird-like houses with big chimneys in the middle of the roofs, sloping tiles, Elizabethan beams – what are these houses trying to say? Is it harking back or a more positive statement? It's small-time English nationalism manifested in archi-tecture – end-of-empire melancholy. Either that, or they're statues to a giant suburban turkey god. (Who might the turkey god be? Possibly an Egyptian lesser deity.) There is an Environment Agency van, and two wiry blokes in green overalls are heaving shopping

294   trolleys onto a mesh trailer which is already full of trolley brothers
and sisters covered in pond weed.

I go over to talk to them/annoy them with inane questions.
'Are you fishing them out of the river?'

'Sure am,' he says. Maybe it was anti-supermarket eco-
warriors, a supermarket trolley liberation group who
set the trolleys free. I think how easy it must have
been in the old days to clog the rivers up if, even in
today's supposedly more enlightened society, we are
callous and lazy enough to just dump things anywhere. It's human nature, I suppose, to pile wheeled shopping carriers in watercourses.

Further up, a crowd of executives are whacking balls to
relieve the stress at World of Golf. World of Golf is open to the
public seven days a week. I wander in, and look around the strange
artificial world of the World of Golf. A sloped fairway raised up to
green plastic greens. Four-wheel drives stand in the car park.

The river has disappeared from view. Down below, almost
underneath the road, is a strange settlement, a funny little world
down there in the 'catacombs', like a forgotten mountain village. On
the path is a single red rubber glove. What does that mean? Some
sort of fetishist Loyalist paramilitary group? Nearby is a V reg.
Mitsubishi Colt with a KKK number plate. The little main street of
the village runs pretty much parallel to the river before it sweeps to
the east and crosses under the A3.

I'm walking past a nice garden and notice an old woman and
decide to go back and talk to her.

'Excuse me. I was just wondering ... do you ever get used to the
traffic noise round here?'

She looks up slightly surprised and puts down her garden sheers.
She has fierce but friendly eyes, a hook nose and a big smile.

'Oh, you get used to it. I don't even notice it these days. In fact
it would seem strange if the traffic disappeared. It's like an old

friend. I'd feel very lonely without it. When my husband and I
moved in here after the war the main road was just three lanes.
You could cross over to go to what then was the other side of the
village.'

'What's the village?'

'Combe, I suppose it would be called.'

I explain that I'm walking the Beverley Brook and ask if she
knows anything about it.

'There was a little river, or I should say more of a stream than a
river, which joined the Beverley Brook on the other side of the A3.'

'Can you remember what it was called?'

'Think it was the Po.'

'Isn't that in Italy?'

'Is it? Oh well. It's something like that.'

She then tells me about her experience of the war years in real time.

Half an hour later and I'm on my way into Raynes Park. I haven't
been back since I left in December 1996 in a van driven by a racist
middle-aged bloke. It's a nice day and Raynes Park doesn't look half
bad. Have I forgotten how bad it really was? The centre has had a
facelift – or maybe just a bit of regular moisturiser. There are more
new shops on the main drag, a couple of new cafes, and the big
Raynes Park Tavern has been painted.

I cross under the subway to my old bit of Raynes Park and it's a
different story on 'Grand' Parade. If anything it's gone downhill.
Even more of the shops have been boarded up. The little grocer's
shop near Dupont Road, which had been run by two elderly gents
since the end of the eighteenth century, has closed down and been
replaced by a timber warehouse. Has someone spotted a gap in the
market? Are we all running out of wood? It's sad. Twenty-five years
ago, most of Britain was overrun with little grocers such as this,
shops run by hairless old men with specs who stocked only four or
five products, covering the basic nutritional requirements. These
minimalist general stores were as ubiquitous as McDonalds today.

296   And those old fellows in shops always had stories to tell – of run-away steam trains and daring dawn raids on Jerry (or in some cases, dawn raids on the Boers).

I used to enjoy going in the little Raynes Park grocer shop for a 'packaged food nostalgia browse'. The main item was jelly. They had several flavours, in a nice display. Jelly, as these two clever businessmen no doubt realized, always comes in handy. They also had an extensive range of soups, covering all the flavours that matter – tomato, vegetable and exotic oxtail. Sometimes there were corn-flakes too. As in many such pairings, one old gent was nice and one was nasty. But I could never tell which was which. And I suppose now I never will.

The model railway shop is also not there, nor the tiny, frail home-less man. My head starts to ache at the mental torture of the sub-urbs. Now there's graffiti everywhere, and not of the good or interesting kind. When I go into my old newsagents, the tall man behind the counter says 'All right there?' as if it's been three or four hours since I last came in.

'How are you doing?' he says. 'Hey, see that guy that just went out – he started banging on about ganja. Hey, all the rich people smoke it, I've got nothing against it. Everyone in the House of Lords has to smoke it by law, you know.'

'I thought so,' I say. He still goes off at tangents. He's older and more knackered but has still got a spark. His wife, the famously foxy-eyed one, also looks knackered and they're both greying but holding the fort.

'Or the *Fortean Times*, my friend, ha ha ha,' as the newsagent would say. I go down Dupont Road to see my old house again. I look in the window and the whole thing is being renovated and painted. It feels weird, I can't remember living here. Maybe I never actually did or else I've wiped it from my memory banks. I feel melancholy. It's time to move on.

I sometimes get the feeling that I am living parallel lives. Or at least that alternative versions of my life are running simultaneously to this one. I've lived in many parts of London and when I visit them they're all pretty much the same as when I lived in them – except for the fact, that I don't live there any more. I'm like a visiting ghost. And it makes me think that if I'd stayed there I wouldn't have known or thought about the other Tims. Except that now I'm travelling around, I'm seeking them out. They have to hide away when I'm around. But maybe I never really left the places I lived in – Muswell Hill, Walthamstow, Stamford Brook, Westbourne Park, Raynes Park, Hammersmith – just dreamed it, and kept dreaming about moving on. My worst nightmare is that this is all a dream and that I'll wake up and I'm stuck in the past. Would it cause big problems if the other Tims and I met up? Like Michael J. Fox when he goes back to the mid fifties and is on for giving his mum one and the other Michael J. Fox has to stop him, but can't meet him face to face and ... never mind.

I head towards Wimbledon Common along the A3 briefly, with endless, mindless streams of traffic flowing past. This should all be renamed Woodpark City. A small stream runs into the trees. Woods and forests are often full of Cubs and Scouts out camping. I spent a few years brainwashed by that sect, with their strange practices – toggles and woggles and badges, tying knots. We were called Wolf Cubs, but wolves have pups not cubs. So what's going on? Baden Powell was the God of Cubs. Wasn't he a proto fascist? 'Cubs do your best, we will do our best,' we'd say, then sing the national anthem as the Union Jack was lowered at the end of the evening and we'd clutch our little uniforms. Or was it the Lord's Prayer we said? I'm surprised we weren't given weapons. We were basically a private army.

Richmond Park is grassland, with avenues of trees along the little roads, and cars roaring past on their way somewhere important. It's a through road, like a national park rather than a typical clean-cut London park. Over on the left are deer, old and young, basking in the shade of a something tree (check up in my *I Spy Book of Trees*

298 when I get home). Their heads look like lots of branches sticking up. I get closer to do a drawing, but not too near. They see me and

Whit ir you lookin' it, Pal?

some stand up as if to say aggressively, 'Whit the fuck ir you lookin' it, pal?' Glaswegian deer. They watch me as I retreat through the wild grass.

You get a good idea of what the now buried rivers would have looked like before the development of London by walking along Beverley Brook – trees on banks jut out into the river and the park stretches off to the north-east as far as the eye can see – browny green grassland, lots of trees dotted around and the odd bit of traffic streaking by. I cross over the road and continue alongside the river. This is the pure essence of summer feeling that reminds me of being a kid, stuck in the car in intense heat, being driven to some park or monument or country house, feeling car sick, arguing with my brother, the back of my legs sticking to the plastic seats, the smell of ham sandwiches, melting ice cream in your hands, sand in your toes. All that rushes into my mind when an old green Austin Maxi, so similar to our old car, goes past. It should have a soundtrack by Teenage Fanclub.

Here, Beverley Brook goes under a wall through a metal grille. I could go right over the bridge out of the park or keep going on this side of the wall. I keep going (though this turns out to be a mistake). I cross over a little dried-up tributary stream that goes into the wall – it's very marshy round here, what's on the other side of this little wooden plank?

There are voices coming from behind the wall – well-bred Roehampton and Richmond types. At last I come out at a gate, but it's the wrong one – it's East Sheen. I've gone too far. I turn into a backstreet and it's pre-war semis world again. A kid – about eleven or twelve – in full hip-hop regalia, superbaggy jeans and sloppy T-shirt, is doing his skateboard moves. Except he's shit. There are crazy East-Sheen-style crap tags on the bottle bank and water hydrant. These crazy middle-class kids live in a smart rich suburb and they're hooked on US black urban culture.

There in front of me is the Beverley Brook, slowly meandering along. Over Creek Bridge then through into a little meadow with grass already brown. Zippo's Circus is here. A stalwart of the London park scene, Zippo has been to Stoke Newington and Finsbury Park in the last year. Clown, Ringmaster and Cockney Pearly-King urchins hang out in the parks.

The final stretch of Beverley Brook goes through the playing fields of private clubs which are all locked up. I have to go back through Barnes Common past Zippo and his mates again, who are bound to laugh, because they're all clowns. 'Hiyaa hiyaaa,' says a circus bloke inside the big top. Through old Putney Cemetery now, which soon becomes thick forest, and I'm treading on gravestones. I stub my toe on a little cross sticking up from a gravestone. There are lots of topless skinhead biker muscle boys hanging around. Maybe it's one of those Hardcore-Drum-Beating Men's River Walking Societies.

I turn into a playing field with a gate at the end, past a small circus tent – maybe the clowns' private bar – and up into another part of the wood where a bloke and girl are looking for somewhere to lie down. The river suddenly gets wider and opens out into a lovely pool. And then the last stretch, under a little humpbacked bridge – at last, I see a tributary stream enter the Thames. It feels good. Now I've lived. Determined Germanic-looking men and women jog by in tight lycra. Up on the boatyard balconies toothy fleshy people look down on the passers-by.

About three days after the walk, I finally got several films developed and there was one set with lots of eight-year-old photos of

300   Raynes Park. Me in an old life, different house, different relation-
      ship. Same haircut. The film must have been kicking around in an
      old box for years. Very weird. Very Hole-In-Pan-Dimensional-Space-
      Time.

𝕒 𝕒 𝕒

Film Idea: The John Major Story

A four-hour epic, directed by Oliver Stone. John is at nets practice
when he's seduced by feminist water nymphs like the scene in
O Brother Where Art Thou?, and his team mates are turned to stone
and sold as garden ornaments. He vows to become Prime Minister
to avenge them and has many triumphs along the way. Eventually
there is a big naval battle at the mouth of Beverley Brook which
Major wins.

George Clooney – John Major
Holly Hunter – Norma Major
Helen Mirren – Margaret Thatcher

London Stories 13: 30-Love in the Time of Henmania

How was tennis ever invented? I imagine fops at the court of Louis XIV pranced about one day at Versailles. See, it's called a court for that reason. It's a metaphor for courtly debate, knocking an idea backwards and forwards. Public-school types like debating societies and public-school types like tennis. Anyway, it was hot and one of them happened to drape his fancy cloak across the room. Then, as they were wittily and cruelly discussing some subject like, say, whether a man will save his wallet or his wife from a burning building, with lots of savage but subtle attacks on each other, someone said, 'Chaps, let me have all the knicker elastic in the room and I'll scrunch it up into a ball that can represent the multi-faceted strands of our conversation.'

Wimbledon fortnight was always a depressing time of year. Strawberries, cream, hot weather, suffocating Englishness, suburban life, mowed lawns, flies buzzing in the kitchen, egg sandwiches, salad cream mingling with the vinegar from pickled beetroot. It always got me down. Wimbledon is also a brilliant metaphor for Englishness in the sporting arena. Plucky English lads and lasses galumphing about with their big legs and rosy cheeks and getting walloped by the more sophisticated sporting machines of the USA, Australia, Germany, Russia, Eastern Europe, France, in fact just about anywhere.

And then there was the one success, that insane hallucinatory year of 1977 – government crumbling, just got a loan from the IMF, Lib-Lab pact keeping them in power, Queen's Silver Jubilee sandwiches and little Union Jack flags, the Sex Pistols getting to number one (not that anyone in Lincolnshire noticed it). But Virginia Wade, average and nice, won Wimbledon. She somehow subverted Englishness, manifested by the milk-maid looks and jolly hockey niceness of Sue Barker. Virginia Wade was sort of Italian-looking and, according to my gran, 'a gilwill'. I presume this must be an old English tennis technical term.

Anyway, here's a typical interview with the current darling of the scene, Tim Henman.

Interviewer: Tell us about the game, Tim Henman.
Tim Henman: Well, I was pleased with my game. Thought my serve and volley

was good. He's a difficult opponent. I had a plan and I followed it through. 'This is Tim Henman's game,' I said to myself. My carbohydrate glucose levels stayed constant throughout the match. The carbon tungsten fibres of my racket held up well. Tim Henman's got to be happy with that.

Tennis isn't really a sport because blokes don't talk about it in pubs. Nobody I know takes it seriously. I mean, what can you say? Andre Agassi had some nice shorts on today. Did you see Henman's shot that went in? Didn't Venus Williams do a good smash? It's pointless. My only good memory of Wimbledon was when Pat Cash won in the eighties. At the end of the game he started climbing up

though the crowd, up and up, and I thought to myself, my God he's going to keep going, jump onto the roof of Centre Court and shout, 'This is pointless!' at the top of his voice then keep climbing, up and up, until he's plucked out of the air by a waiting spaceship and whisked off to a more sensible planet.

But he just kissed his parents.

THE RIVER THEY COULDN'T KILL

The story of the Wandle

Once upon a time London was a city of sweet babbling brooks, dingly dells and bunny rabbits.

But by the Victorian era, most of the streams had been buried by fanatical men with whiskers.

HA HA!

A few survived. One of these was the Wandle, which still flows from Croydon to Wandsworth.

It was once a famous trout stream but became polluted into a great big stinking flowing mess of shite.

THE COMPLEAT ANGLER

However, it has survived and prospered thanks to groups like the Friends of the Wandle...

FRIENDS OF THE WANDLE

...who have to watch their backs with the Wandle Liberation Army and Wandle Defence Association.

WLA   NDA   WDA

Even more secretive is a sect called Free the Rivers. They dig up buried streams at night.

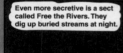

Their goal is to restore all the rivers to their former glory so that London will become like Venice.

Farringdon Street

The Fleet

If they succeed, all houses will be built on stilts. So Londoners will be OK when sea levels rise.

However, a sensible Thames Water spokesman comments:

THE RIVERS BROUGHT DAMP, FOG, DISEASE AND DEATH. BRINGING THEM BACK WOULD BE HUGELY IRRESPONSIBLE

In the interests of balance, a connoisseur of hallucinogenic high-strength lager says:

THE RIVERS ARE LOVELY. LET'S FREE THEM!

Anyway, back to the Wandle. As Ruskin famously said of the stream... "There..." Oh, we've run out of space.

SUPER!   £12.99

FREE THE RIVERS

£12.99

DIG FOR D MI

WHILE STOCKS! LA

16b. Sorry to Keep You

It's time for my weekly session with the Thames Water switch-board. I'm asked for my account number as usual, then when I say I want to be put in touch with the Swindon office because I want to go down into the sewers, I'm put on hold. A Mozart track drones on. Then a voice appears.

'We are sorry to keep you. Your call is important to us – however, we are currently experiencing high call volumes. You are moving up the queue and your call will be answered as soon as possible. Thank you for your patience at this busy time.'

Pause. Scratch arse. Look out of window.

'We are sorry to keep you. Your call is important to us – however, we are currently experiencing high call volumes. You are moving up the queue and your call will be answered as soon as possible. Thank you for your patience at this busy time.'

Pause. Pick nose.

'We are sorry to keep you. Your call is important to us – however, we are currently experiencing high call volumes. You are moving up the queue and your call will be answered as soon as possible. Thank you for your patience at this busy time.'

Pause. Stare off into space.

'We are sorry to keep you. Your call is important to us – however, we are currently experiencing high call volumes. You are moving up the queue and your call will be answered as soon as possible. Thank you for your patience at this busy time.'

Pause. After 20 minutes I finally get through but the woman I talk to can't help me and I'm put back into the Mozart queue for another 20 minutes, then put through to operations. They can find the log of my letter arriving but that's it. I'll try and find out if anyone knows anything, says Operations Woman. She puts me back onto Mozart hold.

17. The Tim Team

• Falcon Brook from Tooting to Battersea

The bastard TV people haven't got back in touch about my river walks idea so I'm now doing my own TV history show, walking along the route of Falcon Brook dressed as a Celtic warrior and with an imaginary TV crew accompanying me. It's the Tim Team.

Dear_____

A few months ago we met to discuss a possible TV project about walking the routes of London's buried rivers. Seeing as I haven't heard from you, I've gone ahead and written up one of the episodes. I hope you like it.

Yours
Tim Bradford

Voiceover: One of the most famous Celtic finds in London is the Battersea Shield, which was found in the Thames, near Battersea. Experts believe a Celtic warrior was lying on the beach sunbathing and the shield floated away, all the way to the Wandsworth Museum, where it is now kept. I imagine that the Celtic

310 warrior walked to the Thames from the sacred source of the Falcon Brook, so I plan to walk in his footsteps and, on the way, talk to local experts and enthusiasts, noting sites of historical interest.

Celts wore baggy trousers and brightly coloured tunics. Their hair was bleached with lime and worn in a spiky, punk-like style. After much research effort I come up with a modern equivalent, some green combat trousers and a Hawaiian shirt (my black one with yellow and red flowers). The hair is perfect, thanks to the heat and sweat and the fact that I hardly ever wash it.

Scene: I'm in Tooting trying to get through to Thames Water on my mobile. All I can hear is a pre-recorded message.

'We are sorry to keep you. Your call is important to us – however, we are currently experiencing high call volumes. You are moving up the queue and your call will be answered as soon as possible. Thank you for your patience at this busy time.'

Scene: Me in a street looking around. I begin the walk on Tooting's Furzedown Road, where the spring is located. Two women are sitting on a low wall. They are obviously pagan high priestesses guarding the sacred spring of the Falcon. One is Welsh, in her late forties, with red hair and big tits, the other in her sixties looks like a granny. They appear to be waiting for something. I strike a majestic pose and ask them to tell me where the sacred spring is located.

Hello Love

HIGH PRIESTESSES of THE FALCON

Granny: Are you with the water board, love?

Me: Ha ha no (*glancing down at my magnificent Celtic outfit. I tell them about the river walking idea, and some stuff about Danish punk music.*)

Welsh bird: (*getting quite excited*) That's a

really good idea. It is. A really good idea. Oh, what a very interesting
project!.
Voiceover: I think maybe she fancies me.
(*I stand there, not so much majestic as smiling awkwardly and looking
around.*)
Me: So ... do you know where the spring is then?
Welsh bird: The spring?
Granny: What spring is that, dear?
Voiceover: Come on, old woman, do I look stupid?
Me: The start of the river is round here somewhere. Maybe under-
neath one of these houses.
(*I brandish my ancient map, the* A to Z, *with the Falcon scrawled on
in blue biro, as if that will prove what I'm saying is true.*)
Welsh bird: Ooh, how interesting!
Voiceover: Did she just wink at me?
(*I decide that the spring is most likely directly underneath where they
are sitting, and tell them so. They both start giggling. I have a choice.
To persevere and wangle out of them the whereabouts of the river's
source, inevitably entailing me having to snog the Welsh bird to get
information, or leg it. I look around again, sniffing the air.*)
Me: I'd better be off.
(*They wave goodbye, the Welsh woman smiling and shouting, 'It's a
really good idea!'*)

Scene: About 100 yards further on, I sit down next to a wise old
woman on a bench and ask her if she knows anything about the
buried Falcon Brook.
Old woman: (*In a rasping voice she quotes what must be an old local
poem from the Tooting Myth Cycle. Ancient flute music plays in background.*)

There is an old river
But it's in Streatham.
Not round here.
No underground rivers
Round here, love.

Scene: I walk back towards Tooting Bec Road and cross over. The road next to the path is called Dr Johnson Avenue.

Dr Johnson: *(gravelly voice)* Oh yes, I have shat in the Falcon Brook many a time. Think I had too many snipe for breakfast.

Voiceover: On the right is Tooting Common. On the left is Tooting Graveney Common. There's a stream called the Graveney that flows into the Wandle and a cricketer called Graveney who played for England.

Scene: People lie around the edges of the common, flaking out. Kids are playing football and the adults are lying around in the sun with their shirts off. Dogs chase around. Bikes lie on their sides.

Voiceover: Here we are at Elmbourne, its name suggesting elms by the river.

Cut to: Picture of an elm tree

Voiceover: Then onto Wimbourne Court, suggesting wimmin by the river.

Cut to: Picture of women bathing in the river.

Voiceover: ... and Byrne Road, a derivation of bourne,

Cut to: Picture of river

Voiceover: or burn, some sacrificial offerings,

Cut to: A bonfire.

Voiceover: or after that floppy-haired Irish actor that was in *The*

Usual Suspects. And you think all along it was him that set up the
others. But by the end you have to watch it all again.
Cut to: Picture of Gabriel Byrne in *Usual Suspects* publicity shot.

๑ ๑ ๑

Scene: Me walking along boring road.
Voiceover: At Cornford Grove there's a tree that looks like Eddy
Grant. *Close-up to camera*: There was a ford in the river here, nearby
a grove of trees. They had lots of corn, enough for everyone. Great
mountains of it.
(Visual 3-D artist's drawing of cornfields in style of TV football graphics)
Voiceover: It was a perfect world. The leader of their little rural
commune was an Eddy-Grant-like figure with dreadlocks. After we
cross the main road, we reach Ravenslea Road, a field filled with
London's magical black birds. Perhaps guarding the corn. On the
right is the Bedford Arms. I went to a few comedy nights there
around a decade ago when comedy was at its height. It was what
you did. You'd 'have a laugh': Fancy a pint or a laugh? Ooh, a laugh
please.

Scene: At Balham Station there are some interesting sculptures on
the wall, of commuters in what looks like a pre-orgy scene. I take a
photo. People start looking at me.
Locals: Bloody hell there's a sightseer in Balham. That is just too
confusing. Kill him. Kill him.
*(Before the mob has a chance to gather, I am off again at speed, my
camera safely tucked away.)*

Scene: Balham High Street and Chadwick's Traditional Meat,
Poultry and Game.
Voiceover: Edwin Chadwick's family were originally into public
health and poor law application, but his sons went into the meat
trade.

'Helping the poor? Very nice. So, how about a
snippet of ham shank for tha' supper, fayther?'

Edwin: But what about the health of the poor?

Little Edwin: Bugger that. I'll do you ten sausages for sixpence, fayther.

Edwin: (*pause*) Alright then – and throw in a few pounds of tripe as well.

Scene: A launderette on the left, a video shop then the Las Vegas boutique, bringing forties-style purple and peach nylon threads back to the masses.

Voiceover: The proprietors stand around outside, looking to drag customers in off the streets. World War Two is over, lads!

(*I'm crossing over the main road to Chestnut Grove.*)

Scene: Picture of what Falcon Brook would have looked like in the eighteenth century. Then cut to today's scene – three late twenty-something sunburnt, topless blokes, with that layering of fat that follows quite quickly if men stop playing sport and carry on boozing, swagger out of the Balham Tup pub and waddle up the street. In the other direction, a green tractor trundles slowly down the centre of the road 'controlled' by a rather scared-looking unshaven bloke in a matching green polo shirt.

Talking to camera: The river goes underneath a school so I have to

go on a detour. *(I turn right down Mayford Road and keep going.)*
The road follows the river exactly and runs along in a little valley
here where the roads to the right and left go up.
(At a crossroads. Lots of big Victorian houses)
Voiceover: I'm now in the wide open spaces of Nightingale Lane,
where I can see the river valley properly. This is where the two main
branches of the Falcon Brook meet, the other coming from somewhere near Streatham (waves hand in general north-eastish direction).
Talking to camera while walking: Now we're on Hendrick
Avenue. If you look up at the top of these big red Victorian houses
here you can see strange Arts-and-Crafts-style coats of arms on
little triangles at the front of their second-floor windows. Most
have just an urn with grapes and leaves, but four have their own
design. One has a cross with a circle on each square of it; one a
diagonal line with a flower on each side; one the same except with
Prince of Wales feathers one each side; one a St Andrew's-style
diagonal cross. What do they mean?
Cut to: Image of big question mark.
Voiceover: The London Basement Company is hard at work on
one, and the soft moist clay churning out of their pump splatters
into a big yellow skip.
 *(I look to make sure there's no one around then plunge my hand
right in, squeezing it hard and bringing out a lump of Falcon Brook
clay.)*
Talking to camera: It's got a funny smell, perfumed, musky – actually it smells of sex.
 *(The clay dries almost immediately on contact. I walk on, still sniffing
my fingers.)*
Voiceover: The river runs in a perfect valley directly underneath
Northcote Road to Clapham Junction. *(Serious voice)* This area has
experienced severe and crippling gentrification over the last few
years. Northcote Road used to boast a famous fruit and veg market
but is now home only to ciabattas, sun-dried tomatoes and countless

316 fancy restaurants. A good test is how long it takes to find a hardware shop. If it's more than ten minutes' walk, an area is beyond the point of no return. You end up using olives instead of screws. And here we are at Honeywell Road – perhaps there was a spring nearby.

Ↄ Ↄ Ↄ

Scene: A smart woman climbs out of a sporty green BMW, all legs and tan and little black top. I go into a bookshop and ask about their local history section. They haven't got much. I tell the owner about the Falcon Brook and she seems surprised.

Heavily pregnant woman browsing in the bookshop: There's a man on Bellevue Road near the common who sells old pictures on a Saturday and Sunday and he has some river stuff.

Me: Great

Heavily pregnant woman: Also, I overheard a conversation in a nearby estate agent that you shouldn't buy in Belleville Road because it's got a river underneath it.

Me: Great! Thanks.

Scene: I cross the road to the estate agent's at the bottom of Belleville Road. The two women in the office look at each other, telepathically trying to work out the best strategy.

Woman 1: Ooh no, we've never heard of Falcon Brook.

Woman 2: Falcon Brook. No. No.

Me: But it flows right underneath Northcote Road.

Woman 1: Does it? Strange. We've never heard of it. Have we?

Woman 2: No. What was it called again?

Me: Falcon Brook.

Woman 1: Sorry.

Me: Well, I've seen it on old maps. *And* it's mentioned in the *Anglo-Saxon Chronicles*.

(They shake their heads. I make a 'sad' face. One of them takes pity on me.)

Woman 2: *(brightly)* I have heard of Honey Brook and Alder Brook. And in hot summers we've had surveys that have come up with strange goings on underground ... *(She trails off as her colleague shoots her a look).* But there's nothing round here, oh no.
Me: Where are Honey Brook and Alder Brook then?
Woman 1: Oh, miles away. In Streatham.
Me: So there's never been a problem round here then?
Woman 1: *(looking at woman 2)* Oh no. Not that we've heard of.
Me: Hmm. A friend of mine who lives in a street parallel to Belleville has a basement which is constantly damp.
(They look at each other embarrassedly and shrug. I give up, thank them and wave them goodbye.)

Scene: St. Tropez-y perma-tan people are sitting outside a Pitcher and Piano. There are loads of offices and estate agents, antique shops, a Tai Chong Peking Cantonese takeaway, Seafare Fish bar, Signor fish with Italian guys sitting outside, Akash Tandoori. A big fat woman, like a tinker Earth Mother, sits outside the Kidney Trust charity shop on top of a pile of suitcases, tricycles, toys, clothes, books, holding a glass of wine in one hand, watching the world go by. She has a coloured hanky in her hair and slightly wonky lipstick. Deli organic Holy Drinker chrome stuff funky stuff Boiled Egg and Soldiers posh café Wok Wok Chinese Gourmet Burger Kitchen Fiction Starbucks coffee All Bar One fruit and veg stalls Fine Line Buona Sera white building with veranda and conservatory Osteria Antica Bologna ...
Talking to camera: I once had Roman stew here, made to a 2000-year-old recipe, at least that's what the chef said. Bloody good it was too.

Scene: The camera pans past fishmongers, health food shops, the Glaister bistro, and a funky bar; people moving and shaking and eating and sipping and making light conversation in fashionable clothes.

318 **Voiceover:** As we cross over Battersea Rise towards Clapham Junction it's a different vibe. Gone is the hint of brown bread bohemia and it's back to chain-stores: Woolworths, Boots, building societies, cheap jewellery shops, amusement arcades and Superdrug. The people are different, too. Fatter and a bit less pleased with themselves.

Talking to camera: I'm now standing outside the Falcon pub near Clapham Junction station. A plaque on the wall says it was built in the late nineteenth century as a hotel but this can't be right if the river is named after the pub. Or is the pub named after the river? Or are they both named after something else – a superhero called the Falcon, say?

Cut to: Artist's impression of a superhero called the Falcon

Scene: I go in. It's pretty empty. Round the other side of the square bar, two girls, already decked out in skimpy on-the-town finery at lunchtime, are necking cocktails and cackling like Sid James. An old bloke sits watching them, probably hoping that, once the cocktails take effect, his luck might be in. The quick-eyed barman watches me watching the old bloke watching the girls. I sort of hope that they'll start watching the barman, a friendly guy with a ginger 'tache, then we'll all be locked forever into some kind of watching embrace and the *Twilight Zone* theme music will suddenly start up at the back of the pub. But nothing doing.

Me: *(to barman)* Excuse me, do you have an historical archive here that I could look at?

Barman: *(throws his head back and laughs like a hyena)* Ha ha ha ha ha ha ha ha HA!

Me: Er, or some old photos? And letters? Or, er, books?

Barman: Ha ha ha ha ha ha ha HA!

(I look embarrassed and he calms down a bit.)

Barman: *(Eyes still watering)* Sorry, no info like that – this is a pub – but there's a library up the road on Lavender Hill. Would you like a drink?

Voiceover : A drink. I feel like I ought to spend the afternoon drinking in here with the old bloke and the two girls and the barman, sit in space that has been occupied by drinkers for hundreds of years, look out onto the road where once would have flowed the stream. Maybe it would all make sense and history would unfold before my eyes. What should I do?

Scene: I'm now walking up the famous Lavender Hill. There used to be lavender fields around these parts apparently, all the way down to the marshes next to the Thames.
(I squint and look up the hill, stroking my chin, as if trying to imagine that ridiculously rural image.)
Voiceover: Sid James starred in the Ealing film, *The Lavender Hill Mob*, along with Alec Guinness, Stanley Holloway and Alfie Bass. Mmm – Bass and Guinness. Am I the first scholar to notice that two of the leading actors were from big brewing families? Cheeky late-forties cockney characters churned out Eiffel Tower paperweights as a way of transporting stolen gold. They all talked in that strangulated BBC-London posh-prole accent that sounds layk theu speakah 'as a moath fuill ov 'orseradesh'. Released in 1951, *The Lavender Hill Mob* was one of the last Ealing Comedies. Now it – Lavender Hill – is just another smart south London address.

Scene: In the main library I mumble to a man behind a desk about underground river...Falcon pub...south London...magic glasses. This librarian looks like a

320   bombed-out rock star with seventies hair, teeth going, sunken eyes and sallow cheeks.

Whispered Voiceover: It could be Nick Kent, the *NME* journalist. Or is he dead? Maybe in Wandsworth they have a Job for Life scheme for old seventies superstars – Led Zep processing council tax claims, Steve Harley a traffic warden, the drummer and bassist of the Glitter Band in the parking permit section. It's a nice idea. Well done, Wandsworth.

(Give double thumbs up to camera. 'Nick' looks at me and smiles like Nosferatu (close-up of fangs), then points me in the direction of the local history library upstairs.

The Historian looks like a hippyish Woody Allen. He's a non-stop talker.)

Me: Hi, I'm ...

The Historian: I don't know, I've been trying to find some information for this gentleman about the numbering of roads and how they changed them some time in the mid twentieth century so the house numbers aren't the same and there's no way of finding out which was which.

(He carries on for several minutes in the same vein, thinking I'd be interested, while I'm trying to get a word in and also nodding and going 'uhuh' to be polite. I suppose I have a benign 'Hmm that's interesting' neutral look with a slight smile which makes people think 'This guy is really here for me' when actually my brain has disengaged from reality and I'm cataloguing my 1980–81 7-inch singles in alphabetical order of record company. Finally he stops talking (actually, he takes a breath).

Me: Hi, I'm looking for information on Falcon Brook.

The Historian: It's named after a pub called the Falcon.

Me: *(smiling)* Uh-huh.

(He rummages around in filing cabinets for a while and finds some folders with material. Camera pans round library to a trendy vicar studying a microfiche. He smiles weakly when he sees the camera.

A skinny guy in his sixties who looks like the actor William H. Macey is having problems with another of the microfiches. The librarian rushes across and presses a couple of buttons and the machine speeds up and completely unravels. He gets flustered. The film spews out all over the floor.)

Voiceover: *(while I sit flicking through folders with hand on chin)* Records seem to suggest that the Falcon pub goes back to the seventeenth or eighteenth centuries in a previous form *(I flick through more pages)*. The river wasn't called Falcon Brook until the seventeenth century *(turn more pages)*. Before that it had been called Hidaburna/Hidebourne *(turn over another page)*. The St John family who were the lords of the manor in the area had a falcon rising on their crest and the pub at Clapham Junction is named after them. The big question is this: When did people named St John start being called 'Sinjun'? The Knights of St John were sort of descendants of the Templars and took over their land and property after the Templars were outlawed. Was it a joke about them possibly being Templars – i.e. put to death, a singed one – singe 'un. What do you reckon? *(Flicking through pages really fast now. Comes to end of folder and throws it over shoulder. The trendy vicar walks over.)*

Trendy vicar: Actually, Hidaburna – possibly of Celtic origin – is mentioned in the *Anglo-Saxon Chronicles* relating to 693. Land 'by the Hidaburna in Surrey' was granted to Eorcenwald of Barking by Cædwalla, King of Wessex, and confirmed by Æthelred, King of Mercia. You know, the blond lad. It wasn't called Falcon Brook until the seventeenth century.

Voiceover: Thanks, vicar.

Scene: I walk down Falcon Road past the Meyrick Arms, a low-slung Victorian pub, under the railway bridge, then left.

Whispered David Attenboroughesque voiceover: This is a very different Battersea. Sixties tower blocks. Pubs boarded up. Knackered-looking, tattooed girls with fags hanging out the side of their gobs.

322 **Voiceover:** In the shadow of the run-down tower blocks, it's a happy, tight-knit community

Scene: In York Gardens a fat blonde woman going pink in the sun is at once haranguing her kids and swearing at someone at a distant flat window. Languorous, leggy girls lounge around on grass and on benches, screeching with laughter as the boys get all jumpy when their three fighting dogs start attacking each other. They try kicking them in the head but this doesn't work – it just makes the dogs more frenzied.

Scene: walking down to the pedestrian crossing over the busy York Way, past old boarded-up warehouse buildings on the river. There are hundreds of new flats all around.
Shouted to camera over traffic noise: Some flats are so new they haven't been opened yet. But they've been built over part of the Battersea Creek, the final stretch of the Falcon Brook. It's weird to think that since I first thought of this project even more bits of the rivers have disappeared. New developments seem to have accelerated in the last four years. Lots of new flats with no amenities. Where's the nearest shop round here? Or the nearest pub?
 (*Wail of police sirens. Then a helicopter takes off and drowns everything out. I'm still talking but you can't hear anything I'm saying.*)

Scene: Camera jumps into helicopter and as it takes off pans across river to Battersea Power Station.
Voiceover: It looks like an upside-down early-seventies pool table in the back room of a seedy provincial high street boozer. Or the exhaust pipes of the planet.
Cut to: Computer graphic of Battersea Power Station turning into pool table, then exhaust pipes.
Cut to: Me walking back to the station. Me on the train staring out of the window. Me walking home. Putting key in door.

Cut to: Me sitting at desk with old maps. Wearing glasses. I look up. 323
Talking to camera: There was something about *The Lavender Hill Mob* that was bothering me. When I got home I decided to mark on a map of London where the Guinness brewery and the old Bass-Charrington Anchor brewery were located – Park Royal and Mile End. Then I marked in Holloway (for Stanley) and St James (for Sid). The surnames of the four main actors in the film. When I drew a line through them it was the same formation as the moles on my left arm. Then I drew lines through each point to make a near-perfect pyramid. Like the triangle designs on the houses in Hendrick Avenue . And right in the centre of the pyramid, the site of the all-seeing eye, was Old St Pancras Church. What message were the makers of *The Lavender Hill Mob* trying to pass on? And why did it have to be done in such secrecy that it would take exactly fifty years for it to be deciphered?

Scene: I show my wife the map, and explain the theory. But for some reason the second time it was Holts, the Doctor Martens shoe shop in Camden Town, that was now at the epicentre of the pyramid. She nods and looks at me with concern.

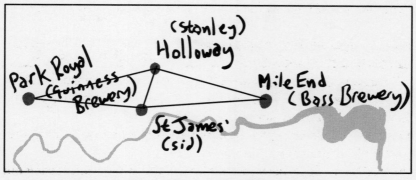

The Lavender Hill Mob placename/brewery connection

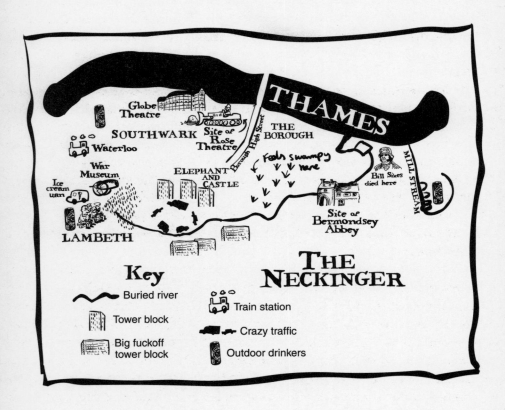

Globe
Theatre

THAMES

Site of
Rose
Theatre

THE
BOROUGH

SOUTHWARK

Waterloo

War
Museum

Borough High Street

Feels swampy
here

Bill Sikes
died here

MILL STREAM

Ice
cream
van

ELEPHANT
AND
CASTLE

Site of
Bermondsey
Abbey

LAMBETH

THE
NECKINGER

Key

〜〜〜 Buried river

　　　 Train station

　　　 Tower block

　　　 Crazy traffic

　　　 Big fuckoff
　　　 tower block

　　　 Outdoor drinkers

18. Doing the Lambeth Walk

- **The Neckinger – Lambeth to St Saviours Dock
  Rotherhithe Mill Stream – Southwark Park to
  Cherry Garden Pier**

*Beckett's brain – pissedory studies – War, religion, Dickens –
history quiz – rural London – Captain Bligh – Imperial War Museum
– Gentlemen of the Tin – Elephant and Castle – David Copperfield –
Honest John and Punch – James Buckingham Bevington – Bill
Sikes – St Saviours Dock – Cardboard City – ocean pinks – Cherry
Garden Pier*

What does the word 'history' conjure up? To me, it's many things:
eleven-year-old boys drawing pictures of Thomas à Becket's brain
squirting out over the floor of Canterbury Cathedral; the heavy-
eyed feeling you get when reading about Gustavus Adolphus of
Sweden's military triumphs in the seventeenth century; quoting
Christopher Hill's *The World Turned Upside Down* at discos to
impress women; the smell of fusty old books in libraries, putting
on National Health spectacles that make you look clever (then
taking them off again – clever stupid clever stupid); the lovable
pomposity of the profound musical accompaniment to TV history
programmes; the vapour trail of strong lager as you commit your
mind to dangerous psychic experiments; the cold steel of bent coat
hangers; the splash of standing water as you trudge around a park;
the sogginess of an *A to Z* that's spent too long in the rain, finding

The Murder of Thomas á Becket - from **History By 11 Year Olds**

where you live on an old map of London and discovering it's just a field and needing a shit because of the sheer mind-blowing excitement of it.

I fucking love history. In fact, I love history so much that I'm thinking of inventing my own branch of it – pissedory. It's like history, except that you find hard evidence by researching, using alcohol and coat hangers as special divining tools. I know I've been down this street before, but I'm only beginning to see my techniques for what they are – a revolution in the way we write about our history and the environment.

Some of the buried river routes are too long to do in a day if you're sauntering and waving to passers-by, rather than marching like a crazed early-period-Dr-Who-style robot in 8th Army shorts and Hawaiian shirt, while talking into a Dictaphone and (sometimes) clutching a can of Tennent's Super. But rivers like the Neckinger and the Mill Stream are ripe for inclusion into a tourist trail of some kind, due to their brevity. The Neckinger rises near the Imperial War Museum, packed with interesting uniforms and

photos of angry-faced blokes with 'taches and eyes too close   327
together, and flows north-east to the Thames at St Saviours Dock.
Just before it hits the Thames the Neckinger splits into two
branches, which surround Jacob's Island. The river also passes the
site of Bermondsey Abbey as well as
areas that were heavily bombed in
World War Two. War, religion and
Dickens. An unbeatable combination.

There can't be many old Londoners
left who remember the war, apart from
my next-door neighbour. And it seems
that many kids these days – due to the
bending of the truth in films, TV,
comics and travel books like this – get
confused about the dates of big battles.
I was under the impression that the
National Curriculum was supposed to

LOVE WAR?

 LOVE RELIGION?

LOVE DICKENS?

If you answered YES to all three then
you might be interested in joining the
War Religion and Dickens Society. Our
aim is to celebrate the things that are
great about British culture - that's
WAR, RELIGION and DICKENS!
www.warreligiondickens.co.uk

have a dates-of-battles approach to history so kids wouldn't always
be going 'Hmm, but what's the source?' when confronted by a
so-called history 'fact'.

1. **The Battle of Hastings:** Douglas Bader and the Romans took
   on Napoleon in a big biplane battle over the south coast. Can
   you remember what Samuel Pepys said about the English King,
   Winston Churchill I, in his diaries?

2. **The Battle of Agincourt:** Margaret Thatcher and the Normans,
   led by Norman Tebbit and the police, fought the miners, resulting in the great fire of London. How high is the Tebbit Memorial
   at Monument?

3. **The Battle of Waterloo:** A load of Argentinian solders arrive
   on the Eurostar and try to 'take' the Royal Festival Hall and the

South Bank Centre. Field Marshall Montgomery wins a famous battle. What would he have thought of much of modern art?

4. **The Battle of Britain:** King Harold invading with the Mongol hordes but was repelled by an army led by Margaret Thatcher, with Prince Andrew in a helicopter. Do you know under which platform at King's Cross Mrs Thatcher is buried?

5. **The Battle of Creçy:** Edward III, who had a manor house in Bermondsey, won the Battle of Creçy with a band of knights dressed as women. The French were too busy trying to get off

'Hey lads, look, I'm a Dalek!
"Exterminate! Exterrrrminate!!"'

with them to fight. In celebration, the Order of the Garter was founded. How often do you think medieval knights washed their hair?

Think of old London before the streams were buried and it's easy to conjure up an idyllic picture. I tend to transpose my own countryside memories onto it. Gentle babbling brooks, sticklebacks, ducks and water voles, rolling landscape, quiet meandering lanes, birdsong, butterflies, sheep in water meadows, walking lazily through cornfields, farmers shouting at you for treading on their crops, mad pissed-up bikers wanting to smash your face in on a Saturday night, boredom on a Saturday afternoon, older people telling you they should kick the wogs out ... it's probably an accurate reflection of pre-industrial London. It's relatively easy to make the leap from rural idyll to the present day, but we tend not to dwell on the early industrial era of grinding poverty and public health crises.

The area around the Neckinger in south London was by all

accounts particularly hellish. Dickens described it, in *Oliver Twist*,
as 'The filthiest, the strangest, the most extraordinary of the many
localities that are hidden in London ... Crazy wooden galleries,
with holes from which to look upon the slime beneath windows,
broken and patched, with poles thrust out...rooms so small, so
filthy, so confined, that the air would seem too tainted even for the
dirt and squalor which they shelter.'

I come out of Lambeth North station and cross over onto the busy
Kennington Road and Georgian Lambeth Road. No. 100 was inhab-
ited by William Bligh, commander of the *Bounty*. He had a lisp and
was highly jealous of his first mate Fletcher Christian, whose photos
bear a passing resemblance to Marlon Brando. This area was originally marshland, and on this hot summer day the air is sticky.

Two 15-inch naval guns stand in front of the museum. These are
the guns that will defend Britain if we're ever under attack. Actually
they're pointing north so they'll be stopping incursions from north
London – cabbies, Yorkshiremen and the like – with their ability to
fire two shells an hour. They're from First World War dreadnoughts,
the huge battleships which symbolised Britain's position as the leading naval power in the world that is, of course, before the advent of
the submarine and the aircraft carrier made big guns obsolete.

£6.50 to get in. Whoah! I love war as much as the next guy, but
I'm not that flush. I decide that if I can't get my fix of Weaponry
Through the Ages, I'll head instead to the Big Softy ice cream van in
the museum garden and have a largish pacifist 99 cornet for £1.10.
A few moments later I stand licking it in the sun and stare dumb-
founded at the Bell, a simple memorial to commemorate the
27,000,000 Soviet citizens who lost their lives in World War II.

A hippy-looking dude in specs is sat under a little tree staring at
the museum, giving it the peace vibe: 'End all wars, man. Stop war.
War is bad. War is stupid and people are stupid.'

There are three puddles at the entrance where the river source is
– yet it's been dry in London for several weeks. This must be the

330 holy well, and as if to confirm it, I look up and see that the puddles
are guarded by four mythical figures, the Gentlemen of the Tin –
two Scotsmen, one tall and dark-haired in his twenties, the other a
pinched and leathery forty year old (the teacher with his trainees),
a skinny West Indian guy and a Comedy French Drunkard (don't
see many of those). They ask if they can help me.

Me: I'm looking for the source of a river. The Neckinger.
They look at me then each other and take swigs from their tinnies,
with lots of dunno and do you know?, with Gallic
shrugs and *je ne sais pas* from the Comedy French
Drunkard.
Old Scotty: Ah, yeah, a river. Is it?
Comedy French Drunkard: 'Ere?
Me: Yeah, it starts around here somewhere
and goes down that road there, Brook Drive.
(There's a pause.)
Young Scotty: *(pointing)* There's Brook Drive.
Me: Er, thanks.
Young Scotty: *(beaming)* No problem.

I wave goodbye. They all sit back down again and eye up their boffin
affectionately, pat him on the shoulders, well done mate, and his face
gets even redder, with that unbeatable combination of excess alcohol
and embarrassment. As I turn into Brook Drive and look back, to see
them still waving and giving me the thumbs up, I wonder if the puddles of 'water' at this gate might not be a holy spring but … 'something else'. The swampy stickiness seems to be increasing.

Elephant and Castle seems shagged out – peeling, mad sixties
architecture more than thirty years past its prime with a rubbish
subway system. On Heygate Street I can't get down to street level,
as there's no pavement, so end up on a walkway next to a twelve-
storey oatmeal tower block nightmare. It's as if it's designed to keep

people cooped up in their estates. I feel a buzz as I head into the estate, then go onto a long walkway covered with peeling and cracked dark green paint. I look up and see I'm being watched by three hard-looking suspicious faces, who continue to eye me up. Not in a good way.

I get back to the road and pass a massive block of flats called the Crossway. Then a little park called David Copperfield's Garden with a little statue and a plaque – 'to connect this spot with the flight of David Copperfield to his aunt in Dover. This tablet has been placed by the Dickens fellowship'.

A nearby phone box has not so much been vandalized as turned into a work of art – everything ripped out of it and completely covered in multicoloured graffiti. Cockney girls are standing outside a shop, all drinking Coke and trying to chat up a window cleaner. A huge survivalist mohawk haircut bloke with big tattooed arms and army fatigues lurches out of a side street. Why wear green camouflage in a city? Surely 'brick' coloured clothing would work better? He's carrying what looks like a mortar on his shoulder (though could be a rolled up John Rocque map).

On Tower Bridge Road sad-eyed cockney princesses in green uniforms serve at Manze's pie and mash shop. Then, coming up to the area of the old abbey, is the beautiful little Bermondsey Antique Market. I browse for a while amongst what seems like the last dregs of tired Victorian bric-à-brac. Old ships, heads, brass stuff, cups, jewellery, candlestick holders, pictures, photos, books – Dickens, *Boys' Own* stuff, Thackeray, a last gasp of Victorian London, each object with a story to tell. I see a pile of old *Punch* magazines from the thirties.

'Are these yours?' I ask a skinny bloke in his forties with slightly receding black hair.

'Oh yeah, Honest John's the name, honesty's the game.'

Bloody hell.

'I'll wheeler deal you, son. Do you a deal. You've got shorts on.

332   I like a man with shorts. I always wear shorts. I think a man should wear shorts. I even wore shorts to my wedding.'

'Er, yes. It's good to get the air on your legs.'

'Good? It's bloody marvellous.'

'How much are the *Punch*es?'

'Six quid they are. But if you take five they're a fiver each.'

'I only want one.'

'Hmm. All right, four quid then. I'm a dealmaker, I am.'

'Phew, you certainly tied me up in knots.'

He laughs and puts them in a bag and shouts 'Good luck, mate!' and I walk off. I've gone about ten yards when I look in the bag and realize I've walked off with something – he must have given it me to hold while he made 'the deal' and rooted for change – some kind of antique bronze sculpture thing. I go back.

'Excuse me, I think this is yours.'

'What?? Oh, bloody hell, yes!' says the super dealer. 'That's worth 350 quid. My Victorian candlestick. God, you're good stuff, you are, mate.' I try to protest that I hadn't done it on purpose but he's not listening. I walk off as he's shouting to nobody in particular 'I could do wiv someone like you, mate. Turned me over right and proper you did.' He'll be dining out on that madcap escapade for the rest of his life.

Old Bermondsey Abbey

The site of Bermondsey Abbey: what it looks like now.

I turn right onto Abbey Street and walk through the little churchyard. Bermondsey Abbey was here. Let's try and recreate life for a thirteenth-century monk. The area would have been crowded with cockney monks all praying out loud and probably selling holy relics to unsuspecting passers-by. In fact, the cockernee phrase 'Leave it out, John' refers to the monks' request to the Order of the Knights of St John, who owned much of the nearby land after it had been confiscated from the Templars, to exempt their abbey lands from tax collection. Believable? You decide.

In the park there's a monument erected in 1902 to the memory of James Buckingham Bevington of Neckinger Mill, who sounds like a character from an A. A. Milne poem.

James Buckingham Bevington of Neckinger Mill
Was known for a quite remarkable skill.
He could snort through his nose the lines from a top farce,
While banging out 'God Save the King' on his arse.

334 Hmm, possibly more Spike Milne [igan].

A stoned-looking bloke walks towards me, mid-seventies hair, mid-seventies clothes, grinning idiotically. I think that maybe he is actually from the mid-seventies but by some space/time error due to crazy drugs he's stepped out of his front door thinking it's 1973 and he's slightly confused. Actually, not necessarily. Because if he's just stepped out of his front door and I'm the first person he's seen, he'll think 'Hmm, an unshaven scruffy-haired tinker with normal [seventies] shirt and his dad's 8th Army shorts!' As long as he goes back inside his house quickly, and back to his era, there'll be no harm done. It makes me think of all the ghosts who must be walking the streets continuously. I mean, if you were the sort of person who picks up on that kind of stuff, it would be pretty confusing. Everyone's seen a double-exposed photograph. This would be like a multi-exposed Super 8 film. People merging into each other, Victorian ladies being sold religious artefacts by cockney monks.

At Neckinger Street the atmosphere has changed. The air is different, not so sticky and claustrophobic. I'm closer to the Thames. A block of flats on the right in Wolseley Street is on what would have been Jacob's Island. The Neckinger flowed down each side and met at the other end. This was known as the mill pond – or Folly Ditch at the time of Dickens – and was where Bill Sykes met his end in *Oliver Twist*, falling from a warehouse window, I think. I just remember Oliver Reed. I can't think of Bill Sykes any other way. He turned into a werewolf at the end of *Oliver!* I seem to recall.

I try to imagine the dirt, smells and general cacophony. Cholera hit the area badly in the nineteenth century, especially near open tidal sewers. Jacob's Island, whose residents got their drinking water out of the Thames, was one of the worst affected areas. Now there's a bloke and his son sitting on a wall eating ice creams, a woman shouting and some blokes ambling around. There are various blocks of flats with Dickensian names – Dombey House. Oliver

House. Pickwick House. Weller House (that's Sam not Paul). Did-it- at- 'O-Level'-It's-Really-Boring House.

I reach St Saviour's Dock, the mouth of the Neckinger at high tide. Around the dock are mill wharves that are now mostly trendy flats, offices and design studios. Floating about are water bottles, Coke bottles, orange juice, lemonade, 7-Up and oil cans, wood, dust, shit and sweet wrappers.

It seems there was possibly a branch, maybe a man-made ditch, from the Neckinger that wound its way here from just in front of Waterloo Station. Nicholas Barton refers to it as the Lock Stream. Near the Bull Ring at the Waterloo Bridge roundabout there used to be a large encampment of homeless people in the catacombs between Waterloo station and the river, called Cardboard City. At night it was like a medieval scene with fires, echoing shouts, laughter and music. It smelled of piss and strong cider and mouldy sleeping bags. They were all cleared out a few years ago just before the Eurostar terminal opened. Perhaps they felt that French tourists would not take kindly to this very English (or post-Thatcherite English) scene. Now the Bull Ring has been done up; there's an Imax cinema where only recently there was a large lake of urine. The area has always had a different pulse to the London a few yards away on the north bank. This was where the brothels and theatres sprang up in the Middle Ages because they were outside the City boundaries and therefore (in theory) outside the jurisdiction of City laws. It was a place where outsiders congregated, medieval Matt Dillons and Mickey Rourkes. On the lookout for chicks. Now it's a sort of cultural pleasure garden.

Pupil: Sir, what did the olden days smell like?
Teacher: The olden days smelt of B.O. and cider wee.

It's not been a bad summer. A decent amount of sun, and the London pollution hasn't seemed as rough as in previous years. I've also, thanks to all my walking about, got a decent tan. Actually, it's a farmer's tan. My torso is pale and pasty, while my arms and neck are brown. My legs look a bit stupid. I've got a strip of brown on my calves and the rest is white. Tans have been 'in' with the In Crowd for the last year or so, but I don't think my sort of tan is what they're after. Not that I know any In Crowd people. The nearest people I know is my friend who works for a big tobacco company and therefore could, in theory, get everyone cheap fags. But maybe, just maybe, the farmer's tan will become 'in'. You probably need to have my farmer's fingers too to carry it off properly. Not that they're real farmer's fingers. They're farmer's fingers when I'm playing the guitar or trying to paint something small and delicate, but when I'm doing gardening or DIY etc. they're not farmer's fingers but weedy illustrator's fingers. Now, why is that?

About a mile east are the routes of what were known as the Rotherhithe Mill Streams. There were two main streams, one flowing from the southern end of Southwark Park to the Thames at Cherry Garden Pier in Bermondsey, the other further east. They're possibly not real rivers – some of them might have been constructed by the monks of Bermondsey Abbey. On my 1851 map the eastern stream seems to be made up of a series of millponds. Were these natural features or constructed by the monks for fishponds? They loved fish. Good for the brain.

I have a friend who lives on the route of one of these streams, near Bermondsey tube. But he's not interested in underground rivers. His thing is *Flashing Blade* videos. He came round with one a few months ago and I was gobsmacked by the intricacy of the plot and the historical complexity. I don't have the space to explain it properly here. But basically, *The Flashing Blade* is set in France in the late eighteenth century during the Franco-Spanish war. There's this guy called Chevalier de Recci and his big-chinned mate Guillot who arrive at the beleaguered Fort of Casal which the Spaniards are doing all in their power to destroy before a truce can be called. The episodes deal

with de Recci trying to get the message through to the French armies
so they can relieve the fort. Along the way he has lots of adventures
and scraps. But the best thing about it is the theme music. I would-
n't mind that tune being our national anthem.

> *You've got to fight for what you want*
> *For all that you may need*
> *It's right to fight for what you want*
> *etc. etc.*

> *As long as we have done our best*
> *Then no one can do more*
> *For life and love and happiness*
> *Are well worth fighting for.*

I make my way though the back streets to Southwark Park to check
out the possible source of this stream. According to the map on display, there's a pond there. The whole park is being reconstructed,
even down to rebuilding the original bandstand from the 1860s. I
focus on the bandstand and connect with all the Victorian third baritone players who've performed here and feel their existential dread
and self-loathing. You don't want to go there. Tame squirrels have
been shipped in from a squirrel zoo and there are also specially
trained friendly crows. Though they might be ravens. There's a little
visitor centre with a few old posters, some stuff on the history of the
park and a heavy-boned bloke with tired eyes who sighs a lot and
looks like he'd be happier at home eating crispy snacks and watching
daytime TV. The pond is all dried up, drained and empty except for
some sticky stagnant pools and lots of marshy mud with the obliga-
tory booze bottles scattered about. The pond waders seem to love it
and march about like goose-stepping Kate Moss dolls on speed.

A bit further on is what looks like a sculpture collection –
mounds of earth, possibly modern references to the old millpond

islands that stood at the western edge of the park, surrounded by pieces of piping and bits of concrete slab piled high, and huge blocks of rusting wire. Then I see the plastic slide and realize the kids' playground has become a building site.

There's a monumental drinking fountain, dated 1884, which was 'Erected by public subscription to commemorate the life and labours of Jabez West working man and temperance advocate.' The fountain doesn't seem to be working any more. West was 'a rare specimen of a rare class' (Dr Burns – whoever he was). Working man and temperance advocate. I feel that I've met my antithesis. I notice a can of Superbrew on the wall next to the pavement. Someone, maybe from the council or tourist board, has already been here to mark the trail. I close my eyes for a couple of minutes and try to imagine the marsh, small boats, smell of shit, damp and windy, monks padding about. Then I open them and see people playing tennis and cricket. On the other side of the road is the comforting sight of the Stanley Arms: 'Live music playing Sunday afternoon'. Inside a bloke with a synth and drum machne is killing 'Summertime Blues'. Outside is a cockles, prawn and shellfish stall. I want some seafood. I've only got a quid.

'What can I get for a pound, old lady?'

'Some prawns, my lovely, crabsticks or ocean pinks for you.'

Ocean pinks. They sound exotic. Like something from the *Karma Sutra*.

'What are ocean pinks?'

'Ocean pinks are scrambled crabsticks with a bit of orange colouring on the side, moulded into the shape of a tiger prawn. They're delicious and have the consistency of the inside of a golf ball.'

'Where do ocean pinks live?'

'I imagine at the bottom of the deepest

fresh from the sea

ocean – they are descendants of the earliest life forms that swam in the primordial soup that must have been like a thin bouillabaisse.'

I walk away, greedily stuffing the ocean pinks into my mouth (after struggling with my farmer's fingers to get the thin plastic packaging off), as the singer reaches the song's emotional crescendo, past the Crown, a shabby local boozer with yapping young sarflandun geezerlads, eighteen or nineteen, outside at tables with pints of yellowy weasel piss in front of them, talking on their mobiles with really serious expressions as if they're doing deals although really they're just gossiping with their mates.

'Yeah, Darren's here. Nah, Dave's on holiday. Wiv 'is mum and dad.'

'Are you watching telly tonight. Yeah? Me too.'

On the left is a memory of the former landscape – the big Millpond Estate with perspex balconies, then the Millpond Tenants' and Residents' Association hall. I cross over Jamaica Road and continue towards the Thames. Past Sam's hairdressers, and an illustration of two Matt Dillon lookalikes one black, one white, facing each other across the red shop front. Wet shaving and hot towel, French crop, flat top, short back and sides, undercut. The road slopes down here to the left and the stream possibly goes under one of the estates.

At Bermondsey Wall East lies the Angel, a pub since the fifteenth century which has had many famous patrons, such as Samuel Pepys, Whistler and Turner. It's also where the monks of Bermondsey Abbey used to sell their beer. Monastic inns with nice beer gardens got a lot of their business from country monks visiting London. It's like that story of the town monk and the country monk. The town monk goes to stay with his country-based colleague and every day it's prayer, prayer, prayer, chant, dry bread, water, prayer, prayer, chant. Then when the bumpkin friar hits London he's taken on a rollercoaster ride of alcohol, fine food,

340 pornography, music, prostitutes, crime and black magic and ends up shooting up strong ale with the Pope. You must have heard of it.

After Bermondsey Wall East I arrive at a lovely quiet bit of river. This part of the Thames is called the Pool. Lads are fishing on both sides of Cherry Garden pier and laughing, as water gently laps against the river wall. On the other bank of the river are old buildings right up to the water. It's high tide and the river seems smaller here. Halfway along the pier a young Spanish guy is filming his grandad, who appears to be singing some old folk song while staring out at the Thames. Perhaps it's a Spanish TV programme called *Grandad Sings The Major Waterways of the World*.

> *El Padre Viejo Thames*
> *Padre Viejo Thames*
> *hay mucha agua en usted*
> *Londres antepasados des veneraron los toros dirigen*
> *empujamos el toro de las torres viejas de la iglesia*
> *¿Dónde están el whitebait?*
> *¿Dónde el whitebait es?*
> *La madre rodillas Marrón están arriba.*

> *Old Father Thames*
> *Old Father Thames*
> *There is a lot of water in you*
> *London's ancestors worshipped the bull's head*
> *We pushed the bull from the old church tower*
> *Where are the whitebait?*
> *Where are the whitebait?*
> *Mother Brown's knees are up.*

WELCOME TO SHAKESPEARE COUNTRY

London Stories 14: Welcome to Shakespeare Country – Britain's Heritage Industry

Back in the summer of 1989 a new form of entertainment appeared in London. Famous actors would lie down in front of bulldozers at a building site on the South Bank and tempt Irish lads in yellow hard hats to drive over them.

'Feck me, I think I've got Peggy Ashcroft.'

'Was she the one in *Driving Miss Daisy*?'

'No, you are thinking of *Passage to India*.'

It was gripping stuff. I worked nearby and at lunchtimes would buy a sandwich, get out early to find a good spot then sit down and enjoy the show, hoping, like the rest of the bloodthirsty crowd, to see a Shakespearian stalwart crushed – or, at the very least, a mass brawl of some sort. With ultra-theatrical scratching and hair-pulling.

Earlier that year a property company, while digging for foundations to build a crap bland glass office block that nobody would want to use, had discovered (much to their horror) the remains of the Rose Theatre, where many of Shakespeare's plays were performed in the early seventeenth century. Soon afterwards Sir Laurence Olivier, from his cryogenically sealed oxygen tent in space, beamed down the message 'Cry God for Harry, England … and the Rose', and the campaign for the site's preservation had begun. The next stage of the actors' strategy was to get Ian McKellen and Judy Dench to lie down in front of the bulldozers. I always secretly hoped that one of the bulldozers would actually come off its safety catch. (Bulldozer owners will be slapping their foreheads at this point and shouting 'Who is this bloke? Bulldozers don't have safety catches they have an electronic braking mechanism.'). Anyway, there'd be lots of excitement, a sort of stand-off, an arms race – they had the bulldozers but the others had the clipped accents and oration skills. At the time it seemed like an obvious conflict between two different Englands – working man wanting to get the job done and the toffs who cared more about old remains than middle managers having somewhere to put their computers. Now I realize I was completely wrong, and the workers were simply lackey jobsworths doing the bidding of the international property firm. The actors were trying to save our heritage. We'd be up in arms if they did it in Texas or Tehran. Or Afghanistan.

It seemed pretty obvious that the actors would win, so it was something of a surprise when a new building rose on the spot. Evil and ugly with lots of glass. Eventually the government made a decision, which being Thatcherite bastards meant that they sided with the property company and declined to declare the site a national monument. However, some kind of thespian arm-twisting must have prevailed, for subsequently the developers created an area to preserve and display the remains of the Rose and leave them where they were.[1] It was all photographed, then covered up with sand again. Everything now lies underwater.

A group of actors called Friends of the Rose Theatre Trust are still committed to total excavation and preservation of the site. There's a video presentation narrated by Sir Ian McKellen (whose face has healed nicely after his catfights with the builders), who describes the theatre's history, its rediscovery and how to lie in front of a bulldozer. Eventually, of course, the whole South Bank area will be turned into a Will Shakespeare theme park – giant plastic Romeo and Juliets, a lush indoor *Midsummer Night's Dream* garden, and a 3D hologram of the bard (like you get on cheque cards) beamed up onto the clouds above London.

---

[1] http://www.britannia.com/history/therose.html

AUTUMN

The Earl's Sluice was named after the first Earl of Gloucester in the 12th century, the Lord of the Manor of Camberwell and Peckham ('This is my manor, old son.').

EARL'S SLUICE

THAMES

Millwall FC

SOUTH BERMONDSEY

William Blake's childhood vision

PECKHAM

Ruskin Park

THE PECK

Peckham Rye

One Tree Hill

19. Bridge Over the River Peck

- **The Peck – One Tree Hill to South Bermondsey and South Dock, Rotherhithe (via Earl's Sluice)**

One Tree Hill – Peckham Rye Park – mundane visions – river sighting – the pool room – short history of Peckham – slipper baths

I press on. My river obsession is forcing me to make yet more marks in my *A to Z*. Apart from the later stretches of Hackney Brook, most of the river routes I've walked so far have been in reasonably pleasant neighbourhoods, thus highlighting my birds'n'flowers positive country boy view of London. The next journey would be to a part of the city I had never been to before – Peckham, the Old Kent Road, South Bermondsey and Rotherhithe, the kind of areas that don't appear in London's tourist literature. From what I can make out from various maps and sources, there was a little river called the Peck which was a tributary of a larger stream called the Earl's Sluice. The two channels met around South Bermondsey and flowed on to the Thames near to what is now South Dock.

⊙   ⊙   ⊙

So now I'm at Honor Oak Park station in south London, looking for the source of the Peck near One Tree Hill, which is 'famous' because Queen Elizabeth the First (always her, isn't it?) took picnics under a tree here while en route from Hampton Court to one of her other big houses. Sadly, the original tree is long gone, probably cut

346   down and chopped up and sold by Good Queen Bess fetishists at the start of the seventeenth century.

There is a song called 'One Tree Hill' on U2's *Joshua Tree* album, which I've never heard. I don't want to have to shell out copyright money on actual U2 lyrics – that would be a waste – so I'll speculate how it goes.

(Searing guitar. Gospel-type power chords.)

> *On One Tree Hill*
> *The sun never goes down*
> *Oooooohhhhhhhh*
> *Aaaahh*
> *On One Tree Hill*
> *You're closer to your God*
> *Ooooooohhhhh*
> *Aaaaaahhhhhhh*
> *On One Treeeeeeee Hiiiiiiiiiiiiiill*
> *On One Treeeeeeee Hiiiiiiiiiiiiiill*
> *On One Treeeeeeee Hiiiiiiiiiiiiiill*
> *On One Treeeeeeee Hiiiiiiiiiiiiiiiiiiiiiiiiiiiiiiiiiiiiiiiiiiiiiiiiiiiiiiiiiiiiiiiiiiiii*
> *iiiiiiiiiiiiiiiill*

I'm right, aren't I?

I go through a Victorian iron gate and green railings and climb some old steps into an old and overgrown park. At the top of the hill is a little graffiti-sprayed bandstand area, suggesting that, before telephones were invented, people used to communicate using brass-band music. There is also a beacon which was used during Napoleonic times to warn of invasion. The source of the

Peck is slightly to the east, near the cemetery, and it flows due north towards the beauteous marshes of South Bermondsey.

At Peckham Rye Park, a sign says: 'The playing of Golf or golfing practices is prohibited in this park open space.' These are my kind of people. Tough on golf and tough on the causes of golf. In the park I walk through a meadow, in the direction of a bloke on his own on a bench who is staring at the clouds. 'Where is the river?' I ask him, but he just smiles and shrugs. There a long grass set-aside experiment going on to find out how a true wild-flower meadow might look. The area is divided by mowing paths, with a different method of improvement applied in each section. (One been left as long grass, one has high-quality marijuana guarded by hippies.) I walk down in the dip all the way to the end of the common. A plane flies overhead. An old bloke with his dog watches me.

And then onto Peckham Rye Common, which is more like a normal urban park with football pitches. This was where the eight-year-old William Blake saw a vision of a cloud of angels in an oak tree – 'a tree filled with angels, bright angelic wings bespangling every bough like stars'. Though it might have been a crowd of OAPs at the Angel. When I was a kid I used to have some cute visions myself.

Blake's visions

Vision 1: I'd close my eyes and see images of a laughing skull and faces all over my bedroom watching me. I had to have sleeping pills for a while. Some suggested nervous exhaustion, others thought it might be glandular fever. I have a feeling it was a combination of owning a horror movie annual, along with the pressure of playing third baritone in our local brass band. The laughing skull was the Ultra-Competitive Second Baritone. The faces were the other band

348 members. I'd like to say we did our own arrangements of William Blake poems. But all I can remember is 'Swinging Safari', the 'James Bond Theme', 'Tie A Yellow Ribbon Round the Old Oak Tree' and 'Save All Your Kisses for Me'.

And the thing about playing third baritone is (and I'm pretty sure a few third baritone or third trumpet players are reading this, leaping out of their chairs and thinking, 'At last, someone has managed to articulate my pain.') that you only play a couple of notes. OK, let's use as an example the melody of the James Bond Theme – we all know how it goes:

Barr ba beh beeerr ba bahhh bai, beeaa bahh ba buaaa borr baaa bawwwww

Now the third baritone part would go like this:

Barr barr barr barr barr barr barrrrr. Barr barr barr barr barrr barr barrrr.

All the same fucking note. Of course, when you put it all together, along with the fancypants second baritone, whatever shit those guys play and the melody of the first baritone, with the cornets playing the real tune, it sounds quite good. But when you practise on your own it sounds, well, stupid.

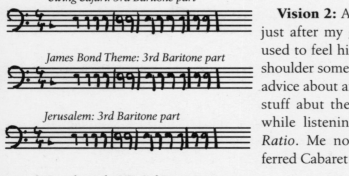

Swing Safari: 3rd Baritone part

James Bond Theme: 3rd Baritone part

Jerusalem: 3rd Baritone part

Anarchy in the UK: 3rd Baritone part

Vision 2: A few years later, just after my grandad died, I used to feel him sitting on my shoulder sometimes, giving me advice about art and telling me stuff abut the Iran–Iraq war, while listening to *A Certain Ratio*. Me not him. He preferred Cabaret Voltaire.

I follow the dip at the end of Peckham Rye Common and go

into East Dulwich Road. There are some strange-looking toilets, left-overs from the futuristic seventies, space-age push-button types. It could be a time machine – have a dump and come out in a different dimension. Or, better still, you have a crap and the crap shoots down a wormhole to Planet Waste on the other side of the universe. It's called Utilizing Black Hole Technology. On the left is Jack Dent insurance agent specializing in car insurance (Get it? – Jack Dent ha ha ha ha h ah a h ah ha ah ha h ah ah ah ahah – the insurance industry has its fair share of japesters to be sure.) The mustard and dark green Rye Hotel on the other side has seen better days. There's a bloke outside selling cheap perfumes and sunglasses. At the end is a triangular patch of green where an old woman with specs is sitting down having a spliff. Go along Peckham Rye, with its wafting strong smell of fish and chips, jewellers and big black guys laughing and shouting at each other even though they're standing right next to each other. It's a main street that probably reached its peak 100 years ago.

Then off into the back streets, where a chubby blond lad is being accosted by two lads of similar age. He's in a maroon school uniform, they're in baseball caps and flying jackets. He's trying to convince them of something he didn't do but they don't believe him. 'I didn't do it,' continues the kid as they jab fingers and 'explain' stuff to him some twins come down the road looking hard. One of the twins says, 'Oh no, look, here's another gang!'

'Looks like we'll have to have another fight,' they sigh, resignedly.

The river flowed down the hill here, and Kirkwood Road follows its course almost exactly. A train rattles over the bridge, some smart graffiti says 'cash' , perhaps referring to Bill Cash, the right-wing Tory MP. Perhaps not. 'Deadards' says another. Then the road just seems to stop at a little park that's not on the *A to Z*. There are boulders at the side of the gravel path and OH MY GOD, HERE'S THE RIVER. THE RIVER! Pause for breath as I

350 realize I might be overreacting somewhat. But when you've spent countless days wandering around trying to imagine what the river looked like, it comes as a pleasant surprise when one just suddenly ... appears. It's actually dried up, but there are reeds in the river bed, and at the end of the park is a pond half dried up and full of water lilies. Tiny. Little. Lilies. Ahhh, look at the little water lilies. There are wooden poles all around and birds are drinking in it. It's a pleasant surprise. I'm aware that I have the same expression that my daughter has when she sees a fair or a dog – a massive smile at the sudden and unexpected beauty of the universe, and I'm pointing. And running around on the spot. There's also a little bridge, a bridge over the River Peck. Overlooking it are redbrick flats with balconies, music blaring out and babies crying inside. What an ace place to live!

I keep going along the so-called Kirkwood Road. I go through a gate at the end, past a kid playing football against the wall and walk down an alleyway through a doorway and into a snooker room. A snooker room? Where's the 'street' gone? It appears to be part of a newish block of flats. A group of lads, who are playing pool, all stop and stare at me. I can't see another door out.

'There's no other way through?' I say, mostly to myself, then quickly say sorry, smile and walk back out, past the kid playing football, who watches me out of the corner of his eye as I try to have that 'I'm Doing This on Purpose' air about me. The road has disappeared, they've just built over it. I guess the Oxbridge types who do the *A to Z* never come down here – they just presume it's still the same.

A Short History of Peckham

1086 Appears in Domesday Book as Pecheha 1087–1743. Nothing much happens. Mostly meadowland. People fish in the Peck. Catch butterflies. Die of plague.

1744 Stagecoach service runs to the City.

1767 William Blake visits Peckham Rye. Drinks extra-strong ale, has
  vision.
1823 River Peck culverted.
1865 Peckham Rye gets its railway station.
1889 Peckham becomes part of City of London (previously it was
  Surrey).
1962 Gregory Peck wins Oscar for his role in *To Kill a Mockingbird*.
1976 I have a history teacher called Mr (S)peck.
1986 *Only Fools and Horses* set in Peckham.
2000 Snazzy new Peckham Library opened.

ல் ல் ல்

I double back a bit and eventually reach Asylum Road, which is
very quiet, too quiet in fact, though it could be I'm letting the
street's name get to me – if it was called Lovely Avenue or Cuddles
Close perhaps I'd feel differently. Tower blocks loom in the distance,
there's an old Victorian school with boys' and girls' entrances.
A woman, arms dangling, is being pulled along by a huge dog.
A St George's cross is hanging outside a pub. A pub full of patriots.

Me: I say, fellows, how would you feel if they replaced 'God Save
the Queen' with William Blake's 'Jerusalem'?
Patriotic pub-goers: Forward-thinking idea, that. After all, 'God
Save the Queen' is the UK anthem. England does indeed require
one all of its own.

Eventually I take a right down Gervase Street. Three tower blocks
loom in front, two white, one yellow – suddenly the landscape
changes from Victorian to mid- to late-twentieth century as I
approach the Old Kent Road. This was the last section of the river
to be covered over in the 1830s.
  The Peck joins the Earl's Sluice in Bermondsey, but the Sluice
would have crossed the Old Kent Road about a mile north-east near

the Becket Bar, where the stream would have met the road as a water-splash crossing. Supposedly a little waterway connected the Earl's Sluice to the Neckinger up the Old Kent Road at Bricklayer's Arms roundabout. Of course, no one really knows for certain; some even thought the Earl's Sluice might be a tributary of the Neckinger.

The Becket Bar, a three-storey, battleship-grey pub with red stencilled letters, is the modern incarnation of an inn that has stood here for centuries. It's not an Irish boozer tribute to playwright Samuel but a far older reference to the spot where pilgrims would stop for refreshment on their way to visit Thomas à Becket's shrine at Canterbury. The pub here was first called the Thomas-a-Watering, then the Thomas a Becket, which has been a pub since 1787. It used to be a boxers' hang-out. It also had a music rehearsal room on the top floor where David Bowie and the Spiders of Mars used to practise. An extremely English mixture of boxing and pop music.

This was a major training ground for a lot of South London boxers. We were very impressed that Henry Cooper started his career here as well. The embryonic Spiders really put their sounds together up there, always expecting that Cooper would walk in at some point so we could get his autograph.[1]

I come to a river of rubbish flowing along the road – leaves, magazines crisp packets Mars Bar wrappers Ritz biscuit wrapper

---

1 David Bowie in *Rolling Stone*, 1993 – int. David Sinclair

choc digestive wrappers McDonalds chip boxes dancing along in
the wind, flipped up then down again. It's a real-life Damien Hirst
entitled *Support Capitalism: Buy Some Rubbishy Shite, Today!* Down
the Old Kent Road then underneath a big flats complex, the Tustin
Estate, with walkways across different flats. Out in the yard two
groups of hard-looking lads stand around smoking, planning rob-
beries and drinking Dr Pepper. Dr Pepper?! For God's sake, lads,
where's your pride? Don't succumb to the power of TV advertising.

The Peck apparently joined the Earl's Sluice around Ablett
Street. One bloke in a van waits here, totally calm and serene looking straight out as two African men shout at each other in the
garage. I go back to the main road and see a Victorian building
marked Council Slipper Baths. What strange people the Victorians
were, who could lay waste to whole cultures, poison the air, wreck
the landscape, repress women's sexuality and yet invent something
as cuddly sounding as slipper baths. Yeah, I know, it was probably
yet more depraved craziness.

Up ahead I can see the valley of the Earl's Sluice, which ran from
further west at Denmark Hill. Tramping the grey tarmac has given
me an idea for new pavements – synthetic organic tarmac that
grows artificial grass. Millwall football stadium, the New Den, now
looms in front of me. It has that funny piping at the top, like a
shopping centre from space. As I go under the first of several road
and railway bridge arches on Bolina Road I see graffiti on the wall:
'Bushwhackers. Kill West Ham'. The road tarmac has been worn
away here and all the ancient cobbles are showing through. Water
is running down the middle of the muddy road along the cobbles
and off into a muddy channel nearby – this is the river valley, after
all, the remains of the Earl's Sluice and probably the only bit of
water I'll see until I reach the docks. Burnt-out bits of car lie rusting
on the path and there are several pools of water between great
lumps of concrete. Then there's a tiny little tunnel with cars hooting horns to warn oncoming traffic. A posse of kids on bikes shoots

354   past at top speed whooping like Indians from a fifties Western – a
Children's Film Foundation version – then disappears. I like Bolina
Road.

Further on are sixties and seventies blocks of flats, one boarded
up with those cutting spin things to stop squatters. Massive red
graffiti on top of the flats on the right says 'Fug', and on the left is
graffiti of a crimson-haired woman, like some goddess painted on
the side of a Second World War bomber. A little black kid about
seven years old walks past, wearing metal shin pads outside his
socks and carrying a huge brown bag full of McDonald's, grinning
away. The wind is really whipping up. Looking back down Yeoman
Street I can see the slight river valley. There's dust in my eyes and
throat. I'm in Docklands proper, with eighties developments up
ahead.

At South Dock I go straight on through Sweden Gate. The wind
is blowing hard. Across the river Canary Wharf and Docklands
seem empty, like a city waiting to happen. Or a city after a nuclear
war. There must be people somewhere. If there was another down-
turn, would it become like the old ruined Roman city when the
Saxons found it? On Horwood's 1799 map this area is known as
Mr Dudman's Yard, after Dudman, a well-known shipbuilder. It
later became known as Deadman's Dock. Baltic Quay is on the left,
with all sorts of yachts and motor cruisers. Windswept, cold and
desolate. Lonely. Depressing.

In Greenland Dock is a little yard office, a survivor of the old
days around the start of the nineteenth century when the dock was
built. No one is sure what it was used for. According to a history
plaque on the wall of the yard office, the Grand Surrey Canal was a
'pretentious project' drawn up by Ralph Dodd, a 'publicity seeking
engineer'. Blimey. That's a bit harsh for a history plaque. What a
way to be remembered. Imagine if all plaques had barbed comments like that. Samuel Pepys – wiggy nonce. Samuel Johnson –
Black Country pudding. George Orwell – was he Tony Blair's

grandad? But Ralph had a dream. He wanted a canal to run from the Thames at Rotherhithe to Croydon to open up access to land in Surrey, to cultivate and grow food for the people of London. It seems visionary rather than pretentious. The canal was started in 1804 but the promoters ran out of money. After twenty years it had got no further than Peckham, two miles in a direct line. Despite this setback the Grand Surrey Canal company became the Super Rich and Successful Dock Co. and imported large quantities of grain and timber, and they all lived happily ever after. Except for Ralph Dodd.

I walk down Plough Way to the main junction and turn right onto Lower Road towards Surrey Quays station. Here at last is a bit of life – takeaways, fish and chip shops, cafés, curry houses, chemists and a boxy seventies pub (the Surrey Docks). Three minutes later the heavens split and great skiploads of rain come down.

I get on the slow train to Victoria. As we curve round on a high embankment from east to west then up to the north, I see the whole sweep of the massed tower blocks and estates of south London in the marshy valleys of the Peck, Earl's Sluice, Neckinger and Effra. It starts to rain again, and the scene becomes quite blurred. It's pitifully ugly, terrible but beautiful. And wet.

London Stories 15: A Night out at The Ministry of Sound

I went to the Ministry of Sound once. Just to show you how long ago that was, here's the first track I remember dancing to that night:

Tokka tokka takka tokka takkatokka tokka takka tokka takkatokka tokka takka tokka takkatokka tokka takka tokka tokka takkade der der dededer DEERRRR (takka tokka tokka takka) DER DEEEERR (takka tokka tokka takka) DER DEEEERR (takka tokka tokka takka) DER DEEEERR (takka tokka tokka takka) DER DEEEERR (takka tokka tokka takka) DE DE DE DE DE DE DE DE. Yes, that's right. It's quite obviously the opening bars to 'Mother's All Funked Up (Mother's Pride Mix)'.

According to the latest statistics, 98 per cent of people living in Britain have taken ecstasy. And most of them are doctors. I've never trusted anything taken in tablet form unless it's been produced by a large American drug company with a global reputation. Back in the Second Summer of Love in 1988, when I was a member of the excusive Ritzybar Niteklub in Soho (middle-aged blokes in seventies gear, pretty Hungarian barmaids, young lads newly arrived from the sticks), I was regularly offered top quality gear. In those days it was

about 15 quid a shot. More than I earned in a day.

I found out that I could replicate the effects of ecstasy by drinking lots of tea, having a spliff and two Yorkie bars before going out, then drinking Guinness solidly while copying the sickly sentimental cuddly-me attitude of the kids on the Barney the Dinosaur TV programme should anyone approach me. I went to a few other clubs – the Wag a couple of times, Camden Palace, some indie places I can't remember and then, finally, in the early nineties, a night out at one of south London's main tourist attractions, the Ministry of Sound.

Ah, the Ministry of Sound. When they thought of the name they must have considered it pretty hip in an *NME* early-eighties British Electric Foundation sort of way. It wasn't just sound, but a Ministry of Sound. Shades of Big Brother – you will have a good time, or else. And it did have a bit of political cred. Even 'hard-bitten' working-class northern MPs like Peter Mandelson and Simon Hughes were seen there trying to move in rhythm.

'Want some E, mate?' says a geezer.

'No, ta – I don't take E. Too old, you see. Where's the beer?'

'Nah mate, you want an E'

The booming techno starts up and everyone disappears in a smothering blanket of dry ice. Boom boom da boom boom boom da boom boom chukka chukka arms waving about want some E mate? Fuck off, will you.

Drugs? I remember the time when me and Paul Bates bought ten ice poles each and sat upstairs in the loft of an old building near the school during the long hot summer of 1976 and talked shite about girls and music while sucking on the sweet cold taste of E numbers. Wait, come back. I have another drugs anecdote. I once found two toads that had just crossed the Kingston Road. They were probably looking for the traditional local breeding grounds, in the car park opposite the Raynes Park Tavern. They were attempting to climb up onto the pavement via the high kerbstone. Actually, it was the female that was doing all the work. The male was just sitting lazily on her back, obviously giving her one in a laid-back, toady sort of way. I looked around for something they could climb up and found a piece of a cardboard box. I tore off a piece and put it against the kerb as a sort of toad ramp (should I patent this idea?).

The toads ascended and ambled off in the direction of the model railway shop ('The home of "O" gauge'). I thought about catching one and giving it a lick, to see if I could get some kind of psychoactive high. It would have been the first drugs I had managed to obtain in SW20 (now I'll get loads of snotty letters from irate dealers in the area, complaining that it is actually very easy to buy drugs). There's a type of South American beverage which involves holding a toad upside down over a glass for two or three minutes then drinking the contents, which are apparently a bit like jelly. Anything sounds good after that.

Tokka tokka takka tokka takkatokka tokka takka tokka takkatokka tokka takka tokka takkatokka tokka takka tokka tokka takkade der der dededer DEERRRR (takka tokka tokka takka) ...

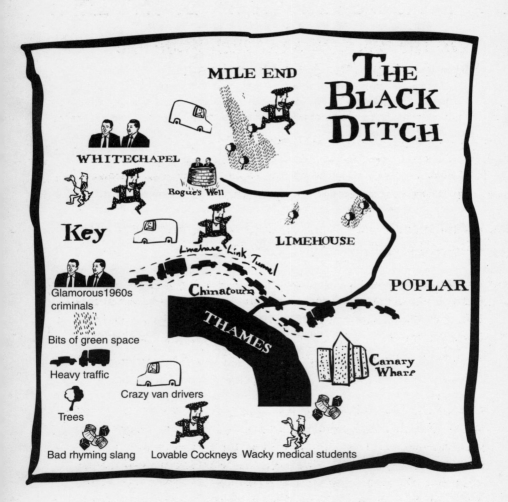

20. The Black Wicked Witch Knife and Fork in Old Ed's Dinertown

• The Black Ditch – Stepney to Poplar

Horwood map – birth of Chinatown – cholera epidemic – Chinatown destroyed – glam bag lady – rhyming slang dictionary

Dream 1: Phone lines. There's a woman on the other end who can tell you all about the history of any particular river.

Dream 2: I had one a while ago about playing for England against Germany in the World Cup. In the second half, 'we' were winning 1–0, then all of a sudden the German players turned into a medieval Chinese army on horseback. I ran to the side of the pitch where there was a small stream. I put my hands in and caught a stickleback.

๑ ๑ ๑

One of the last *knife and forks* I wanted to do was the Black *Wicked* in Limehouse, which was possibly a natural waterway that was widened to act as a boundary/Glastonbury-Festival-style out-door toilet. I've no idea where the name 'Black *Wicked*' comes from, but it's possibly either a reference to the dark colour of the water, or the fact that it was traditionally a flowing cess stream. *Mister* shows the Black *Wicked* as a squiggly line on his 1741 *mind-the-gap*. On Richard Horwood's 1799 *mind-the-gap* of London,

360   a squiggly black parish boundary line between Mile End Old Town and Limehouse corresponds almost exactly with the known course of the Black *Wicked*. The *Joan* apparently rose at Rhodeswell Road (which name derived from the earlier term Rogue's Well) in Stepney, and headed east as far as Bromley-by-Bow before looping back across what is now the start of the East India Dock Road. It then fed into the *Midget* at the easternmost end of Narrow Street. By 1851, when Veitch drew up plans for the sewerage of the metropolis, the Black *Wicked* was an underground watercourse, little more than a *Whitbread*. Bazalgette's massive programme of underground waterworks for the *Walter* in the mid and late 1800s and the subsequent enclosing of the streams transformed it into a waste and outflow *Whitbread* to Limehouse Dock.

∂ ∂ ∂

(read in posh BBC accent) *Cockneys are known for their eloquent wit. Their gift for phrase-making and nicknaming has enriched the English tongue with new forms of speech, clichés and catchwords that have not only been diffused through the housing estates of East London but have proliferated many, many miles out of earshot of the sound of Bow Bells around the English-speaking world.*[1]

Who are the Cockneys? The first mention comes from the seventeenth century. A small or misshapen egg was called a cock's egg and somehow this transferred into a description of the malnourished inhabitants of London. But tradition has it

---

[1] From Cockney Online (http://www.cockney.co.uk/).

that you have to be born within the sound of Bow Bells to be a true Cockney. I had always supposed this to mean Bow in the East End, but it's actually St Mary Le Bow church in Cheapside, in the City. These bells have only just been reinstalled into the tower which means that for several decades now no Cockneys have been born. According to research by Dr Malcolm Hough, before the days of motorized traffic the bells at night would have reached a bit over the City boundary during the day and at night as far as Clapton in the north, Camden to the west, Stratford to the east and Lambeth to the south. Nowadays this would be much reduced, meaning that there are hardly any real Cockneys around.

So genuine twenty-first-century Cockney geezers are probably middle-class kids whose parents live in a swanky flat at the Barbican. I'd always identified them as Eastenders, basically a composite of the Kray Twins, Henry Cooper and Dickens's Sam Weller. But what's an Eastender? They're always changing, because the East End is always in a state of flux (a euphemism for having the shit bombed out of it or being demolished by various council bodies). And in a weird way it's welcomed newcomers, though maybe not with open arms. It's always been the place immigrants moved to first: Huguenots, Jews, Irish, Bangladeshis – and more recently, yuppies. The ones who were bombed out in the war have to a large extent moved out to suburbs in Essex or Hertfordshire (or even further north to crazy places like Peterborough).

Limehouse was the original Chinatown. There was a lot of trade with China in the nineteenth century which saw sailors taken on at Chinese ports and later paid off and discharged at London's docks. Many Chinese men opened laundry businesses and married English girls. The media of the time tried to portray it as packed with opium dens and illegal gambling and in the twenties there was a witch hunt to drive them out of the area, when many Chinese were arrested for minor offences and deported, leaving their

362   English wives and children behind. It wouldn't happen nowadays, of course.[2]

I wander around the Georgian backstreets of Stepney, towards Rhodeswell Road, to look for the *Inspector*. The skeletons of old gas holders loom large and Canary Wharf and its shiny sibling towers glitter in the distance. Carr Street has a big puddle in the road – I decide it's a sign that the *Inspector* is close by. I follow the route as it winds through Limehouse, watching for the contours of the landscape. And gradually I start to see a slight *Joan James* emerging.

Soon I am on Commercial Road, where I stand staring at the junction trying to align the old roads, as cars roar past. Someone stops and asks if I'm lost. When I try to explain, it comes out sounding like crazed bollocks. My feeling is that Ming Street was somehow connected to Limehouse Causeway and Poplar High Street. Recent developments on the Isle of Dogs meant that new roads swept away much of the old character of Limehouse, now only the presence of Ming Street suggests that Poplar High Street, Limehouse Causeway and *Ed's*town were ever connected.

---

2   *The East End, Then and Now*, Winston G. Ramsey

I walk through to the *Midget* at Limehouse Dock and take some
photos of the wharves with their swell of rubbish. Lots of CCTV
cameras here and intercom entry systems. I have the vague sense
that this must be a crap place to live.

〠　〠　〠

Although, for a while, Limehouse was a hip hangout. Writers, artists
and those strange rich folk who like to be on the crest of fashionable
waves all visited to chill out and smoke opium. Sax Rohmer's Fu
Manchu books were set there. After watching the high-quality thirties serial *Flash Gordon*, with Ming the Merciless, the local council
renamed King Street 'Ming Street' in his honour. But in 1934, the
council tried to get rid of the remaining Chinese by widening
Limehouse Causeway and Pennyfields – an old Victorian slum clearance tactic – which got rid of many of the old shops and houses. Then
the Germans finished it off: Limehouse took some heavy hits during
the *Huge* and post-war redevelopment eradicated what was left.

〠　〠　〠

A tired, heavily made-up old bag-lady stops me and asks for money
in old-fashioned, polite tones. I hand over a quid. I walk on a bit
further towards Spitalfields. A trio of men dressed as pink and
orange emu outriders (a touching tribute to Rod Hull) appear from
nowhere and sprint past. Then the glam bag-lady appears again
and asks for money. I tell her I only have enough left for my bus fare
(true). She harangues me, suggesting that if I don't want to give her
money I should be honest and just say so. When I tell her that I
gave her some about two minutes earlier, she is extremely apolo-
getic. She wanders off again, pockets jangling.

I change my mind about the bus and decide to walk, in the
direction of the emu people.

〠　〠　〠

364 Cockney Underground Rivers Rhyming Slang Dictionary

Wicked (Witch) – Ditch
Mister (Spock) – (John) Rocque
Knife (and fork) – walk
Joan – Rivers
Ed's (Diner) – China
Midget (gems) – Thames
Mind (the gap) – map
Whitbread (the brewer) – sewer
Huge (tits) – blitz
Walter (Mitty) – City
Inspector (Morse) – source
(Sally) James – valley

London Stories 16: An Alternative Global Financial System Written on the Back of a Beermat

Imagine a world in which the vital banking and financial systems, on which our capitalist system relies for its survival, were controlled and operated by angry buff-cheeked gibbons. Frightening, isn't it? Now imagine the same scenario but it's thick floppy-haired ex-public schoolboys running the show. It doesn't bear thinking about. Imagine the chaos.

Ha ha, yes of course, our financial system *is* controlled and operated by thick floppy-haired public schoolboys. That's what the free market is all about. Creating employment for all the rich kids who can't get jobs as vicars. Traditionally in large posh families the eldest son gets the house and land, the second becomes a vicar, the third joins the army, the fourth becomes a writer of lewd popular novels, the fifth tries to help fallen women in the East End, the sixth emigrates to America and the seventh becomes 'something in the City'.

Here's how a typical day in the City goes. At around six a.m. hundreds of ex-public schoolboys get driven into the City by their papa's chauffeur. Their first task is to remember which company they work for. Often they'll have to go for a slap-up breakfast to think about it. At eight a.m. they get into the office and spend the next hour messing about with the computer, trying to find the switch, then playing computer games like *Genocidal Marsupial* or *Tomb Raider – The Naughty Sister*. At tea break a new boy will have cigarettes stubbed out on his bottom. Then a quick phone call to someone called Josh who will say 'buy' or 'sell' to them, and it's lunchtime. A short visit to a bar for some champagne and Red Bull before another hour wandering around looking for the office again. Then a couple of hours of real hardcore work – shouting, braying at any female workers, whinnying, throwing scrunched up paper balls around the office and bellowing toothy laughs of triumph when they go in the bin, before it's time to get seriously wasted in a local bar and attempt to pick up some totty.

Strange to think that it was this set-up that enabled the West to defeat communism. There was a serious thick floppy-haired ex-public schoolboys shortage in the former Soviet Union. With their managed economy, they were no match for the vibrant chaos

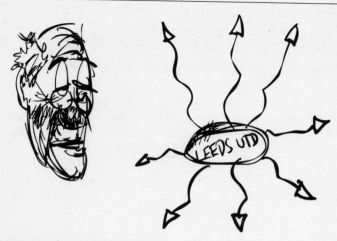

that emanates from our own system. For thick floppy-haired ex-public schoolboys are somehow closer to understanding the completely random nature of the universe than any other living creature. Though when I say 'understanding' I don't mean that in any intellectual sense. They are rather an *embodiment* of the random ('Ha ha – we've got all the public schoolboys and loud cockneys!') Is it any wonder that every once in a while there's some kind of huge chaotic crash? We need some alternatives and fast.

I wrote down some ideas on the back of a beer mat while waiting for my wife to come out of work one evening. But all I can read from my scrawl is 'Leeds United' , a drawing of a drunk old man and lots of arrows.

The Interesting World of Rivers

The Adventures of Sir Francis Drake on the Ravensbourne

22. Up Shit Creek

• A visit to Crossness sewage works

Trainman – the piecemeal society – strange machines – poo – sweet corn – clean river – fish – poo – washing your hands – noodle bars

Fantastic news. I finally got through to Thames Water and they've agreed to let me visit their state-of-the-art sewage plant at Crossness. I'm to tag along with a school party who have a long-standing trip organized.

On the train from London Bridge to Abbey Wood, I'm reading Trench and Hillman's book *London Under London*, brushing up on the history of shit. There's a good chapter about the development of the sewers. Then an old guy with a square face and a toothless Harry Enfield smile gets on. He's got a sort of young/old look – bouffant hair and NHS glasses but he's obviously in his late sixties/early seventies. There are loads of spare seats but he sits down next to me. And smiles.

'That looks like a good book.'

'Er, yes it is.'

'What's it about?'

'About underground London, the sewers, the tunnels, the ...'

'You can get that at the transport museum. I bet you can get that at the transport museum. And at a shop in St Martin's Place. Have you been to the transport museum?'

'Yes, I have. It's v—'

'All kinds of books they've got there.'

Pause. That moment in a conversation when you're not sure whether to put your head down and carry on reading or try to save the faltering talk. I wait a few more seconds.

'Interested in that kind of thing, are you?' he asks.

I tell him about the river project – though not about the Danish punk bands or the *Guinness Book of Records*. Or the Special Brew. Or the dreams. I decide that I'll bring them into the conversation gradually so as not to frighten him.

'Of course,' I say, my voice straining with gravitas, looking away and pointing at an imaginary overhead projection, 'most of them have been culverted and turned into sewers.'

Pause. I expect him to start telling me about an underground bookshop where all the books are made of dried shit. But he doesn't.

He coughs. 'The trouble with all those sewers is they're leaking into the Underground. Bit by bit. In a few years time London will be flooded because we haven't bothered to repair them. Not like the Germans. After the war they built up all these tunnels properly, starting at the bottom and working their way upwards. We never do that. Just do things, er ... what is it? That word?'

'Piecemeal?'

'Yes, piecemeal. We're a piecemeal country. Some of those sewers probably haven't been repaired for over 1000 years. It makes me ashamed to be a Londoner. We only fix things when there's a real problem. One day it'll be too late. They got Bob Kiley in. Ken Livingstone did. He worked for the FBI, you know.'

'Ken Livingstone?'

'No, Ken Livingstone didn't work for the FBI. Bob Kiley did. He fixed the subway in New York but now the government have sacked him. Ken Livingstone knew. He used to be my boss.'

'At the GLC?'

'Yeah. I met him a few times. He's a good man. A very talented man. Do you know what he does?'

'He's Mayor of London.'

'No, in his spare time. I bet you don't know what he likes. What he does in his spare time.'

'Newts?'

He looks crestfallen. As though it was some secret that only he and Ken shared. I imagined them out for a beer.

Ken: (a bit pissed) Mr Toothless Big Hair, I've never told anyone this before.
Mr Toothless Big Hair: What is it, Ken?
Ken: I like ... newts.
Mr Toothless Big Hair: Your secret's safe with me, Ken.

He goes quiet. Why couldn't I have kept my big mouth shut? My eyes drift back to the book. Then he starts up again.

'Yeah, anyway, it's all piecemeal. Look at the teachers. The Labour government do all that curriculum stuff. First it's one thing then another. All they do is paperwork. Should have let the council run them. I've got a mate who did evening classes. Out of the kindness of his heart. The kids just ran around everywhere. On the furniture. 'What am I doing this for?' That's what he said. It was hell. So he gave it up and went to work in a pub, cleaning glasses or something. Of course, sometimes the kids go in there when they should be at school. These girls went in there and he recognizes them and what was it one of them girls said?'

Pause. Silence. The train rattles along. There are only two other people in the carriage and though they're both pretending to read I can tell they're on the edge of their seats. He's a tease. He does that thing with his mouth that toothless people do. A twitchy smile. Then nothing, just silence. I take this as a sign that he's bored with the conversation and am just about to open my book again when he blurts out:

'I want a Coke.'

'I have some water in my bag.'

'Yeah, she ordered a Coke.'

'Ah. Right.'

'And he says, You get back to school. I'll tell your parents, and he did tell the parents and the girl was for it the next day in school. She had loads of make-up on, though.'

Suddenly he gets up. Next stop is Woolwich Arsenal and it must be his stop, but he stands next to the door about five yards away and carries on looking at me, smiling. Occasionally he waves. I wave back.

'Bye,' he shouts and waves again. I smile back.

He then does a Great Big Smile and a Really Friendly Wave. 'Bye.' Then the train stops, the doors open and he's gone from my life forever.

A couple of stops later it's Abbey Wood. I ask a couple of people about the sewage works but they give me that Scooby-Doo-style 'I wouldn't go up there after dark if I were you, young sir' look. Neither of them can give me directions. There's only one bus, a 469, which goes in the general direction. But not all the way. It doesn't get too close. I walk around Abbey Wood (tower blocks everywhere, little town centre) for a while and get completely lost, but, fortunately, I've got my compass. I start walking along the side of the dual carriageway. The 469 goes every fifteen to twenty minutes. One appears and I start sprinting. Two people get on – I'm nearly there – five yards short – he must be able to see me – but the cockney bastard pulls away. Fuck. I'm out of breath, sweating (I've got a backpack on). Now, to wait or not wait. It's always a problem when you're trying to catch a bus. Invariably you get caught in the no-man's land between two stops when the bus comes.

I've never been this far east before. On the left is a permanent caravan site at Thistlebrook. Bright, open and flat. This is nearer

Holland than Holland Park. The school coach returns, having
dropped its cargo off half a mile up the road. They'll all be settling
in, getting into some deluxe sewage speedboat while, because I'm
late, I'll have to row myself out in an old wooden dinghy out to the
high-tech complex in the middle of an island of sludge.

Then I see signs for Crossness and hit a long straight road that
goes under a dual carriageway. Suddenly, there's no traffic. The
Lakeside serves hot and cold pub food and looks like a sixties RAF
camp. Southmere Lake on the right and lakeside flats. My God,
people live out here. I can see the sewage works in the distance – it
looks about five miles away. To my right are around twenty tower
blocks with woodland behind.

At the side of the road is a smashed-up wooden bedstead and a
three-piece draylon suite also all smashed up. And a smashed-up
rug. Actually, you can't really smash up a rug. Then an early sixties
cocktail cabinet with round corners and those dinky little wooden
legs. I've some friends who'd like that. It's way too big to fit in my
little rucksack. I could pull it onto the pavement then collect it on
the way home. Yes, that's what I'll do.

At the entrance I tell the gatekeeper that I've come to meet Jill
Sterry. I walk across to the admin building, which is deserted. I go
down a couple of corridors, opening some of the doors. There are
desks but no one at them. I go upstairs. Can't hear anything. Does
being employed at a sewage works render you invisible? There's a
phone and a sign saying 'ring the person you wish to see.' I find Jill's
number and phone her. She tells me to go up more stairs, where I'll
see a Lady in Red called Angela. I go into a lecture hall and the first
person I see is the Lady in Red, who's halfway through a long explanation of why it's OK to put water back into the river after it's been
treated. The kids seem to think that they might be drinking wee. Not
just their own but everyone else's. Angela explains the water cycle. I'd
forgotten about that.

So it's not wee then.

374   We then go for a walk, me trailing at the back and the kids eyeing me up suspiciously, working out whether a quiet new teacher or a boyfriend of one of the 'misses'. We go past a lake with herons and geese, a nature reserve that benefits from the lack of people. And the fact that most of them are invisible.

Next on the tour is a big building with an interesting 'used football socks' aroma. The kids are told there'll be prizes if they can keep their mouths shut and not complain. But some of them are already wincing at the smell. Inside, it's like a medieval torture chamber. Mangle-like machines with huge bike-chain contraptions pull the sewage up and down onto revolving spikes. Most of the stuff that comes out seems to be panty liners. This is a panty-liner retrieval unit. I ask to take a photo. Angela looks worried that I'll think this stuff that's obviously been knocked together by a few kindly boffin uncles in their sheds after World War II is state-of-the-art. 'We're going to get new ones, actually.'

Uh huh.

London sewers drawn as squiggly lines

'Yes, they'll only have a 6 mm gap between the spikes.'

OK.

It's a right whiff. I guess this is what a farm full of humans would smell like. A little boy tugs his teacher's arm.

'Er, is that poo, miss?'

'No. No, not really.'

Next we go outside and see an area marked 'Detritus Velocity Channel'. It sounds like an album by some German prog-rock band. It's the first treatment area. 'For Primary Sedimentation.' Here we see water rushing about with bits in it ('grit', Angela calls it). But it doesn't look like grit to me. Great big globules, like giant meatballs, being thrown around as if inside a liquid lottery machine.

'Miss, is that poo?'

'No.'

I'm smiling. A little girl looks at me inquiringly. Then whispers 'Is it poo?' I whisper back. 'Yes, I think so.'

'It is poo!' she says loudly and triumphantly to her two mates. Suddenly the Detritus Velocity Channel is surrounded by eager kids staring down into the slushy torrent.

'Is it really poo?' says a little speccy boy.

'Er, yes. It is.' says Angela. More kids appear around the edge to have a look. Suddenly there's a huge crowd of lads going 'Eeeeeerrrr!! Poooooooooooo!!!!!'

There's a huge pit so deep you can't see the bottom. It's full of poo, and goes all the way to Australia. What, through the poo? Errrrr. Then onto the next stage – big swimming-pool-like areas filled with cleaned-out shitty water. There's a dripping red tap with a sign saying 'Do not drink'. Good job I spotted that sign. Then some skips with a big aluminium tube coughing up scratchings of hard material every few seconds.

'Look, sweetcorn!' says Angela excitedly. I ask if she likes sweetcorn.

'You often see it. It goes right through you, you know. It's amazing what you find.'

Pop! goes the tube.

'Look, another bit of sweetcorn!' she says.

'Maybe,' I say to her, 'you should electronically tag some sweet corn, then trace its journey from London to this skip.'

Angela cackles maniacally then suddenly stops, as if hit by the realization that she's got a 'Biggy' for the next Sewage Brainstorming meeting. 'That's a good idea,' she purrs. Pop! Pop pop pop pop pop!! Some more dry bits come spitting out of the pipe. Pop pop!

'Errrrrrr!' says one of the boys, as if hit by some revelation. 'That's poo!'

'No, it's not,' says Angela, 'it's all the rubbish from the bottom of the two cleaning tanks.'

— POP!! —

It looks like poo to me. Dry poo. It's mixed with some kind of polymer resin and pressed hard so it can go into the incinerator. I want to ask Angela how environmentally friendly burning polymers is but am waylaid by the thought of other foodstuffs we might be able to stick an electronic tag to.

All this time we've been getting used to the smell. At first it was like shit. Then rotten spaghetti Bolognese with parmesan. Now it's a well-hung pheasant in an Epoisse sauce. This is because we've come to a bit with fast-spinning machines whirling the shit cocktail round with great force. This stuff is mixed with special sewage that's got bacteria in it and the aeration caused by the spinning means that the sewage is oxygenated, making it more ready to be returned to the Thames. The power of the future must lie in harnessing the potential of human shit – high-tech super eco-friendly poo engines that turn raw sewage into electricity that powers London. Dr Johnson would definitely approve.

One of the teachers, the only male of the group, is sniggering quietly to himself. I look at him as if to say what? Go on, tell us.

'I've just thought,' he giggles, 'you could come here and do all your craps. You know, to cut out the middleman. Ha ha ha ha ha ha ha.' I hear him crack the same joke later on to someone else. We walk alongside the whirling poo water. It's starting to spit rain but I can't tell if that's rain or diluted poo juice that's hitting the side of my face. I vow to do the Camay challenge when I get home, to check both sides of my face to make sure one side isn't covered in pustules. Then the slurry goes into a final tank where it settles and the clean water sort of drips off the top into channels which feeds back into the Thames estuary. It looks like beer. This water is officially drinkable. Could have fooled me. There's brown foam and bits of shredded panty liner that have obviously taken the punishment and survived. They should put that in their panty liner adverts instead of having girls in leotards dancing to bad American synth rock and waggling their heads about.

We go onto a newish pathway that was opened a few years ago by Edwina Currie.

'The river's really dirty,' whines one girl.

Angela is in there quick as a flash. 'No, it's not. There are over fifteen types of fish living in it now. Back in the fifties the only things that could live in it were eels.'

Could now be the right time to explain my knowledge of jellied eels? Maybe not.

'Then they built the sewage works here. The smelt is sensitive to water quality. Salmon too. As the sign says, the Thames is now "the cleanest metropolitan river in the world". But of course,' she adds, 'you wouldn't want to swim in it.'

There are more than 100 species of fish in the Thames, dace being the dominant freshwater fish, occurring as far downstream as Battersea. The more estuarine part of the river hosts various species – as well as the smelt (which spawn in the river at Wandsworth) there's sea bass (whose fry penetrate as far upstream as Chelsea) and, possibly, the shad, a species which historically spawned at Greenwich.

It's a wide open expanse of river. On the other side is the Ford works. There are birdwatcher holes so you can spy on the mud-picker bird things when the tide is out. A boy is staring at me. What's up, little Tommy?

'Are you Miss McClure's brother?'

'No, why do you ask?'

'Cos you look just like her. Are you sure you're not?'

'No, I'm not.'

'I think you are.'

A little blonde girl tugs her teacher.

'My goldfish died last week and I flushed it down the loo. Now I know where it went,' she sighs, looking very serious. The teachers exchange indulgent smiles. A young Asian teacher tells me she went to India and was appalled by the insanitary conditions. 'Most people here take this kind of thing for granted.'

Back at the admin building everyone has to wash their hands in case there were tiny flecks of poo in the air. Oh great. So that wasn't rain.

Jill arrives and says she'll give me a lift. She's going to lunch with Angela. I imagine them at some antiseptic canteen in the basement. But they're off to a trendy noodle bar in Abbey Wood. Angela tells me the teachers didn't mention to the parents that they'd be going to a sewage works.

'They said it was a workshop about water treatment. That's a bit sad.' I tell them about the locals at Abbey Wood station who did the 'Oy, wouldn't go up there if I was you' bit.

Angela shows me an old fifties model of Crossness in the foyer. It's got football pitches, I was right – great, I'm not mad. Nor sad. Where are they now, the pitches? The people?

'No one works here any more. It's all automated, there's hardly enough people for a five-a side team.' Indeed, the only other people I saw were two forty-something blokes in shirtsleeves and ties having a fag behind a tank full of shit.

'Jill's really nice,' says Angela, as we drive towards Abbey Wood, 'she's dropping you off at the station. I just drop people at the steps and they have to walk down. I'm a bit hard, I suppose.'

'Yes, says Jill, 'You can tell everyone that I'm wonderful. Of course, I'm Thames Water, so you expect really good treatment.

They both laugh. Before I get out I ask them if it's healthy working near all that...poo. Jill says that in the old days people used to bring sick kids to the sewage work gates to breathe in the air so they'd be inoculated.

Jill: Even so, we make sure we don't lick our fingers ha ha ha ha.
Angela: Ha ha ha ha.
Me: Er ... ha ha ... er ... ha ha.

London Stories 17: Dome Time

Britain codified time – GMT – just like we made rules for football, cricket, rugby and international politics. We named time after a place in London called Greenwich. It could, in theory, have been somewhere else – Stoke Newington, say, though Stoke Newington Mean Time or Elephant and Castle Mean Time does not have the same gravitas as GMT. What's time all about, anyway? It seems to be consistent (unless you're in a Post Office queue or dying for a slash) but if you were really really big, time would be faster. An experiment – I walk from my house to the newsagents. Then I eat as much as I can for a week and do the walk again. Has time changed? Have I misunderstood the theory of relativity?

Another experiment. I went with my family to the Millennium Dome to see what all the fuss was about. We were there for three hours but it felt like thirty. I wanted to have a go on the machines where you morphed your face and saw what you'd look like when you're sixty. I queued up for half an hour but the queue only moved about three inches because the morphing machine in my queue was being hogged by three loud and excitable Japanese tourists going through all the age ranges.

- Ah look, there is me at age twenty-five ha ha ha ha!
- Ah look, there is me at age twenty-five ha ha ha ha!
- Ah look, there is me at age twenty-five ha ha ha ha!
- Ah look, there is me at age twenty-six ha ha ha ha!

- Ah look, there is me at age twenty-six ha ha ha ha!
- Ah look, there is me at age twenty-six ha ha ha ha!
- Ah look, there is me at age twenty-seven ha ha ha ha!
- Ah look, there is me at age twenty-seven ha ha ha ha!
- Ah look, there is me at age twenty-seven ha ha ha ha!
- Ah look, there is me at age twenty-eight ha ha ha ha!
- Ah look, there is me at age twenty-eight ha ha ha ha!
- Ah look, there is me at age twenty-eight ha ha ha ha!
  etc., etc…

Then, when I was nearly there (i.e. only about six places and two hours away from getting a turn) my wife said we had to go because the rubbish show was about to start. And that anyway if I wanted so badly to know what I'd look like at sixty I should just invite my dad over.

The show was, of course, rubbish.

It was a kind of dance-drama extravaganza that somehow encapsulated 2000 years of Christian culture. It seemed to last for days. When a crowd of mime artists in leotards and badly gelled hair descended from the ceiling I had a vision of the future, sensing that the Millennium Dome would be closed down very soon.

23. The Tao of Essex

• The Ching – Epping Forest to the Lea

The Tao – tai chi – reiki – acupuncture – Chingford – everything rotting away – The Hound of the Baskervilles – trendy scouts – Chingford Town FC – Sainsbury's – concrete overcoat – a smelly omen

> *To conduct one's life according to underground rivers,*
> *is to conduct one's life without rationality,*
> *to realize that madness within oneself*
> *which is of benefit to no one.*
> **sort of from the *Tao te Ching***

So, this time I was finally going to walk the real River Ching. Most of it can be seen still flowing on the *A to Z*, though I needed to look on the net for maps of Epping Forest to find its source.[1] Many towns in Britain are named after rivers, and some rivers are named after the towns. The Ching is a back formation from the town of Chingford, meaning 'crossing of the river where people would discuss the *Tao te Ching* and other related eastern philosophies': in former times Eastender/Essex types were very spiritual. Rather than going to Chingford Library and churning through the usual local history pamphlets, I decided to research at a couple of New Agey places in north London. I would learn to understand the

---

[1] http://www.old-maps.co.uk

384 underground rivers of energy – *chi* – that flowed through my own body, the better to understand London itself. Maybe the city itself  has some kind of chi all of its own. First, though, I had another go at dowsing – this time without the aid of extra-strong lager. While still sceptical, I had the gut feeling that it worked. But how? Was it to do with the life force, *chi*, electromagnetic currents, quantum gravity, or tiny Raquel Welch clones in miniaturized submarines floating through my bloodstream? When I closed my eyes, I could see patterns. Could these be the energy channels given off by the underground rivers?

I went to a healer called the Barefoot Doctor, a skinhead with a nice flat in West Hampstead, who pushed and pressed my belly and talked in a nice soft voice and somehow got me talking about women. I also did his tai-chi class for a while. It's top-class self-defence. Someone throws a punch, but rather than shouting in a loud drunken voice, 'You fuckin' wanker, I'll 'ave you!' then swinging and missing, you respond really slowly, standing on one leg and making a bird's beak shape with your hands – but somehow the space-time continuum (yeah yeah, like in *Back to the Future*) gets affected or something and to your attacker you seem to be moving at lightning speed. The main point of it, as far as I could see, was that by learning to use my *chi* I would have got my potential assailant to buy me a pint long before he had any thoughts of beating me to a pulp. But I had to give it up. I didn't have enough time to become a Taoist warrior and pick up my daughter from the childminder too. So I bought the Doctor's video instead, but became paranoid that the woman across the road was watching me and having a good old laugh.

But, now, I have created my own tai-chi move. *Chi* Sandwich – Drunk Man Dowses. Here's some diagrams of how my system might work. It's a fighting tool, the drunk stuff, enabling you to wave your arms around a lot and make noise while urinating on

your opponent and making a dowsing rod shape with your fingers. Go forward and live in peace and tranquility in a tidy space. Find lots of water.

Next, I went to a reiki therapist in Hackney. Reiki is a Japanese healing thing in which the therapist puts her hands close to your body and taps into the *chi*. I went up some rickety stairs and lay down on a trolley in a tiny old room, while the hippy girl set up some crystals then waved her arms around for half an hour.

'I can see a spirit figure coming out of your body.'

Uh-oh. Hippy shit. Or was this the extensive fee I was about to part with?

'It's a small person, quite mischievous. It looks like a leprechaun.'

'What is it doing?' I asked.

'Just sitting there smiling. Now it's gone.'

'Do you often see spirits?' I said.

'Not that often. But that was very vivid. Does it say anything to you?'

I told her that I once drove around Ireland in a Kerouacian adventure with a felt leprechaun toy, then hummed the little tune it sang when you pressed its belly. She nodded seriously.

'You are like a coiled spring,' she said. 'There's a lot of energy inside you trying to get out.' Psychologically-and-emotionally-buried-stuff-underground-rivers-what's-that-all-about-then-eh?-

386 palm-slapping-moment-of-enlightenment! Fucking great. I walked home from the session thinking about the clutter inside me that I am always trying to get out. And it's a physical thing too. I do keep lots of clutter – mostly bits of paper with ideas and drawings that are manifestations of the inside clutter made physical. My study is like a part of my mind. I also put this down to the fact that my grandad's family house was bombed in the Second World War and all the family documents – papers, photos, memorabilia, the lot went up in flames. Some of the more obscure family members have thus disappeared from our memories. So I feel that it's my job to keep all the crap that others might throw away. After this, though, I bought a book on how to tidy your room. Normal people wouldn't need a book about that, but I do. It's now in a big pile of books in a corner of the room surrounded by a wall of paper.

My final adventure into the realms of rivers of energy was at the Stoke Newington Alternative Health Centre. I have always had moles on my arms. But I'd only recently noticed a delta symbol made up of four small moles (see earlier chapter): was there something wrong with my (*does rabbit ears with fingers*) energy pathways? Maybe acupuncture would sort it out. The acupuncturist asked me a few questions about myself and my diet, then I lay down and she stuck some needles in my legs. Suddenly a wave of relaxation and elation washed over me. 'Turn off your mind, relax and float downstream' she said. It sounded as if there was a clothes peg on her nose. Then I dozed off and dreamt about football. Twenty minutes later I handed over the dosh and floated home.

A couple of days after the snooze therapy, I dozed off and all of a sudden I was about to achieve enlightenment. I was being told that the way I see things is only a small part of what there is to see. My body can see things, my whole being can 'see' things. Not seeing just through your eyes but seeing or experiencing through every particle of your being. Unfortunately the explanation never got finished because I suddenly woke up before I could fully take it all in.

It seemed jumbled. Is that it? God comes to you in your dreams and talks like a New Age guru. Awake, all I can think of is something about belly-button fluff and a theory of the universe – it all grows from nothing. And pebbles. We are all pebbles.

๑   ๑   ๑

In Search of the Ching: a Journey in Haikus

From Chingford Station
I walk fast to Whitehall Plain
to find the Ching's source.

In Epping Forest
black ground is soft underfoot.
I am all alone.

Tree split by big wind
looks like a huge dead dragon.
Water trickles by.

River is black smudge.
Two small planes fly overhead.
World War II fighters?

Rotting nuts and seeds:
A bag of high-class muesli
scattered on the floor.

Hear the birds chatter.
Feel the forest's energy.
Seems like I'm floating.

388

Swarms of butterflies
Then a field of dragonflies,
Meadows of crickets.

I pick up a large stick
And take it for a staff.
It pushes the ground.

Hedges and long grass
by the winding sandy path.
Crunch of my footsteps.

A milkshake bottle
Stuffed with a packet of crisps
Lies next to the ditch.

In the Dark Ages
The Saxons sailed up the Thames
And along the Lea.

Then up Hackney Brook
Hacka and his mates got off.
The rest carried on.

Then they reached the Ching
and sailed as far as they could
towards the Ching's source.

They cut the boat up
and rebuilt it much smaller
for the little Saxons.

When river ran out,
In high-pitched voices they said,
'Hey, let's found Essex.'

I have dropped my map.
Oh shit – when did that happen?
Still, I won't get lost.

My loose change jingles.
My stick thuds against the path
Feet trudging along.

Sound of plane engine.
Crickets cheeping near the path
Merges into one.

Jingle trudge thud cheep
Jingle trudge thud cheep jingle
Trudge thud cheep jingle.

Trudge thud cheep jingle
Trudge thud cheep jingle trudge thud
Cheep jingle trudge thud.

Nyeeeeeeeeeeeeeeeeaaaaaoooouuugggghhhhhh. (That was a plane.)
Jingle trudge thud cheep jingle
trudge thud cheep jingle.

Some teen Scouts in shorts
(mostly sixteen-year-old girls)
Appear on the path.

It's Brigitte Bardot!
Not how I remember Scouts.
Almost looks like fun.

(Ahhh – 'Cubs do your best!'
'We will do our best!' we'd chant
In Dalek voices.)

A fatal mistake.
Concentration affected
I take the wrong path.

Smell of strong horse shit.
I should have brought my compass.
I go back. More tracks.

Er, that can't be right.
I use the sun for bearings.
Fuck this, where am I?

Flies buzzing round me
Then I see the Scouts again.
Is this the right way?

I have to turn round
Past the Scouts, having a laugh.
'Ha ha mate, you're lost!'

I pretend I'm fine
Looking at stuff. But they know
I'm a lost fuckwit.

After half an hour
at last it's Connaught Water.
I sit down. Thank fuck.

Then I cross the road.
The path follows the river.
Smell of rotting leaves.

What's this? Stone buttons.
What are they? Burial mounds?
Or boundary stones?

On top of a mound
A sign says 'hole 6, par 5'.
It's Woodford Golf Course.

Chingford Town FC
Play on a pitch to the left.
That's a funny tale.

(Back in the forties
The club formed and bought a field
At the edge of town.

Unfortunately,
The Ching ran in a big ditch
Straight through the middle.

The club pulled down trees,
moved the river eighty yards,
and laid a new pitch.)

392   *Now I'm at a road*
       Crappy stores, flats, car showrooms,
       And a sandwich shop.

       Chicken mayonnaise
       Has been in the sun too long
       But I'm so hungry.

       Down a forest glade,
       river to my left, steep banks
       Some kids climbing trees.

       At a lake, two blokes
       Talk about supermarkets.
       (They don't like Asda.)

       A Daily Mail
       Lies charred black in a sewer.
       Ritual slaughter?

       A girl with huge breasts
       Walks along the road, bouncing.
       Traffic slows to look.

       Tippex graffiti
       Love poems, all signed by 'Sean'.
       A well-brought-up kid.

       At a big sports field
       Sainsbury's shopping trolleys
       Lie in the river.

Walthamstow Dog Track
And then Charlie Chan's night club.
The river winds on.

But the path has gone.
Sainsbury's is up ahead.
The Ching disappears.

Inside Sainsbury's
I ask 'Is the river here?'
A speccy bloke grunts.

'No – have a nice day.'
(It's customer services)
'But…' 'Have a nice day!'

Which way to go now?
Then a stocky old woman
asks if I need help.

'Where is the river?'
'In a concrete overcoat.'
New road. New estate.

I walk up a bank
To the North Circular Road
Maelstrom of traffic.

I feel for the Ching
Encased beneath the tarmac
In this bleak wasteland.

Gasholders, pylons,
Small factories, reservoirs
And too many cars.

Then I find the Lea.
The piped Ching flows in somewhere
Near the moored old boat.

๏ ๏ ๏

There's a nice little omen on my doorstep. It's big, brown and smelly. I'd say it was dogshit but it seems a bit too big and hard for that. On closer inspection I decide it's human. Someone is trying to freak me out – either the fast-talking Geordie fish sellers, the Yugoslavian refugees, the Hardcore Feminist River Walkers, the Masons, the yellow hats, the Jehovah's Witnesses, the Unemployed Homeless Jiffy Cloth Sellers, the bloke from Virgin, the Arsenal FC historian, or, most likely of all, the ghost of Dr Johnson somehow manifesting itself in the physical world just long enough to crap in my front garden.

Film idea: The Chingford Town Story

A football team moving the course of the River Ching? Could be a film. This is a remake of Werner Herzog's *Burden of Dreams* (about the making of his film *Fitzcarraldo* in which he recreates the moving of an old paddle steamer over a hill in the Amazonian jungle). An arty European director is doing some heavy black-and-white film about Chingford. So he has to recreate the moving of the Ching and decides to dig up Chingford Golf Course. But he can't locate Chingford so travels all over north and east London, with a big film crew, digging up golf courses. There's a big *Blazing-Saddles*-style scrap at the end between the film crowd and some hard golf-club types.

Directed by Guy Richie

Starring:

Jean Luc Godard as the arty director;

Vinnie Jones as himself playing a footballer;

Pele as himself playing another footballer;

Gwyneth Paltrow as herself playing a young Essex Girl;

Steven Seagal as a golf club member.

London Stories 18: The Eighties were Shit But Free-Jazz Pool Was Great

In the exciting and heady days of late summer 1988 when we were all so punch drunk from nearly a decade of Thatcherism and our anger had knackered us out, the most exciting thing most of us could remember for ages was when pub opening hours changed to allow all-day drinking (clever Tory plot – keep them pissed and quiet). And when I say 'us' I mean me and my friends who didn't have what society would call 'proper' jobs.

Y'see, in the eighties (cue heavy synth bass. Elephant-crashing synth drums. Synth power chords. An army of blokes with gelled mullets marching over the horizon, frowning), the Yuppies had all the 'proper' jobs. Though what many people don't know was that the Yuppies were actually a subtle guerrilla marketing campaign by the anarchist punk group Crass. They were trying to show how shallow everyone would become through free-market capitalism. Unfortunately for Crass, people seemed to like it. I think it was the big mobile phones that got them hooked.

When I first came down to London it seemed that everybody else in the city was in on some big money-making secret. They all had loud voices, shiny suits, smart flats in Clapham and Battersea and, of course, mobile phones the size of cake tins.

Anyway, once the Great And Beautiful All Day Drinking was introduced, me and my 'resting between jobs' friends would go round the corner to the Lorne Arms, our local boozer in Walthamstow for beer and pool. The pub was always quiet and we'd get slowly and deliciously drunk, whilst whacking balls into pockets (or not, in my case), talking about women we fancied and testing each others' pop-music knowledge. Although some were good pool players whatever, most of us were ONLY any good when we were plastered. Our games thus became infamous in the Lorne, for we introduced free-jazz pool playing.

'What am I? Am I yellow?'

'No, I'm yellow.'

'But you've only got two balls left.'

'That's because I've potted them all, Tim.'

'When was that then?'

'While you were standing there staring into space.'

Then, with about seven pints of

Guinness inside me, I'd go up to the table and start thrashing the pool balls anywhere in a spontaneously improvised manner, without caring where they ended up. It was remarkably effective. Your subconscious takes over, and you can hold a conversation or, say, operate heavy machinery while still playing top quality pool. And, of course, as soon as you concentrate, you're fucked. It's great for lulling a more naturally gifted opponent into a false sense of security.

Sometimes I'd stand there pinging the balls all over the pub and wondering to myself is that all there is? Am I missing out by not having a 'proper' job? But the Free-Jazz Pool Style was also a rebellion against the shiny conformity of the eighties. We weren't going to play by anyone else's rules.

So what happened to the Yuppies? Where did they go? Perhaps they've all got Yuppie Flu. Or they were driven out by global warming.

Funnily enough, most of the blokes I knew who had 'proper' jobs at that time have taken their foot off the pedal. Whilst many of those who dossed through the eighties are now hyper rich. The layabouts, drinkers and perpetual students are now the go-getters. Which suggests there are only so many high-powered hours in a man's life.

Women are different. All the women I knew walked straight into high-powered jobs in the eighties and they've all gone on to success. None of them have fucked up. None of them have burnt out. None of them have formed a country and western band.

And I know very few couples in which the blokes are the major wage earners. My feeling is that it's because men have reached a higher stage of evolutionary consciousness – we have rebelled against the work ethic of our parents' generation and realized that there's more to life than work. Like what?

Well, free-jazz pool, for one.

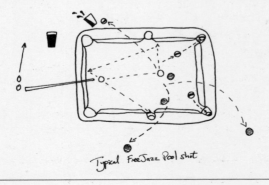

Typical Free Jazz Pool shot

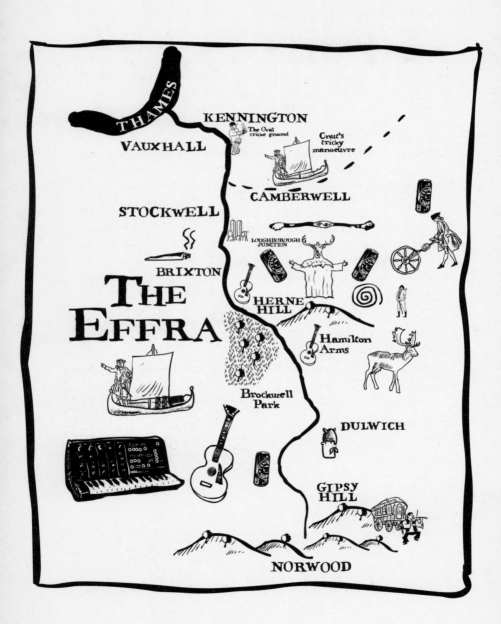

THAMES

KENNINGTON

The Oval cricke ground

Cnut's tricky manoeuvre

VAUXHALL

CAMBERWELL

STOCKWELL

LOUGHBOROUGH JUNCTION

BRIXTON

THE

EFFRA

HERNE HILL

Hamilton Arms

Brockwell Park

DULWICH

GIPSY HILL

NORWOOD

24. Smoke on the Water

• Effra from Dulwich through Brixton to Battersea

*Musical dream – South London – Culturally aware – Korg MS-10 –
Deep Purple – West Norwood – Boring Dulwich – Effra
Redevelopment Agency – Crazy Estates – Lumberjack Man –
Brixton – Stockwell – Kennington – songs for rivers – world turned
upside down*

Last night's dream was about a musical
instrument – I blew into the mouthpiece
on a little curved metal tube with a
mouthpiece leading into a big box
with lots of pipes inside. It might
have been water-cooled. Like the
rivers. Just as my breath was running
out, I could hear the sound of space.
Did the instrument represent London?

The Effra, which flows from Norwood to Vauxhall, is the most
culturally venerated of the smaller London rivers. By this, I mean
that the communities along its route seem to be aware of its presence and celebrate it, whether through books, art exhibitions or
campaigns to get it brought back to the surface. Local history

400 seems to be big in this part of town. I'd saved up the Effra walk
until the end of the summer because I was hoping that I might be
accompanied by a local historian, the Brixton Society's Alan Piper,
who's written books and pamphlets about the stream.
Unfortunately it didn't work out as planned – Alan was simply too
busy – so I roped in a stand-in historian, my mate Doug, who used
to live in Brixton. I had a simple plan. Walk the first half of the river
really quickly, meet Doug at Brixton's Phoenix cafe for lunch, then
let him take me on a history walk. A few months earlier Doug had
lent me a pamphlet about the Effra by Ken Dixon, which described
the route in great detail with some handy maps. The stream had
several tributaries, but the main one rose in the exciting hills of
West Norwood. This meant another rail journey deep into the deep
South.

The Effra is known as a royal river. King Canute apparently sailed
down it to take the Saxons from behind (someone had to) and seize
London in 1016. And always PR-aware, Elizabeth I sailed down the
stream over 500 years later, to visit Walter Raleigh at his house in
Brixton and have a smoke on his new potato/tobacco invention.

I'm beginning to realize that travel writing can't quite sum up the
underground rivers, so I've been contemplating using a more broad-
brush multimedia approach. This would involve a CD, with a different piece of music for each river. I thought maybe I could get an Arts
Council lottery-money grant. So I sent off for all the forms but I just
couldn't be arsed to fill them in. Instead I decided to do one tape
and describe it, so that the reader could imagine the music.

I plugged my Korg MS10 into an amp and pressed a key.
Ffffttthhhhhhhhhhhhhhhh it went. Ssssssshhhzzzhzhhhhhhhhhhhh.
Hmm. Sort of riversy. I stared out of the window for a few minutes
thinking I might be the new Steve Reich – sswwwwwwweeeeeeeee
eeeeeeeeeeeeeeeeeessssshhffffffffffffffzzzzzzzzzzzzzzzzzzzzzzzzz
gzgggggggghhhhhhhhhhhhhhh – then turned off the Korg MS10.
Maybe electronic music was the wrong approach. Perhaps I should

try and create some London songs, a sort of twenty-first-century
Music-Hall style but without any mockernee-sparradom. I should
try and write some sensitive acoustic numbers based on
London and showcase them at a small acoustic music
night in Islington. Strum strum strummity strum
Ooooh the rivers flow Ooooh where
do they go? But Nick Drake has
already beaten me to it.

Ftttttttthhhhhh

(strum strum strummity strum ...)

    Going to see the river man
    Going to tell him all I can
    About the ban
    On feeling free

    If he tells me all he knows
    About the way his river flows
    I don't suppose
    It's meant for me

    Oh, how they come and go
    Oh, how they come and go.

See. The same but better.

It was on a hot and balmy night in the summer of 1996 that, Doug
and I formed a country band called Magic Orange. The name came
from an incident on a tube when I gave up my seat to an old
Chinese man; in gratitude he gave me an orange, which I decided
had magical powers. Our first song was called 'Girl with the Yellow
Face'.

Girl with the yellow face
You're not really a member of the human race
Are you?
'Moo' says the cow with the Van Morrison mask
I'm too shy and polite to ask
You out.

With Doug on Paul McCartney-style bass and
me on four-chords-but-don't-know-what-they're-
called acoustic guitar, we practised our six-song
set diligently over the autumn until by the start of
the next year we were ready. We played our first proper gig at the
Hamilton Arms on Railton Road, an old-style pub usually full of old
Jamaican guys.

🌀 🌀 🌀

I come out at Gipsy Hill station, past the Gipsy Hill Tavern, where the
gipsies used to meet up every summer before descending on the West
End to sell lucky heather to the unsuspecting masses. An old bloke
shuffles past me: 'Colder, innit? Winter's coming, eh?' The source of the
Effra is around here somewhere. I just have to choose a likely spot. I'm
sniffing the air like the childcatcher in *Chitty Chitty Bang Bang*. Except
that my sense of smell isn't that great since I broke my nose. The sound
of kids' voices floats over on the wind. It gets louder as I go down the
road – there are three schools right next to each other and it's deafening.

(in unison)

Kids 1: Eaeaaaaa ashout shout areeee!

Kids 2: Scream yaaaargggh bloowww!

Kids 3: Eeeeieeeieee oooo eeeee!

Kids 4: Aaah aahhhhhhh hhhhhhh!

Kids 5: Screech screeeeeeechhh!

I pass a bloke who can only have been a burned-out rock star, a handsome but haggard greyhair in denims, he was probably in some late-sixties band like Deep Purple – in fact, maybe it's Ian Gillan. He still wears kaftans though, I think, so maybe not. Deep Purple were big with the lads who played guitars in school music rooms – 'Smoke on the Water' ERR ERRR ERRRRR ERR ERRR ER ERRRR and that other riff da da da daa (da da da da daaa da).. What was it? I've asked a few people over the years and they don't know. Maybe Cream. In 1979 heavy metal was big again, I bought Deep Purple's greatest hits and had *Deep Purple in Rock* on tape. And Thin Lizzy's *Live and Dangerous* LP, and er, that's it. But I was a punksoulboy, never a rocker. It's important for me to say that. Maybe this whole search for underground rivers would be more interesting if it was an ex-bassist from Deep Purple doing it.

ᓚ   ᓚ   ᓚ

Rockin' with the Rivers – the magazine for heavy metal fans of underground streams

Hi folks. John Lord here, looking for the streams underground, like the streams of consciousness when you're flyin' high. Me and the guys – Ritchie Blackmore, Ian Paice, Roger Glover and Ian Gillan – took some instruments down in the sewers. We were just settin' up for this gig, yeah, but then we saw that Whitesnake were down there as well. Hey guys, this is our thing, said Ritchie. Nah man, said Whitesnake overdude David Coverdale, we were here first, Ricardo. Then there's this fight between Ritchie and Dave until

Deep Purple in shit

one of the Thames Water fellas starts gettin angry, 'cos like, he'd taken us down on this trip but he goes I thought you guys were serious river researchers, I'm gonna take you back up now, and we go no way dude, so then we all start running and Ian's drum kit starts floating away. We take a few turnings to get away from the water man and soon we're lost and Dave says wow that's all your fault, Ritchie, you little turd and Ritchie says I'm gonna get you Coverdale, but then me and Gillan say hey, the acoustics in this bit are pretty cool let's set up here, so we get the amps up onto a big ledge thing and Ian's using his head for drums but then, shit, we realize we're totally lost. I'm writing this by the light of a spliff: we've been down here for three years living on rats and Whitesnake are about 50 yards downstream so, if anyone gets this note, hey guys, get us out of here ...

Right onto Convent Hill and down a passageway into the wood. Except it doesn't go into the wood, it goes into a school. A load of kids stand around glaring: 'What are you doing?' shouts one boy. 'This is a school!' So I retrace my steps past a little orchard and get lost in the maze of streets. Eventually I get out to Crown Dale. A football pitch on the right feels like a good place for the source of the Effra. However, there's already some sort of river valley here. I cross into Norwood Park. The valley runs almost due south through here – there's an avenue of oak trees that looks as though it marks the route. I take a photo then skirt through the park, past the Park Tavern, a tatty old boozer, and arrive at Elder Road, which leads into Norwood High Street. The river would have curved around what is now the road. The undulations encourage me to imagine a gentle rural landscape not all that far back in time. And there's the river valley. No, there it is! It's over here now! An old fellow stops and asks if I'm lost. Ha ha, I say, I'm looking for an underground river. Do you know it? Very good, young man, he smiles, walking off as quickly as he can. Twenty yards further on a young bearded guy is begging at the side of the road. He too asks if I need help so I show him my *A to Z* with the Effra's course marked on it in red felt tip. The thick red line, like an artery, seems to unsettle him.

'See – although it's actually got more of a curve and a wind than I've drawn on the map.'

'O...K,' he says.

On the right is Pilgrim Hill and a little cottage called the Boathouse which I presume must have been on the river when it was built in the early Victorian era. I follow the hill down into a housing estate. This is like an eighties recreation of a medieval village, with winding lanes and little houses up to the edge of the path all packed in tightly. I'm holding the *A to Z* up to my face trying to keep to the route.

'Are you lost, love?' says a woman coming out of her house.

'I'm looking for an underground river.'

'Ah ... yeah ... right.'

But, as if to confirm it, I see a can of Tennent's Super lying on the path. I go back out to the main road, past the cemetery gate. After the cemetery is Norwood Library so, always keen to get in a spot of extra research, I go and have a nose about. There's information about the gypsies of Norwood, especially Margaret Finch, the so-called Queen of the Gypsies, who used to sit under a tree on Gypsy Hill with her chin resting on her knees like Olga Korbut, telling fortunes and dispensing wise words. When she died they couldn't straighten her out so they buried her in a box. The gypsies were eventually driven out by the enclosure acts. That's what I love about libraries. You find out useful stuff that you can bore people with at parties. There's also a scale model of the set of the Ealing film *Passport to Pimlico*, which was built around here somewhere.

I also learned about an art exhibition on the Effra on in Brixton. It sounds like it's one of those multi-media jobs in which an artist has encouraged local people to express their own feelings about the river. This is what I mean about river consciousness. I can't imagine a similar project about the Hackney Brook.

Towards Dulwich (Old English meaning 'small village of the very dull Saxon people'), the roads start to widen into villa-style terraces. I give two West Indian grannies directions to some housing estate (remember, an *A to Z* is power). Although I'm getting nearer the centre of London it's getting increasingly suburban. It's dull. The railway that runs

parallel to the road follows the line of the river. I'm now heading into Herne Hill, past a dead television and a big pile of junk that is possibly part of some local Effra Art installation.

ʢ   ʢ   ʢ

Before my wedding I'd been thinking about having a stag night. I've been on countless stag nights over the last fifteen years and, apart from a rather leisurely and sedate trip to Edinburgh with a crowd of Nick Hornby types, they've been pretty miserable – fights, girls in French waitress outfits, headbutts, best man shitting in someone's garden, fights, vomit, fights. Stag nights are Saxon rituals in praise of the horned God. Who or what this horned God represented I'm not sure. But it's certainly a Saxon thing and a result of the blending of Anglo-Saxon and Celtic traditions. In Germany before a wedding they slice each other's faces with fencing swords then dress up in marble-wash denim and try to 'tag' the groom's mullet. Over here there was the tradition of the Love Stick, a painted mystical branch with carved female and male figures on either end, which portended great fertility and good fortune for the couple in question.

Going over what I've learned from folk history (i.e. some half remembered excerpts from the ITV series *Robin of Sherwood* starring Michael Praed – the one with the Clannad theme music ... Rooooooooooooobin – (ding ding) – THE HOODED MAN!!!), the

horned god was called Herne the Hunter. Herne lived deep in the
forest and spoke with a faintly northern RSC accent. Whenever he
appeared, there was lots of mist and atmospheric drum music. A
fight invariably ensued soon after-
wards. There were witches too
with their Northern European
voodoo – big soups and stews
full to the brim with exotic creatures
and herbs of the forest. And dead chickens
and lots of blood. I'm not that interested in
Robin Hood but the idea of Herne the Hunter
is appealing. It's doubtful that such an important
god could have lived in the East Midlands.
Herne Hill would be the place. You've got
the marshy mists, you've got the chicken
blood pouring out of the shops and stalls of Atlantic Road just a bit
further north, the drug dealers, the violence, the vibrant music
scene. And a magical river – the Effra.

Woooooo!
Wooooo!!

๑ ๑ ๑

A crowd of men on the benches just inside the park are all drinking
cans of Skol Super. A fat bloke in a tatty suit is carrying loads more
in a yellow bucket. It's as if they've been sponsored by the brewer.
Branded pissheads. The Prince Regent Tavern has a massive picture
of the Prince Regent at the top of it, looking like Alain Delon. Or
Chevalier Recci from *The Flashing Blade*. This was where Magic
Orange would retire to after our practices to discuss strategies for
record industry domination. At the crossroads I turn off the main
Effra route to check out the course of one of the stream's tributaries
mentioned by Ken Dixon in his pamphlet. It begins at the ponds in
Brockwell Park and would have flowed north, then east at Brixton
Water Lane, meeting the main branch of the river at the Dulwich
Road junction.

408   At the start of Water Lane there are some old villas which give you an idea of early nineteenth-century rural Brixton. I walk down past various ponds – brown murky water with a film on top. A really desperate person has tried to paint graffiti on the hedge. After the ponds a little stream appears, a thin trickle with plants and grass growing all round it. This is a recent development – local people lobbied to have this part of the Effra brought out of its pipes. It disappears again quite quickly, just before a kids' playground.

The Effra Redevelopment Agency, based in Brixton in 1992, put forward the idea that the river could be brought back to the surface and turned into a local feature. They took over a disused shop on Norwood Road, under which the Effra flows, and opened a visitors' centre with models, exhibition and video and encouraged local people to take part in the discussions about the river, describing themselves as 'redevelopment experts'.

But it turned out that the 'Effra Redevelopment Agency', was actually an art project produced by a London-based group called Platform.

> We executed a local and national press campaign which spread the idea of unearthing the river further ('plan to revive forgotten river', 'river deep – a vision', 'dream to make the Effra flow', 'wet dark and buried'). Our aim was to have the word 'Effra' on as many lips as possible. At a public debate towards the end of ERA's tenure on Norwood road, heated arguments arose between supporters of the Effra who – for many diverse reasons – had decided to welcome the thought of a river in their part of the city, and dissenters, who worried about – amongst other things – where they would park their cars if a river were to run down their street. More adventurous local supporters began plans to start the Effra's unearthing at a point where the river ran underground in the local park. Thus, as the Effra Redevelopment Agency disappeared quietly one Saturday night, the debate continued and continues along the river's banks.

I follow the river bank back through some neat but plain Victorian terraced streets, towards Coldharbour Lane. A big pub on the corner here is called the Effra Hall Tavern. I explore Coldharbour Lane towards Loughborough Junction. Loughborough Junction is Brixton without the sex appeal, the shouty blokes, the wobbly bike riders, the big-hipped ladieez, the chicken blood on the streets, the obvious drug dealers, the hip little cafés, the militant squatters and the funky music blaring out of shops and car stereos. So what has it got? Er, middle-aged men holding cans of extra strong lager who stand and stare and big young lads with hard stares who walk quickly along the pavement and ... stare, and grimy-looking blocks of flats (from which, I'm sure, all kinds of people stand and stare).

The area is marked on John Rocque's 1741 map. Then again, I reckon Rocque chickened out of going to Hackney so he probably didn't show his face in Loughborough Junction either. Not that it was called Loughborough Junction then. Nor was it especially dodgy. On Rocque's map it's marked as part of the Effra Farm Estate. So he might have got savaged by a chicken.

I notice for the first time the crazy graffiti above the majestic, but closed down, Brady's (formerly the historic Railway Hotel) on Atlantic Road. And the incredible housing estate at the start of Coldharbour Lane with huge slabs of massive concrete, tiny windows and mad walkways. It's Buck Rogers meets Richard Rogers. It's got to be a listed building. God knows what it's like to live there but it looks great. Unlike Buck Rogers. Now what

410 was his sidekick called? Not the little robot that went 'beelee beelee beelee'. Wilma Deering. She was nice. Wore a tight spandex all-in-one uniform.

A bit further up there's a rather special patch of grass with a hedge around it, full of empty oil cans and Special Brew tins. A hidden alchemical drinking experiment is being conducted there and I try not to interfere. A middle-aged guy in a lumberjack shirt stands guard, staring.

> **Me:** *(jaunty)* Hi. How's it going?
> **Lumberjack man:** *(staring straight ahead)* ....
> **Me:** *(stupid grin)* I don't suppose you know any-thing about an...underground river?
> **Lumberjack man:** *(eyes turn to look at me then turn back)* What?
> **Me:** *(ready to run)* An underground river?
> **Lumberjack man:** *(shakes head, frowns)* ....
> **Me:** *(quiet voice)* No problem. Cheers (walks away quickly)

At the Phoenix Café I meet Doug, who is going to take me around the historic streets of Brixton. First we try to find the Effra exhibition, but it's closed, so we visit the nearby Effra Hall, which was once a grand mansion with huge grounds but now hidden away amongst other buildings, is falling apart. Doug then points to the headquarters of some secret sect he's recently joined called the Brixton Society. It's the Masons, isn't it, Doug? No no, they do history walks and really good stuff like that. He then takes me up towards Tulse Hill, past Rush Common, 'Bits of green ... once a huge common ... big villas ... babbling brooks ... lovely.' and tries to find Walter Raleigh's house, the fabulous palace that Elizabeth I visited. Some say it's a load of bollocks, but there is a Raleigh

House – a residential block of flats in a Tudorbethan style. With a   411
swimming pool. I wonder if the story of Raleigh putting his cloak
down so the Queen could walk over a puddle might be a reference
to the Effra – maybe he bridged it for her. In fact, this event
allegedly took place at the site of the Brixton Academy (coinci-
dentally, the last gig I saw there was Beck – an obvious river reference). Then we cross the road, past some grotty second-hand
shops and up to the windmill, a miraculous survivor of old
Brixton, with a kids' nursery and a few shacks next to it. Then we
head back into central Brixton. When the first immigrants from
Jamaica were welcomed here in the fifties, the area was a scruffy
district of grand Victorian villas that had been split up into rented
bedsits, rooming houses and dingy B&Bs. Now it's dead funky
and particularly good for sixties suits, cheapo chickens, fresh fish
and getting your mobile phone nicked. We catch up with the Effra
route again, over Coldharbour Lane and under the railway, along
the stalls of Popes Road then back to Brixton Road. The Effra
would have flowed parallel and just to the east.

Doug: *(pointing)* Look at those old houses.
Me: Uh-huh?
Doug: See how they're at an angle to the road?
Me: Uhmmm.
Doug: That's because they were built on the banks of the Effra,
which wound its way along here, rather than in a straight line.

We go past a big Bar Lorca which apparently was an ancient coaching inn called the Coach and Horses. These people have no shame.
They'd turn the Tower of London into Bar Lorca if they had the
chance.

ꙮ ꙮ ꙮ

412   One morning I was forlornly looking on the net for some sign of
the Hardcore London Feminist River Walkers. I'd typed in 'lost
rivers of London' and come up with an electronic band called Coil
who, in their *Untitled III* album, had a track called 'Lost Rivers of
London'. A couple of days and about £12 later, the album arrived
in the post. I excitedly put it on. Deep growly synths and a high
harpsichord synth doing a horror-film-style two-note arpeggio (can
it be an arpeggio?), then a bloke comes in going 'ahhhh ahhh
ahhhh' with lots of reverb as if in an old farmhouse downstairs
toilet with tiles on the floor. Then he starts reciting poetry. Guitar
with echo and flange comes in. Then another synth starts up dee
der der dee just two notes. A wind sound (you can do it quite easily
on a Korg MS10 and a few patch leads), the sort of thing we used to
do when we were seventeen.

'I have sat there and watched the winter days end their short-
spelled lives,' says Mr Coil. It's fantastically damp, depressing and
dreadful.

Then another 'Ahhhh aaaaaaahhhhhhhhhh ahh ahhh ahhhhhhh
ahha ahhhhhhhhhhhhhh'.

Then poetry again. 'sluggishly drowsy so it seems ... Colourless,
factless, blurred. The soil dark lifeless elms. Rotting.'

Deep synth growwwl growwwwl guitar cranked up plays it
through twice and I start to feel a black dog coming on, so go and
make a cup of coffee and stick on *King of Snake* by Underworld.
Ahhhhhh. Fun and laughter. Sexy rhythms. Dancing. Is that what
happens to people who spend too long messing in their minds
with the Lost Rivers of London? I wonder what Nicholas Barton
would make of it all. Ahhhhhhhhhh. Wind. Shoooooowwww
eeeeeeeeooooooo. Ahhhhhhhhhhhhhhh. ahhhhhhhhh. ahhh ahh
ahhhh ahhhhhhh ahhhhhhhhhhhhhhhhhhhhhhhhhhhhhhhhhhhhhh
hhhhhhhhhhhhhhhhhhhhhhhhhhhh (fade out with reverb).

I decide to phone him and ask. I've had his number for ages but
been too chicken to call. The phone rings for a while. I feel a bit like

the class snitch. Sir, Sir, little Tommy Coil has gone and done an 413
ambient jazz album, Sir, and he's written a track about you.

> **Barton:** Is this true, Coil?
> **Coil:** *(wind sound)* shooowwwwweeeeeooooooooooo
> **Barton:** Right, detention for you
> **Coil:** Ahh ahhh ahhhhhhhhhhhhhhhh.
> **Barton:** Write out a thousand times, 'I will not take the piss
> out of the Lost Rivers of London.'

Fifteen rings. I put the phone down.

ゆ　ゆ　ゆ

New River: slow harpsichord four-note arpeggio. A radio is being
tuned in. Didgeridoo sounds.

Hackney Brook: xylophone plonkings.
Massed choir sings, 'You're shit and you
know you are', on a continuous tape loop.

Dagenham Brook: Danish punk thrash.
My mate Stevey P. sings the words from
the Environmental Agency flood warning
leaflet.

Fleet: maudlin squeezebox as Dr-
Johnson-style vocal does voiceover.

Moselle: Ray Davies of the Kinks does a special acoustic ballad
about growing up in Muswell Hill.

Walbrook: brass band reworking of 'Maybe It's Because I'm a
Londoner' at half speed.

414   **Tyburn:** olde English folk song style with Morris dancers' bells in the background.

Westbourne: three-chord guitar thrash by a punk 'supergroup', lasting for about a minute. The only lyrics are 'Westbourne Westbooooourrrrrne'.

Counter's Creek: church organ playing deathly waltz. Maudlin choir intones names of people who are buried in Kensal Green cemetery.

Stamford Brook: Japanese pop-thrash Elvis impersonators do version of 'God Save the Queen'.

The Brent: massed close harmony female choirs.

Beverley Brook: cut-ups of John Major's voice over East Sheen hip-hop massive thing beat.

Wandle: small fish attached to primitive synthesizer to create Throbbing-Gristle-style white noise.

Falcon Brook: eighties AOR power ballad about house prices.

Neckinger and Mill streams: drunk monks chanting.

The Peck: Chas 'n' Dave do a medley using William Blake poems as lyrics.

The Black Ditch: some of Reggie Kray's poetry set to the tune of Spandau Ballet's 'Gold'.

The Ravensbourne: old-fashioned sea shanty about Francis Drake.

The Ching: eastern gong music. Bamboo percussion. Bloke from
Sainsbury's Customer Services Department reads from his diary.

ᘒ   ᘒ   ᘒ

As we come up Brixton Road, still complaining about ruined pubs
and crap planning and unearthed rivers, Doug's mobile rings. It's
Sarah telling us to get to a TV because a plane has just gone into one
of the World Trade Center towers. Dazed, we walk up Brixton Hill
trying to unscramble our brains, but it's too late – they're being
rewired. Rushing into the nearest pub – the Hanover Arms – we
watch as the towers collapse. Then everything slows down. Doug
goes home. I walk the last bit of the Effra route, past the Oval cricket
ground, under which the Effra flows, and which lies in an area of
marshland deemed permanently unsuitable for building. A school. A
pub (the Beehive), another pub (Durham Arms). Down Vauxhall
Grove past a closed-up Elephant and Castle pub and under the
subway (I don't remember because my mind went numb, but I just
talked robotically into the Dictaphone). I get to Vauxhall Bridge and
look down at the Effra tunnel, where a trickle of slimy water spills
out onto the little beach and down into the Thames. And I stare hard
because, in a previous existence, this would have been a good
moment, but now seems unbearably trivial, and I think to myself,
'What does it all fucking mean?'

25: Black Sewer, Crimson Cloud, Silver Fountain

Letting go of rivers

Dream: I'm in a subterranean post-apocalyptic world, with lots of tunnels and corridors leading to ancient train systems. I wander through a labyrinth of tunnels. Hundreds of signs point to various stations and places, but they are all pointing in the wrong direction, and thousands of people are shoving and milling about.

ҩ ҩ ҩ

I'm in Star Nergiz café on Blackstock Road looking out onto the old junction where the New River used to be carried on stilts over the Hackney Brook. It's my favourite part of Highbury Vale: I like to sit near the window and watch the world go by. I'm eating a bacon sandwich. The pretty Turkish waitress comes over and stares at my manuscript.

'What are you doing?'

'I'm going through these papers making notes.'

'Is it a book?'

'Yes.'

'Did you write it?'

'Yes.'

'What sort of stuff do you write?'

418 'I'm a sort of travel writer.'

Sharp intake of breath – she goes over to the counter and gabbles to someone in the kitchen, then comes back.

'What's it about?'

'It's a description of the routes of underground rivers in London.'

'Hmm. Is that interesting?'

(In John Majorish voice) 'Oh yes, it's VERY interesting.'

'It doesn't sound interesting to me.' *(She's cross)*. 'Why are you writing about London? It's all ugly buildings and noise. There are so many beautiful places. If I was a travel writer I'd go somewhere nice.'

I smile. So does she and runs off to the kitchen. Five minutes later she's back, fiddling with the ketchup holders. She replaces the brown sauce.

'Would you like another coffee?'

'Ah, go on then.'

She brings the coffee and mucks about with the ketchup bottle again.

'Are you a famous writer?'

'Ha ha, no.'

'What's your name?'

'You won't have heard of me.'

'What's your name then?'

'Tim.'

'Tim what?'

'Tim Bradford.'

'Naa. Never heard of you.'

She rushes back to the kitchen.

Just like last autumn, the rains have started to come again. Up at Finsbury Park the drains are backing up and there's a river running down Stroud Green Road, along Seven Sisters and down Blackstock Road. Old rivulets that weren't on anybody's map have come alive.

Nowadays, they are only seen when torrential rain causes flooding,
but they are there just the same, forming a large part of the
Victorian sewer system that still serves London. Streams with no
name, so I didn't bother about them. I'll call this one Hallal Brook.
If the weather carries on like this for the next few years the old
Victorian drainage system won't be able to take it.

I've decided to put something back into society by becoming a
car mover. I go jogging round the neighbourhood and push cars
that have broken down out of harm's way. So far I've done three. It
feels good. I just hope my back can take it.

ð ð ð

Some good news. My sister-in-law has been asked to join a pub ska
band in Derby. Course, she's gone and nicked my old trombone.
Slide's knackered, love, I said to her, but she wouldn't listen. To
help her out I worked on a ska arrangement of the *Panorama* theme
tune for about five minutes in the pub, but she wasn't interested.
Then it occurred to me that we could finally end all wars if only all
national anthems were played in a ska style.

ð ð ð

In Victoria Park I meet a vibrant man in his late eighties who
says he fought the fascists in the pre-war East End using jujitsu.
He says he slashed the face of William Joyce (Lord Haw Haw).
Later he helped the Labour Party get elected in Hackney for the
first time.

'When I was a little boy I planted a cherry tree and now look –
it's huge.'

Back in our own park Cathleen and I plant a plum stone and
check it every day for signs of growth.

ð ð ð

420 I wonder what I've learned, if anything, over the last few months. That one can travel and have adventures in London. Except that I don't really have adventures, as such. If you hung out with me the nearest you'd get to an actual adventure would be if I meant to spend all day in a library but got drunk instead.

My so-called history technique consists of piling on lots of stuff – anecdotes, song lyrics, illustrations, dreams, shopping lists, diaries, snatches of dialogue from the kids' TV shows my daughter watches, things people have told me at parties, bus tickets, a bit of fact copied from a library book and mixing it all together into a big pot of simmering wordsludge, then hoping that the reader digests it all, sleeps on it for a bit then wakes up one day (possibly several years later, by which time I am sleeping rough under Waterloo Bridge), slaps their forehead and says, 'That's it!'

ə ə ə

Finally, at the end of the summer, someone from Thames Water got in touch to say I could go down into the Fleet. 'But I don't know if there's a gang available … and I don't control the gangs.'

1. Relaxed and lucid

2. Strange buzzing sound in head

3. Explosion of unrelated trivia

Control the gangs? Was this like LA? At last I was getting somewhere. There were gangs of river enthusiasts like me working for Thames Water and possibly living down in the sewers.

Whatever, we were to meet at New Bridge Street at 12.30 p.m. a couple of days later. I turned up and had to get changed into white plastic overalls, wader boots that came up above my thighs with thick weighted soles, red rubber gloves and a hard hat. A white one. Then I put on a safety harness in case I needed to be winched away from a raging torrent or testicle-eating killer rat. I got the bloke who was helping me – a chirpy bloke called Brian – to take a photo of me in the hard hat. Something to show the grandchildren. ('Ah yes, we had man's jobs in those days, like.')

Then I went down a manhole. Never done it before. No secret to it. You just go down a ladder. One rung at a time, nice and slow. It was pitch black down there. Then a light appeared at the end of a tunnel. It was on someone's head, a big sweating person with specs like the guy out of *Seinfeld*. He led me to another manhole and we climbed even lower. A long ladder, this one. Down into a huge cavern where I could just about make out a couple of other figures in the darkness. Thames Water people. Then I was introduced to Rob, the gang leader.

And there in the dark it was, the silver glint of the Fleet. Like some caged animal. Could it smell my fear? We waded through shallow water at first, then into a big river down the tunnel in about two feet of water. It was humid, echoing, sticky, with a terrific rumble overhead. The District Line was directly above us. Then there was a swoosh of water and everyone stopped dead.

422   'What was that?' Rob said, more to himself than me.

Whatdoyoumeanwhatwasthatyourtheexperty
oushouldknowwhatitisandreallyrelaxeddownhere
showingmearoundIcanleavenowifyouwant. I took a
deep breath. 'It sounds like water.' I said.

'Ah, it's just a boat. If it was a flood you'd just hear a
rush of wind.'

'And then get out in a calm and orderly fashion?'

'Ha ha, no. You'd have to leg it. In seconds.'
I lift up one of my weighted boots and gave
out a little silent whimper. But it did feel
exhilarating, the thought of being down there
under the city. At the end of the tunnel was a big iron door.

'What's on the other side of that, then?' I squeaked.

'That's the river.'

Fuck.

'As you can see, the river's a couple of feet higher than the water
level in here... So if it came through we'd be finished.'

WATER

WATER   WATER

Primal fears realized

Later, the speccy bloke told me about the possibility of explo-
sions. Then it was back to the crunch and splosh of weighted boots
as we walked along. Rob told me to follow his line. He worked one
foot at a time; right foot, then dragged his left after it. It was hard
work. I didn't have a light so had to follow the light from their
heads. Sometimes they turned to me and it shone blindingly in my
face. I saw flashes of rusting Victorian iron work, an old sluice gate,
big cogs.

Was I searching for my dark side? Underground Tim. The smelly
bit that I don't want to show. The speccy bloke farted and shook his
head.

ॐ   ॐ   ॐ

I volunteer to do a sponsored walk for the Cecil Housing Trust, a
charity for homeless women. The walk is from London Bridge to
Richmond, about 17 miles. I'd seen a poster in our local laundrette
while I'd been chatting to the middle-aged Irish woman who
always gives my clothes 'special care' without telling her boss. But a
few days before I'm due to go I stand on an old Victorian floor tack
which takes a deep slice out of my foot.

I set out with a crowd of well-meaning feminists and even with
my rather exaggerated limp, I've soon overtaken all of them, apart
from a skinny woman who looks like a Deep Purple bassist and her
punkish Japanese friend, who stick with me for a while until I lose
them in the Wandsworth one-way system. It's low tide and on the
north bank I pass by the sewer tunnels and river mouths of the tributaries – Fleet, Tyburn, Westbourne, Counter's Creek, a small
hatch and bank undulations near Parr's Ditch, Stamford Brook and
the large mouth of the Brent. I realize that I should have done this
at the start of my 'project', to get an idea of the scale of London and
its waters, and to fix a map in my head. But now I feel like I'm
saying goodbye to old friends.

The rich have appropriated most of the river. Luxury flats are

everywhere, bland and empty boxes conceived by soulless architects and planners.

At Old Deer Park a crowd of women walks slowly towards me,
with the sun behind them. Their hair is shining gold. Am I deliri-
ous? Is it the Hardcore London Feminist River Walkers at last? They
are all beautiful and have come for me to take me to their underground water world. As they get closer I realize they are just a
group of German tourists in expensive leisurewear. After four and a
half hours I arrive in Richmond but there's no one there to greet me
so I bugger off home. But, strangely, my foot feels much better.

᷍ ᷍ ᷍

I meet Northern Dave at the Tup in Stoke Newington and we sit out
in the beer garden. I want to talk about Hackney Brook and I have
brought along copies of Rocque's map as well as various Ordnance
Survey maps. But Northern Dave is having none of it. He pulls out
The Anatomy of Melancholy and shows me various snippets, then
just when I'm ready to tell him about poor drainage in the
Clissold Park area he reveals a cleverly concealed Edie
Sedgwick biography. (Northern Dave and I have the same
taste in dead actresses and models from the sixties.) He's
marked out the important drug haze passages for me to
read, then we dwell admiringly on the black and
white photos of Edie. After our third pint, we depart
for Abney Park Cemetery. On the way I buy a can of
Tennent's Super Dowsing Ale – my last ever, I have
decided – while Dave takes a more prosaic Red Stripe
view of things. But inside the gates Dave has one last
surprise. He's brought along his treasured copy of the *Tao te Ching:*
we take it in turns to find a verse at random and read it out whenever the dowsing rods come together.

᷍ ᷍ ᷍

Looking back on the last year, I see all the small rivers I didn't walk, **425**
like the Graveney, the Quaggy, Salmon's Brook and Pymme's
Brook. I'm glad I got the cold shoul-
der from the *Guinness Book of
Records*. Also, various people never
replied to my letters and emails –
Ken Livingstone, Prince Edward and
all the Beverly Brookses. But no
matter, my real regret is not taking a
mate's advice and walking around
London in a paper 'boat' outfit.

Now I should be finishing the
book but I'm watching the sun set
slowly from the upstairs window.

Hackney Brook walk, Abney Park Cemetery

Burning bread dough, sand dunes, turquoise and yellow fire of a
furnace. Hornsey, Finsbury Park, Blackstock Road and Highbury
Vale have become magic kingdoms of light. My neighbour is out in
her garden with her camera. But no one will believe her when she
tells them about this sunset and when she shows them the photo
there'll be nothing there, just a few clouds.

The sky goes a deeper crimson, a tower block shifts into silhou-
ette. A police car over on Seven Sisters Road speeds east. I look out
over Hornsey Wood and imagine what the New River would have
looked like, its water red reflecting the sky. There's nowhere else you
get skies like this.

The next afternoon I'm walking through Clissold Park. It's
another humid day. As I get to the little mound with a drinking
fountain, which (I like to think) taps straight into the New River, I
notice streams cascading down into the grass below. As I get closer
I see that someone has left the tap on and the water is spilling
down, filling up the top basins then the lower inset basins beneath
a watery pulsating film. I stand staring at it for a while, slightly
mesmerized, hypnotized by its sound. Then I move further in and,

426   as the water splashes over my shoes. I reach for the tap and close it off. The basin settles down. It's quiet now and I walk quickly away, as the water seeps down into the park's soil. I continue walking home, a smile on my face, my step a little lighter than before.

ə   ə   ə

From: Beverley Brooks
Date: Tuesday, November 6, 2001 4:20 pm
Subject: Beverley Brooks

Hi Tim,
I'm a Beverley Brooks. What's the scoop?

Appendix

Flow rates

A friend, after I'd explained what this book was about, asked if there would be a lot of information about flow rates of the different rivers. I didn't know what to say, mainly because I didn't know what he was talking about. Just for him I have included a heavily researched flow rate diagram.

ॐ ॐ ॐ

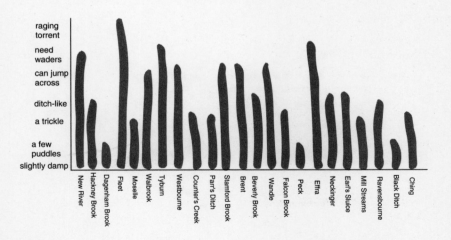

Highly Scientific Diagram of Flow Rates

428 What is London?

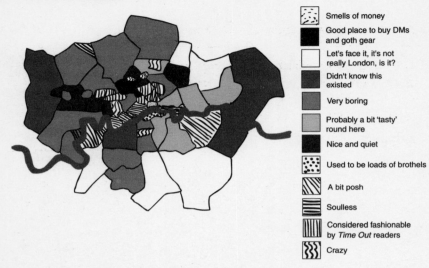

(dotted pattern)	Smells of money
(solid black)	Good place to buy DMs and goth gear
(white)	Let's face it, it's not really London, is it?
(dark grey)	Didn't know this existed
(medium grey)	Very boring
(light grey)	Probably a bit 'tasty' round here
(black)	Nice and quiet
(dotted)	Used to be loads of brothels
(diagonal lines)	A bit posh
(horizontal lines)	Soulless
(vertical lines)	Considered fashionable by *Time Out* readers
(crazy pattern)	Crazy

London is typically described as a collection of villages rather than a large city. But it's more a collection of different atmospheres (which may or may not be connected to the layout of the buried tributaries).

London weather

London now only has two seasons - summer (orange-grey pollution) and winter (damp and depressing)

Summer

Winter

(sun symbol) Bright sunshine

(people symbol) Fat blokes ogling girls in the park

(skull cloud symbol) Pollution death clouds

(rain cloud symbol) Pissing it down

(sad symbol) Feelings of melancholy and madness

Some Top London Buskers

1. Dying baby whale sings 'Soul Man'

A small, punky-haired Japanese  girl stands outside the Hippodrome on a damp spring morning and sings strange sad versions of soul songs in a mad, high-pitched squawk. People hesitate as they walk past but few stop to put money in her little cup. I can't tell whether this is terrible or the sound of genius.

2. Flying-V hippy man at Camden Lock

No discussion of London buskers could be complete without the flying-V hippy man at Camden Lock. Years ago, he used to stand near the

entrance to the old lock market, flared legs wide apart, long curly hair flowing, and blasting out Hendrix riffs from a red (or was it white?) flying-V guitar plugged into a practice amp and a big muff fuzzbox. At that time most buskers were of the 'Let me take you by the hand' school. He was special.

3. Classical duo at Hammersmith shopping centre

Tall sandy-haired speccy bloke and tall longdarkhaired posh bird in nice clothes play along to

classical 'hits'. Shoppers shuffle past eyeing them up suspiciously. Occasionally someone will ostentatiously tip some coins into the open violin case as if to say, 'I know this one. I'm a classical music buff, don't you know.' A group of track-suited kids take the piss from a safe distance.

4. Misty-eyed with cans

Four drunk blokes loiter at the side of a park in Holloway. One stands singing Irish folk songs – 'Molly Malone', which segues into 'Rivers Run Free' – in a croaky voice, the other three squat around him misty-eyed, clutching cans. I sense a pool of urine slowly expanding behind them.

5. An earnest black girl with an acoustic guitar

An earnest black girl with an acoustic guitar gets on the District Line southbound train at Fulham Broadway and belts out a few acoustic numbers.

Unbelievably, for a train busker she's pretty good. 'That was pretty good, I say. She tells me that a record company is after her. What, has she nicked stuff from them or something? No, they want her to sign. Blimey, busking's not what it used to be.

6. Twiddlynote accordion bluster

Victoria Line going north. Two cheery blokes with watery eyes swagger through the interconnecting door between the carriages, followed by a quiet-looking little kid. The two men flash smiles and are off, one playing the accordion, the other a kind of bazouki thing. Despicably upbeat it's completely inappropriate for the London Underground. The boy follows on with his hand out, asking for money.

7. Sid Griffin at the South Bank

Not strictly speaking a busker. Sid had been hired to play at a Fans United Love-In Get Together at the South Bank, before the 1998 World Cup. Sid, former frontman of the 'Big in 1985' country rock band, the Long Ryders, seemed mighty peeved to be playing to a handful of speccy ex-Marxist football fans. At the end of the set he tried to flog some CDs. I never fall for this standard busker cash-grabbing tactic, but I felt so heartbreakingly sorry for him, I bought two. What a mug.

8. Wake guitarists

In Hammersmith one evening I hear familiar sounds coming from the subway. South American guitar music. Beautiful. What a strange feeling. When I get down the steps there are two guys playing in front of a little home-made paper plaque for Felipe Romero, a busker. It's been his funeral today. This is their little tribute. Ba da da da dang. Diddle de di dang dang twaaaaaaaaang.

Bullshit Detector Detector

*Places you can't buy **Bullshit Detector** volume 1*

I'll never really know the whereabouts of my copy of *Bullshit Detector*. Maybe it sank a few yards downstream. But I do know where it isn't – various second-hand music shops around North London.

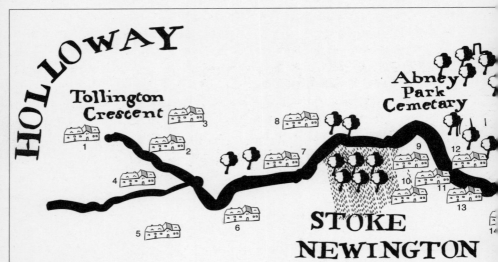

1. **The Plough**
Tollington Park and Hornsey Road

2. **Bedford Tavern**
Corner of Burman Road and Seven
Sisters Road

3. **Red Rose**
North side of Seven Sisters Road.

4. **The Tollington**
Hornsey Road and Tollllington Road

5. **Clancey's Pub**
Junction of Benwell Road and
Albany Place

6. **The Drayton Park**
Drayton Park.

7. **The Arsenal Tavern**
Mountgrove Road

8. **The Brownswood Tavern**
Green Lanes

9. **The Stoke Tup**
Stoke Newington Church Street

10. **The Auld Shillelagh**
Stoke Newington Church Street

11. **The Daniel Defoe**
Stoke Newington Church Street

12. **Jolly Butchers**
Stoke Newington High Street

13. **The Cricketers**
Northwold Road

14. **London Tavern**
Junction of Rendelsham Road and
Maury Road

15. **The Earl Armhurst**
Amhurst Road

16. **The Railway Tavern**
Morning Lane.

17. **The Globe**
Morning Lane

18. **Duke of Wellington**
Morning Lane

19. **The Kenton Arms**
Kenton Road

20. **Price of Wales**
Wick Road/Barnabus road

21. **The Eagle**
Wick Road

22. **The Tiger**
End of Wick Road

23. **The Victoria**
Eastway. Big brick boozer

Like Hackney? Like drinking? Here's the walk for you.

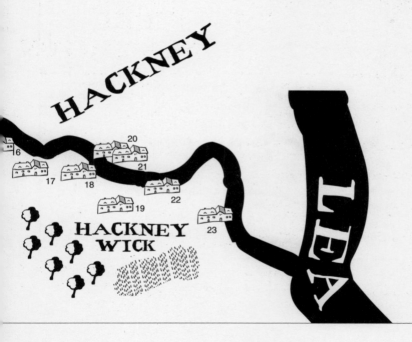

THE
HACKNEY
BROOK
PUB CRAWL

HACKNEY

LEA

6
20
17
18
21
22
19
HACKNEY
WICK
23

Spot a river

Here are some of the more obscure London rivers. Tick the box when you spot them. Hours of fun. ✓

Quaggy River ☐

Strawberry Vale Brook ☐

Pymme's Brook ☐

Salmon Brook ☐

The Graveney ☐

River Roding ☐

Hogsmill River ☐

Yeading Brook ☐

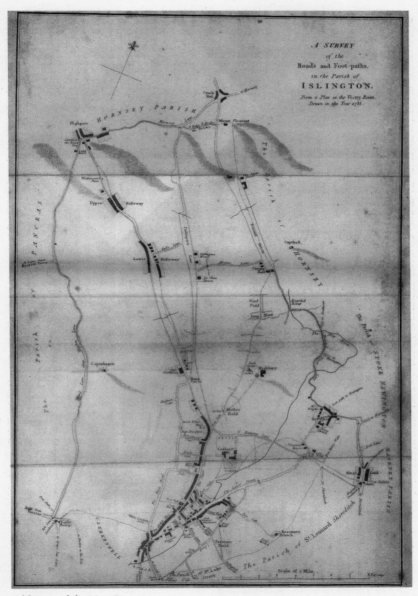

Old Map of the New River.

436 **The Etymologists of Bishopsgate Library**

As suggested in the text, the names of many of the Thames tributaries have changed over the centuries and none are especially ancient (compared to, say, the Thames). Take the Tyburn. At various times it has been known as Ayebrook, Ey Brook, Mill Ditch, Kings Scholars Pond Sewer, Tatchbrook, Tiburn, Teyborne, Maribourne. Even Nonce's River. (No, that was a test one to make sure you're concentrating.)

I went to Bishopsgate Library to do some 'research'. What I found were old magazines packed with letters from respectable gents, about underground rivers. It's not healthy. What taxed the greatest minds of the Victorian and Edwardian eras was not how to reconcile being ethical and moral while having an empire, the state of the poor, urban pollution, or looking for cures for disease, but working out how the Tyebourne got its name. It's actually scary. I have this vision of the British Empire crumbling because its top brains were writing to gentlemen's publications about river etymology. I suppose they were the nineteenth-century version of internet message boards.

The first blast in this war of words was back in the 1870s...

'Tyburn was doubtless originally Ey-burn. It was also called Aye-brook or Eye-brook. The first part of the name is said to be preserved in the neighbouring Hay Hill and may be compared with the River Y at Amsterdam, and the Wye and Wey in England. The vocables ey, eye, aye, wey, wye, are derived from the British ui, au, aw, av' Welsh, gwuy (A.S ecí, ig' Plat: awe' Dan.,aa' Is., á, aa' Gothic., ahwa' Sp., agua), corrupted from "aqua".

(R.S. Charnock, Grays Inn. 8 March 1873)

Then it all went quiet, as the various parties retired to their chambers for a while (nearly thirty years) to consider their responses.

"Tyburn was a brook, which ran from Hampstead to the Thames.
(Rev W.J. Loftie, 16 March 1901)

This seemingly innocuous sentence, in a letter written by the Victorian river expert, the Reverend W.J. Loftie, in the March 1901 edition of *Gentleman's Quarterly*, blew the roof off the genteel world of London river enthusiasts. In fact it was just the first blast in what was to become one of the bloodiest internecine wars amongst gentlemen amateur academics ever witnessed in England.

Mr H.A. Harben wrote (20 April 1901) 'Will M.R. Loftie be so good as to give his authority for the following statement? ... That Tyburn was a brook which ran from Hampstead to the Thames.'

'In regarding the word bourne (burn, burne &c.) only in the sense of stream (rivulet), is there not the danger of forgetting another meaning of the word – viz., limit, boundary (Fr. borne, Webster)? ... When the poet wrote of "that" bourne from whence no traveller returns, one does not imagine he was thinking of a rivulet.' (W.H.B. 1 February 1902)

'I would never call it the Tyburn, except in a conventional way, for, with the exception of a doubtful passage in a charter of uncertain date, there is ... little evidence to show that the King's Scholars' Pond Sewer was ever known as the Tyburn.' (W.F. Prideaux 8 March 1902)

BALDERDASH!

'With regard to the name bourne, otherwise burn, brun, in the sense of limit, boundary ... May it not possibly be because the idea limit, boundary, originally always underlay the thought stream, rivulet? and this perhaps through the fact that the first natural limits and boundaries regarded by men would most frequently be streams and rivulets ... where bourne or burn is the name received from old time for a stream or river, may not that name point back to that old function of boundary marking.' (W.H.B. 8 March 1902)

'Mary bourne/Mariborne was invented by the *Marylebone Mercury* in the late 19th century. For many years past I have endeavoured to investigate the history of my native parish, and have never met the "Mary Bourne" mentioned in any authentic document. But, occurring as it does in an accepted textbook (Mr Arnold Foster's little school-reader *Our Great City*), I feel no doubt that fifty years hence the name will be championed...' (Prideaux 5 July 1902)

There is a hiatus of six years, during which the correspondents get on with their lives and perhaps become more well-rounded individuals, before Col. Prideaux can't take it any longer and, in 1908, hits back with a huge letter to *Notes and Queries*.

"In the course of a correspondence which took place some years ago (16 March 1901) on "Executions of Tyburn", the Rev. W.J. Loftie asserted, inter alia, that "Tyburn was a brook, which ran from Hampstead to the Thames"' whereupon Mr H.A. Harben asked for his authority for that statement. No reply was given, and I doubt if one could be found. [uh-oh – this is going to kick off. Calm down lads...] 'My own opinion is that... "Teoburn" means not the stream, but the Manor'

He recalls that the earliest mention of the river is in the Charter of King Edgar in the year 951, conferring a grant of about 600 acres of land to the Church of St Peter of Westminster: 'of Cuforde upp andlong Teoburnam to thaere wide heres-street' (from Cowford up along Tyburn to the wide military road)

(Prideaux adds) "much ink has been spent in discussing the meaning of the prefix "teo". I belive it to be a form of "tweo", which is equivalent to "twá", the fem. nom. plur. of "twgen", two, and which we find in the word "betweonung" or "betweonan", between. The word "Teoburna" would therefore signify the land situated between the two burns, which modern topography call the Westbourne and the Tyburn. 'The truth seems to be that the residents in the manor of Tyburn naturally called the stream the

Tyburn Brook, while those in the Manor of Eye called it the Eye brook ... No one called it the Tyburn till the nineteenth century was well on its way to maturity'.

(Col. Prideaux 31 October 1908)

"I think Col. Prideaux is in error saying that no one called the brook the Tyburn "until the nineteenth century was well on its way to maturity". There are two MS. plans in the Crace Collection at the British Museum, dated 1732 and made by J. Hanway, jun., in which the brook is marked "Tybourn" and "Ty-bourn" (portfolio xiv. 22, 26). Another question which suggests itself is whether, assuming the etymology to be "Twyburn", the name would not rather denote a "twofold" or "two-forked" stream than the land between two comparatively distant streams.' (H.A. Harben, 28 November 1908)

"I regret that my absence from England prevents me from reply-ing in detail to Mr H.A. Harben's criticisms, but

Poppycock!

may I venture on one or two remarks. [Several pages later...] "What I actually sug-gested was that the name signified the land lying beween the two burns – that Teooburna, to compare small things with great, represented to the Anglo-Saxon mind what Mesopotamia (the land lying between the two great rivers, the Tigris and the Euphrates) represented to the Greeks and Romans ... I think it is to be regretted that before writing his "reply" H.A. Harben did not refresh his memory by again reading the notes on 'Executions at Tyburn,' which were respectively written by Mr W.L. Rutton and myself." (W.F. Prideaux, Grand Hotel, Locarno 19 December 1908)

'I have discussed the evidence for the supposed extension of Tyburn manor to Bayswater in a paper on London's First Conduit System,' published in the *Transactions of the London and Middlesex Archæological Society*, within the last two years. I there point out that all the evidence shows is the existence of a very small detached part of the manor of Tyburn in the common fields of Westbourne. I must refer those interested to that paper, as I have no opportunity to go over the evidence again at present. (A. Morley Davies 19 December 1908)

A new kid on the block...

'I was ... wholly puzzled to imagine how the proposed derivation from the Anglo-Saxon "twëo" could be sustained ... the w in tw (or other combinations) is never lost unless the sound of o or u follows. But the sound of eo had nothing of the nature of an o or about it. The etymology is simple enough, viz., from the verb to tie, Anglo-Saxon "tígan" and it must be remembered that tígan was itself derived (with the usual vowel-mutation) from the sb. téag-, nom. "teah", a tie, band, also an enclosure or paddock which was itself derived from téah, the second grade of the root-verb "téohan", which is cognate with the German "Ziehen" and the well-known Latin "dúcere". (etc. etc. for quite a lot longer) ...' (Walter Skeat, 9 January 1909)

But Colonel Prideaux isn't going to take this lying down ...

'Prof. Skeat's statement that the w in tw cannot be lost unless the sound of o or u follows, is, of course, conclusive, and it is therefore hardly worthwhile to discuss the pronunciation of the word Tyburn ... It must be remembered that Tyburn is only a book word and that it fell out of common speech ... considerably more than a hundred years ago. Prof. Skeat, in suggesting the derivation from Anglo-Saxon "tígan", does not explicitly say that the earliest spelling of the word that we know of, namely, "Teoburna", is another form of "Tig-burna" but I presume that that is his meaning. Of course, if

the compound could signify a "tye", or piece of land enclosed
between two burns, it would suit my main hypothesis as well as the
derivation I originally suggested." (W.F. Prideaux 13 February 1909)

'But "de Tyburne" appears to be genitive, not ablative (the "e"
being for œ I and therefore to the real "of Tyburne" not "from"
Tyburn. I ... would interpret Tyburn as originally the general name
for the many streams that issued from the Hampstead springs. In
the far-off Saxon days when "Teoburna" was invented, we can
imagine a great tract of forest and swamp percolated by these
numerous and undistinguishable rivulets,which the natives on their
small clearances knew only as "the divided burn".

Ty in Tyburn may have its simplets equivalent in tye – a word in use
for an enclosure, or even for its antithesis, a common, and thus a tract
... and when we are led to a root-verb "teohan", we seem to have the
evolution from Teoburna to Tyburn. May we then "rest and be thank-
ful" in the solution, the tye-burn, or the 'burn of the tye'? And thus
have we not the name of the burn rather than the name of the tye?'
(W.L. Rutton 13 February 1909)

Brilliant.

'Since Domesday the name has been indeclinable, and Tyburne
is not the genitive form, even if we can conceive of the preposition
de governing the genitive. Can Prof. Skeet or some other authority
say what is the exact force of the termination "born" in the German
place-name Paderborn?

'In conclusion – and the Editor and readers of N.&Q. will be glad
to learn that I really intend on the present occasion to conclude my
remarks on this thorny subject – I may point out with reference to
Mr H.A. Harben's question (10/x. 431) as to the existence of Tyburn
in the Bayswater district, that in a pedigree given in Mr F.A. Crisp's
Visitations vol. XV., Lord William Murray, third son of the third
Duke of Atholl, who died 31 Dec. 1796, is stated to have been
buried on "St. George's Cemetery, Tyburn, co. Middlesex." ... the

442 title-deeds of this burying-ground as well as of the older buildings in the neighbourhood would, I feel no doubt, corroborate my view that originally the manor of Tyburn extended as far as the Westbourne.

'In reply to the query of Col. Prideaux, I may say that "Born" is the Low-German form of the High-German "Brunnen", cognate, of course, with metathesis of r, with Eng. "bourn". (H.P.L 24 April 1908)

'... although "Tyburne" is not ablative, I will not further claim it as genitive ("Tyburne" for "Tyburnae"), being assured on trustworthy authority that invariably de commands the ablative ... I may add that my classic authority, unaware of the argument, thought "Tyburne" to be vernacular, not declined Latin." (W.L. Rutton 24 April 1909)

[This correspondence continues for several more volumes ...]

Further reading

If you've become obsessed by underground rivers and want more in the way of real facts, here's a selection of source material which will provide a good starting point for your own explorations.

The Lost Rivers of London Nicholas Barton
Up there with the 1972 *Topical Times Football Book* as one of the great texts of the twentieth Century. Concentrates more on the bigger streams. Particularly good on industrial uses for the rivers. Some great old illustrations.

London Under London Trench and Hillman
Similar book to the above but takes a wider view – sewers, tubes lines etc – so less detail about the streams.

Some Lost Rivers of London Alan Ivimey
A chapter in the *Wonderful London* series of books. Short (but to the point) romantic view of the lost rivers, with some nice diagrams. Probably hard to find – I'd lend you my copy but I'm always lending my favourite books to people and not getting them back. So get your own.

Springs, Streams and Spas of London A.S. Foord
Wide-ranging survey and history of London's wells. It's an early twentieth-century volume so long out of print, although most

444   history libraries seem to have a copy. Would be worth updating or someone writing a more contemporary version. But not me.

The Growth of Stoke Newington Jack Whitehead

Mostly of interest to locals, nevertheless an interesting way of approaching local history (ie. bung in loads of old maps and charts).

The Fleet: its River, Prisons and Marriages JE Ashton

Victorian era study of the Fleet's history. Lots of stuff about conditions in the prisons. Beautiful old map in the front.

Address to the Auctioneers Institute of the United Kingdom J.G. Head

A short pamphlet published in 1907 – a time of peace and prosperity when lots of people were interested in mad stuff like underground streams. It concentrates on the problems of building above lost rivers.

Walks Around Hackney Benjamin Clarke

Mid nineteenth-century East End bloke talks about how great London was in the good old days.

The New River: A Romance of the Time of Hugh Myddleton Edmund Fitzgerald

When I saw this 1920s novel in Haringey History Library I nearly fell off my chair. Shit, I thought, there's nothing new to say, is there. So much for my great film ideas.

Review of the New River Metropolitan Water Board

Big book with lots of black and white pictures of water. Only of interest to obsessive types.

The Water Supply of the County of London from Underground Sources Buchan

Well, I must have looked at this because I took some notes but I
don't really remember it. Another Haringey History Library classic.

Prehistoric London: Its Mounds & Circles E.O. Gordon
A 1925 study of London's ancient ritual places. A must for all
Druids of the inter-war period.

Other useful books and journals:
> *The History of Muswell* Hill Ken Gray
> *People and Places Lost Estates in Highgate, Hornsey and Wood
> Green* John Schuster
> *Notes & Queries* Various
> *The Effra* Ken Dixon
> *Brixton* Alan Piper
> *Lights Out for the Territory* Iain Sinclair
> *The Pickwick Papers* Charles Dickens
> *London Placenames*
> *Dictionary of London*
> *History of Islington* John Nelson
> *Islington Past* John Richardson
> *The London Scene* Lewis Melville & Aubrey Hammond
> *Clissold Park* Abney Park Cemetery Trust
> *Leylines* Danny Sullivan
> *The Geology of Islington* Islington Council

Fictional books
> *Perambulations Along the Watercourses of Our Great Metropolis*
> C. F. Talgutt
> *Shitting My Way Around London's Rivers* Samuel Johnson

446 Useful websites for the underground river walker

http://www.cityoflondon.gov.uk/leisure_heritage/libraries_archives_museums_
galleries/guildhall_art_gallery/ – Guildhall Art Gallery

http://www.hertsdirect.org/infoadvice/comvol/enviro2y/envnaturereserve/70214?
view=Heritage – New River Action Group

http://www.leyman.demon.co.uk/dowsing.htm – dowsing

http://www.isleofavalon.co.uk/edu/archive/ndlstone/02dowse.html – dowsing
and archeology

http://www.greatdreams.com/penlearn.htm – dowsing with a pendulum

http://www.goddessmound.com/ – the goddess mound experience

http://www.stanford.edu/dept/english/victorian/dickens/marsh/page4.htm

http://www.braincourse.com/dreama.html – lucid dreams

http://www.cix.co.uk/~joc/hhs/index.htm – hornsey Historical Society

http://www.leyman.demon.co.uk/polter.htm – underground streams and
poltergeists

http://www.n16.com/paper3/fourteen.htm – the Growth of Stoke Newington by
Rab McWilliam

http://www.muswell–hill.com/muswell/history/woodland/ – Haringey's ancient
woodland

http://www.thames.org.uk/guide4.htm – the Swiftstone Trust

http://www.lib.virginia.edu/exhibits/dead/otherworld.html–The Tibetan Book of
the Dead

http://www.moonstonerp.com/assistant/comp.html#tea – English Tea Gardens

http://www.shu.ac.uk/schools/cs/fineart/research/jordan/jordan.htm – Still
Waters project

http://www.thames–online.co.uk/ – Thames Online

http://www.ukrivers.net/ – UK Rivers Network

http://www.geocities.com/TheTropics/Cabana/9424/ – London Alleyways by Ivor
Hoole

http://www.buchwald.dircon.co.uk/planam.html – London place names

http://www.krysstal.com/londname.html – London place names

http://www.flamemag.dircon.co.uk/herne_the_hunter.htm – celtic London

http://www.civicheraldry.co.uk/lcc.html – civic heraldry

http://www.guinnessworldrecords.com/ – Guinness book of records   **447**

http://www.greenchannel.com/slt/substant.htm – creating a sustainable London

http://www.csp.org/chrestomathy/strange_fruit.html – Strange Fruit (Alchemy, Religion and Magical Foods)

http://www.deadbeat.dk/ – Deabeat Magazine

http://www.bathspa.ac.uk/greenwood/lplaces.html – Greenwood's 1827 map of London with place names

http://www.handprint.com/HP/WCL/artist04.html – William Blake

http://www.sca.org/heraldry/laurel/names/engplnam.html – History of English place names

http://www.motco.com/Map/81005/imageonea.asp?Picno=81005000 – Horwood's London Map 1792–9

http://www.parliament.uk/commons/lib/contactingmp.htm – How To Contact Your MP

http://freepages.genealogy.rootsweb.com/~genmaps/genfiles/COU_files/ENG/LON/Norden_london_1593–small.pg.jpg – Norden's 1593 Map of London

http://freepages.genealogy.rootsweb.com/~genmaps/genfiles/COU_files/ENG/LON/Rocque/rocque_index.htm – John Rocque's 1746 London map

http://www.unpopular.demon.co.uk/lpa/organisations/lsc.html – London Street Commune

http://www.greenspun.com/bboard/q–and–a–fetch–msg.tcl?msg_id=005Ryr – source of the East End Bear story

http://www.red4.co.uk/Folklore/trevelyan/welshfolklore/chapt7.htm – plants, herbs and flowers

http://www.geocities.com/greenwitchcraft/WitchesBrew.html – witches brew

http://www.geocities.com/lavenderwater37/red.htm – red magick

http://www.keru.freeserve.co.uk/FH/Middlesex%20Text.html – History of Middlesex

http://www.wandleindustrialmuseum.freeserve.co.uk/common.htg/frame.htm – the Wandle trail

http://www.fdavidpeat.com/bibliography/essays/artenv.htm – Art and the Environment

448   http://www.nbtsc.org/~julieclipse/instar_proposal.html – Environmental Art
http://www.vauxhallpark.org.uk/Detail–3URL.html – Vauxhall Park History
http://www.brixtonsociety.org.uk/trailsix.htm – Effra walk
http://www.bbc.co.uk/otr/intext93–94/Reynolds7.11.93.html – BBC Interview
    with Albert Reynolds
http://www.fantompowa.net/Flame/issue_ten_contents.htm – Flame Mag Online
http://www.tanton.ndirect.co.uk/crossness/ – the Crossness Pumping Station
http://www.theplumber.com/eng.html – the history of plumbing
http://www.politicalcompass.org/ – the political compass
http://www.davidric.dircon.co.uk/1832chol.html – the 1832 cholera epidemic
http://www.chinatown–online.co.uk/pages/guide/history.html – London's
    Chinatown
http://www.leevalley.co.uk/EastEndFestival/history/chinese.html – Chinese
    Limehouse
http://www.lbp.org.uk/hathames1.htm – London biodiversity Partnership
http://www.urban75.net/ – London forum
http://www.londonancestor.com/misc–hist.htm – history of Bermondsey
http://www.mike–stevens.co.uk/maps/1860/index1860.htm – waterways of
    Englandand Wales
http://www.xrefer.com/entry/249447 – John Ruskin
http://www.guardian.co.uk/weather/ – the Weather
http://www.londonlandscape.gre.ac.uk/ – London landscape
http://www.landscapeplanning.gre.ac.uk/rivers.htm – river restoration
http://www.wildtrout.org/WTT/library/features/lostLondon.asp – the Wild Trout
    Trust
http://wwwsul.stanford.edu/depts/hasrg/ablit/britlit/brcatalog.html – London
    sanitary reform
http://www.london–lodges.org/ – London freemasonry
http://www.britannia.com/travel/london/cockney/cable.html – the Battle of
    Cable Street
http://www.cherryred.co.uk/books/meektxt.htm – Joe Meek
http://www.ph.ucla.edu/epi/snow/watermap1856/watermap_1856a4.html – old
    Hackney Brook map

http://www.unpopular.demon.co.uk/lpa/words/british.html – British

http://www.clas.ufl.edu/users/gthursby/taoism/ttcstan2.htm – Ta Te Ching

http://www.morrissociety.org/statement.html – William Morris Society

http://www.aocarchaeology.com/blackf.html – Archaeology in Blackfriars

http://www.storyoflondon.com/article1007.html – bathing in London

http://www.fidnet.com/~dap1955/dickens/dickens_london_map.html – Dickens
London map

http://www.shcarter.freeserve.co.uk/talons/4s4.htm – Dr Who and London rivers

http://www.fountain–international.org/colin/chapter1.htm – Dowsing the
Dragon by Colin Bloy

http://homepage2.nifty.com/~k2/cv/holl_rep.html – Fleet Prison

http://www.nytimes.com/books/first/u/uglow–hogarth.html – Hogarth

http://www.curriculumvisions.com/place/LondonTour/
000TimeLine.html – London Time Line

http://www.cf.ac.uk/encap/skilton/nonfic/town/townint.html – 19thC London
and Literature

http://www.bath.ac.uk/lispring/sourcearchive/fs1/fs1cp1.htm – The River of
Wells by Chesca Potter

http://www.towerhamlets.gov.uk/templates/index.cfm – London Borough of
Tower Hamlets

http://www.lordmayorsshow.org/hist/gogmagog.shtml – Gog and Magog

http://www.findagrave.com/pictures/5634.html – Anton Walbrook's grave

http://www.eng–h.gov.uk/ArchRev/rev95_6/poultry.htm – excavations at No.1
Poultry

http://www.chr.org.uk/anddidthosefeet.htm – The Celts

http://www.museum–london.org.uk/ – Museum of London

http://www.well.com/user/davidu/mithras.html – Mithras Mysteries

http://www.ukpaganlinks.co.uk/links/druid.shtml – UK Pagan Links

http://elvispelvis.com/epicsoundtracks.htm – Epic Soundtracks

http://www.buzzcocks.com/SecretPublic/SP_main/newsindx/SP_16/body_sp_16.
html – The Buzzcocks

http://www.marcus–beale.co.uk/pages/merton.html – Merton Abbey

http://www.environment–agency.gov.uk/ – Environment Agency

450 http://www.sutton.gov.uk/lfl/heritage/wandle/index.htm – the River Wandle

http://www.lbwf.gov.uk/wmg/ – William Morris Gallery

http://www.lbhf.gov.uk/external/thamesstrategy/ – Thames Strategy

http://dspace.dial.pipex.com/town/terrace/kam82/merton/WandleTrail.html – The Wandle Trail

http://www.sutton.gov.uk/council/magazines/LBSMag/summer2002/wandle.htm – The Wandle Group

http://www.keith.emmerson.btinternet.co.uk/guide.html – East London Pub Guide

http://www.southwark.gov.uk/discovering/ – Discovering Southwark

http://www.swarming.org.uk/recl/recl.htm – reclaim the beach

http://www.bookstore–cool.com/A_CainN1.html – how to write a non–fiction book

http://www.angelfire.com/al/thewritesite/block.html – Writer's Block Guildhall Art Gallery – London

இ இ இ

If you feel that your underground river deserves the special Effra treatment, do get in touch with Platform....

PLATFORM
7 Horsleydown Lane
Bermondsey
London, SE1 2LN

info@platformlondon.org

REWARD OFFERED

LOST RIVER

MISSING

Last seen around 1872. Answers to the name of 'Hackney Brook'. Please help us find our special watery friend.

Credits

The author and publishers would like to express their gratitude to the following for permission to reproduce material: Universal Music for permission to quote from '1977', 'London Calling' and 'White Man (In Hammersmith Palais)' by the Clash, written by Joe Strummer and Mick Jones; Minder Music Ltd for 'Leave The Capitol' by The Fall, written by Mark E. Smith, Marc Riley, Craig Scanlon, Paul Hanley; Crass for 'Do They Owe Us A Living?'; Kassner Associated Publishers for permission to quote from 'So Long' by Ray Davies; Dabe Music Ltd for 'Let Me Be'; by Dave Davies; And Son Music Ltd, London WC2H OQY for permission to quote from 'London Traffic' words and music by Bruce Foxton (1977); and Spike Milligan Productions for 'Rain' by Spike Milligan from *Silly Verse for Kids*.

We have made every attempt to find the copyright holders of quoted material, apologise for any omissions and are happy to receive emendations from copyright holders.

Pubs that appear in the text

italics – former pubs

Index

461